CHALO DELHI

Writings and Speeches

1943–1945

Netaji Collected Works Volume 12

CHALO DELHI

Writings and Speeches 1943–1945

SUBHAS CHANDRA BOSE

Edited by
SISIR K. BOSE AND SUGATA BOSE

NETAJI RESEARCH BUREAU · CALCUTTA

Orient BlackSwan

CHALO DELHI: WRITINGS AND SPEECHES 1943–1945

ORIENT BLACKSWAN PRIVATE LIMITED

Registered Office
3-6-752 Himayatnagar, Hyderabad 500 029, Telangana, India
e-mail: centraloffice@orientblackswan.com

Other Offices
Bengaluru, Chennai, Guwahati, Hyderabad, Kolkata,
Mumbai, New Delhi, Noida, Patna, Visakhapatnam

First published in Hardback
by Permanent Black 2007
First paperback printing 2008
Second impression published by Orient Blackswan Pvt. Ltd 2021
Reprinted 2023

ISBN 978-93-5442-041-2

036781

Printed in India at
Yash Printographics
Noida 201 301

Published by
Orient Blackswan Private Limited
3-6-752 Himayatnagar, Hyderabad 500 029, Telangana, India
e-mail: info@orientblackswan.com

Contents

Letters

Illustrations

(between pp. 76 and 77)

Dr Sisir Kumar Bose and Netaji's Work[1]

Netaji's charioteer during the Great Escape on those two fateful nights of 16 and 17 January 1941 left us all bereft on 30 September 2000. In the second week of December 1940 Netaji had called Sisir Bose to his side and asked him in Bengali: '*Amar ekta kaj korte parbe*?' From that magical moment Sisir Bose never stopped doing Netaji's work. All morning on 30 September 2000 he was working away in the chairman's office next to Netaji's bedroom, making certain that the generations to come would continue to learn from Netaji's book of life. On his last visit to the Netaji Research Bureau Netaji's friend Dilip Kumar Roy had said: '*Sisir, Janoto loyalty kathatar kono Bangla sathik pratishabda hoyna, karon amra Bangalira loyal hote janina. Tumi kintu loyalty kake bale ta dekhie diyechho.*' (Sisir, there is no exact Bengali equivalent of the word loyalty because we Bengalis do not know how to be loyal. But you have shown what loyalty truly means.)

For the crime of 'assisting Subhas Chandra Bose' Sisir suffered imprisonment in Calcutta's Presidency Jail, Delhi's Red Fort, the Lahore Fort and Lyallpur Jail between 1942 and 1945, the years covered in Volumes 11 and 12 of Netaji's Collected Works. In the post-independence period, alongside his untiring work as one of India's leading pediatricians, he devoted himself to the task of preserving the best traditions of India's freedom movement.

What Dr Sisir Kumar Bose tried to achieve, through the Netaji Research Bureau, to preserve and protect Netaji's historic legacy is best expressed in a Bengali poem 'Uttraradhikar' that he wrote on his 80th birthday on 2 February 2000:[2]

[1] Dr Sisir Kumar Bose did not live to see Volumes 11 and 12 of Netaji's Collected Works in print. This is a brief tribute to his lifelong devotion to a cause.

[2] Translated by Sumantra Bose.

This life of ours
A portrait of fulfilment,
The task of preserving the inheritance
was a heavy one indeed.
But it was achieved,
that's a story unto itself.
Fifty years of struggle,
hand in hand, together,
Recording history, reading politics,
and above all keeping alive the mission
of patriotism, public service.
This life of ours
is blessed
with love, dedication and, service.

In the words of our great poet-philosopher Rabindranath Tagore: '*Shikha theke shikha jwalate hoy. Tanr sei paripurna jeeban theke amader agni grahan koorte habe.*' (A flame has to be lit from a flame. We must receive a spark from his life of fulfilment.)

The founding father of this 'great institution' (President K.R. Narayanan's phrase in his condolence letter to Sisir's wife, Mrs Krishna Bose) is no more. But we can take solace from the words Rabindranath Tagore spoke about his father Debendranath Tagore in one of his Santiniketan lectures: '*Mrityur dwarai sei mahapurush tanr jeebanke sampurnabhabe uthsarga korechhen—tanr samasta badha dur hoye gechhe—ei jeebanke niye amader kono samsarik prayojaner tuchchata nei, kono loukik o samaoyik sambandher kshudrata nei. Tanr shange kebal ekti matro sampurna jog hoyechhe, se hochhe amriter jog. Mrityui ei amritake prakash kare.*' (It is through death that this great spirit has completely dedicated his life to us. All barriers have been broken. This life of ours is no longer constrained by any worldly trifle, nor the insignificance of any mundane or temporal relationship. We have only one complete connection with him—the tie of immortality. It is death which reveals this immortality.)

If I may take the liberty of paraphrasing Rabindranath a little: '*Ekdin . . . tini ekla amritajeebaner deeksha grahan korechhilen, sedinkar sambad khub alpa lokei jenechhilo . . . tanr ekdiner sei eklar deeksha aaj amra sakale mile grahan korbar adhikari hoyechhi. Sei adhikarke amra swarthak kore jabo.*' (One day he had alone received initiation into this life immortal; very few people knew of that day's conversation. The sacrament that was given to him alone on that day is to be shared by all of us today. We pledge to fulfil that responsibility.)

Let me conclude with that pledge in Dr Sisir Kumar Bose's own words:[3]

THE WORK GOES ON

It happened on a winter afternoon,
I was called, bidding me to sit beside him,
He asked, I have some work,
Can you do it?
He looked with a serene, quiet, intent gaze,
Hoping for my answer,
What could I say?
What work? Post a letter?
Draft a telegram?
Or take care of a guest?
No, a secret task, to be his companion
On a secret journey, no one must know!
Except Ila.
Well, what was about to transpire?
I remembered Father saying
A couple of years ago
The boy has fallen under Subhas's spell,
Were his words coming true!
That was the commencement of work, the work goes on,
It will go on.

SUGATA BOSE

[3] Translated from the Bengali poem 'Kaaj Chalchhe' by Sumantra Bose.

Acknowledgements

We warmly thank Professor Krishna Bose and Professor Leonard A. Gordon for their editorial advice, Mr Kartik Chakraborty for secretarial assistance, the late Mr Naga Sundaram and Mr Sukhamoy Chowdhury for archival support, and Manohar Mondal and Munshi Das for unstinted practical help in running the Netaji Research Bureau's publication division. The research assistance of Shona Ganguly, an undergraduate at the University of California-Berkeley, during the summer of 2005 was of great help in getting the final manuscript ready for publication. For help in gathering material included in this volume over many decades we are grateful to a very large number of people in South, South East and East Asia, including S.A. Ayer, Abid Hasan Safrani, John A. Thivy, Mohammad Zaman Kiani, Prem Kumar Sahgal, Gurbaksh Singh Dhillon, Janaki Davar Athinahappan, Brahmachari Kailasam, Pratima Pal, Satiavati Thevar, Anand Murti (nephew of Rama Murti), Yoichi Yokobori, and Mrs Emori.

The task of editing Volume 12 was more difficult than the rest. For the other volumes we could generally rely on original manuscripts, documents and letters in the archives of the Netaji Research Bureau (NRB). For Volume 12 we have, of course, drawn in the first instance on letters as well as audio and video recordings of some broadcasts and speeches preserved in the NRB archives. But many of Netaji's speeches in South East Asia between 1943 and 1945 were delivered extempore in Hindustani. Fortunately, the Indian Independence League and the Provisional Government of Azad Hind had competent Departments of Publicity which published English translations of many of these speeches even during the great turmoil of the war of independence. There were, in particular, three publications between 1943 and 1945 that are available with the NRB: Narayana Menon (ed.), *On To Delhi:*

Speeches and Wrtings of Subhas Chandra Bose (Bangkok: Indian Independence League, 1944); Subhas Chandra Bose, *Blood Bath* (Singapore: The Publicity and Propaganda Department, Indian Independence League Headquarters, 1944; reproduced Lahore: Hero Publications, 1947); and *India Fights On* (Bangkok: Provisional Government of Azad Hind, 1945). Narayana Menon, the editor of *On To Delhi*, states in his preface that he has done his best to provide as authentic versions as possible of Netaji's speeches, but also acknowledges that Netaji himself was too busy to check the manuscript before publication. So we cannot be absolutely sure that Netaji would have rendered his Hindustani speeches into English in exactly the way that his Publicity Department did. In addition to the publications that were issued while Netaji was alive, there are at least two important compilations of his speeches made soon after the end of the Second World War: Arun (ed.), *Testament of Subhas Bose: Being a Complete and Authentic Record of Netaji's Broadcast Speeches, Press Statements, etc. during the Years 1942–1945* (Delhi: Rajkamal Publications, 1946) and S.A. Das and K.B. Subbaiah, eds (with a foreword by John A. Thivy, Minister of State and Secretary, Provisional Government of Free India), *Chalo Delhi! An Historical Account of the Independence Movement in East Asia* (Kuala Lumpur: The Economy Printers, 1946). The *Testament* edited under the pseudonym Arun was based on materials made available by INA personnel, but also appears to have had the benefit of access to British transcripts of Netaji's radio broadcasts. The compilation edited by Das and Subbaiah can also be considered reliable as it was issued with a foreword by John A. Thivy, a Minister in the Provisional Government of Azad Hind, and the author of an excellent chronicle of the activities of the Azad Hind movement. The Das and Subbaiah account also conveys some of the atmosphere at the public meetings addressed by Netaji. We have also read the transcripts of some of Netaji's broadcasts made by the British government and now available in the National Archives of India. These are broadly congruent with the speeches as published by organs of the Azad Hind movement to which we have given precedence in cases of minor discrepancies. We have needed to use only two of the colonial government's transcripts of broadcasts made in October 1944, as these were not available in the literature produced by the Azad Hind movement.

Overall, we offer as accurate and definitive a volume as possible of Netaji's speeches and writings between 1943 and 1945. Yet, even more than sixty years after the tumultuous events of the Second World War, new material keeps coming into our hands. The letters to Sri Rama Murti were, for instance, acquired only as late as 2005. We know that Netaji made broadcasts to the United States of America from Japan in November 1944, but have not yet been able to locate them. It is possible that another round of research in US and Japanese archives will unearth a few more speeches and letters, which we will then add in a future edition of the Collected Works. Dr Sisir Kumar Bose had launched the mammoth project of publishing Netaji's works in 1961 with the help of Benode C. Chaudhuri and he began the twelve-volume Collected Works project in 1980. In the year of the diamond jubilee of India's independence we have the satisfaction of having redeemed our pledge to bring the corpus of Netaji's works before the public eye—not wholly or in full measure, but very substantially.

We take this opportunity once again to express our deep appreciation to Netaji's wife Emilie Schenkl and their daughter Anita Pfaff for having generously assigned the copyright in Netaji's works to the Netaji Research Bureau.

Introduction

SUGATA BOSE

On 6 May 1943, after a perilous 90-day submarine voyage, Netaji Subhas Chandra Bose reached Sabang on the coast of Sumatra. The journey had begun on 8 February 1943 at Kiel in Germany and included a daring transfer from a German to a Japanese submarine in the Indian Ocean off the coast of Madagascar on 28 April 1943. Subhas Chandra Bose autographed a photograph with the crew taken just prior to disembarkation: 'It was a great pleasure to sail aboard this submarine . . . I believe this will mark a milestone in our fight for victory and peace.'[1]

Netaji had come across half the globe to accept the leadership of the Indian independence movement in South East Asia. After his escape from India in January 1941 he had gone to Europe in an attempt to win over Indian prisoners-of-war in German and Italian hands to the cause of Indian freedom. The German invasion of the Soviet Union in June 1941 had upset his plans. The Japanese military advance across South East Asia in December 1941 and early 1942 opened the eastern frontier of India to the army of liberation of his dreams. A conference of Indian expatriate patriots at Bangkok on 15 June 1942 had issued him an invitation to lead them in South East Asia. At the time he had been able only to send them a message underscoring the need to 'link up Indian nationalists all over the world'.[2] A year later he was at last among them, providing that link in person. The presence of well over

[1] Sisir Kumar Bose, Alexander Werth and S.A. Ayer, *A Beacon across Asia: A Biography of Subhas Chandra Bose* (Bombay: Orient Longman, 1973), pp. 163–4.

[2] 'Link up Indian Nationalists all Over the World', message to the Bangkok conference, 15 June 1942, in Sisir K. Bose and Sugata Bose (eds), *Azad Hind:*

two million, if not three million (as claimed by the Azad Hind movement), Indian civilians in the region gave his movement in Asia a very large social base of support. From Sabang he first flew to Tokyo to garner support for his armed struggle and Japanese recognition of Indian independence. This twelfth and final volume of Netaji's Collected Works opens with his statements and stirring radio broadcasts from Tokyo. 'Only when the blood of freedom-loving Indians begins to flow,' he declared, 'will India attain her freedom.'[3]

On 2 July 1943, Subhas Chandra Bose arrived in Singapore—once 'a bulwark', now 'a graveyard' of the British Empire. He was greeted with the song: '*Subhas-ji, Subhas-ji, woh jaan-e-Hind aagaye, woh naaz jispe Hind ko, woh shan-e-Hind aagaye.*' This was just an early indication of the affection and pride that Indians in South East Asia felt for their leader. Two days later, at an enthusiastic representative assembly of Indians in South East Asia held in the Cathay theatre, Netaji accepted the leadership of the Indian Independence League from Rashbehari Bose. The English translation in cold print of his speech in Hindustani on that historic occasion can hardly capture the passion of the delivery and the enthusiasm of the audience's response that can be seen in the film recordings of that day. In ringing tones and elegant Hindustani he told those who were prepared to follow him that he could offer 'nothing but hunger, thirst, privation, forced marches and death' on the journey towards the Red Fort of Delhi.[4] The following day, 5 July 1943, was 'the proudest day' in Netaji's life as he had 'the unique privilege and honour of announcing to the whole world that India's Army of Liberation' had 'come into being'.[5] In the months that followed he electrified massive audiences of civilians and soldiers with his speeches in Hindustani and elicited an overwhelmingly positive response to his call for 'total mobilization'. His speeches were instantly translated into

---

Writings and Speeches, 1941–1943, Collected Works of Netaji Subhas Chandra Bose, Volume 11 (Calcutta: Netaji Research Bureau and Delhi: Permanent Black, 2002), pp. 115–16.

[3] See below, 'The Blood of Freedom-Loving Indians' [Broadcast from Tokyo, June 1943].

[4] See below, 'Hunger, Thirst, Privation, Forced Marches and Death' [Presidential Address to the East Asia Delegates Conference at Singapore, 4 July 1943].

[5] See below, 'To Delhi, to Delhi!' [Speech delivered as the Supreme Commander of the INA at a Military Review of the INA in Singapore on 5 July 1943].

Tamil. 'Indians outside India', he told a mass meeting in Singapore on 9 July 1943, 'particularly, Indians in East Asia, are going to organize a fighting force which will be powerful enough to attack the British army of occupation in India. When we do so, a revolution will break out, not only among the civilian population at home, but also among the Indian Army, which is now standing under the British flag. When the British government is thus attacked from both sides—from inside India and from outside—it will collapse and the Indian people will then regain their liberty.' He had already given his soldiers the slogan 'Chalo Delhi', reminiscent of the 1857 rebellion in India, in the course of his speech on 5 July. From the Indian civilians in South East Asia he called for 'total mobilization for a total war'. In return for such mobilization of men and women, money and resources, he promised 'a real second front for the Indian struggle'.[6]

A large majority of Indian expatriates in South East Asia responded with great emotional fervour to this patriotic call for a revolution. At least 18,000 civilians, mostly Tamils from South India, excluded by the British from their mythology of martial races, enlisted in the Indian National Army (INA). They received military training alongside professional soldiers from the north-western regions of the subcontinent. Some 40,000 soldiers of Britain's Indian Army forsook their allegiance to the King-Emperor and professed a new loyalty to Netaji and the cause of India's freedom. 'When Netaji arrived in Singapore,' Shah Nawaz Khan explained at the time of the Red Fort trial of November 1945, 'I watched him very keenly . . . I heard a number of his public speeches, which had a profound effect on me. It will not be wrong to say that I was hypnotized by his personality and his speeches. He placed the true picture of India before us and for the first time in my life I saw India, through the eyes of an Indian.'[7] Many tens of thousands of civilians joined the numerous local branches of the Indian Independence League that provided support functions of various kinds to the army of liberation.[8] While travelling in the submarine, Subhas

[6] See below, 'Why I Left Home and Homeland' [Speech at a mass meeting in Singapore, 9 July 1943].

[7] Moti Ram, *Two Historic Red Fort Trials* (New Delhi, Roxy Printing Press, 1946), pp. 109–10.

[8] Leonard A. Gordon, *Brothers against the Raj: A Biography of Indian Nationalists Sarat and Subhas Chandra Bose* (New York: Columbia University Press, 1990),

Chandra Bose had dictated a speech to Abid Hasan which he planned to deliver to a women's regiment of the INA of his dreams. A torpedo attack had not been permitted to interrupt the dictation.[9] The speech was eventually given to the first recruits of the Rani of Jhansi Regiment of a thousand young Indian women from Malaya and Burma—mostly but not exclusively Tamils.[10] In July 1943 the seventeen-year-old Janaki Davar (Thevar) went to hear Subhas Chandra Bose speak at a rally in Kuala Lumpur. At the end of the meeting people rushed forward to give money, jewellery, and anything else they possessed to Netaji. Janaki took off her earrings and gold chain and put them in Netaji's hands. Her parents learnt of what she had done from a photograph on the front page of the local newspaper the next day. When Lakshmi Swaminathan came recruiting for her regiment, Janaki persuaded her father to grant her permission to join. She went with the regiment to Burma in January 1944 and was one of the hundred women who retreated on foot with Subhas Chandra Bose from Burma to Thailand in May 1945.[11]

Netaji undertook a whirlwind tour of various South East Asian countries, galvanizing support for his cause. 'From 1925 to 1927,' he said during a visit to Burma in August 1943, 'I used to gaze from the verandah of my cell in Mandalay prison on the palace of the last independent king of Burma and I used to wonder when Burma would be free once again. Today Burma is an independent state and I am breathing the atmosphere of that liberated country.'[12] Netaji tried to

---

p. 498; Peter Ward Fay, *The Forgotten Army: India's Armed Struggle for Independence, 1942–1945* (Ann Arbor: University of Michigan Press, 1993), pp. 214, 525–6.

[9] Abid Hasan Safrani, 'A Soldier Remembers', transcript of a taped interview in the archives of the Netaji Research Bureau, 1976, part 5, printed in *The Oracle*, 7, 1 (January 1985), p. 21.

[10] See below, 'Empire that Rose in a Day will Vanish in a Night' [Speech delivered at a meeting of Indian women held under the auspices of the Women's Section of the IIL, Singapore Branch on 12 July 1943].

[11] Puan Sri Datin Janaki Athinahappan, 'The Rani of Jhansi Regiment', in *The Oracle*, 2, 2 (January 1980), pp. 29–32, and editors' conversations with Janaki Athinahappan (*nee* Davar [Thevar]). See also Fay, *The Forgotten Army*, pp. 219–21.

[12] See below, 'Independent Burma' [Press statement on the achievement of Burma's independence, 1 August 1943].

send rice from Burma to Bengal which was being decimated by a terrible man-made famine, but his offer was nervously suppressed by the British in India.[13] On 26 September 1943, a ceremonial parade and prayers were held at the last Mughal emperor Bahadur Shah's tomb in Rangoon to signal the INA's determination to march to the Red Fort of Delhi. 'We Indians, regardless of religious faiths, cherish the memory of Bahadur Shah', Netaji said, 'not because he was the man who gave the clarion call to his countrymen to fight the enemy from without, but because he was the man under whose flag fought Indians from all provinces, Indians professing different religious faiths, the man under whose sacred flag . . . freedom-loving Hindus, Muslims and Sikhs fought side by side in the war that has been dubbed by English historians as the sepoy mutiny, but which we Indians call the first war of independence.' That spirit of dynamic faith-inspired unity, not listless secular uniformity, was what he wanted to see emulated in 'the last war of independence'.[14]

On 21 October 1943, Netaji proclaimed the formation of a Provisional Government of Azad Hind (Free India) in Singapore. S.A. Ayer has described how Netaji wrote the proclamation himself well past midnight on 19–20 October 1943 drawing on Indian history and elements of the Irish and American declarations of independence. 'Then I witnessed a phenomenon,' Ayer has written. 'I had a glimpse of the great man. He took hold of a bunch of quarter-sheets of blank paper, took a pencil in hand, and started writing.' As Netaji delivered each handwritten page, Ayer typed it up to be sent to the printers. 'Having goaded Indians to desperation by its hypocrisy,' Netaji began, 'and having driven them to starvation and death by plunder and loot, British rule in India has forfeited the goodwill of the Indian people altogether and is now living a precarious existence. It needs but a flame to destroy the last vestige of that unhappy rule. To light that flame is the task of India's Army of Liberation.' Ayer has described the writing process during that night: 'He did not lift his eyes from the paper in front of him, silently handed to me the first page as soon as he finished it, and I walked out of the room and sat at the typewriter. Abid [Hasan]

[13] See Krishna Bose, *Charana Rekha Taba* (Calcutta: Ananda, 1982), pp. 66–7.

[14] See below, 'At Bahadur Shah's Tomb' [Speech on 26 September 1943].

and [N.G.] Swami went to his room in turn and brought me the proclamation manuscript, sheet after sheet, as Netaji finished it. What amazed me was that he never once wanted to see any of the earlier pages that he had written. How he could remember every word that he had written in the preceding pages, how he could remember the sequence of the paragraphs. In the entire manuscript there was not one word corrected or scored out, and the punctuation was complete.' In the final paragraph came the exhortation to the Indian people:

> In the name of God, in the name of bygone generations who have welded the Indian people into one nation, and in the name of the dead heroes who have bequeathed to us a tradition of heroism and self-sacrifice—we call upon the Indian people to rally round our banner and strike for India's freedom.

'The Provisional Government is entitled to, and hereby claims', the proclamation said in an echo of its Irish predecessor, 'the allegiance of every Indian. It guarantees religious liberty, as well as equal rights and equal opportunities to its citizens. It declares its firm resolve to pursue the happiness and prosperity of the whole nation equally and transcending all the differences cunningly fostered by an alien government in the past.'[15]

By June 1944, 230,000 Indians took written oaths of allegiance to the government in Malaya alone.[16] Netaji achieved remarkable success in forging a spirit of unity and solidarity among different religious communities and linguistic groups. He did so without asking his followers to give up their multiple identities in pledging their loyalty to the Indian nation.

Bridging the disparities of class posed a somewhat greater challenge. Poorer Indians initially responded to Netaji's call with greater alacrity. Netaji could barely conceal his exasperation with the niggardliness of a few of the richer Indians, even though there were also to be stunning instances of millionaires choosing to become fakirs. 'When the INA

[15] See below, 'Proclamation of the Provisional Government of Azad Hind', 21 October 1943, and S.A. Ayer, *Unto Him A Witness: The Story of Netaji Subhas Chandra Bose in East Asia* (Bombay: Thacker and Co., 1951), pp. 163–4.

[16] Bhulabhai Desai, 'Address of Counsel for Defence, Red Fort Trial, Delhi, 1 December 1945', in *The Oracle* 15, 4 (October 1993), p. 34.

is getting trained either to march to victory or to spill its last drop of blood on the way', he said to the Chettiars and other merchants on 25 October 1943, 'the rich people are asking me whether total mobilization means 10 per cent or 5 per cent. I would ask these people who are speaking of percentage whether we can tell our soldiers to fight and spill only 10 per cent of their blood and save the rest.'[17] In the end the Provisional Government gratefully accepted 100 per cent from the enthusiastic and settled for 10 per cent from the reluctant. Netaji turned out to be a very successful fund-raiser ensuring receipts of nearly two million Straits dollars a month by the close of 1943.[18] The Chettiars from Tamil Nadu were among the big contributors to the coffers of the Azad Hind government.

When priests of the main Chettiar temple in Singapore had come to invite Netaji to a religious ceremony, they had been turned away because of their inegalitarian practices. He acceded to their request only after they agreed to host a national meeting open to all castes and communities. Abid Hasan could not remember the speech that Netaji gave on that occasion. 'The memory I retain,' he wrote much later, 'is one of an invigorating music as that of a symphony dedicated to the unity of the motherland and the common purpose of all Indians to be united in their efforts to establish their identity.' It was the echo of that music that was to sustain him during the disastrous retreat from Imphal in late 1944.[19] The Azad Hind government inculcated this sense of unity with a subtle sense of purpose. 'Jai Hind' ('Victory to India') was chosen from the very outset as the common greeting or salutation when Indians met one another. Hindustani, an admixture of Hindi and Urdu, written in the Roman script became the national language, but given the large South Indian presence translation into Tamil was provided at all public meetings. Even the proclamation of the Azad Hind government was read in Hindustani, Tamil and English. A simple

[17] See below, 'Where is your Bank Book?' [Speech at the All Malai Chettiars and other Indian Merchants Conference, 25 October 1943].

[18] Fay, *The Forgotten Army*, p. 215. For detailed reports of contributions collected at local branches in Malaya, see, for instance, *Young India* (Sunday, 19 September 1943, archives of the Netaji Research Bureau), pp.12–13.

[19] Abid Hasan Safrani, *The Men from Imphal* (Calcutta: Netaji Research Bureau, 1971, 1995), pp. 11–12.

Hindustani translation of Rabindranath Tagore's song 'Jana Gana Mana' became the national anthem. A springing tiger, evoking Tipu Sultan of Mysore's gallant resistance against the British featured as the emblem on the tricolour shoulder-pieces on uniforms. Gandhi's charkha continued to adorn the centre of the tricolour flags that INA soldiers were to carry in their march towards Delhi. Three Urdu words—*itmad* (faith), *ittefaq* (unity), and *kurbani* (sacrifice)—encapsulated the motto of the Azad Hind movement.[20]

Overwhelmed by the enthusiastic response to his speeches in the latter half of 1943, Netaji had rashly promised at a public meeting that the INA would be on Indian soil before the end of the year. Fortunately, the Japanese handed over de jure territorial control over the Andaman and Nicobar islands to the Azad Hind government in late December 1943. Netaji visited the Cellular Jail to pay tribute to the revolutionaries who had suffered imprisonment there and renamed Andaman as 'Shaheed' ('Martyrs') and Nicobar as 'Swaraj' ('Freedom') island.[21]

In early January 1944 the headquarters of the Provisional Government were moved forward from Singapore to Rangoon. Having first seen action on the Arakan front in February 1944, the INA moved into north-eastern India towards Imphal and Kohima on 18 March 1944. With 'Chalo Delhi' on their lips the Azad Hind Fauj crossed the Indo-Burma frontier and carried the armed struggle on to Indian soil. Netaji issued a lyrical order of the day on that historic occasion in which he dwelt on the theme of sacrificial patriotism:

> there, there in the distance—beyond that river, beyond those jungles, beyond those hills lies the promised land—the soil from which we sprang—the land to which we shall now return. Hark! India is calling—India's metropolis Delhi is calling—three hundred and eighty eight millions of our countrymen are calling. Blood is calling to blood. Get up, we have no time to lose. Take up your arms. There, in front of you is the road that our pioneers have built. We shall march along that road. We shall carve our

[20] See below, 'Unification of the Indian Nation' [Resolutions of the meeting of the Council of Ministers of the Provisional Government of Azad Hind, 9 December 1943].

[21] 'Netaji in Andaman, 29–31 December 1943: A Report', in *The Oracle*, 16, 1 (January 1994), pp. 11–13.

> way through the enemy's ranks—or if God wills, we shall die a martyr's death. And in our last sleep we shall kiss the road that will bring our Army to Delhi. The road to Delhi is the road to Freedom. CHALO DELHI.[22]

The most detailed justification of his course of action during the World War II was given by Netaji in his radio address to the Mahatma on 6 July 1944. Since Gandhi's decision to launch the Quit India movement, the two leaders had drawn closer in their aims and ideology. Netaji sought 'the blessings and good wishes' of the 'Father of Our Nation' for the 'holy war' that was then raging in north-eastern India.[23]

Elaborate plans were drawn up for civilian administration of territories in India that fell to the INA.[24] An Indian millionaire in Rangoon, Abdul Habeeb Saheb, donated all his assets valued at more than ten million rupees, and Shrimati Betai did much the same, earning thereby the decoration of 'Sewak-i-Hind' or 'Servant of India'.[25] Largely thanks to Netaji's mesmerizing oratory, the Azad Hind bank was able to raise 200 million rupees from Malaya and Burma.[26] The promised march to Delhi was, however, halted in Imphal. The British and Britain's Indian Army with American air support were able to break the siege of Imphal after three and a half tense months and beat back the Japanese forces and the INA from the outskirts of Kohima as well. The torrential monsoon had already cut off the supply lines of the INA soldiers fighting around Imphal and Kohima when Netaji and his followers gathered once more at Bahadur Shah's tomb on the emperor's death anniversary on 11 July 1944. Their solace on this sombre occasion, in addition to a Bahadur Shah couplet about a warrior's faith composed after the collapse of the 1857 revolt, was a well-known verse in English: 'Freedom's battle once begun, bequeathed from bleeding sire to son, tho' baffled oft, is e'er won.'[27]

[22] See below, 'Indian National Army in Action' [Addresses to the INA and statements issued by Netaji during the months January to March 1944].

[23] See below, 'Father of Our Nation' [Message to Mahatma Gandhi, broadcast on 6 July 1944].

[24] Gordon, *Brothers against the Raj*, p. 511.

[25] Ibid., p. 510.

[26] Bhulabhai Desai, 'Address of Counsel for Defence', p. 42.

[27] See below, 'The Great Patriot and Leader' [Speech at Bahadur Shah's tomb, 11 July 1944].

The military debacle in Imphal by July 1944 was followed by a harrowing retreat speckled with a few determined rearguard actions by the INA in Burma during late 1944 and early 1945. Netaji publicly acknowledged the failure of the Imphal offensive in August 1944, but hoped to regroup to fight the next round. In October 1944 he described the war in Burma as 'a fight between the human spirit on the one side and steel and armour on the other'. 'In no revolution in the world's history', he reminded his tenacious followers, 'have the revolutionaries ever had superiority either in numbers or in equipment. Nevertheless the revolutionaries have, in most cases, succeeded in overthrowing the foreign yoke. This will also happen in the case of India.'[28] Away from the battlefield, Netaji found one last occasion to give his views on the fundamental problems of India when he was invited to address the faculty and students at Tokyo University in November 1944. He argued in what is called his 'Tokyo thesis' that the creative faculty of its people and their determination to resist imperialist domination gave ample proof of India's vitality as a nation. He dwelt skilfully on the theme of Indian modernity and offered finely etched assessments of Mahatma Gandhi and Rabindranath Tagore. The speech had some glaringly weak points, especially in its discussion of caste in India. But Netaji was able to delineate with clarity for a foreign audience what he thought would be the three most urgent tasks facing free India—national defence, eradication of poverty and provision of education for all.[29]

Netaji desperately wanted to resume his march towards Delhi. Even though he continued to hope that Britain's Maginot Line in Imphal could be breached with a second assault, talks with the Japanese appear to have convinced him that he could not expect any further help in those plans from that quarter. It is in November 1944 that Netaji tried to establish contact with the Soviet Union through their ambassador Jacob Malik in Tokyo. He anticipated conflicts between the Soviet Union and the Western allies and wanted to reopen a line of communication with a country which had never really helped him in the past except to grant him passage through Moscow in 1941. In Tokyo Netaji

[28] See below, 'The Human Spirit is More Powerful than Steel and Armour' [Broadcast on 'Army Day', 18 October 1944].

[29] See below, 'The Fundamental Problems of India' [An Address to Faculty and Students of Tokyo University, November 1944].

also met the young men he had sent there to receive the best training as cadets in the military academy in Tokyo. Netaji's letters from this period reveal his special solicitude and concern for these Tokyo cadets and the young women who had joined the Rani of Jhansi Regiment. 'My dear boys', he wrote on 29 November 1944 (his daughter Anita's second birthday), 'On the eve of my taking off from the soil of Nippon, I want to send you my love and good wishes for the success of your work. I have no son of my own—but you are to me more than my son—because you have dedicated your life to the cause, which is the one and only goal of my life—the freedom of "Bharat mata."'[30] He returned to Burma to carry on the fight via Taipei, Saigon, and Singapore. 'Today a gentleman is going from here to Tokyo,' he wrote to the Tokyo cadets from Saigon on 14 December 1944. 'I am taking the opportunity of sending a bundle of "papar" for you. I could have sent a few other things, but he could not carry any more weight.'[31] His letters to M. Satiavati Thevar show his willingness to deal with the minutest details concerning the organization of the women's regiment.

'It was the battling with no hope along the Irrawady, not the battling with high hope about the Manipur basin', Peter Fay has plausibly argued, 'that justified the freedom army and gave it in the end such moral leverage.'[32] One might add that it was Netaji's historic retreat with the soldiers of the INA and the women of the Rani of Jhansi Regiment from Burma to Thailand—a dangerous trek under constant enemy fire for 23 days—in April and May 1945 that left an indelible imprint on popular memory about the sacrifices made by these warriors to pay the price of freedom. 'At this critical hour', Netaji told his soldiers on the eve of his departure from Burma, 'I have only one word of command to give you, and that is that if you have to go down temporarily, then go down fighting with the national tri-colour held aloft; go down as heroes; go down upholding the highest code of honour and discipline. The future generations of Indians, who will be born, not as slaves but as free men, because of your colossal sacrifice, will bless your names and proudly proclaim to the world that you, their forbears, fought and suffered reverses in the battles in Manipur, Assam, and Burma, but

[30] See below, Letter to the Tokyo cadets, 29 November 1944.

[31] See below, Letter to the Tokyo cadets, 14 December 1944.

[32] Fay, *The Forgotten Army*, p. 556.

through temporary failure you paved the way to ultimate success and glory.'[33]

If General Slim could gloat over turning 'defeat into victory' in a military sense,[34] Netaji was already considering how the INA could return the compliment on a political plane. In his first public address upon reaching Thailand on 21 May 1945, Netaji drew on examples from the history of Turkey and Ireland in urging Indians to fight on for freedom. 'It may be that we shall not go to Delhi via Imphal', he told those he had roused to unprecedented patriotic fervour with his slogan 'Chalo Delhi'. 'But the roads to Delhi are many,' he assured them, 'like the roads to Rome. And along one of these many roads we shall travel and ultimately reach our destination, the metropolis of India.' He was naturally disappointed that Indian soldiers had once again played a crucial role in the military re-conquest of Burma, but he clearly noticed something new that promised a different future:

> There is, however, one silver lining in the cloud that has overtaken us, and that is, the British Indian Army of today is not the British Indian Army of the last war. Soldiers of the Azad Hind Fauj have had numerous opportunities of coming into close contact with members of the British Indian Army. Very often our soldiers were told by the latter that if they (i.e. Azad Hind Fauj) succeed in advancing further, members of the British Indian Army would then come and join them. There is no doubt that at heart large sections of the British Indian Army sympathize with the Azad Hind Fauj and its fight for freedom. But the British Indian Army is not yet prepared to take the risk and line up with the revolutionaries. As a result of foreign rule, members of the British Indian Army have lost their self-confidence and they are afraid that the British might ultimately win, in which case they would be in a difficult situation. Moreover, they have been influenced, to some extent, by the propaganda of our enemies that the Azad Hind Fauj (Indian National Army) is a puppet army of the Japanese. After coming into Burma, the eyes of the British Indian Army will be opened. They will see for themselves what the Provisional Government of Azad Hind and the Azad Hind Fauj have done and how they have fought for India's freedom. They will hear 'Jai Hind', which is the greeting of all free Indians. They will also hear India's inspiring

[33] See below, 'The Future Generations of Indians Will Bless Your Names' [Special Order of the Day, 24 April 1945].

[34] William Slim, *Defeat into Victory* (London: Cassell, 1956).

> national anthem sung by freedom-loving Indians in Burma. The effect of this experience on the British Indian Army, and all other Indians, who have come into Burma alongside of the British, is bound to be great in the days to come.[35]

He said much the same thing in a private letter to Brahmachari Kailasam on 10 June 1945: 'The fight goes on, despite what has recently happened in Burma. We shall win and India will be free.'[36]

In late June 1945 Netaji made a series of broadcasts urging Indians at home not to compromise with British imperialism. He argued the case for a three-pronged strategy in pursuing the goal of Indian independence: (1) continued armed struggle outside India, (2) resistance rather than compromise inside India, and (3) diplomacy in the international field. Since the almighty British Empire had gone down on its knees to seek American help, he felt he had done nothing wrong as the leader of an enslaved and disarmed nation in allying with Japan. No country had won freedom without some degree of foreign help. Far more important than his analysis of the Wavell offer were the grounds on which he felt entitled to offer advice to his countrymen at home:

> I and my comrades here are engaged in a grim struggle. Our comrades at the front have to play with death. Even those who are not at the front have to face danger every minute of their existence. When we were in Burma, bombing and machine-gunning were our daily entertainment. I have seen many of my comrades killed, maimed and injured from the enemy's ruthless bombing and machine-gunning. I have seen the entire hospital of the Azad Hind Fauj in Rangoon razed to the ground with our helpless patients suffering heavy casualties. That I and many others with me are still alive today is only through God's grace. It is because we are living, working and fighting in the face of death that I have a right to speak to you and to advise you. Most of you do not know what bombing is. Most of you do not know what it is to be machine-gunned by low-flying bombers and fighters. Most of you have had no experience of bullets whistling past you, to your right and to your left. Those who have gone through this experience and have kept up morale dare not even look at Lord Wavell's offer.[37]

[35] See below, 'We Fight On' [Speech delivered in Bangkok on 21 May 1945].

[36] See below, Letter to Brahmachari Kailasam, 10 June 1945.

[37] See below, 'Cooperation with Japan' [Broadcast from Singapore on 26 June 1945].

4th July may be the date of the American Declaration of Independence, but it was no less significant in the history of the Azad Hind movement in East Asia. On the day he had taken over the leadership of the movement in 1943, Netaji addressed a large gathering in Singapore for two hours in Hindustani where the audience reaffirmed their determination to achieve liberty or death. On 8 July 1945, Netaji laid the foundation stone of a memorial to the martyrs of the INA who had laid down their lives in the cause of freedom. Cyril John Stracey of the INA built it in record time on the seaface in Singapore bearing the words of their motto—*itmad* (faith), *ittefaq* (unity) and *kurbani* (sacrifice).[38] The atom bombs on Hiroshima and Nagasaki in early August 1945 brought the war in East Asia to an abrupt end. On the day of Japan's surrender on 15 August 1945—exactly two years before India's independence—Netaji issued his last order of the day and a special message to Indians in East Asia. 'The roads to Delhi are many', he told his soldiers, 'and Delhi still remains our goal. The sacrifices of your immortal comrades and yourselves will certainly achieve their fulfillment.'[39] And to the Indian civilians who had responded with unprecedented enthusiasm to his call for total mobilization, he had this to say:

> Sisters and Brothers,
>
> A glorious chapter in the history of India's Struggle for Freedom has just come to a close and, in that chapter, the sons and daughters of India in East Asia will have an undying place.
>
> You set a shining example of patriotism and self-sacrifice by pouring out men, money and materials into the struggle for India's independence. I shall never forget the spontaneity and enthusiasm with which you responded to my call for "Total Mobilization". You sent an unending stream of your sons and daughters to the camps to be trained as soldiers of the Azad Hind Fauj and of the Rani of Jhansi Regiment. Money and materials you poured lavishly into the war chest of the Provisional Government of Azad Hind. In short, you did your duty as true sons and daughters of India. I regret more than you do that your sufferings and sacrifices have not borne immediate fruit. But they have not gone in vain,

[38] Cyril John Stracey, 'How I came to join the INA', in *The Oracle*, 4, 1 (January 1982), pp. 53–6.

[39] See below, 'The Roads to Delhi are Many' [Special Order of the Day, 15 August 1945].

> because they have ensured the emancipation of our motherland and will serve as an undying inspiration to Indians all over the world. Posterity will bless your name, and will talk with pride about your offerings at the altar of India's Freedom and about your positive achievement as well.

Urging them never to falter in their faith in India's destiny, Netaji expressed confidence that 'India shall be free and before long'.[40]

At the end of the war in 1945 the independence movement in India was at a low ebb. At that crucial moment Netaji's soldiers descended upon the Red Fort of Delhi as a godsend. The trial of some of their leading officers reached the saga of the INA and its Netaji to every Indian home. 'The whole country has been roused', Gandhi observed, 'and even the regular forces have been stirred into a new political consciousness and have begun to think in terms of independence.'[41] Netaji had succeeded in his strategy to knock out the keystone of British imperialist domination over its Asian colonies by supplanting the loyalty of the Indian soldiers to their enslavers with a new loyalty to their country's freedom. 'Whether we survive or not, whether we individually live to see India free or not,' he had declared in one of his speeches, 'India shall be free.'[42] As he tried to move from one battlefield to another after the Japanese surrender, Netaji tragically died as a result of an air crash in Taipei on 18 August 1945. His disdain for self-preservation and his supreme self-sacrifice at the climactic moment of the war of independence meant that his ideas lost out in the fashioning of post-colonial India. But as the 'Father of Our Nation' said about his 'prince among patriots', 'Netaji's name' had become one to 'conjure with'. 'The lesson that Netaji and his army brings to us,' Mahatma Gandhi wrote in *Harijan* on 12 February 1946, 'is one of self-sacrifice, unity—irrespective of class and community—and discipline.'[43] Netaji himself had composed his last testament even before his *mahanishkraman*, the

[40] See below, 'India Shall be Free' [Special Message to Indians in Malaya, Thailand, Indo-China, Java, Sumatra, Borneo, Philippines, Japan and other parts of East Asia, 15 August 1945].

[41] D.G. Tendulkar, *Mahatma: Life of Mohandas Karamchand Gandhi, Vol. 7, 1945–1947* (New Delhi: Publications Division, Government of India, rpnt 1988), p. 113.

[42] See below, 'Netaji at the Assembly of Greater East Asia Nations', November 1943.

[43] Tendulkar, *Mahatma*, p. 68.

great escape, from Calcutta in January 1941. 'The individual must die,' he had written to his British captors on 26 November 1940, before launching a hunger strike in prison, 'so that the nation may live. Today I must die, so that India may live and may win freedom and glory.' He genuinely believed that 'nobody can lose through suffering and sacrifice'. 'If he does lose anything of the earth, earthy', Netaji had written prophetically, 'he will gain much more in return by becoming the heir to a life immortal.'[44]

Edward Farley Oaten, the professor of history against whom the young Subhas had struck a blow in 1916, wrote the best obituary comment on the mortal end of India's deathless hero in the form of a poem:

Subhash Chandra Bose

Obiit 1945

Did I once suffer, Subhash, at your hand?
Your patriot heart is stilled! I would forget!
Let me recall but this, that while as yet
The Raj that you once challenged in your land
Was Mighty; Icarus-like your courage planned
To mount the skies, and storm in battleset
The ramparts of High Heaven, to claim the debt
Of freedom owed, on plain and rude demand.
High Heaven yielded, but in dignity.
Like Icarus, you sped towards the sea.
Your wings were melted from you by the sun,
The genial patriot fire, that brightly glowed
In India's mighty heart, and flamed and flowed
Forth from her Army's thousand victories won.[45]

[44] 'My Political Testament', letter to the Governor, Chief Minister and Council of Ministers, 26 November 1940, in Sisir K. Bose and Sugata Bose (eds), *The Alternative Leadership: Speeches, Articles, Statements and Letters, June 1939–January 1941: Netaji Subhas Chandra Bose Collected Works Volume 10* (Calcutta: Netaji Research Bureau and Delhi: Permanent Black, 2003), p. 197.

[45] Facsimile reprint in Oaten's own hand in Krishna Bose, *Itahaser Sandhane* (Calcutta: Ananda Publishers, 1972).

1

What British Imperialism Means for India

[Statement at a press conference held in Tokyo on 19 June 1943][1]

Gentlemen! At the outset, I may say that it is, for me, a great pleasure to offer you my cordial greetings since I have been, for a long time, connected with journalism in my own country. You may be wondering what has brought me to this part of the world and at such a time. For many long years British jails in India and Burma had been my residence. But the fact that today I am standing before you in the heart of Nippon instead of sitting idly in a prison house in India is symbolic of the new movement that is now sweeping over my country.

It was in accordance with the will of my countrymen that I left home and homeland more than two years ago, and whatever I had done since then was also in accordance with their will. During the last World War our leaders had been bluffed and deceived by the wily British politicians. That was why we took the vow more than 20 years ago never again to be deceived by them. For more than 20 years, my generation had striven for freedom and eagerly awaited the hour that has now struck—the hour that is for the Indian people the dawn of freedom. We know very well such an opportunity will not come again for another hundred years and we are therefore determined to make the fullest use of it.

[1] Narayana Menon (ed.), *On To Delhi: Speeches and Wrtings of Subhas Chandra Bose* (Bangkok: Indian Independence League, 1944), pp. 15–17, and audio and video recordings of the press conference in the archives of the Netaji Research Bureau.

Gentlemen! We have so often heard of war that is being waged for freedom and democracy. But you can very well imagine what my countrymen think of those Powers that talk of freedom and democracy and deny the same to one-fifth of the human race—the Powers that reply to the demand for liberty by terror and brutality and by the massacre of unarmed men, women and children. British Imperialism means for India moral degradation, cultural ruin, economic impoverishment and political enslavement.

Is it any wonder, therefore, that the Indian people have at last solemnly resolved to end the British yoke? The present world conflict means for the Indian people the struggle between the forces that want to maintain the status quo and those that are determined to overthrow it. Can anyone blame us if in such conflict our sympathy lies with those powers that stand for change—for the New Order? And when these powers support our demand for freedom it is but natural that our sympathy for them should deepen into enthusiastic support.

The Tripartite Powers have rendered the greatest help to India's struggle by waging war against our eternal foe. And they have earned our lasting gratitude by offering us not only sympathy but active support and assistance. Nevertheless, it is our duty to pay for our liberty with our own blood. The freedom that we shall win, through our sacrifice and exertions, we shall be able to preserve with our own strength. We, therefore, feel strongly that we should actively participate in the war against our common foe.

The enemy that has drawn the sword must be fought with the sword. Civil Disobedience must develop into armed struggle. And only when the Indian people receive the baptism of fire on a large scale will they qualify for their freedom.

You may be eager to know the sentiments of Indians towards Japan. Japan was the first country which prevented the people of an alien continent from committing aggression in the Asian continent. Japan's victory over Russia in 1905 was the first harbinger of Asian resurgence. That victory was hailed with great joy not only by the Japanese but also by the Indians. Therefore, Indians feel that the existence of a strong Japan is essential for the reconstruction of Asia.

It is true that India's views on Japan underwent some change following the Chinese affair. But after the beginning of the great East Asia war the situation has become different. Today Japan is waging war against our common enemy; Chungking has joined our enemies. Any Indian who is participating in the struggle for liberating India is bound to be friendly with that country which supports his cause. Further, Indians are now asking why Chiang Kai-shek has not come to some honourable settlement with Japan, and why he is relying on and serving as a tool of the Anglo-Americans even after the announcement of Japan's new policy on China.

India and Japan have in the past been bound by deep cultural ties that are about twenty centuries old. In recent times these ties have been interrupted because of the British domination of India. It is, however, certain, that once India is free these ties will be revived and strengthened.

2

Our National Honour

[Broadcast from Tokyo on 21 June 1943][1]

Countrymen and Friends! In April last, you heard my voice over another radio in another part of the world. Now I am in Tokyo, and I am accepting the hospitality of the broadcasting station here in order to speak to you again. Since I spoke to you last no important change has taken place in the general war situation. In the western theatre, the Anglo-American forces have scored a success, and the fighting in North Africa has come to an end. The Anglo-Americans have followed this up by occupying a few small and barren islands in the Mediterranean. As is customary with Anglo-American propagandists, they had been rending the skies with their boasting and bragging, subsequent to this small military success, which they achieved. Prior to this, they have been boasting about the Anglo-American landings in North Africa and claiming that an African victory would finally determine the result of the war. Now that allied victory has been achieved in North Africa they are still as far from winning the war as they were at the end of 1940. These propaganda tactics make it clear that they badly need some success—however insignificant—to bolster up the sinking morale of their people. If one were to listen to the broadcasts from England and America after the campaign in Tunisia, as I have been doing, one would think that the Anglo-American forces have already won the war. This type of propaganda had brought good results during the last world

[1] Arun (ed.), *Testament of Subhas Bose: Being a Complete and Authentic Record of Netaji's Broadcast Speeches, Press Statements, etc. during the Years 1942–1945* (Delhi: Rajkamal Publications, 1946), pp. 54–8.

war, when radio broadcasting was virtually unknown. That is why the Anglo-Americans have been indulging in it again. They are, however, blissfully oblivious of the fact that the world is not as unsophisticated today as it was in 1915 and 1916, and that broadcasting has now enabled people in every corner of the globe to listen to both versions of the story on every point. Moreover, the Indian public, having been repeatedly deceived by cunning and lying British propaganda, has now become extremely cautious, and is not likely to be influenced at all by one-sided enemy propaganda. I have, therefore, no doubt in my mind that so far as my countrymen are concerned, they will never be deceived by what London or New York or Boston might say.

After the Anglo-American occupation of some small and barren islands in the Mediterranean like Pantelleria and Lampedusa, enemy propagandists have given the whole world the impression that a landing on and occupation of the European continent is now a question of a few days. When I was in Paris, soon after the first Anglo-American landing in French North Africa, I heard from many Parisians that Anglo-American radio stations had given them the impression that Anglo-American troops would be in Paris in a fortnight's time. Those Frenchmen who were elated over this news naturally suffered a severe disappointment when the Anglo-Americans did not appear in France again after the shameful debacle at Dieppe. I am afraid that all those people who are still hoping for the miracle of an Anglo-American victory have painful disappointment in store for them. These optimists will soon realize that the occupation of the European continent is still as remote as the occupation of the moon.

Friends, you will certainly remember that when the campaign in Africa was going on, I repeatedly told you that for the ultimate outcome of the war, the African campaign did not play an important role, though it had been fully utilized by the Anglo-Americans for propagandist purposes. You will now realize that what I said then was no exaggeration. The campaign in North Africa has ended, but we have not come any nearer to the end of the war, than when fighting was going on in the Cyrenaika or Tripolitania or Tunisia. The fact is, as I told you more than once, that the fate of the war depends on the situation in Europe, in Asia and on the high seas. And so far as India is concerned, what is the most important of all is the situation near India. No amount of Anglo-American propaganda can either ignore or hide the fact that, after achieving brilliant victories in Hong Kong, in the Philippines, in the East Indies, in Malaya and Singapore, and in Burma, the forces of the Imperial Japanese Army now stand on the frontier of India.

During the whole history of British rule in India, it has never struck one single British general that at some time in the future some enemy of Britain may appear on the Eastern frontier of India. The whole attention of Britain's military strategists had, therefore, been concentrated on the Northwestern frontier of India. Hence, with the naval fortress of Singapore in their possession, our rulers thought that India was safe and secure in their hands. But the phenomenal advance of the Japanese brought victory and opened the eyes of the world to the worthlessness of British strategy. Since then General Wavell has been making feverish attempts to put up fortifications on the Eastern frontier of India. But what the Indian people today are asking is this: 'If it took 20 years to build Singapore, and only one week to lose it, how long will it take the ever-retreating British Commander-in-Chief or his successor to withdraw from his eastern fortification?'

You have seen that during the course of the present war, Anglo-American Powers have time and again made themselves the laughing stock of the world by beginning a military campaign to the accompaniment of boastful propaganda and extravagant claims. They are now doing this in connection with their contemplated occupation of the European continent. They did it some months ago when General Wavell started operations on the Indo-Burma frontier and marched into Burma. At that time, it was advertised all over the world that the campaign for the re-conquest of Burma had begun. But what face could the British Commander-in-Chief show when his troops had to run back to India, leaving all their bag and baggage behind as soon as the powerful Japanese Army began its counter-offensive? General Wavell has subsequently invented all kinds of excuses in order to cover his defeat. Even the British Prime Minister, during his recent visit to America, was at pains to explain away the ignominious failure of his Commander-in-Chief to retake Burma. But what one cannot understand is why the Anglo-American Powers repeatedly indulged in premature bragging. In contrast to them, the Axis Powers talk less, and instead of beginning a military campaign with a bumptious propaganda campaign they leave actual events to speak for themselves. When the German forces occupied the Channel Islands, which lie between the French and the English coasts, in 1940, German propaganda never claimed that through the occupation of these islands, the German Army had come nearer to an invasion of England. If, as Anglo-American propaganda is now trying to make out, the occupation of Pantelleria has made landings on and the occupation of Sicily a reasonable certainty, why could not the Anglo-American forces make that attempt from the island fortress of Malta, which is as near to Sicily as Pantelleria and has been always in their possession? No, friends, the fact is that the Anglo-American Powers are in such a hopeless situation that they have somehow to bolster up the sinking morale of their people, and in order to do that, they feel constrained to resort to premature boasting again and again. Such tactics may be a necessity for their propaganda, but that is no reason why the world, which is now wide-awake, should be duped by them. For India, what is of primary importance is not what is happening in Tunisia and Timbuctoo or in Lampedusa and Alaska, but what is happening inside India and across her frontier.

What is of primary importance to us is that the much-advertised reconquest of Burma has ended in shameful retreat, that the victorious Japanese army is standing on our eastern frontier, that the Government of Japan, through its worthy Prime Minister, General Tojo, has repeatedly declared its fullest support to Indian independence and its firm resolve to see Anglo-American power and influence expelled from India. And, lastly, that Japan's Prime Minister has offered active assistance, should the Indian revolutionaries need it, in their struggle for complete national independence. What is also of direct importance to India is the policy of British Imperialism towards our country.

You know as well as I do that when this war broke out some of our friends thought that since the British Government would soon find itself in serious difficulties, it would feel constrained to sue for peace with the party that controlled the cabinets in eight out of 11 provinces in British India. According to these friends, all that the Congress had to do was to hold itself in patience till the British Government was compelled to make the first advance. A year rolled by but there was no evidence of this change of heart on the British side. Then those friends considered it necessary to exert mild pressure on the British Government in order to bring about a compromise. Various steps were taken in this behalf, but no tangible results followed. Even the fall of Singapore, 'the greatest disaster in British military history' according to Mr. Winston Churchill, and the loss of Burma did not bring about any appreciable change. British Imperialism goes on forever—that is what our rulers continue to think. You may call this lack of statesmanship or political bankruptcy or midsummer madness. But, this midsummer madness has its own explanation. The British Empire has grown out of India. The British people, no matter to which political party they belong, have grown fat on the spoils, the wealth and the resources of India. To them, the empire today means India. They are now fighting in order to preserve that empire. If they are to win the war at the cost of recognizing India's independence, it will amount to winning the war by losing the empire. Consequently, no matter what fate overtakes Britain during the course of this war, the average Englishman will endeavour to the very last to hold on to his empire, that is to hold on to India. Therefore, if I were to speak frankly, I should say that it is not midsummer madness that British politicians refuse to recognize India's independence, though they are in a terrible plight. It is midsummer madness that we should expect the Englishman to voluntarily give up his empire, simply because he has fallen on evil days. There is another factor that accounts for the unrelenting policy of British imperialists. As the Foreign Minister of Germany said the other day in his inimitable style, the British Empire has been losing one part of its territory to its enemies, and another part of it to its friends during the course of the present war. Moreover, in his frantic efforts to maintain his empire, John Bull is now bleeding himself white. The only hope of even partially making up for this colossal loss is to exploit India more ruthlessly when the war is over. Therefore, according to imperialistic logic, the worse England's position becomes during this war, the more difficult will it be to retain a firm grip over India. British Imperialism will ultimately break, but it will never bend. That is how empires have always behaved in the history of mankind. Consequently, no Indian should ever cherish the illusion that one day England will be induced to recognize India's independence.

But that is not to say that British politicians will never again attempt a compromise with India. Another attempt at a compromise will be made any time, whether under the pressure of a worsening military situation, or in order to placate the liberal elements in England and America. Personally, I expect another such attempt sometime this year. But what I want to point out more emphatically is that in attempting a compromise British politicians will never recognize India's independence but will only try to bluff the Indian people, and through protracted negotiations will only try to sidetrack the issue of independence and thereby undermine the national will, as they did between December 1941 and July 1942. The negotiations carried on by Sir Stafford Cripps during the last year did not harm the British Government in any way. It only interrupted our struggle for freedom. Therefore, we should once for all set our face against any compromise with British imperialism. Friends, independence admits of no compromise. Freedom has only one connotation, namely, that the British and their Allies must quit India for good. And those who really want liberty must fight for it, and pay for it with their own blood.

Countrymen and friends, let us, therefore, carry on the fight for liberty inside India with all our strength and vigour. Let us continue the battle with resolute heart, and with unshakeable faith, till one day under the combined attack of our friends and allies, and of ourselves, Anglo-American imperialism will be overthrown, the British Empire will be broken up, and out of its ashes a new India will once again emerge as an independent nation. In this struggle there is no going back, there can be no faltering. We must march forward and forward, till victory is achieved and freedom won. Inquilab Zindabad! Azad Hind Zindabad!

3

The Blood of Freedom-Loving Indians

[Broadcast from Tokyo, June 1943][1]

While I am in Tokyo, I desire to address a few words to you, and I have no doubt that you will give them due consideration. In the first place I desire to thank you most heartily for the warm and enthusiastic welcome that you have given me on the occasion of my public appearance in East Asia, and for the assurance you have given me of your wholehearted support to our effort to liberate our dear Motherland. I feel overwhelmed at this manifestation of your burning patriotism and spirit of sacrifice. I have received numerous telegraphic, telephonic and postal messages from you directly, while other messages I have read in the press and all these messages have given me great joy and satisfaction.

You know that I have always been an optimist. Nevertheless, I must say that the response that I have received has exceeded my fondest expectation. I can only say in reply that I am proud of you. Since the outbreak of the war in Europe and East Asia, I have been saying repeatedly that we, the Indian people, could not have wished or even dreamt of a better combination of circumstances for helping us achieve our liberty. When world forces are helping us in this way, our task automatically becomes very much easier than what it would have been otherwise. This fact should further strengthen our self-confidence and optimism and hearten us considerably in the fight that lies ahead of us. I am

[1] Audio recording of Netaji's broadcast in his voice (archives of the Netaji Research Bureau).

overjoyed to see that you have already realized the responsibility of winning freedom lies at home. It is but natural that they should bear the brunt of the burden, and they have been doing so already. But, at the same time, every Indian—no matter where he is living at the present time—has a duty towards his country and he must contribute his due share towards the final victory.

I am convinced that India cannot hope to be free until Indians living abroad perform their duty in this momentous world crisis. Owing to the fact that the Tripartite Powers have been giving their fullest support to Indian independence, it is comparatively easy for Indians who are now abroad. I expect Indians living in Axis countries or in countries controlled by the Axis powers to play their part in the national struggle and consequently I expect that they will render maximum service to the Motherland. Here in East Asia, you have seen yourself how deep the interest and sympathy is for Indian independence. The readiness of the Imperial Nippon Government and nation to render any assistance in our national struggle we may need has lightened our task to a considerable degree. Consequently, there can be no possible excuse why any Indian in East Asia should not put his whole might into the present struggle.

But though the Axis powers in general, and Nippon in particular, are prepared to help us at any time and have been actually doing so already, the task of liberating India is ours, and ours alone. That responsibility we shall not cast on anybody else, because that would be against our national honour. Moreover, we have no right to ask for or expect help from any quarter until we ourselves have first of all done our very utmost. Our sisters and brothers at home have been doing their very best in the circumstances in which they have been placed. But the enemy is ruthless and desperate and he is armed to the teeth. Against such a brutal foe, no amount of civil disobedience or sabotage or revolutionary terrorism can be of any avail. If, therefore, we want to expel British power from India, we have to fight the enemy with his own weapon. The enemy has already drawn the sword—he must therefore be fought with the sword. But it is not possible for our countrymen at home to organize an armed revolution and to fight the British army of occupation with modern arms. This task must therefore devolve on Indians living abroad and particularly on Indians living in East Asia.

Friends! If you compare the history of our national struggle with the histories and struggles in other parts of the world, you will realize we, in India, have up till now lacked one thing and one thing alone. We lack an organization whereby we can meet force with force. It is our task to supply this one want and thereby eliminate once and for all the only drawback in our national struggle. I therefore desire that all able-bodied Indians living in East Asia should volunteer to fight with me for the liberation of our Motherland.

This is our supreme task and duty, before which no other type of service counts for much. All those countrymen of mine who are prepared to fight for the liberation of India will please get in touch with me at once, directly or through their local organizations. I am confident that with the help of my countrymen in East Asia, I shall be able to organize such a gigantic force as will be able to sweep away the British power from India, in conjunction with those who have been already fighting at home. The hour has struck, and every patriotic Indian must advance towards the field of battle. Only when the blood of freedom-loving Indians begins to flow, will India attain her freedom.

4

This War and its Significance

[Broadcast from Tokyo on 24 June 1943][1]

Countrymen and Friends! I want to deal, in the first place, with the meaning if this war, and the historical facts lying behind it. Well, this war is a clash between the forces that want to maintain the status quo in the world and the new forces that are determined to destroy it in order to usher in a new order. The former includes the Anglo-American imperialistic powers that have been masquerading under the cloak of freedom and democracy. Victory to these imperialistic powers would mean the perpetuation of our servitude as well as the continued enslavement of many other unfortunate nations.

Some of my countrymen have been expecting that under the pressure of an international crisis, the imperialistic powers like Britain might be induced to recognize the independence of enslaved countries like India, but all such expectations have been completely falsified. Likewise, all attempts previously made by some people to avoid war, and somehow to arrive at a compromise between the two parties, have proved to be fruitless. The result is the present war, which is being fought to a finish, and there is very high chance of it being a more prolonged struggle than the last World War.

In this titanic conflict our national interest clearly lies in allying ourselves with those young and virile nations, who are determined to

[1] *On To Delhi*, pp. 9–14. A slightly modified and a more lyrical and stirring version of this speech was broadcast in Bengali. An audio recording of that speech is available in the archives of the Netaji Research Bureau. The final sentence is worth quoting in full in the original Bengali: '*Swadheen Bharate sakal karagarer louha kapat unmukta hoibe ebong Bharatmatar sreshtha santanera takhan karaprakashther andhakar hoite nirmal aloke bahir hoiya jayamalye bhushita hoiben.*'

overthrow the status quo and thereby give us a chance of winning our liberty. It should be fully evident that the Tripartite Powers by fighting our age-long enemy and inflicting terrible defeats on him have been indirectly helping our national struggle to a remarkable degree. If our enemy had not been mortally wounded by these powers, our task of achieving liberty would have been a hundred times more difficult than what it is to-day. We are grateful for this, but we are even more grateful that the Tripartite Powers are not only content with giving us indirect help, but have been offering active support and assistance in our fight for freedom.

I know that there are some countrymen of mine who, having been brought up in English institutions and having been influenced by English propaganda, doubt the merits of the Tripartite Powers. I WOULD ASK THOSE COUNTRYMEN TO PUT THEIR TRUST IN ME. FOR THE POWERFUL BRITISH GOVERNMENT THAT HAS PERSECUTED ME ALL MY LIFE AND HAS IMPRISONED ME ELEVEN TIMES, HAS NOT BEEN ABLE TO DEMORALISE ME. NO POWER ON EARTH CAN HOPE TO DO SO. AND IF THE WILY, CUNNING AND RESOURCEFUL BRITISH POLITICIANS HAVE FAILED TO CAJOLE AND CORRUPT ME, NOBODY ELSE CAN DO SO.

In all the Axis countries I have visited, I have not only studied very closely the public opinion in regard to India, but I have also acquainted myself at first hand with the attitude and policy of the three Governments. Friends! The latest declaration of Premier Tojo made at the Imperial Diet on 16th June, 1943, which I had the privilege of hearing personally, following my interview with him on 14th June, was absolutely clear and unequivocal. In the course of that statement which will live in history for all time as an epoch-making declaration, His Excellency said: 'Japan is firmly resolved to extend all means in order to help to expel and eliminate from India the Anglo-Saxon influences which are the enemy of the Indian people, and enable India to achieve full independence in the true sense of the term.'

Friends! I know that some anti-Axis people have been making efforts to mislead the Indian people by suggesting that it is unbelievable that the Axis powers should become so generous as to support India's demand for independence. But to me the attitude of every Axis Power is traditionally both natural and easily understandable. Today, the Axis Powers and India have a common enemy, and therefore a common interest and objective.

The Axis Powers must, in their own interest and in order to ensure their own freedom and prosperity in the future, defeat and overthrow the British Empire. In order to achieve that aim they must expel Anglo-American Powers and influence from India, and they must do this even if the Indian people preferred to remain under the British yoke. Knowing, however, that the Indian people have been struggling for their freedom, the sympathy of the Axis Powers naturally goes out to them.

Moreover, if India could achieve her national emancipation from the British Empire, it will be of advantage to the whole world including the Axis Powers. Reason and common sense should, therefore, easily comprehend why the Axis powers have adopted so friendly an attitude towards the Indian Independence Movement. Having been completely foiled in their anti-Axis and anti-Japanese propaganda, the Anglo-American Imperialists and their hirelings have fallen back on their last subterfuge. Referring to Premier Tojo's repeated declarations, they have been saying that these declarations are the embodiment of policies intended to bluff the gullible and credulous people. There is an old saying in Sanskrit which you all know—ATMAWATH MANYATE JAGATH—which means that a man would judge the world according to his own nature. Being hypocrites themselves, these people think that everybody else is a hypocrite.

However, Premier Tojo has given the most effective and crushing reply to such vile propaganda by declaring to the whole world that before the end of the present year both Burma and the Philippines will have independence in reality. I wonder what new arguments our enemies can possibly invent for their anti-Axis propaganda when this year is out.

Countrymen! You are aware that towards the end of 1940 since I saw that Mahatma Gandhi had at long last launched civil disobedience campaign, I felt that the honour and prestige of the Indian people had been vindicated, and it was necessary to plan the Indian revolution on a larger scale and in an effective manner in order to bring it to fruition. But for that it was necessary to have information on the international situation and to establish contact with the Axis Powers and to secure the active assistance of our countrymen abroad. Today I am in a position to announce to you that all these objectives have been fully achieved.

Firstly, we know the international situation at first hand and we are, therefore, convinced of our ultimate victory. Secondly, we know at first hand that the Axis Powers in general, and Japan in particular, are the best friends and allies that the Indian people now have for their struggle for freedom. Thirdly, all Indians outside India, who are not living in countries directly under the control of our enemies, have now been brought together into one well-built organization. They are following closely developments inside India and on the other hand they are keeping unimpeded contact with international events. They are making all possible preparations to bring at the right time the maximum assistance to you who have been carrying on this struggle at home in spite of internment, persecution and brutality.

Friends! You may remember that I have in the past assured you more than once that when the hour strikes, I, and many others like myself, will be by your side to share the glory of fighting and suffering side by side and to share with you the joy of victory as well. The British Broadcasting Corporation, through its speaker Mr. Brenwood, said that I did not have the slightest intention of fulfilling my pledge. I would like to tell them that my pledge, which had been given not to the BBC but to my countrymen, would be redeemed in the fullness of time. Now, I have taken the third step, and I am not far from the Indian frontier. No power on earth was able to hamper my movements since January 1941; and no power on earth will be able to prevent my crossing the frontier once again in order to participate in the last phase of our national struggle.

Countrymen and Friends! In conclusion, let me convey through you to our comrades in prison and in internment my brotherly greetings. Tell them to be of good cheer. They have upheld the honour and prestige of our country. Through their sufferings, they have declared to the whole world that enslaved India is at war with Britain. I, and all those who have been working outside India, are proud of them. Not a day passes without our paying humble homage to their noble martyrdom. I assure them once again that their suffering will not be in vain.

India shall be free—and before long. And a free India will throw open the prison gates so that her worthy sons may step out of the darkness of the prison cells into the light of freedom, joy and self-fulfilment.

Inquilab Zindabad! (Long Live Revolution!)
Azad Hind Zindabad! (Long Live Free India!)

5

The Fable about India

[Press interview, 28 June 1943][1]

Erwin Wickert will now give our German listeners an account of the talk which we had yesterday with Mr. Subhas Chandra Bose.

'This fable that India is divided into castes, parties, religions, communities and races and therefore, cannot rule herself has been invented by British propaganda. Communism has worked in India for British interests ever since 1939, when Germany concluded a non-aggression pact with the Soviet Union. The Indian people have proved in practice that they are capable of governing themselves. Just as sure as the victory of the Tripartite Powers is the fact that India will gain her freedom in this war.'

These phrases are the main points of an interview which Subhas Chandra Bose, the leader of the Indian Independence Movement, granted to listeners of the German Radio. Calmly and deliberately Bose answered all the questions put in the German language. With sharp, decisive gestures he underlined his words. The discussion was based on the fact that Subhas Chandra Bose employed the Radio as the principal propaganda weapon in the struggle for a free India. We in East Asia clearly remember how Bose, following his escape from prison and before his arrival in Germany, spoke over the Free India Radio only a few days after British propaganda claimed that Subhas Chandra Bose was dead. When asked as to which parts of the Indian nation were particularly affected by his movement, he answered that like National Socialism his movement embraced the entire Indian population. Then followed these questions and answers.

[1] *Testament of Subhas Bose*, pp. 144–7.

Q. When the arrival of Your Excellency in Tokyo was announced ten days ago, there was not one among the Indians in Free East Asia who did not welcome this event with great joy. All the great Indian communities in China, the Philippines, Japan, Indo-China, Thailand and Malaya sent you congratulatory telegrams. How does this fact tally with the British claims to the effect that the Indian people are disunited, split up into castes, religions and races, which are fighting each other?

A. This is a typical example of lying British propaganda. In my National Movement the religious question does not exist. I have followers among all Indians, in particular among the Mohammedans who, according to the British, pursue separatist aims.

Q. When looking at the political map of India, you notice the relatively large states of the Indian Princes besides those parts of the country which are directly under British control. What is the role of Indian Princes in the policy of Your Excellency?

A. The Princes will not be able to stop our movement and its victorious end. They either voluntarily submitted to Britain or are under British pressure. Contrary to what happened in the last World War, they are not playing any political role in the present one. During the last 20 years and under the very eyes of the Princes a national movement for India's independence began throughout the Indian states. It is the people who count today. It is in the Indian states that my movement has found many followers.

Q. Is there any other Indian group which hampers unity to any significant extent? For instance, how about the Communists to whom, apparently on Moscow's pressure, Britain has granted more freedom in India during the last few years?

A. The Third International has been fighting in India for British interests ever since the outbreak of the war in 1939. Since that moment, it lost all chances of success with the Indian people. Its political significance has thus decreased. In spite of its alliance with Britain, we do not fear to fight against it. The only real danger facing our movement is the desire to bring about a compromise with Great Britain, a wish which is still being voiced by some people in India who have not yet realized facts.

Q. Britain's propaganda bases the claim for domination on the fact that India is not able to govern herself.

A. Bose only smiled and said that it was difficult for him to take this old British argument seriously. He added: When the British came to India we had for a long time our own successful governments. We have an age-old history, much older than the British. Apart from this fact, Indian Congress Ministries in the recent past functioned in eight Indian Provinces. Though we were not free, we were able to do more for our people during that short period than the British did in the course of their entire domination. Then, the social problem of India was, for the first time, seriously tackled. This fact has given the Indian people the necessary self-confidence. We know that we are more capable of administering our country than the British authorities. In 1939, when the war against Germany broke out, the British Parliament took away from the Congress Ministries the rights of self-government, because further progress was considered too dangerous.

Subhas Chandra Bose then emphasized the similarity between the fate of Germany and India, and pointed out that in the 17th century Britain, according to the motto *'divide et impera'* repeatedly tried to exploit the discord, which formerly prevailed in Germany and Europe in favour of her so-called principle of 'balance of power.' Britain has been doing the same thing in India for a century, and, as formerly in Europe, she plays one Indian party against the other. Though the differences between these parties are not really significant, Britain aggravates them and tells the whole world that India is incapable of governing herself. Britain alone is responsible for the wrong picture, which even many well-meaning people still have of India. 'I know,' Bose said, 'that the Germans, having had personal experience of Britain's policy, understand India and her fight better than any other nation in the world. I am, therefore, convinced that our fight is closely connected with the struggle now being waged by Germany and the other Tripartite Powers. Should we be alone, our fight against Britain would be very difficult.'

Bose concluded the interview with the words: 'I am firmly convinced that the Tripartite Powers will be victorious, and I believe just as strongly that India will attain independence in this war.'

—BERLIN RADIO, 28 June 1943

6

Subhas Chandra Bose Takes the Lead

[Address to the INA at Singapore on 2 July 1943, and proceedings of the meeting of the Committee of Representatives of the Indian Independence League, 4 July 1943][1]

On July 2, Sri Subhas Chandra Bose stepped off a plane from Tokyo at the airport at Syonan and was accorded a royal welcome by the leaders of the movement and the representatives of the Indian National Army. A guard of honour composed of the members of the INA was drawn up on the courtyard. He was overcome with emotion when he saw with his own eyes India's Army of Liberation. 'The only thing we have been lacking so far in our fight for independence is an armed force to fight against the British. You, patriotic warriors, have come forward and provided that armed force', he said, addressing the guard of honour. 'Let us all march forward together, ready to lay down our lives and thus win the freedom of our Motherland.' The men of the INA, in reply, gave him three resounding cheers.

Remarkable scenes of patriotic fervour and enthusiasm were witnessed at the meeting of the Committee of Representatives of the Indian Independence League in East Asia held in Syonan on July 4, when

[1] S.A. Das and K.B. Subbaiah, eds (with a foreword by John A. Thivy, Minister of State and Secretary, Provisional Government of Free India), *Chalo Delhi! An Historical Account of the Independence Movement in East Asia* (Kuala Lumpur: The Economy Printers, n.d), pp. 123–5, 130.

Sri Subhas Chandra Bose assumed office as President of the League in East Asia. From early morning large crowds thronged all approaches to the Cathay Cinema, not minding the steady drizzle, to catch a glimpse of their leader Subhas Bose, who on arrival at the Cinema accompanied by Rash Behari Bose, were greeted with thunderous ovation from the crowds. The Hinomaru (Rising Sun flag) and the Indian National Tri-colour flag adorned the dais. On Subhas Bose's entry into the meeting hall, the whole assembly rose up and greeted him with cheers. From all parts of the hall cries of 'Subhas Bose Ki Jai,' 'Rash Behari Bose Ki Jai,' 'Mahatma Gandhi Ki Jai,' 'Moulana Abul Kalam Azad ki Jai,' and 'Pandit Jawaharlal Nehru Ki Jai' rent the air.

The proceedings commenced with the garlanding of the two leaders by girl students of the Ramakrishna Mission. Miss S.N. Saraswathi delighted the gathering with the singing of Indian national songs.

Deafening cheers filled the air as Rash Behari Bose announced the appointment of 'Deshsevak' Subhas Chandra Bose as President of the Indian Independence League in East Asia. Sri Rash Behari Bose's address was translated into Tamil by Lt.-Col. S. A. Alagappan.

Before he commenced his address, Sri Subhas Chandra Bose paid a well-deserved tribute to the retiring President in Hindustani, which was translated into Tamil. It was indeed a touching scene, Subhas Bose said:

'During and before the last Great War, people in India knew him (the Retiring President) very well, but the present generation may have forgotten him. His marvellous services at the risk of his life during the last war for the liberation of India are not only fresh in our memories but are also in the records of the British Imperialists.'

Subhas Bose asked the retiring President to continue his activities in the League as the President's Supreme Adviser and to guide him in leading this movement.

7

Hunger, Thirst, Privation, Forced Marches and Death

[Presidential address to the East Asia Delegates Conference at Singapore, 4 July 1943][1]

Mr. Rash Behari Bose and representatives of the Indian Independence Movement in East Asia! Sisters and Brothers!

I thank you from the bottom of my heart for the honour you have done me, by appointing me to the leadership of the Indian Independence Movement in East Asia. I accept this responsibility—but I do so with a feeling of extreme humility and I pray that God may grant me strength to fulfill my duty, to the entire satisfaction of my countrymen at home and abroad.

If you were to hear my experiences—at home and abroad—since the outbreak of the present war, you would feel, as I do, that the hand of Providence has been protecting us from harm and has been guiding our efforts along the path leading to victory and freedom. This has increased my optimism and self-confidence a hundredfold.

Friends, the time has now come for freedom-loving Indians to act. Action in a war-crisis demands, above all, military discipline, as well as unflinching loyalty to the cause. I, therefore, call upon you, all my countrymen in East Asia, to line up in one solid phalanx under one leadership and prepare for the grim fight that is ahead of us. I am confident that they will do so.

[1] *On To Delhi*, pp. 22–30, translated from the original Hindustani. Audio and video recordings of Netaji's original speech in Hindustani are available in the archives of the Netaji Research Bureau.

I am glad to tell you that the momentous step taken today serves to unite in a common bond, not only the patriotic Indians in East Asia, but patriotic Indians all over the world as well. I have today the confidence and support of all freedom-loving Indians abroad, who are actively working for the emancipation of our Motherland. Even Indians now living in enemy countries, where they are unable to work actively for India's freedom, are morally with us in the work that we are doing. Within my knowledge, this is the first time in recent history that Indians living abroad have been united in one organization, for the attainment of one common goal.

What is perhaps even more remarkable is that patriotic Indians abroad are working in complete harmony with their countrymen at home. I have publicly declared several times that, when I left home and Homeland in 1941, on an important mission, it was in accordance with the will of the vast majority of my countrymen. Since then, despite all the restrictions imposed by the CID—that is, the Secret Service—I have remained in constant touch with my countrymen at home. Today, I can go so far as to inform you that during the last twelve months, a large number of our representatives have been sent to India from outside, from all directions. Some of them have been captured and shot, for which we shall, in due time, exact full revenge. But many more have been able to evade arrest and, according to latest reports, they are working satisfactorily. Thus, patriotic Indians abroad have been working as genuine trustees of the freedom fighters at home. I can assure everybody once again that whatever we have done up till now, or may do in future, has been and will be for the freedom of India, and we shall never do anything that is either against the interest of India or will not be in accordance with the will of our people.

I shall now deal with the question as to how we can win our liberty. Some of my friends at home had hoped, at one time, that at the pressure of an international crisis, the British Government would, in its own interest, accede to India's demand for independence. These friends must have been disillusioned by now—because it is transparently clear that both during and after the War the British Government intends to exploit India more ruthlessly than ever before. That is why Field Marshal Lord Wavell is being sent as Viceroy and Governor-General. I have noticed that certain circles at home are extremely dissatisfied over this appointment, and they would have probably preferred a man like Lord Halifax as Viceroy, but I do not share their view. For me, the appointment of Field Marshal Lord Wavell as Viceroy is a prophetic event—a writing on the wall. This ever-retreating Commander-in-Chief is destined to be the last Viceroy of India. Moreover, the military, political and economic exploitation of India, which he is bound to intensify, will further embitter the Indian masses and thereby strengthen the gathering forces of revolution.

But though India is in for a period of military dictatorship under the new Viceroy, I anticipate, nevertheless, that in future another attempt at a compromise with India will be made. This attempt will be nothing more than a bluff—or a hoax—and our countrymen at home should be prepared in advance to see through it—as they did when Sir Stafford Cripps offered empty promises to India in April, 1942. Mr. Winston Churchill, the supreme representative of British people, recently gave an indication of his mentality when he told the Lord Mayor of London that he did not like even the expression 'British Commonwealth', preferring the expression 'British Empire' instead. The last Imperialist Prime Minister of England will, no doubt, do his very best to preserve that Empire and any offer that he will make to the Indian people will be only for the purpose of deceiving them. But there is no sense in even thinking of a compromise with an Empire that will soon disappear from the face of the earth.

Those of you who have studied the history of freedom-movements in other lands—as I have done—must have observed that for the achievement of independence, two conditions are essential—firstly, a favourable international situation and, secondly, necessary sacrifice and effort. The first condition has been already fulfilled. If India had to fight single-handed with the British Empire, our task would have been exceedingly difficult. The Tripartite Powers are determined to carry on the war until Anglo-American Imperialism is overthrown.

Friends! For more than two years I have been constantly travelling with a view to studying the war-situation at first hand. From this study, I am convinced that, however long this war may last, there can be one outcome—namely, the complete victory of the Tripartite Powers and their allies. I am not blind to the many difficulties that have to be overcome before Anglo-American Imperialism could be defeated. I am also aware that in a long war, temporary ups and downs are unavoidable and that at the present moment, the Anglo-American Powers are enjoying a temporary advantage in certain unimportant theatres of war. But the general war-situation—and the strategic position in particular—remains greatly advantageous to the Tripartite Powers, and you will see that, as the days roll by, the Anglo-American Powers will have to suffer one defeat after another.

Friends! The British Empire, in spite of all its power and might, has been seeking and obtaining help from every possible quarter. It is, therefore, but natural that we, too, should look out for sympathy and assistance, wherever it is available. Moreover, every freedom-movement in history has had to seek some help or other from abroad, before it could achieve success. The logic of events, in the present case, has made the Tripartite Powers our natural allies and there is nothing wrong if we accept their sympathy, or even their help, should we need it.

I know that some of my countrymen, who are under the influence of British propaganda, doubt the sincerity of the Tripartite Powers in their attitude towards India. But common sense should tell them that it is the most natural thing for the enemies of British imperialism to support India's demand for liberty. Moreover, with the exception of England, a free India will be an advantage to the whole world, including the Tripartite Powers.

The Tripartite Powers have in the past, often, clarified their attitude towards India. In addition, the Japanese Government, through its worthy Prime Minister, General Tojo, has repeatedly proclaimed its policy towards the Philippines, Burma and India. British politicians and propagandists, being themselves hypocrites, have been describing Japan's attitude as insincere and hypocritical. But Prime Minister General Tojo has dealt a crushing blow to Anglo-American propaganda by boldly declaring before the world that independence will be a reality in Burma and in the Philippines—not after the war but before the end of the current year.

Japan's attitude towards Burma and the Philippines will be the most convincing proof of her sincerity and good faith. But apart from this, as a normal human being, I see no reason why I should have any doubt or mistrust with regard to Japan's intentions. Japan was the first Asiatic Power to successfully resist foreign aggression—and Japan knows, more than any other Asiatic power, that, so long as the enslaved Asiatic nations are not emancipated, no Asiatic nation can feel completely safe from the menace of aggression. Moreover, there is in Japan, today, what one might call an Asiatic consciousness, which manifests itself in a desire to help other Asiatic nations to achieve their liberation. This is a unique development, which affords a golden opportunity to all enslaved nations in Asia to emancipate them and set up a new order based on freedom, justice and morality.

If anybody has still any doubt in his mind on this point, I should ask him to place his trust in me. My loyalty is to India and to India alone and not even our enemies will have the audacity to urge that I am capable of betraying my country. And as I said in Tokyo the other day, if the British Government could not demoralize me after persecuting me all my life, nobody else can do so. And if cunning British politicians could neither cajole nor deceive me—no one else can hope to do so. Every Indian should realize that the victory of the Anglo-American Powers will mean for India continued enslavement and more ruthless exploitation. Our only hope of freedom is therefore in a Tripartite victory. But we should so conduct our own struggle that an Axis victory may simultaneously bring us our liberty.

Friends! We have now the most favourable international situation and the most happy combination of circumstances. Consequently, all that is needed for winning freedom is sufficient effort and sacrifice. Our record in this connection is by no means unsatisfactory. You may remember that in May last year after the departure of Sir Stafford Cripps from India and exactly 85 years after the outbreak of our first war of independence, I declared that our national struggle was entering upon a most significant phase. Since then, we have passed many a milestone on our onward march—the most important of these being the intensification of the Civil Disobedience Movement and the commencement of sabotage activities after the arrest of Mahatma Gandhi in August last. In the history of India's struggle, August 1942 will, therefore, remain an unforgettable landmark, indicating the psychological transition from passive to active resistance. Not content with a civil disobedience campaign, the Indian people are now morally prepared to employ other means for achieving their liberation.

The time has, therefore, come to pass on to the next stage of our campaign. All organizations, whether inside or outside, must now transform themselves into a disciplined fighting organization under one leadership. The aim and purpose of this organization should be to take up arms against British Imperialism, when the time is ripe and the signal is given. In order to mobilize all our forces effectively, I intend to organize a provisional government of Free India. It will be the task of this provisional government to lead the Indian Revolution to a successful conclusion. To this end, the provisional government will have to prepare the Indian people—inside and outside India—for an armed struggle, which will be the culmination of all our national efforts since 1883. When the revolution succeeds and Anglo-American Imperialism is expelled from India, the task of the provisional government will be over. It will then make room for a permanent government to be set up inside India, *in accordance with the will of the Indian people.*

When all our preparations for the last struggle are complete, it will be possible to bring the Indian struggle into line with the common struggle of the Tripartite Powers against the common foe. By participation in this common fight, we shall be qualifying for our freedom. By shedding our blood in a sacred cause, we shall be paying the price of liberty and, at the same time, we shall be laying the only enduring foundation for our national unity. And last but not least, by winning freedom through our own efforts and sacrifice, we shall be acquiring the strength whereby we shall preserve our liberty for all time.

Friends! In conclusion, I thank you once again from the bottom of my heart for the confidence you have reposed in me, for the assurance of unflinching support that you have given me. I warn you that, though we are absolutely sure of our final victory, we can never afford to underestimate the enemy and we should even be prepared for temporary setbacks. We have a grim fight ahead of us—for the enemy is at once powerful, unscrupulous and ruthless. In this final march to freedom you will have to face hunger, thirst, privation, forced marches and death. Only when you pass this test, will freedom be yours. I am confident that you will do so and thereby bring freedom and prosperity to your enslaved and impoverished land. When we hold our victory parade in the Red Fort of Delhi, no one can say who among us will be there, who among us will live to see India free. Whether we live or die, that is of no consequence. The only thing that matters, the only truth, is that India shall be free.

Inquilab Zindabad! (Long Live Revolution!) Azad Hind Zindabad! (Long Live Free India!)

8

To Delhi, to Delhi!

[Speech delivered as the Supreme Commander of the INA at a military review of the INA in Singapore on 5 July 1943][1]

As the President of the Indian Independence League in East Asia Srijut Subhas Chandra Bose took the salute at a parade of the Indian National Army on the ground opposite the Singapore Municipal Offices on July 5. Representative detachments of the Army took up their positions an hour before the parade began. Looking smart in his khaki military uniform, Srijut Subhas Chandra Bose, accompanied by an INA bodyguard, arrived at the parade punctually at 10.30 a.m., when the troops presented arms and the bugle sounded. The President then ascended the dais and from there surveyed the serried ranks of the warriors who had sworn to sacrifice their lives in the fight for India's freedom.

Led by the Chiefs of the Indian National Army and accompanied by Srijut Rash Behari Bose, his Supreme Adviser, Srijut Subhas Chandra Bose went round inspecting the Army. The President then returned to the rostrum and delivered a stirring message to the officers and men of the Army. Thunderous shouts of 'Inqilab Zindabad', 'Mahatma Gandhi Ki Jai' and 'Subhas Chandra Bose Ki Jai' punctuated his address.

The President said:
Soldiers of India's Army of Liberation,

Today is the proudest day of my life. Today, it has pleased Providence to give me the unique privilege and honour of announcing to the

[1] *Chalo Delhi*, pp. 135–8.

whole world that India's Army of Liberation has come into being. This Army has now been drawn up in military formation on the battlefield of Singapore, which was once the bulwark of the British Empire. This is not only the Army that will emancipate India from the British yoke; it is also the Army that will, hereafter, create the future national army of Free India. Every Indian must feel proud that this Army—his own Army—has been organized entirely under Indian leadership and that when the historic moment arrives, under Indian leadership it will go to battle.

There are people who thought at one time that the Empire, on which the sun did not set, was an everlasting Empire. No such thought ever troubled me. History has taught me that every empire has its inevitable decline and collapse. Moreover, I had seen with my own eyes, cities and fortresses that were once the bulwark, but which became the graveyards of by-gone empires. But standing today on the graveyard of the British Empire, even a child is convinced that the almighty British Empire is already a thing of the past.

When France declared war on Germany in 1939 and the campaign began, there was but one cry, which rose from the lips of German soldiers 'To Paris, to Paris.' When the brave soldiers of Nippon set out on their march in December 1941, there was but one cry, which rose from their lips 'To Singapore, to Singapore.' Comrades! My soldiers! Let your battle cry be 'To Delhi, to Delhi.' How many of us will individually survive this war of Freedom, I do not know. But I do know this that we shall ultimately win and our task will not end until our surviving heroes hold the victory-parade on another graveyard of the British Empire—the Lal Kila or Red Fortress of ancient Delhi.

Throughout my public career, I have always felt that though India is otherwise ripe for independence in every way, she has lacked one thing, namely, an army of liberation. George Washington of America could fight and win freedom, because he had his army. Garibaldi could liberate Italy, because he had his armed volunteers behind him. It is your privilege and honour to be the first to come forward and organize India's National Army. By doing so, you have removed the last obstacle in our path to freedom. Be happy and proud that you are the pioneers—the vanguard—in such a noble cause.

Let me remind you that you have a two-fold task to perform. With the force of arms and at the cost of your blood, you will have to win liberty. Then, when India is free, you will have to organize the permanent army of Free India whose task it will be to preserve our liberty for all time. We must build up our national defence on such an unshakeable foundation that never again in our history shall we lose our freedom.

As soldiers, you will always have to cherish and live up to the three ideals of faithfulness, duty and sacrifice. Soldiers, who always remain faithful to their nation, who perform their duty under all circumstances, and who are always prepared to sacrifice their lives, are invincible. If you, too, want to be invincible, engrave these three ideals in the innermost core of your hearts. A true soldier needs both military and spiritual training. You must—all of you—so train yourselves and your comrades that every soldier will have unbounded confidence in himself, will be conscious of being immensely superior to the enemy, will be fearless of death, and will have sufficient initiative to act on his own in any critical situation, should the need arise. During the course of the present war, you have seen with your own eyes what wonders, scientific training, coupled with courage, fearlessness and dynamism, can achieve. Learn all that you can from this example and build up for Mother India an absolutely first class modern army.

To those of you who are officers, I should like to say that your responsibility is a heavy one. Though the responsibility of an officer in every army in this world is indeed great, it is far greater in your case. Because of our political enslavement, we have no tradition like that of Mukden, Port Arthur or Sedan to inspire us. We have to unlearn some of the things that the British taught us and we have to learn that which they did not teach. Nevertheless, I am confident that you will rise to the occasion and fulfill the task that your countrymen have thrown on your brave shoulders. Remember always that officers can make or unmake an army. Remember, too, that the British have suffered defeats on so many fronts, largely because of worthless officers. And remember also that out of your ranks will be born the future General Staff of the Army of Free India.

To all of you, I should like to say that in the course of this war, you will have to acquire the experience and achieve the success which alone can build up a national tradition for our army in future. An army that has no tradition of courage, fearlessness and invincibility cannot hold its own in a struggle with a powerful enemy.

Comrades! You have voluntarily accepted a mission that is the noblest that the human mind can conceive of. For the fulfilment of such a mission, no sacrifice is too great—not even the sacrifice of one's life. You are today the custodians of India's national honour and the embodiment of India's hopes and aspirations. So conduct yourselves that your countrymen may bless you and posterity may be proud of you.

I have said that today is the proudest day of my life. For an enslaved people, there can be no greater pride, no higher honour, than to be the first soldier in the army of liberation. But this honour carries with it a corresponding responsibility and I am deeply conscious of it. I assure you that I shall be with you in darkness and in sunshine, in sorrow and in joy, in suffering and in victory. For the present, I can offer you nothing except hunger, thirst, privation, forced marches and death. But if you follow me in life and in death—as I am confident you will—I shall lead you to victory and freedom. It does not matter who among us will live to see India free. It is enough that India shall be free and that we shall give our all to make her free. May God now bless our army and grant us victory in the coming fight!

Inquilab Zindabad! Azad Hind Zindabad!

9

Fight Shoulder to Shoulder

[Address of welcome made to Prime Minister General Hideki Tojo at a review of the march past presented by the forces of the INA on 6 July 1943][1]

The following day, Tuesday, July 6, 1943, in bright sunshine, and on the former battlefield of Singapore, the Premier of Nippon witnessed a parade of India's Army of Liberation, in the presence of Srijut Subhas Chandra Bose.

Premier General Tojo stood at the top of the Singapore Municipal Offices and surveyed the solid phalanx of the soldiers of India's Army of Liberation. Officers of the Indian National Army, whom the Nippon Premier reviewed, were conscious of the rare honour bestowed on them by Nippon, through General Tojo taking the salute at the parade. They were obviously strengthened by this further evidence of Nippon's sincerity and inflexible determination to give unstinting aid to Indians in their fight against the Anglo-Americans for the complete independence of their motherland.

To the serried ranks of the Indian National Army drawn up on the esplanade, the sight of the Premier of Nippon, General Tojo, and Srijut Subhas Chandra Bose, the uncrowned King of Free India, standing side by side, and taking salute at the Parade was a rare experience and a wonderful tonic to the already high morale.

The following address of welcome was presented to Premier Tojo by Srijut Subhas Chandra Bose on behalf of the Indian National Army:

[1] *Chalo Delhi*, pp. 138–9.

'Your Excellency, on behalf of the Indian National Army I have great pleasure in offering Your Excellency a most hearty welcome this morning. I desire to express our profound appreciation of the great honour Your Excellency has done us by spending so much of your valuable time in order to review our Army. This day will ever remain a red-letter day in the history of the newly organized Army of Free India. Your Excellency's presence among our soldiers today, immediately after sending an inspiring message to the Indian Independence League Conference yesterday, has given a powerful impetus to our revolutionary struggle.

The Army that stands before Your Excellency today knows that it will have to fight for India's liberty. It is also conscious of the many difficulties that still beset the path to victory and freedom. But this Army is determined to achieve India's liberty at the cost of any sacrifice. In this task the Army has the active support of all Indians in East Asia, whose enthusiasm knows no bounds.

In conclusion, I beg to assure Your Excellency of our unshakeable determination to fight with you shoulder to shoulder, through joy and sorrow, through sunshine and darkness, till complete victory is achieved and till India regains her lost liberty.'

10

Why I Left Home and Homeland

[Speech delivered at the mass meeting held at Singapore on 9 July 1943][1]

Sisters and brothers! Let me, first of all thank you for the exceedingly warm and enthusiastic welcome that you have given me today. I am particularly thankful to my sisters who have boldly come forward in such large numbers to give expression to their patriotic feelings. From what I see today, I feel confident that in the coming fight, my countrymen in Syonan and in Malai will play a leading part. What was once a bulwark of British Imperialism has now become a bulwark of Indian Nationalism.

Next, I would like to tell you quite frankly what made me leave home and homeland on a journey that was fraught with danger of every kind. You know that I have been actively working in the independence movement ever since I left the portals of the University in 1921. I have been through all the civil disobedience campaigns during the last two decades. In addition to this, I have been repeatedly put in prison without trial, on the suspicion of having been connected with secret revolutionary movement—whether non-violent or violent—with which I have been familiar. I may also assert without the slightest exaggeration that there is no nationalist leader in India who can claim to possess the many-sided experience that I have been able to acquire. In the light of this experience, I came to the conclusion that all the

[1] *On To Delhi*, pp. 31–6, translated from the original Hindustani.

efforts that we could forward inside India, would not suffice to expel the British from our country. If the struggle at home had sufficed to achieve liberty for our people, I would not have been so foolish as to undertake this unnecessary risk and hazard.

To put it briefly, therefore, my object in leaving India was to supplement from outside the struggle going on at home. Without this supplementary help from outside it is impossible for anybody to liberate India. On the other hand, the supplementary help from outside which the national struggle at home so urgently needs is in reality very small. This is because the defeats inflicted on the British by the Axis Powers have shattered British power and prestige to such an extent, that our task has been rendered comparatively easy.

The help that our countrymen at home needed and still need is a two-fold one—moral and material. Firstly, they have to be morally convinced that their victory is assured in the long run. Secondly, they have to be given military help from outside. In order to do the first, one had to study objectively the International war-situation and thereby find out what the result of the war was going to be. To do the second, one had to find out what Indians outside India could do to help their countrymen at home and also if it was possible to obtain help from the enemies of British Imperialism, should that need arise. Friends! I am now in a position to tell you that both these objectives have been fulfilled. By travelling abroad, I could see things for myself and could study the respective positions of the belligerent powers. Thereafter, when I came to the conclusion that the defeat of Anglo-American Imperialism was assured, I conveyed that information to my countrymen at home. Then, I was delighted to find that my countrymen all over the world were wide-awake and were anxious to undertake their share of the national struggle. I was also gratified to find that the Axis Powers—and Japan in particular—were really eager to see India free, and they were prepared to render any help that was within their power, should the Indian people desire it.

As to the attitude of the Indians abroad, I do not think that there is any man or woman who does not want India to be free and who is not prepared to help the national struggle. As to the attitude of the Axis Powers and of Japan—if anybody has the slightest doubt or suspicion, I can easily convince him with overwhelming proofs that outside the ranks of our countrymen, they are the best friends we have in the world today. Moreover, I can ask you to trust me. Not even my enemies will have the audacity to say that I am capable of doing anything against the interests of my country. And if the British Government could not demoralize me or deceive me or allure me no other power on earth can do so. Therefore, believe me when I say that if you want any external help in your struggle against British Imperialism the Axis Powers will come to your aid. But whether you do need any help or not, is for you to decide—and it goes without saying, that if you could do without any help, it would be the best course for India. At the same time I should add that if the almighty British Government can go round the whole world with the begging-bowl asking for help everywhere—even from the enslaved and impoverished people of India—there is nothing wrong in our taking help from outside, if we are forced to do so.

The time has come when I can openly tell the whole world, including our enemies, as to how it is proposed to bring about our national liberation. Indians outside India—particularly, Indians in East Asia—are going to organize a fighting force which will be powerful enough to attack the British Army in India. When we do so, a revolution will break out, not only among the civil population at home, but also between the Indian Army, which is now standing under the British flag. When the British Government is thus attacked from both sides—from inside India and from outside—it will collapse and the Indian people will then regain their liberty.

According to my plan, therefore, it is not even necessary to bother about the attitude of the Axis Powers towards India. If Indians outside and inside India will only do their duty, it is possible for the Indian people to throw the British out of India and liberate 388 millions of their countrymen. There may be croakers who will say that if 388 millions of Indians cannot expel British power from India, how can three million living abroad hope to do so? But friends, look to the history of Ireland. If three million Irishmen living under the British domination—under a form of martial-law—could, with the help of five thousand armed Sinn Fein volunteers, bring the British Government to its knees in 1921, why cannot three million Indians, backed by a powerful movement at home, hope to throw the British out of India, when the aid of powerful Japan is readily available?

I must, however, say that Indians living abroad and particularly in East Asia, must put forward their maximum effort. In order to do so effectively, it is my intention to set up a Provisional Government of Free India. The task of this government will be to mobilize all the resources of the Indian people and lead the fight against the British Army in India. When the campaign succeeds and India is free, the Provisional Government will make room for the permanent Government of Free India, which will be set up in accordance with the will of the Indian people.

Friends! You will now realize that the time has come for three million Indians living in East Asia to mobilize all their available resources—including money and manpower. Half-hearted measures will not do. I want Total Mobilization and nothing less—for we have been told repeatedly, even by our enemies, that this is a total war. You see before you today a part of India's Army of Liberation—the *Azad Hind Fauj* or the Indian National Army. They held their ceremonial parade the other day in front of the Town Hall. Thereafter, they have resolved that they will not rest till they hold their victory-parade before the red fortress of ancient Delhi. They have adopted the slogan—'Onward to Delhi—Onward to Delhi!' Friends! Let the slogan of the three million Indians in East Asia be—'Total Mobilization for a Total War.' Out of this total mobilization, I expect at least three hundred thousand soldiers and three crores—that is thirty millions—of dollars. I want also a unit of brave Indian women to form a 'Death-defying Regiment' who will wield the sword, which the brave Rani of Jhansi wielded in India's First War of Independence in 1857.

Friends! We have for a long time, been hearing so much of the Sec ond Front in Europe. But our countrymen at home are now hard-pressed, and they are demanding a Second Front. Give me Total Mobilization in East Asia and I promise you a second front—a real second front for the Indian struggle.

11

Empire that Rose in a Day will Vanish in a Night

[Speech delivered at a meeting of Indian women held under the auspices of the Women's Section of the IIL, Singapore Branch on 12 July 1943][1]

Sisters! First of all I want to thank you from the bottom of my heart for the grand welcome that you have given me this afternoon. I am purposely calling it a grand welcome because I cannot conceive of a more magnificent welcome than what you have given me this afternoon. At the same time, I want to thank you also for the great enthusiasm which you exhibited the other day, when we had our Rally at the Padang in front of the Municipal Offices. Not only myself but also the other friends and guests who were with me on the platform were exceedingly impressed by the brave manner in which you stood the rain and inclement weather and stuck to your posts till the very last. I know that some of you had brought your babies also along with you. Your brave attitude and your profound enthusiasm on that occasion have deeply impressed all of us. I have no doubt that after this good beginning your work will progress rapidly from day to day.

You all know, as well as I do, of the part our women at home have taken in the Freedom Movement, especially during the last twenty-two years. From the very beginning of the new awakening in India, our women have taken a prominent part in all spheres of public life. But this has been particularly evident since the year 1921, when the Congress

[1] *On To Delhi*, pp. 44–50.

was reborn under the leadership of Mahatma Gandhi. It is not only in connection with the Congress Movement or the Movement of Civil Disobedience but also in connection with the secret revolutionary movement that our sisters have played a noble part.

In fact, it will be no exaggeration for me to say that there is no sphere of public activity, there is no department of national endeavour, in which Indian women have not played a prominent part. What is more, there is no suffering which Indian women have not gladly and bravely shared along with our men in the course of several decades of our national struggle. Whether it is a work of touring from village to village without food and drink, whether it is a task of lecturing at one meeting after another, whether it is a task of carrying the Freedom message from door to door, whether it is a task of leading processions along public streets in defiance of the official orders and in spite of lathi charges by the inhuman British Police, or whether it is a task of running election campaigns or whether again it is a task of facing bravely imprisonment and persecution, and insult and humiliation of every kind, nowhere have our women been found wanting. And last but not least our sisters, our brave sisters, have also played a prominent part in the secret revolutionary movement, and they have shown that when the need arises they could, like their brothers, shoot very well.

If today I express my fullest confidence in you, in your capacity to suffer and to fight for the freedom of your country, it is not an empty compliment which I indulge in, simply for the purpose of rousing your enthusiasm. If I do so, it is as a result of my personal experience. I know what our women are capable of, and, therefore, I say without the slightest exaggeration that there is no work, there is no sacrifice and there is no suffering which our sisters are not capable of. The time has now come for us to make the last and final effort in order to achieve the liberation of our Motherland. Such an opportunity is indeed rare in the lifetime of a nation. Certainly in our lifetime this opportunity will not come again and perhaps not even for another one hundred years. I must say that it is the Grace of Providence that this opportunity has suddenly presented itself to us. And if we grab this opportunity and make every effort to undergo every sacrifice, we shall be able to achieve once and for all our national emancipation.

I know that among us there are men who have at one time thought that the British Empire was an everlasting Empire, there are men who thought at one time that it is unbelievable that the British Empire can ever cease to exist, but history tells a different tale. History teaches us that every Empire has its fall just as it has its rise. And the time has come for the British Empire to disappear from the face of this world. If you remember, sisters, I told you the other evening at the Padang that at least we who stand on the battlefield of Singapore, at least we should be convinced, and we are convinced, that the British Empire is a thing of the past. We have seen with our own eyes how that Empire has disappeared from this part of the world, and we will see how it disappears from another part of the world also—from India as well. I remember having read years ago a book written by an Englishman called Meridith Conrade. Referring to India, he remarked in that book that once the Indian people are united, it would be impossible for the British to continue their domination over India. And in the course of his remarks, he said that an Empire, which rose in a day, would vanish in a night. I said in one of my radio talks not long ago that it took twenty long years to build Singapore and it took only seven days to evacuate Singapore. Well, I cannot expect that we shall be able to drive out the British from India within a week, but if we calculate mathematically we can find in how many weeks we shall be able to drive the British out of India as well when the final campaign is launched.

Sisters, I hope that each and every one of you has the fullest confidence that the time has come for us to make the final effort for our emancipation. I hope that each and every one of you has the fullest confidence that the ultimate outcome of this war can only be the defeat and overthrow of Anglo-American Imperialism, and it is only out of the defeat of Anglo-American Imperialism that India can hope to win her freedom. That is why I have always been asserting that India's freedom is bound up with the final victory of the Axis Powers. Today both the parties, India and the Axis Powers, have a common enemy, and therefore we have a common goal. We have to fight against the common enemy no matter what the sacrifice involved may be, and through our common suffering and sacrifice to win our liberty.

Even if it is possible to get our liberty without suffering, sacrifice and struggle, I am sure that is not worth having, because freedom that is obtained without sacrifice and struggle would be difficult to be retained even if we are free. Therefore if you want to liberate yourselves from the British yoke and thereafter to preserve your independence, once and for all, if you desire that never again in history should we lose our freedom, then it is necessary that in the course of our national struggle we should acquire that strength whereby we may win, and thereafter be able to preserve our liberty for all time. Therefore we have to pay the price of freedom, and the price of freedom is suffering, sacrifice and struggle. I have no doubt in my mind that we shall be able to put forward the necessary sacrifice and struggle, we shall be able to undergo cheerfully the necessary suffering, and thereby we shall not be able to free ourselves from the British domination, but thereafter we shall be able to retain our freedom forever.

Sisters, the time has come for us to begin our final preparations for the final struggle, in right earnest. We have no time to lose. No one can predict when the call may come, when the march would begin. We must therefore be so prepared that whenever the call comes we should be immediately prepared to begin our march. As I said the other day there is but one thought in our minds, there is but one cry which rises from our lips—'ONWARD TO DELHI, ONWARD TO DELHI!' The campaign which will be begun here in Syonan, which has become the grave-yard of the British Empire, that campaign will end only when we drive out the British from India and occupy our Metropolis. And then we shall parade finally in celebration of our victory before the famous Red Fort of Delhi.

Sisters, we had at one time conservative men amongst us who thought that women had nothing to do with the national struggle, and that it was entirely a man's affair. I hope that there are no such men in our midst today. On the contrary, I am convinced that until and unless Indian women play their due part in the national struggle, India can never hope to be free. And if I am so optimistic today of our speedy emancipation, it is because I am equally optimistic of the part that Indian women will play in the coming struggle.

When I talk of your playing your part in the coming struggle, I do not forget the part that our sisters at home are already playing in the struggle at home. I do not forget that there are hundreds, perhaps thousands of our sisters rotting in British jails in India today, and it is their suffering, it is their sacrifice, which is inspiring the entire youth of our country. I have no doubt that our friends at home, men and women, boys and girls, will go on doing their part, but we know that

that alone will not be enough to win our liberty. All the efforts that they may possibly put forward will not suffice to expel the Britishers from India; therefore, we have a duty to perform and that duty is to bring assistance to India from without.

Here in East Asia we have got a population close upon three million Indians, and I have no doubt that if we can bring about Total Mobilization of our resources, in manpower, in money and in other resources, we shall be able to bring that help to India which will enable our countrymen at home to finally overthrow the British yoke.

12

Subhas Chandra Bose Reorganizes the League

[Circular issued from IIL Headquarters at Syonan for reorganizing the League on 13 July 1943][1]

Soon after his assumption of the office of the President Sri Subhas Chandra Bose issued the following circular for reorganizing the League:

INDIAN INDEPENDENCE
LEAGUE HEADQUARTERS

7, Chancery Lane,
Syonan, 13th July 2603(1943)

In view of the new responsibilities that the Indian Independence Movement has to face in the near future and in view of the wave of enthusiasm that is visible among Indians in East Asia, it has become necessary to reorganize the Indian Independence League. The first step in this direction is to reorganize the Headquarters of the Indian Independence League. For this reorganization, some of the existing departments have to be expanded while other new departments have also to be set up. I am giving below the scheme of reorganization. I shall watch carefully the result of this reorganization and in the light of experience I may make further changes—if and when necessary.

DEPARTMENTS: 1. Military Bureau 2. Recruitment 3. Training 4. Supplies 5. Finance 6. Publicity Press and Propaganda 7. Health and Social Welfare 8. Overseas 9. Women 10. Reconstruction 11. Education and Culture 12. General Secretary.

[1] *Chalo Delhi*, pp. 149–56.

Department of Recruitment. This department will organize recruitment of the *Azad Hind Fauj* (Indian National Army) all over East Asia in a systematic way. This is a new department.

Department of Training. The existing Youth Department will be absorbed in this new Department. The work of this Department will be to provide some kind of training for all recruits throughout East Asia until the Army is in a position to take over these recruits and put them into military barracks.

The existing training institutes will be managed by these departments, and if necessary, more may be started. The present staff of the Youth Department will come under this Department and fresh appointments will be made, if and when necessary according to the amount of work that has to be handled by the department. The head of the Youth Department will become the head of the Department of Training.

Department of Supplies. The function of this new department will be to collect supplies from all over East Asia for the Indian Independence Movement in general and for the *Azad Hind Fauj* (Indian National Army) in particular for present and future use. The existing stores at the Headquarters of the Indian Independence League will henceforth be managed by the Department of Supplies.

Department of Health and Social Welfare. The existing Welfare Department will be absorbed in this Department. The new Department of Health and Social Welfare will have two sub-departments—namely: (a) Medical, and (b) Social Welfare.

The existing Welfare Department with its staff will be absorbed in the sub-department of Social Welfare. The head of the Welfare Department will become the Head of the Sub-department of Social Welfare. The medical Sub-department will be under a Junior Medical Officer. The whole department of Health and Social Welfare will be under a Senior Medical Officer.

Overseas Department. The work of this new department will be:

(a) To direct and stimulate the work of the branches
(b) To establish new branches where necessary
(c) To maintain regular contact between the headquarters and the different branches

Women's Department. This will be a new department. The work of this department will be to organize Indian women throughout East

Asia and direct and stimulate their activities in connection with the Indian Independence Movement. This department will also recruit women for the Army and will organize a Red Cross Department from among Indian women and girls.

Reconstruction Department. The work of this new department will be:

(a) To prepare plans for the future—particularly in connection with future administration in India.
(b) To train men for future administration, etc.

Education and Culture. This will be a new department. The function of this department will be to direct the educational and cultural activities of Indians in East Asia and to provide for additional facilities in this connection, in so far as it is possible for the League to do so.

General Secretary's Department. The function of this department will be:

(a) To maintain liaison with the *Hikari Kikan
(b) To co-ordinate the work of the different departments
(c) To perform any special duties that may be assigned by me from time to time.

This department will have a sub-department, to be called the House Sub-department. This sub-department will deal with problems arising out of the daily work of the Indian Independence League Headquarters, e.g., (a) Transport and Petrol, (b) Building and their equipment, (c) Light, Telephone, etc. at the Headquarters, (d) Medical Staff, and (e) Arrangement for the stay of guests coming from outside. When the work of the House sub-department increases it may be necessary and advisable to convert it into a full-fledged department.

ESTABLISHMENT: Questions with establishments (e.g. allowances, transfer, etc.) will be dealt with by me. The departments concerned will, however, make recommendations from time to time.

- After Major General Iwakuro had departed from Malaya to take up another appointment leaving the Kikan in charge of his successor Col. Yamamoto, the Kikan came to be known as 'Hikari Kikan.' 'Hikari' meaning light and glory.

EXISTING STAFF: The existing staff will all continue to work for the League in future. Transfers from one department to another may, however, be made, if found to be necessary, in order to give effect to the re-organization scheme outlined above.

DETAILED INSTRUCTIONS.—Detailed instructions with regard to the working of each department will follow.

SUBHAS CHANDRA BOSE,
President,
THE INDIAN INDEPENDENCE LEAGUE,
EAST ASIA.

The following circulars were issued by the Departments of Recruitment and Training to provide detailed instructions for the working of each department:

INDIAN INDEPENDENCE LEAGUE
HEADQUARTERS

(Department of Recruitment)

7, Chancery Lane, Syonan.
23rd July 2603 (1943)

SUBJECT: RECRUITMENT

You may be aware by now that the Headquarters of the Indian Independence League have been re-organized and that in order to effect the Total Mobilization of our man-power and resources, several new departments have been started. In accordance with this plan, this department has come into existence, and it is the earnest desire of our President that at least 300,000 men (including women volunteers) be recruited for the coming fight for India's freedom.

Regarding the training of these recruits, the newly formed Training Department will address you separately. I shall only tell you this: that we do not want to call up these recruits at once. In fact, the training will be done in three stages. In the first stage, recruits should not leave either homes or their professional work—and should do only morning or evening drills. In the second stage, they will be brought into camps for whole-time training—when these camps are started in different parts of East Asia. In the third stage, they will be brought into Military Barracks when they will become full-fledged members of the *Azad Hind Fauj* (Indian National Army).

It will be considered a breach of discipline, if any recruit suddenly gives up his professional work, or leaves his home, before he is called up for whole-time training.

To carry on the recruitment of volunteers for the Indian National Army in a systematic way the following machinery is being set up:

1. Under each Territorial Committee, the Chairman of every IIL Branch will be the Recruiting Officer for his own area.
2. Under each branch, the Chairman of every IIL Sub-Branch will be an Assistant Recruiting Officer and will be responsible for recruitment within his area.
3. The Recruiting Officer (Branch Chairman) will supervise and co-ordinate the work of the Assistant Recruiting Officers. In case any Assistant Recruiting Officer fails to do his work properly, the Recruiting Officer will have authority to remove him and appoint a new Assistant Recruiting Officer in his place—after obtaining the approval of the Chairman of the Territorial Committee.
4. The Chairman of each Territorial Committee will be the Chief Recruiting Officer for his area. He will supervise and co-ordinate the work of the Recruiting Officers within his area. In case any Recruiting Officer fails to do his work properly, the Chief Recruiting Officer can remove him and appoint a new Recruiting Officer in his place—after obtaining the approval of the Secretary of the Department of Recruitment of the IIL Headquarters.

DUTIES REGARDING RECRUITMENT

1. Each recruit should fill in an enrolment form and hand it over to the Assistant Recruiting Officer.
2. These forms should be collected and sent to Headquarters through the Recruiting Officer and the Chief Recruiting Officer.
3. Owing to extreme emergency old forms are being made use of, until revised forms are printed by this department.
4. In case of shortage of printed forms, typed enlistment forms may be used by any Recruiting Officer or Assistant Recruiting Officer.
5. Each Officer, either R.O. or A.R.O., who is directly responsible for the recruitment should keep a register of all the recruits who

have applied for enlistment within his area—together with all particulars regarding each recruit.

6. Every C.R.O., R.O. and A.R.O., will please note that there will be no age-restriction for recruits applying for enlistment. Printed forms of enlistment, which contain age restriction, should be amended accordingly.
7. Each Assistant Recruiting Officer should arrange for the Medical Examination of each recruit within his area. If necessary, he will take the help of the R.O. in this connection and the R.O. will, if necessary, take the help of the C.R.O. in this connection.
8. The forms of enlistment duly filled in should be forwarded to Headquarters, together with the Medical Officer's report.
9. No recruit should be rejected by the Medical Officer simply because he does not come up to the Army Standard—provided he is otherwise physically fit.
10. Each Branch or Sub-Branch as the case may be, should meet the expenses in connection with recruitment.
11. Enlistment forms together with the Medical Officer's report should be sent to Headquarters regularly once a fortnight. The first instalment of enlistment forms should be sent up as soon as possible.
12. In order to facilitate and expedite the work of recruitment the Headquarters will send to each Territorial Committee one or more Military Recruitment Advisers. The C.R.O., R.O. and A.R.O. are requested to make the fullest use of these Advisers.

Secretary,
Department of Recruitment.

INDIAN INDEPENDENCE LEAGUE
HEADQUARTERS
(Department of Training)
SUBJECT—TRAINING

1. In view of the total mobilization in which Netaji requires not only the youth, but all able-bodied men to serve irrespective of age, the existing Youth Department has been absorbed in the Training Department.

2. The training being imparted to the Youth Sections by the I.S.I. and the Azad School Graduates at the local centres in Malaya will be continued under the direction of the 'Member in Charge Training' of each branch or sub-branch.

More instructors for local training will be sent to Malayan Branches on demand by the Malayan Chairman.

3. The system of training will mobilize the manpower of East Asia in three successive stages:

1st STAGE: Local training in the nature of part time instruction for 2 hours in the morning or evening, every day as far as possible.

This is the responsibility of the territorial branch and its sub-branches. Recruits should neither leave their profession, nor their homes.

It will be considered a breach of discipline, if any recruit suddenly gives up his professional work, or leaves his home, before he is called up for whole-time training.

Instructors for this purpose will be provided from INA and from men trained in Central Camps.

Officers of the *Azad Hind Fauj* (INA) who are on recruiting or other duty will be utilized wherever possible to supervise such training and to help the local Chairman in matters of Military Training and Organization.

2nd STAGE: Central Training in Central Camps under the Direct Control of this Headquarters.

(i) Ordinary Camps; (ii) Special Camps.

(i) *Ordinary Camps*. Territories will be informed of their quota for ordinary camps as and when camps are ready. Although no high educational qualifications are needed, the best men from local training centres must be selected to make up this quota.

The first ordinary Central Camp will open in Malaya on or about August 15. The total quota of 5000 is allotted to Malaya. Detailed instructions will follow later.

(ii) *Special Camps*. The highest possible educational qualifications are needed for candidates for special Camps.

Three such camps, the Azad School, Syonan, the B.Y.T.C., Kuala Lumpur, and the Swaraj Youth Training Institute, Rangoon, are already in existence.

Another camp, the Azad School, Penang, for 100 volunteers will open during the first week of August 1943. As other territories will not be able to send candidates in time, the quota of 100 will also be required from Malaya.

Other territories should proceed with the task of sifting good material and must send in applications as soon as possible.

3rd STAGE: Training in *Azad Hind Fauj.*

This will be as soon as the Army is in a position to absorb the men permanently.

When the system is in full swing volunteers from the 1st and 2nd stages of training will provide a large reservoir for the INA.

4. *Conditions and Allowances.* In addition to free clothing, board and lodging, men in all central camps will receive a normal pocket allowance.
5. *Training Syllabus and Organization:* for the 1st Stage will remain the same as given in 'Interim Plan' dated 13-4-2603 except that more emphasis will be laid on physical fitness, route marches and military training.

A simple specimen programme for the month of August is given below:

Once a Week: Route March Distance to be increased from 5 to 15 miles.

Daily: P.T. 45 mins., Spiritual Training: 20 mins., Drill: 45 mins. Instruction for next day and rest 10 mins. Total: 2 hours.

Sunday and Holidays: Special lectures for spiritual and political training.

6. *Finance.* The expenses in connection with training will continue to remain a territorial responsibility as far as the 1st Stage of training is concerned.

Secretary,
Department of Training.

13

On Jinnah

[Press statement, 18 July 1943][1]

'I approached Mr. Jinnah for a settlement in 1940, but I came away disappointed. The Muslim League is a pro-British body and is supported mainly by 'yes-men' and traitors. That is why the Viceroy frequently calls Mr. Jinnah and consults him on important matters. It is the British who are the creators of the Muslim League, which is supported by the millionaires and landlords. Had the Congress and the Muslim League come to an understanding in 1940, at the time of the collapse of France, and when British morale was at its lowest, India would have been free now. But, Mr. Jinnah insisted on the materialization of Pakistan, which is detrimental to the interests of India, a demand which hampered our progress towards freedom. The British have long been carrying out a "divide and rule" policy in India. To further weaken our solidarity, the British have engineered the Muslim League demand of Pakistan, which aims at vivisecting India. I can confidently assert that the Hindu-Muslim question is a British creation. This is proved by the fact that though the Indian National Army is mainly composed of Muslim soldiers, there is perfect harmony between them and their Hindu comrades.' Mr. Bose went on to say that the Provisional Government of Free India will shortly take shape and continue functioning until it attains its goal of driving out the British from India. When India is free, this government will be dissolved and a new one will then be constituted by the Indian People. 'I believe', went on Mr. Bose, 'that Mr. Jinnah is doing great harm to the national cause by advocating

[1] *Testament of Subhas Bose*, pp. 189–90.

Pakistan. He is misleading the simple-minded Muslims by lending charm to Pakistan and playing upon their religious fanaticism. We all know that India will be plunged into a welter of chaos and confusion if the Pakistan scheme comes to fruition. The Muslims fail to realize that the British are the enemies of the Muslims and Islam, and their policy has always been directed against them. It was the British who brought about the downfall of the Mughals and enslaved India. Will the British ever liberate India? We think not, they will perpetuate their hold on us and keep us in bondage. It seems to me that Mr. Jinnah is not at all interested in the freedom of India. Had he been sincere and honest towards the Muslims, he would have been in jail with other Muslim leaders. Mr. Jinnah is doing nothing in this hour of India's peril, and he is satisfying his own vanity by delivering flowery speeches. Mr. Jinnah is always surrounded by Muslim landlords and capitalists, who are loyal to the British. However, we resent their activities and condemn them for supporting the British. We are anxious to gain our independence. A Free Indian Army has been organized to deliver India from alien bondage and Indian soldiers will render a great service to Islam by uprooting British influence from their country.'

—BANGKOK RADIO, 18 July 1943.

14

Independent Burma[1]

[i. Press statement on the Achievement of Burma's independence on 1 August 1943]

From 1925 to 1927, I used to gaze from the verandah of my cell in Mandalay Prison on the palace of the last independent King of Burma, and I used to wonder when Burma would be free once again. Today Burma is an independent State and I am breathing the atmosphere of that liberated country.

Right in the midst of a World War, an independent State is born in Asia, out of the ashes of British Imperialism and out of the smouldering ruins left behind by the fleeing British. In November, 1941, the then Prime Minister of Burma was in England, pleading with his British rulers for a small measure of self-rule, but all his entreaties were treated with contempt and scorn. The people of Burma, thereupon, took up arms against the British, co-operated with the armed forces of Nippon and hounded the British out of Burma. They now have their reward for all their suffering and sacrifice.

During the nineteenth century, India through her own enslavement, offered a jumping-off ground to Britain's armed forces for attacking and subjugating Burma. Burma has now repaid us by turning the British out and offering her independent territory as a springboard for India's National Army, in its attack on Britain's Army in India. The pledge given by Japan's worthy Prime Minister, General Tojo, now stands redeemed. While Sir Stafford Cripps gives promises of Dominion

[1] *On To Delhi*, pp. 51–61. Item iii in Netaji's own hand in Bengali is from the archives of the Netaji Research Bureau and translated by the editor.

Status and of Pakistan after the war—and while Sir Dorman Smith claims to rule Burma from Delhi with the help of his typewriter—Burma with the help of ally, Nippon, has succeeded in overthrowing the British and winning her liberty. This has very great significance for India, for Asia, and for the whole world.

The news that India's next-door neighbour, Burma, is now free has thrown our rulers in New Delhi into epileptic fits. They are panic-stricken that the example of Burma will now inspire the Indian people to rise in arms against their alien oppressors, and they are busy devising more ruthless methods for suppressing the nationalist movement. But nothing on earth can keep India enslaved any longer and just as the peacock emblem now flies over the Government House in Rangoon—so the tri-colour will soon fly over the Red Fortress of Delhi.

[ii. Radio speech on 1 August 1943]

Countrymen and Friends! Today is the first of August 1943. Today an event of great historical importance has taken place. Right in the midst of a World War, an Independent State has come into being. Burma—our neighbour has achieved her independence, and she has now her own national Independent Government. Long Live Free Burma!

You all know that when the war in East Asia broke out in December 1941, the people of Burma decided to utilize the opportunity for recovering their lost liberty. Instead of co-operating with the British Government, the vast majority of Burmans did their best to help in expelling the British from the country, and the result is that today, not only has Burma been liberated from the British altogether, but she has actually realized her long cherished goal of independence.

The independence of Burma in this momentous crisis in world history has a two-fold significance for us. It shows, in the first place, what a nation can achieve if it knows how to seize an opportunity which history has offered. Secondly, just as the conquest of India supplied the British with a jumping-off ground for their attack on Burma in the nineteenth century—similarly, the emancipation of Burma has supplied the Indian Independence Movement in East Asia with a springboard, for its attack on Britain's Army of occupation in India, during the twentieth century.

Burma was deprived of her liberty long after India was. Nevertheless, Burma has stolen a march over us and has attained her liberty, while we are still passing through the throes of revolution. On behalf of the Indian people and of myself, I offer my warmest congratulations to the people of Burma on their achievement—and I heartily wish them increasing progress and prosperity in the days to come. I offer also my hearty felicitation to His Excellency Dr. Ba Maw, the head of the New and Independent State of Burma, and I wish him all success in the discharge of the manifold responsibilities which have now devolved on him. It is a source of great pleasure and gratification for me that so soon after meeting Dr. Ba Maw in Syonan, during the first week of July, I can offer him my greetings and congratulations as the head of the new and Independent State of Burma.

Friends, you are aware of the many promises which the British Government has given to the Indian people during the course of their rule in India—promises which have always proved to be mere scraps of paper. You are aware also that these promises have been repeated since the outbreak of the present war and all sorts of silly excuses have been put forward to show that in the midst of a war, transference of power from British to Indian hands cannot take place. As against this example we now see that right in the midst of war, the promise of liberty made by the Prime Minister of Japan, His Excellency General Tojo, on behalf of his Government and nation, has been fully redeemed. Where there is a will there is a way and this statesmanship and generosity on the part of Japan will bring into bold relief the hypocrisy of British politicians—while they will demonstrate the real character of Japan's state policy.

The independence of Burma will, I am sure, be soon followed by the Independence of the Philippines. Asia is now on the threshold of a new era in her history. This is a unique opportunity for all the suppressed nations of Asia to rise and effect their emancipation. It is, above all, the sacred duty of the Indian people to seize the present golden opportunity and fulfill their age-long aspirations.

The liberation of Asia cannot be complete until India is free. The Indian people must, therefore, rise and liberate themselves and thereby help the emancipation of other Asiatic nations. Above all, India must seize the hand of friendship which Japan has offered to India and to other suppressed nations of Asia. Confronted by a common foe, the people of India must march shoulder to shoulder with the brave Nipponese nation, till the enemy is overthrown and India recovers her lost liberty.

INQUILAB ZINDABAD!
AZAD HIND ZINDABAD!

[iii. Message in Bengali, 1 August 1943]

Friends,

Today I desire to send you my heartiest good wishes from the hallowed land of free Burma. Today Burma is free—shall we not be free also? Outside India, India's Army of Liberation or the Azad Hind Fauj is now ready for battle. Even our sisters are training themselves with rifles in their hands. We shall soon set out on our journey and reach the frontiers of India. You must get ready from now so that as soon as we arrive, the fire of revolution may spread out fast to all parts of India. Please tell those who are today in prison that the arbiter of our destiny is now in our favour—the last war of independence is about to begin. Our victory this time is certain. In this our last battle men and women, young and old, must all take part. We particularly want those who are now working under the British flag to join us. There is not much time left—we must complete all preparations quickly and wait for the zero hour. Blood will flow in torrents on the soil of Bengal once the battle is joined. But there is nothing to fear—we must pay for our sins with our own blood. There can be no doubt that our India—more precious to us than gold—will be free this time. Look, the eastern sky is already aglow with the bright rays of the rising sun.

Inquilab Zindabad! Azad Hind Zindabad!

Subhas Chandra Bose

[iv. Speech delivered at the Farrer Park, Singapore, on 15 August 1943]

Indians all over East Asia are meeting today in unprecedented numbers for a twofold purpose. They are first of all celebrating the independence of Burma. They are also reiterating their demand that the British quit

India at once. They are reaffirming their unshakeable determination to continue the struggle till the complete independence of India is achieved.

You may be aware that I had the good fortune to be in Burma when the declaration of independence was made on August 1st, and the new independent State of Burma brought into existence along with the first Cabinet of free Burma. The whole ceremony was a most solemn and impressive one and I am thankful to Providence that I could witness with my own eyes the birth of a new and independent State just across the Indian frontier. By the nemesis of history Burma's independent State was established in the same place, which was the seat of British power and authority in Burma.

As I was witnessing that historic ceremony, I could see vividly with my mind's eye the ceremony of hoisting our national flag over the Viceroy's House in New Delhi and the victory parade which *Azad Hind Fauj* (the Indian National Army) will hold inside the ancient Red Fortress of Delhi—when the British are finally expelled from India.

Friends! You know perhaps that Burma was not new to me and that I had spent two and a half years in prisons in Burma when the British were in occupation of that country. But it was a new Burma and a free Burma that I visited this time. In that free Burma, the Nippon Military Administration has been completely abolished; Dr. Ba Maw is Head of the New State as well as Premier and Commander-in-Chief, and he has formed a Cabinet which will be advised by a Privy Council; independent Burma has declared war on Britain and America who are still dreaming of re-conquering and re-enslaving Burma.

Burma has entered into a treaty of alliance with Nippon. A Nippon Ambassador is already in Burma. Ambassadors of other countries will soon be in Rangoon. Burmese Ambassadors have been accredited to other countries. Nippon has decided to transfer all Anglo-American enemy properties in Burma to the new Burma State. These properties include factories, harbours, railways, telegraphs and telephones. Thus, Burmese will govern the country according to the wishes of the Burmese people. And they have an army manned and officered exclusively by themselves. Last but not least, today the Peacock emblem, the National Flag of Burma—not the Union Jack—is flying over the office and residence of the Head of State—Adipadi Doctor Ba Maw.

Today, my heart is full of my recent experiences in Burma, and it will take me hours and hours if I were to narrate all I have seen and heard there. I shall therefore end this topic after relating only a few things. First of all, about the Rangoon jail. As I lived in the Rangoon jail for several months in 1927, I wanted very much to revisit that place. But I was not allowed to do so as the jail is no longer used for Indian prisoners. It is now used exclusively for British war-prisoners.

Friends! Think of the day when we shall avenge ourselves for the incarceration of hundreds of thousands of Indian patriots by converting all the prisons in India into camps for British war-prisoners. Prepare from now on for that glorious day.

I had the privilege of having long discussions with Dr. Ba Maw and his ministers, and I am glad to tell you that a complete agreement was reached on problems of common interest. Burma and India will now march shoulder to shoulder against the common enemy, and when the common enemy is vanquished and peace established, we shall live in complete amity and accord like good neighbours.

Friends! On behalf of the Indian Independence Movement I desire to offer my warmest congratulations to Adipadi Dr. Ba Maw, to the ministers of the new Cabinet, and to the people of free Burma on the independence that they have won, and I desire also to convey our sincerest good wishes for the everlasting freedom and prosperity of Burma in future. We are fortunate to have in our midst today members of the Burmese deputation who recently visited Tokyo. They are led by His Excellency U Ba Lwin. I beg to offer—on your behalf and mine—the warmest welcome to His Excellency U Ba Lwin and his colleagues, and I request them to convey personally our message to the people of Burma when they arrive in Rangoon.

Friends! The independence of Burma has thrown fresh responsibilities on our shoulders. After the expulsion of the British from Burma the road to India has been opened, and we have to march along that road. Until the British are driven out of India, the freedom of Burma cannot be safe. The freedom of India, therefore, is necessary not only for the Indian people but for Burma as well.

A year has rolled by since Mahatma Gandhi was put in prison for the crime of demanding the withdrawal of the British from India. Since then the civil disobedience movement as well as sabotage activities have gone on with unabated vigour. But we have not won freedom. And we shall not win freedom till we put up a second front on the Indo-Burma frontier and call upon the Indian people and the British Indian army to take up arms against the British and their allies in India.

Providence has ordained that it is the task of Indians in East Asia to put up a second front, which the Indian people have been demanding. For this we need a total mobilization of our manpower and resources in East Asia. I want 300,000 men and women for the *Azad Hind Fauj* (the Indian National Army) including the Rani of Jhansi regiment. I am thankful to the youth of Syonan and Malai for offering themselves for enlistment in such large numbers. But the money that has been forthcoming from Syonan has not been enough. I want from Syonan at least fifty million dollars for our national struggle, and I know this is not too much for you.

I am hoping that the day is not far off when we shall be able to set up a provisional Government of Free India. When this is done we shall march into India under the leadership of our own government. I want to inform my comrades in the army and among the civil population that the Indian National Army is now on the move. It is a long way from Syonan to Delhi—therefore we have to begin our march as early as possible. All those who are fit and ready for action must now being to pack up.

During the next two months a large portion of the army will be on the road to India, and when the army moves the Independence League Headquarters will also move nearer to India. I am longing for the day when our Headquarters will be shifted to the Indo-Burma border.

It is today a very great pleasure for me to see so many of my Muslim countrymen in this gathering of ours. I thank them heartily for the welcome they have given me and for the handsome purse they have offered for the Indian Independence Movement. And let the whole world know, and let our enemies know, that all Indians in East Asia are united regardless of religion or caste, and they are determined to fight for the freedom of their common motherland.

1. Broadcasting to India from Singapore, 1943

2. Speaking at a women's meeting in Singapore, 1943

3. 'Chalo Delhi'

4. Proclamation of the Provisional Government of Azad Hind, 21 October 1943

5. Reviewing the Indian National Army in Singapore, 1943

6. With A.C. Chatterjee, Mohammad Zaman Kiani, and Habibur Rehman

7. In a happy mood at a sports meet

8. Speaking at the Greater East Asia Conference in Tokyo, November 1943

9. A portrait, Tokyo, November 1943

10. Reading the Nippon Times, Tokyo, November 1943

11. Addressing a press conference, Tokyo, November 1943

12. Speaking at a mass rally in Hibiya Park, Tokyo, November 1943

13. The crowd at Hibiya Park, Tokyo, November 1943

14. On his way to see the Japanese emperor, Tokyo, November 1943

15. Netaji addresses the Indian National Army

16. Walking out of the Cellular Jail, Andaman, December 1943

17. Announcing the crossing of the Indo-Burma frontier by the INA, Rangoon, March 1944

18. At the front

19. The last autographed picture, signed in Bangkok, 17 August 1945

20. The last salute, Saigon, 17 August 1945

15

Spiritual and Military Support to Indians at Home

[Press statement, 18 August 1943][1]

Finishing a round of inspection of the anti-British independence movement prevailing in all parts of the Co-prosperity Sphere, Mr. S.C. Bose, President of the Indian Independence League and concurrently Commander-in-Chief of the Indian National Army, dwelt on the prevailing situation at a Press conference and said, 'The present situation in India is becoming more and more precarious. In one year, since the outbreak of the anti-British movement launched by the Indian National Congress, the movement has been crushed by organized British terrorism. Today, it lies smouldering but more or less inactive. We have two alternatives today. One is to give spiritual aid to those patriots who are taking recourse to all possible means to encourage the spirit of their own people. The courage of Indians at home will be doubled if the Provisional Government of Free India is established. The second alternative is to give active military support. It is gratifying to note that the Indian army at home is displaying a more co-operative attitude towards the Indians abroad. I am convinced the time is now ripe to launch, strategically, operations in accordance with the requirements of the domestic movement. The organization of the Independence League lays more emphasis on military affairs. By the experience gained during the recent trip, I have been greatly impressed by the eagerness of all Indians abroad, who are very anxious to establish a Provisional Government. I have personally interviewed Premier Pibul Songgram of Thailand and the Chief of the State, Dr. Ba Maw, of Burma. They have both

[1] *Testament of Subhas Bose*, pp. 148–9.

promised to give me all-out support in the attainment of Indian independence. In order to provide for the forthcoming struggle, every preparation is now ready. For the attainment of the great objective of gaining independence, we strongly avow in the name of all our comrades, to go on undaunted towards our goal in the face of any obstacle.'

—SINGAPORE RADIO, 18 August 1943

16

The Bengal Famine

[Press statement, 20 August 1943][1]

In the course of a broadcast, Netaji Subhas Bose said, 'There is a serious famine prevailing in India, particularly in Bengal and Calcutta. On receipts of these reports from India, the Indian League of Independence in East Asia is extremely anxious about the welfare of the Indian people and is, therefore, trying to do everything in its power to take the necessary measures in order to help them. Today, I am in the happy position to announce that 100,000 tons of rice are waiting to be transported from Burma to relieve hunger in India. This rice is put at the disposal of the Indian people unconditionally. These 100,000 tons of rice are at present lying in a harbour in the vicinity of India. At the moment when the British Government expresses its willingness to accept this delivery, the name of the harbour as well as of the authorities, who will hand over the rice, will be named. At the same time the Japanese Government will be asked for a guarantee of a safe conduct for the ships calling for this quantity of rice.' Mr. Bose further declared that, if this first delivery is accepted by the British Government, further deliveries for the starving Indian population could be sent to India. Mr. Bose expressed the earnest hope that this offer would be accepted, because hundreds of thousands of men, women and children would be saved from starvation.

—RANGOON RADIO, 20 August 1943

[1] *Testament of Subhas Bose,* p. 203.

17

The Servant of 38 Crores of My Countrymen

[Special Order of the Day, issued on the occasion of taking over direct command of the INA on 25 August 1943][1]

Srijut Subhas Chandra Bose took over the supreme command of the Indian National Army and issued the following Special Order of the Day:

'In the interest of the Indian Independence Movement and of the *Azad Hind Fauj*, I have taken over the direct command of our army from this day.

This is for me a matter of joy and pride—because for an Indian, there can be no greater honour than to be the Commander of India's Army of Liberation. But I am conscious of the magnitude of the task that I have undertaken, and I feel weighed down with a sense of responsibility. I pray that God may give me the necessary strength to fulfil my duty to India under all circumstances, however difficult or trying they may be.

I regard myself as the servant of 38 crores of my countrymen, who profess different religious faiths. I am determined to discharge my duties in such a manner that the interests of these 38 crores may be safe in my hands and that every single Indian will have reason to put complete trust in me. It is only on the basis of undiluted nationalism and of perfect justice and impartiality that India's Army of Liberation can be built up.

[1] *On To Delhi*, pp. 62–3.

In the coming struggle for the emancipation of our motherland, for the establishment of a Government of Free India, based on the goodwill of 38 crores of Indians and for the creation of a permanent army which will guarantee Indian independence for all time, the *Azad Hind Fauj* has a vital role to play. To fulfill this role, we must weld ourselves into an army that will have only one goal—namely, the Freedom of India—and only one will—namely, to do or die in the cause of India's freedom. When we stand, the *Azad Hind Fauj* has to be like a wall of granite; when we march, the *Azad Hind Fauj* has to be like a steamroller.

Our task is not an easy one; the war will be long and hard, but I have complete faith in the justice and in the invincibility of our cause. 38 crores of human beings, who form about one-fifth of the human race, have a right to be free and they are now prepared to pay the price of freedom. There is consequently no power on earth that can deprive us of our birthright of liberty any longer.

Comrades! Officers and men! With your unstinted support and unflinching loyalty, the *Azad Hind Fauj* will become the instrument of India's liberation. Ultimate victory will certainly be ours. I assure you.

Our work has already begun. With the slogan, "Onward to Delhi" on our lips, let us continue to labour and to fight till our National Flag flies over the Viceroy's House in New Delhi, and the *Azad Hind Fauj* holds its victory parade inside the ancient Red fortress of India's metropolis.'

SUBHAS CHANDRA BOSE,
Sipah-Salar,
(Supreme Commander)

Headquarters, Sipah-Salar,
Azad Hind Fauj,
25th August 1943.

18

My Individuality

[Speech delivered to INA officers on 25 August 1943][1]

Brother Officers! It is my wish that we should be familiar among ourselves, and all of us should know what is our object, what are our duties and responsibilities and how to discharge these duties and responsibilities satisfactorily.

First of all, I will myself tell you something about me. Because, I wish to let you know what is my individuality and what is my individual life, as in future, we shall have to work together and tread the same path.

After the University career, I entered the political world. The most important question at that time was this: What Indians did during the last war: what was the result and what were the experiences and lessons we got for the future? In India and in England, it was our experience that the policy of our leaders was wrong. Of course, we were depending upon our leaders for action. But we, young men and students, were thoroughly disappointed. In our minds there was only one idea, that the mistake committed by our leaders in the last war should not be committed again. We thought if we get an opportunity in future, we would not make such mistakes.

There was another big question. In Europe, after the war, in the years 1918 and 1919, there were many changes: new governments were coming into existence, which had not existed before the war. The Czechs ceased to be a part of the Austro-Hungarian Empire. Another race, the Poles, formed their own government. When I went to Europe,

[1] *On To Delhi*, pp. 64–7, translated from the original Hindustani.

I had the opportunity of meeting two or three Indian leaders there. They all advised me that if we want to do anything for our motherland, we should study the history of the war and the experiences of such history should be utilized for our fight against Britain. We began to learn and understand things. We came to know how some leaders of Czechs went out of their country for doing propaganda and for getting help from the enemies of Austria and Hungary. They joined hands with Britain and France, and both governments helped these leaders, and even recognized their rights to have free governments after the war. Britain and France assured them of all help and co-operation in their efforts. They began their work in right earnest. They recruited all the Czechs outside their country. The soldiers of Czech nationality of the Austro-Hungarian Army who fell in the hands of the enemy also volunteered for the Czech National Army, which were 20,000-strong. This army fought hand in hand with Britain and France against Austria, Hungary and Germany. The Poles, too, formed an army of 30,000 and took part in the war. It was their fortune that Germany and her allies were defeated, and after the war, they were able to form their own governments. There is no reason why we should not go also by the same path, and taking advantage of the international situation, we should fight shoulder to shoulder with the enemies of Britain to get complete freedom.

The people of Ireland also took advantage of the war. They openly revolted under the Sinn Fein Party against the British. In the city of Dublin, the Sinn Fein Party had an army of 3,000 only. They had also an army of 10,000-strong in the country. Something went wrong with their plans, and the rebellion that started in Dublin did not spread to the countryside. Anyhow, they kept the City of Dublin under their control for eight days. This revolution occurred during Easter, and so the revolution is called the Easter Revolution. Though the revolt did not materialize in 1916, it again broke out in the year 1919, just after the war. They had only 5,000 volunteers. This time it was different. War was over. From England troops could be brought to suppress the rebellion. Even then this army of volunteers numbering 5,000 carried on their fight and in the end the British were brought to their knees.

In 1921, we began working in India with all the experiences that we had from the study of the history of the last war. At that time, as you know, Mahatma Gandhi had launched the Non Co-operation Movement. The Khilafat Committee was also working hand in hand with the Congress. We too took part in the Non-co-operation Movement enthusiastically with the specific idea in mind that, when an opportunity offers itself, we should take up arms against the British. We knew also that Germany would try again to take revenge and then would come our opportunity as well.

We joined the Congress in 1921 under Mahatma Gandhi, because there was no other way to carry on our fight and keep up the honour of the nation in the face of terrible British oppression. Hindus and Muslims were united. But we knew definitely that by the Civil Disobedience Campaign, India would not be completely free. Of course, the movement did create the political consciousness among the people, and it prepared the people for armed struggle. From 1921 onwards we were waiting for an opportunity to take up arms, and that opportunity was a war in Europe.

This is not my individual view but it is the view of many young men who came under Mahatma Gandhi in 1921. Certainly there were a few young men who believed in non-violence, but many of them were strong supporters of violence and they were awaiting the proper time to strike.

I went to Europe in 1933 and remained up to 1936. My idea in going to Europe was to study the situation and to know what was going to happen next. During my stay in Europe I visited Berlin and made acquaintance with certain Government officials. I plainly asked them when they were going to strike at Britain so that we might also take up arms simultaneously against the British. They replied that they were not at all going to fight Britain and they hoped that all their demands would be fulfilled by Britain. They were for a compromise with Britain. However, they expressed their sympathy for Indian freedom. I argued with them about the British hypocrisy and their cunning policy as Indians know best about that by personal experience, and warned them that when Britain thought that the German power was getting stronger, she would openly come into conflict with Germany. In the end I told them: 'Britain is our traditional enemy. We will fight her, whether you support us or not'. But I had no doubt that war would start in Europe very soon. Anybody could understand this, by having a look at the preparations that were going on in Germany. When I went to Europe this time, I reminded them of what I said in the year 1936.

My idea in saying this is that, I came back from Europe with a strong conviction of what was going to happen. The new party that came in power in Germany was always for a fight. I clearly understood that the German demands would not be accepted by the British, and if the British found the Germans growing a bit strong, they would fight the Nazis. In 1938 when I went to Europe, I noticed some changes. Germany was beginning to understand that the British would never fully accept their proposals. In September 1938, when the Germans put forward the case of Sudetan Germans, Mr. Chamberlain rushed to Munich to come to an agreement with Herr Hitler. There was a time when all parleys of international value generally used to take place in London. But when I saw the British Prime Minister, Mr. Chamberlain, going to Germany, leaving his own country and when he accepted the German demands, I realized the secret—Britain was becoming weaker and Germany was getting stronger. It was the first time in the history of the British that a Prime Minister of England, relegating the usual custom, proceeded to a foreign country to accept the demands of another nation.

Then, I started doing propaganda in India that a war in Europe was inevitable and it was the duty of Indians to be alert and to try to force Britain to accept our demands, and if they did not, to prepare ourselves for a fight. I was noticing the reaction of the public to my propaganda, and I was convinced that the full support of the general public was with me. But our leaders were thinking in a different way, particularly Mahatma Gandhi, whose policy was to wait and see. But we young men were not deterred by this policy. We redoubled our propaganda. We were asking the people of India to take advantage of the golden opportunity that would be presented to them in the near future.

In the annual session of the Indian National Congress at Tripuri in March 1939, I tabled one resolution demanding freedom for India within six months and such an ultimatum to be sent to the Government. In case this demand was not conceded in that period, we should prepare the people for a fight against Britain with whatever we might possess.

It was, of course, in the nature of an ultimatum and the resolution was introduced, keeping in view the tense international situation and knowing full well that a conflagration would begin in Europe within six months.

When the war actually started in September 1939, the public began to realize that what I said in March was correct. It was our duty at that time to unite all the nationalist forces and bring pressure on the British Government to concede to our demand, and if unsuccessful, to fight for it. But our leaders were thinking and acting in a different way. They were under the impression that Britain would become weak in the course of the war and to get the Indian help, they would come to an honourable agreement with the Congress. I tried to point out the absurdity of such a notion and told them whatever might be the weakness of Britain during the war they would never allow us to rid them of the power in India. The weaker they grew the more powerful would become their grip on India. Without India they would not be able to prosecute the war successrully. They would begin looting and plundering the country's resources as they got weaker and weaker.

In March 1940, when the Congress Session was in progress, we expected a forward step. But Gandhiji had his own way. He wanted to wait and see. We began to lose our minds and wanted, come what may, to start our own movement. An antiwar movement was started throughout the country. It became somewhat serious; many people courted imprisonment. Meanwhile, I got information that Gandhiji himself would launch a civil disobedience movement in November, as the Government did nothing. I heaved a sigh of relief that if Gandhiji starts a movement, it will have worldwide repercussions. The whole world will come to know that Indians are fighting for freedom. All the nations will think that Indians deserve freedom. We will surely get the sympathy of the world to have saved our honour.

But I thought that by the weapon of Civil Disobedience alone we would not achieve freedom. The movement would surely bring pressure on the Government and hamper its war effort, but the government would never consider our demand. That was my idea. We were thinking what to do. What new method should be adopted? Young men were doing their bit with bombs and revolvers. We got into touch with these young revolutionaries. I knew their strength. They were real revolutionaries with high spirits. But their strength and sacrifice were not enough to achieve complete independence for our motherland.

It was then, we began scanning the pages of history and found many an example and taught many a lesson. The American example was before us. I began to realize, and even came to the conclusion, that without outside help the Indian revolution would not be successful. The United States got a lot of help from France. Even Generals were dispatched from France. In the history of the world, it is not a new thing to get assistance from other nations for winning freedom for one's country.

The news we got in India were twisted and more of a propaganda nature. It was natural that Britain should do so. But to understand the real situation of the world by remaining inside India was not possible. What would be the result of the war and how would the war end and who would win in the end? What were the ideas of Indians abroad, how were they thinking about India's fight for freedom, how to get help from them for India's independence and whether it was possible to get material help from the enemies of Britain? These were the questions which made us think that somebody should be sent outside India. I thought of sending some persons to foreign countries. Certainly it was a most difficult task strictly restricted as our movements were. I thought also that such a person who should leave India [must be one who] the British really 'understand' and whom the Indian people take seriously. At last, I decided myself to get out of India.

I was in jail at that time. To get out of the jail was a difficult problem. To slip away from jail would make it difficult for me to leave the country in view of the British CID. At last I decided to go on hunger strike. This decision was taken after steeling my heart that either I would die or get out of the jail. When my decision was made known to the Government it created a stir in the official circles, as they never wanted to see me die in the jail. The Superintendent of the jail came and entreated me not to undertake hunger strike. He argued that if all the prisoners went on hunger strike the King's Government would come to a standstill, and warned me that if I died in the jail it would be my own responsibility. My hunger strike went on for six days. They tried forcibly to feed me but I was determined to die the way of Jatindra Nath Das. After seven days, a secret conference took place at Government House. They wanted to do something, as the medical report about my condition was serious. They set me free with the idea of re-arresting me after a month. I got information of this in good time. Meanwhile, some arrangements could be made for my escape from India and I left my country.

Experiences, I had a lot, after leaving my homeland. I was listening in to both the radios. I had the privilege from the German authorities to hear the enemy radio and propaganda. I had the opportunity of visiting all the fortifications and other defences all over Europe. After these personal experiences, I have no doubt what will be the result of the war. As I said in your parade the other day, the war will be a prolonged one, but there will surely be one result, that is, the collapse of Britain, and her Empire.

Now the question is this. What is the position of India under these circumstances? The destruction of the British Empire is certain, and the whole map of the world will be changed. What will be the position of India in the new map? The British will be driven out of India, and what should be our position then? We should think about this. There are three alternatives.

One is to keep away from the war and to have a neutral attitude. Second is to go and beg for freedom from the new invader and the third is to take part in the war with the enemies of Britain and qualify ourselves for freedom. I know what alternative you prefer. For us there is but one alternative, that is, to fight hand in hand with the enemies of Britain and contribute our share in the destruction of British Empire.

The internal situation in India is very grave. It is our duty to encourage and support the forces that are in India, doing their bit against Britain. What is the internal situation in India today? The whole population is against the British Government. People are carrying on the fight without arms. To suppress millions of unarmed people, a small army of thousands equipped with all modern arms is enough. When I had the privilege of meeting Herr Hitler, I took the liberty of asking this question of India and sought his advice as to what path we should tread. The Chancellor of Germany, who is himself an experienced revolutionary, giving his opinion, said that a well-equipped army of a few thousands would be able to control millions of unarmed revolutionaries. He added that so long as an external power did not knock at the frontier no change could be expected in the internal situation. We should form part of this external power. We hear so much nowadays of a second front. It is we who should create a second front in India. It would have been possible for them to face us in both the fronts, had not the Axis Powers crippled and maimed them. The Axis Powers had made our work easier. We are thankful to them for doing this, but at the same time, it is incumbent upon us to do our duty towards our motherland. To do this work an army of 50,000 is enough, but we should be prepared to raise an army of 300,000.

The question now is this: What are the duties of this army? There are two duties which this army will have to perform. The first and important duty is, of course, to fight the enemy and free our motherland; the second one is also no less important. After the enemy is defeated, we will have to do tremendous work in India. By freeing India our duty will not be over. Our army is a revolutionary one, and as revolutionaries we have two duties to perform. The first one, as I said before, is to drive the enemy out of India, and the second duty is to form such a powerful army in India that will face any nation or nations put together, and to defend India forever against foreign invasion.

Friends! We all should think that we will never remain slaves. We have already had a very good taste of this slavery. To protect our motherland from any foreign aggressors, it is the duty of all of you to form the strongest possible army in the world. As far as ability and efficiency are concerned, I may tell you that you are second to none. We were not getting proper training and opportunity, but whenever these two things were offered to Indians, they have shown their mettle. Not only in military, but also in politics, economics, science, sports, etc., we Indians are not in any way backward. Indians are efficient and able. The Almighty has created them like that. Of course, we have to learn much from the world, and we are prepared to do so. And with this learning and the natural efficiency and ability of ours and with full confidence, we are forming this army.

For the success of an army, military training only will not suffice. Take the case of France. Up to 1939 the French Army was considered the best in the world. It was really so. They had a lot of materials, aeroplanes, heavy guns, etc. In addition there was the 'impregnable' Maginot Line to protect them. Why then did France fall within so short of time? There was only one reason and that was, there was no *josh* [spirit] in them. After the last war, such a feeling was created in France that they should take rest, as the enemy had been defeated once for all. That was not so in Germany. In Germany, the cry was 'revenge'. One nation was thinking in terms of revenge and sacrifice. That is why the French people had their disastrous defeat. The French people had lost their spirit, and the Germans were seething with the spirit.

After the *Azad Hind Fauj* parade, I had a talk with Premier Tojo who congratulated me for the grand parade. He also said that the success of an army mainly depends on the moral training they get. I assured him that it would be given special attention. The Nipponese attach much importance to this 'spirit'. For instance, see the spirit of the defenders of Attu Island. They knew they could not win against such a numerically superior army. They could have easily surrendered. But they did not do so. It was against the honour and glory of their motherland. The whole garrison of 2,000 sacrificed their lives fighting the enemy.

I may also mention about the brave defenders of Stalingrad. They were at one time surrounded by the enemy and they were even given an ultimatum by the Germans to surrender. They did not surrender and carried on their fight, even though the enemies were 200,000-strong that surrounded them. Such was the spirit of the brave defenders of Stalingrad.

We should create such a spirit in our men. The responsibility of the Officers is great. A sepoy can afford to leave the battlefield but an officer cannot do so. He is a responsible man and only an army led by such responsible officers will be successful in the end. So, your work is tremendous. There is no other work greater and nobler than the work you have undertaken. Our sisters and brothers in India are facing even bigger ordeals with cheer and enthusiasm. For the Indian Independence and for India's welfare, there is no greater work than this.

While in Europe, I tried and I was successful in forming a small National Army. I have brought photos of the army. In Berlin and Rome, Indians are thinking and doing things, as you are thinking and doing here. Everywhere in the world, wherever there are Indians, a new spirit, a new awakening has come among Indians.

19

An Amphibious Monster

[Speech delivered at Kuala Lumpur on 5 September 1943][1]

Friends! I want to thank you most heartily for the purse you have presented to me this evening. It is a handsome purse but I shall call it handsome only if you regard it as a first instalment, considering what other towns are paying and within a very short time, considering also what Ipoh has paid as a first instalment. I am sure that Indians in Kuala Lumpur will be anxious to see that this contribution is multiplied at least five times, and if you cannot do that I am afraid you will be doing a great disservice to your country. You are very proud of your city and rightly too. It is the second city in this part of the world, and if you enjoy the prestige, you must fulfill the responsibilities that follow from that distinction and prestige.

I will now tell you that what we want in cash is only a part of our total requirements. The time has come when we have to give our all in the service of our motherland. The days of minimum sacrifice are over. The time has come when each and every one of us has to think of the maximum sacrifice which he or she is able to offer, and that sacrifice has to be in human life, in money and in other resources which are necessary in order to equip a modern army for its marches, I am glad to know that you citizens of Kuala Lumpur and Selangor State are anxious to do your duty in every respect and my only remark and request to you is to expedite your collections as soon as possible so that our army may be equipped sooner than many expect and be ready to march to the field of action.

[1] *On To Delhi*, pp. 78–85, translated from the original Hindustani.

From my experience, I am convinced that so long as the Indian people remain unarmed, so long as the British Government has a modern army under its control and so long as we do not take up arms for our struggle for freedom, we shall not be able to achieve independence for India. I do not know of one instance—of one single instance—in the whole history of mankind where a nation has been able to achieve full independence without resorting to arms, but apart from history our natural experience in the course of several decades has convinced us that we have to take up arms in the final stage of our struggle if we want full independence and not a diluted form of it. So long as peace reigned all over the world, it was practically impossible for the Indian people to get arms and fight with arms. It was impossible for the people inside India. It was also impossible for people outside India, but thanks to this war, what was impossible four or five years ago has today become possible. If you want arms, you can get them not inside but outside India. If you want to build up a modern army and equip it with all the modern weapons, you can do so today. Five years ago you could not do it even if you wanted to. That is why I say this war has been a God-sent opportunity to us. It has given us a unique opportunity for achieving not Dominion Status or Colonial self-government, but full and complete independence.

The only question I would like to put to you as Indians is whether you really want full and complete independence. If you do so you must pay the price. You must organize a complete modern army and march with that army to India.

Today, the British have one front—the Indian national front—you might call it—inside India. The British with their army are able to cope with this Indian national front. If you can put up a second front—then it will be impossible for the British to maintain their position in the country. I am convinced when the Indian National Army appears on the frontier of India its very appearance will be a clarion call to the people in general and also to the Indian army to rally round the banner of Indian revolution. This is not a wishful dream on my part. I know that people at home are fully aware of our activities in East Asia and the British too are aware, but I do not care. The time has come when we could openly proclaim to the whole world what we have been doing and what we are going to do in the future. Our brethren in the Indian Army who today are standing under the Union Jack are anxiously waiting for the Indian National Army on the continent of India. That is the position at home without any exaggeration. It is therefore our duty to hurry with our work and see that the National Army goes to the aid of India as soon as possible.

Ever since the existence of the Indian National Army was announced to the world and its intention of marching to Delhi, you will be surprised to learn that there has been a complete change in the tactics of British propaganda. Up to recently British propagandists have been saying that today Nippon has become the enemy of India and that its army intends to march into India, but ever since they realized that the Indian National Army had been formed and is getting ready to march into India, there has been a complete change in the attitude and also in the tactics of British propagandists, and now, they are anxiously trying to work up the Indian people to take a stand against the Indian National Army. The British Government knows, as much as we do, what the attitude of the Indian people and the Indian Army will be when our army appears on the frontier of India, and that is why they are anxious to do their best to win over the Indian people to their side so that they may take a stand against the Indian National Army.

But the most unexpected surprise came to me when I was told that British propagandists on the occasion of a Hindu Festival had appealed to the Hindus of India to get ready to fight their brothers who are going to march in from outside. These British propagandists even went so far as to say that the good old days have come back again!

Friends! The Anglo-Americans have found out now a new Napoleon. According to the Anglo-Americans Lord Louis Mountbatten is amphibious. He is a master in land and sea operations. Well, what is the career of this amphibious monster? He is the hero of Dieppe. Dieppe was an attempt by the British army to land in France and to expel the Germans from that part. Within 24 hours they were completely wiped out and there ended all the heroic exploits of Lord Louis Mountbatten. Because of his achievement at Dieppe he has been made Commander-in-Chief of the South East Asia command. I challenge you to show me one country in the world today where promotions are made not for success, not for victories, but for defeats. It is a unique achievement of the British army and its government in this war. I can assure Lord Louis Mountbatten that a much bigger and greater Dieppe is waiting for him in East Asia.

Perhaps, there are some people living in East Asia, and even in Malaya, who are still hoping and dreaming that the British will come back. We have heard of them. There are a few such men in Syonan also. I can only pity them. You know what Syonan was and is today. The British—I do not say it, I only repeat it—took twenty years to build Singapore and how many days to get out? Seven days. This is an achievement and still there are people who believe they will come back! The biggest bulwark of the British Empire is now the biggest graveyard of that Empire and it shall be a graveyard. The days of the British Empire are over. If you have any doubt, turn over the pages of history. Every Empire has had its glory and also its decline. The British Empire had its glory during the last war and since then its decline has become very rapid and we have witnessed with our own eyes the last phase of the decline.

I have always said that the last two wars brought about the disappearance of two Empires, the Ottoman Empire of the Turks and the Austro-Hungarian Empire. This war will see the end of the British Empire and out of the ashes of that Empire will rise a free India. If you want India to be free, you have to work and fight for the overthrow and dismemberment of the British Empire.

British propaganda of late has adopted new tactics, and that is to utilize to the best advantage the small success they have achieved in Africa and Sicily. If you were to listen to the propaganda that British agents have been carrying on all over the world, you would think that with the occupation of Sicily they have already won the war. I know something of Europe, not only of peace-time Europe but war-time Europe, and I know all these places where fighting has taken place. I know also the strength and weakness of the Axis powers in Europe and from experience I want to assure you that whatever may happen in Europe has no bearing on the situation either in India or East Asia. Whatever may happen in Europe, Indians will be ready if only we put forward the required effort. Therefore, do not hesitate for one moment by any propaganda the enemy may carry on to-day or tomorrow and be firm in your belief and faith that it has become possible for Indian people to achieve independence.

First of all, is it a very big effort that we have to bring an army of 200,000 to 300,000 to India? Look at the millions and millions of people fighting on all fronts in different parts of the world. For the salvation of 38 crores an army of 300,000 or even 400,000 is nothing at all and it is possible for the people of East Asia to contribute enough men for this army. It is possible also for the people in East Asia to contribute money and every material for the equipment of this army. Therefore, let us concentrate all our energy on the one task of organizing an army and bringing it to perfection as soon as possible.

Friends, our task today is to bring perfection as soon as possible to the army that exists today, along with it we have to expand our army because the war is going to be a long and hard one. We want more and more young men to come in and get training. I congratulate you that you have in the heart of Kuala Lumpur one of our camps where Indian young men are trained for the coming fight for freedom. Well, it is not only in Syonan and Kuala Lumpur that they are being trained today. Malai is dotted with camps and many of these camps were formerly camps of the British army. They have been turned over to us for our use. That reminds me that even when we go to India, we shall also find ready-made barracks for our national army. We won't have to build new barracks. From Calcutta to Bombay and from Rawalpindi to Madras, there are splendid barracks not for the Indian army but for the British Tommy, but these splendid barracks are going to be taken for our Indian National Army, and I promise to give the British in return all the prisons for their use.

Friends, to defeat Britain we shall need help from outside. The enemy is asking for help all over the world. The almighty British Empire, over which the sun never sets, that mighty British Empire is going round the world with the begging bowl. It is not merely at Washington that they are asking for help but all over the world, even the poor Indian people, the slaved Indian people, are not spared. Even Indian people have to do their share in men, money, munitions and war materials. They are begging even Indian people to help them in their hour of need. We have to fight today not merely the might of Britain but the combined might of Britain and her allies, a most powerful combination. If we are to fight and win, we shall need help and take help when the time comes, but there will be no humiliation in accepting or asking for help when we have first done our duty.

At this juncture, the duty of the people of East Asia is to put forward the maximum effort. Remember you have an opportunity of doing something, which your countrymen in other parts of the world cannot do. What can Indians in Europe, Africa, America, or even in England do? They are helpless. I know many of them are dying to serve and fight for their country's freedom, but it is impossible for them to do so. They are unable to organize an army or join the National Army, but all that is within your reach; if you only make it your mission, you can join the National Army and work for its success. Therefore, when the call of sacrifice reaches your ears, do not flinch. Thank Providence that she has given you of all Indians in the world a unique opportunity to serve your country and fight for your country's independence.

20

At Bahadur Shah's Tomb[1]

[Speech delivered on 26 September 1943]

A solemn and impressive ceremony took place at the Mausoleum of Bahadur Shah, the last Emperor of Free India on Sunday, September 26, 1943. Netaji paid profound homage to the mortal remains of Bahadur Shah, who fought for the overthrow of British rule in India. Amongst those, who attended the function, were His Excellency Dr. Ba Maw and his colleagues.

Your Excellency and Friends! Today, we have assembled here near the tomb of Bahadur Shah, the last Emperor of free India. It is perhaps strange, maybe a lucky coincidence of history, that while the remains of India's last Emperor rest on the soil of Burma, the remains of the last King of free Burma now rest on the soil of India.

We, in India and in Burma, have all along felt bound together historically, by the most profound ties. And this coincidence of history is one of the most convincing proofs of these ties between Your Excellency's nation and ours.

We are, both of our nations, passing through a common fight against our common foe and we therefore consider it to be in the fitness of things to have a small celebration before the mortal remains of our last Emperor so that on the one side we might rouse the fire that burns within us and at the same time strengthen further the ties that have bound Burma and India so long and that will bind us together for all time.

[1] *On To Delhi*, pp. 88–90.

We are profoundly grateful to Your Excellency and to the honourable members of the Government for the honour that has been done us by your gracious presence in this function—a function which is pregnant with important and historical events in the days to come.

As I have done so before, once again, I should like to express our unshakeable determination to fight with our Burmese friends, shoulder to shoulder, assured of the magnanimous help and support of Nippon so that we may bring about the final overthrow of British imperialism, which will, on the one side, bring India her lost liberty and, at the same time, remove once for all the menace to Burma's safety and independence.

This time, we express our unshakeable determination before a sacred memorial, before the mortal remains of the last fighter for India's freedom, the man who was an Emperor among men and, at the same time, a man among Emperors. We cherish the memory of Bahadur Shah. We Indians, regardless of religious faiths, cherish the memory of Bahadur Shah not because he was the man who gave the clarion-call to his countrymen to fight the enemy from without, but because he was the man under whose flag fought Indians from all provinces, Indians professing different religious faiths, the man under whose sacred flag Muslims and Hindus and Sikhs or at least freedom loving Muslims, Hindus and Sikhs, fought side by side in the war that has been dubbed by the English historians as the Sepoy Mutiny, but which we Indians call as the First War of Independence. And now when we are engaged in the last war of India's independence, it is all the more necessary for us to renew our unshakeable determination, to fight this last war for independence to a finish, regardless of all sufferings and sacrifices, regardless of all difficulties on our path, regardless of the length of this war, so that at long last the enemy, the common enemy of Burma and India, will be finally overthrown and we will be free not only within our homes, but free as comrades marching shoulder to shoulder to fulfill the common destiny of mankind.

Your Excellency, with us it is the practice to offer donations and contributions at shrines like this. As a token of our inner feelings and faith, I can think of no better donation or *Nazar* than to offer in the name of the last hero of India's First War of Independence, Emperor Bahadur Shah, a small contribution of Rs. 50,000 to be handed over to Your Excellency as a very small token of our love and admiration for Burma and all that Burma stands for, a small donation which Your Excellency may utilize in a manner considered best by yourself.

And now I shall close these few remarks by quoting the English meaning of a couplet which was composed by Bahadur Shah himself, 'As long as the last particle of faith exists in the souls of India's freedom fighters, the sword of India shall continue to penetrate the heart of London.'

21

Gandhiji's Part in India's Fight

[Broadcast from Bangkok delivered on 2 October 1943][1]

This day, Indians all over the world are celebrating the 75th birthday anniversary of their greatest leader, Mahatma Gandhi. It is customary on such an occasion to relate the life-experiences of the man whom we honour and to whom we pay homage of love and respect. But the Indian people are so well acquainted with the life and work of Mahatma Gandhi that it would be an insult to their intelligence if I were to begin narrating the facts of his life. I shall, instead, devote myself to an estimation of the place of Mahatmaji in the history of India's struggle for independence. The service which Mahatma Gandhi has rendered to India and to the cause of India's freedom is so unique and unparalleled that his name will be written in letters of gold in our national history—for all time.

In order to correctly estimate Mahatma Gandhi's place in Indian history it is necessary to take a bird's-eye-view of the British conquest of India. You all know that when the British first set foot on Indian soil, India was a land flowing with milk and honey, and it was the wealth of India which had attracted poverty-stricken Englishmen from across the seas. Today we find that as a result of political enslavement and economic exploitation the Indian people are dying of hunger and starvation, while the British people who were once so poor and needy have grown fat and rich on the wealth and resources of India. Through sorrow and suffering, humiliation and torture, the Indian people have learnt at

[1] *On to Delhi*, pp. 1–8.

long last that the only solution of their manifold problems is the recovery of their lost liberty.

Turning to the methods of the British conquest of India, we see that the British never attempted to fight the entire Indian population in any part of the country, nor did they try to conquer and occupy the whole of India at once. On the contrary, they always tried to win over a section of the people, through bribery and corruption, before they commenced military operations. This was the case in Bengal, where the Commander-in-Chief, Mir Jaffar, was won over by the British, by offering him the throne of Bengal. At that time, the religious or communal problem was unknown in India. The last independent king of Bengal, Siraj-ud-Dowla, who was a Muslim, was betrayed by his Commander-in-Chief, who was also a Muslim—and it was the Hindu Commander, Mohanlal, who fought with Siraj-ud-Dowla till the very last. The lesson that we have learnt from this episode in Indian history is that unless timely steps are taken to prevent and to punish treachery, the nation cannot hope to preserve its independence. The developments in Bengal did not unfortunately open the eyes of the Indian people in time. Even if after the fall of Siraj-ud-Dowla in Bengal, the Indian people had made common cause against the British, they would have easily succeeded in throwing the unwanted foreigner out of Indian soil. No one can say that the Indian people did not fight in order to retain their freedom—but they did not fight all together. When the British attacked Bengal, nobody attacked them from behind. When later on, the British fought Tipu Sultan in South India, neither the Marathas in Central India nor the Sikhs in the North came to the rescue of Tipu Sultan. Even after the fall of Bengal, it was still possible for the British to attack one part of India at a time and gradually extend their rule over the whole country. The lesson that we have learnt from this painful chapter of Indian history is that unless the Indian people stand united before the enemy, they will never be able to achieve their independence, nor will they be able to preserve it even if they acquire it.

It took a long time to open the eyes of the Indian people. Ultimately, in 1857, they woke up, and they then made a concerted attack on the British in different parts of the country. When the fight began—the fight that the British historians call 'The Sepoy Mutiny' and we call the 'First War of Independence'—the British were easily defeated at first.

But two factors accounted for our ultimate failure. All parts of India did not join in the fight and what is more significant the technical skill of our army commanders was inferior to that of the commanders of the enemy forces. It is a fact that Europe had made considerable progress in the art of modern warfare in the eighteenth century and the Indian people had not kept abreast of the times. Consequently, when the final clash with the British forces took place, our army leaders were found wanting. The lesson that we have learnt from our failure in 1857 is that, in future, the Indian people must keep up intimate contact with the progress made by other nations in every walk of life.

After the defeat in 1857, the British disarmed the Indian people. It was the greatest folly and mistake on their part to submit to disarmament at that time. If the Indian people had not been disarmed and thereby rendered helpless, it would have been possible for them to strike for their liberty once again within a short period of time. Owing to disarmament, however, the Indian people lay politically prostrate and despondent for nearly thirty years. Ultimately, in 1885, a political awakening took place through the birth of the Indian National Congress. The Indian National Congress was in the beginning a moderate body. The leaders of the Congress were, at first, afraid of demanding complete independence and the severance of the British connection. Within a brief span of twenty years, however, new life was infused into the Congress. By 1905, we find leaders like Aurobindo Ghosh demanding complete independence for India. Along with this demand for independence, more extreme methods were adopted for achieving liberty. In Bengal, the boycott of British goods was adopted as a resolution against the partition of that province, and this method of boycott was gradually taken up all over India. Not content with economic boycott, Indian youths next took the cult of the bomb and the revolver. A number of youths were sent abroad to learn revolutionary sabotage in Paris and other European centres, while Indian youths as a whole began to study the revolutionary methods adopted in other parts of the world—notably in Russia and in Ireland.

During the last World War, the Indian leaders were duped by false promises made by unscrupulous British politicians and, as a result, India's blood and money were poured out in the service of Britain and in order to strengthen the chains of India's bondage. It must, however, be said to the eternal honour of the Indian revolutionaries that they did not allow themselves to be deceived by Britain, and they did their very best to work up a revolution in the country. But unfortunately for India, they failed.

When the last World War was over and the Indian leaders began to demand the liberty that had been promised to them, they discovered for the first time that they had been betrayed by perfidious Albion, i.e., the British people and their politicians. The reply to their demand came in the form of the Rowlatt Act—or the Black Act—in 1919, which deprived them of what little liberty they still possessed. And when they protested against that Black Act—the Jallianwalla Bagh massacre followed. For all the sacrifices made by the Indian people during the last World War, the two rewards were—the Rowlatt Act and the Jallianwalla Bagh massacre.

After the above tragic events in 1919, the Indian people were stunned and paralysed for the time being. All the attempts for achieving liberty had been ruthlessly crushed by the British and their armed forces. Constitutional agitation, boycott of British goods, armed revolution—all had alike failed to bring freedom. There was not a ray of hope left and the Indian people, though their hearts were burning with indignation, were groping in the dark for a new method and a new weapon of struggle. Just at this psychological moment, Mahatma Gandhi appeared on the scene with his novel method of Non-co-operation or Satyagraha or Civil Disobedience. It appeared as if he had been sent by Providence to show the path to liberty. Immediately and spontaneously the whole nation rallied round his banner. India was saved. Every Indian's face was now lit up with hope and confidence. Ultimate victory was once again assured.

For twenty years and more Mahatma Gandhi has worked for India's salvation, and with him, the Indian people too have worked. **It is no exaggeration to say that if, in 1920, he had not come forward with his new weapon of struggle, India today would perhaps have been still prostrate. His services to the cause of India's freedom are unique and unparalleled. No single man could have achieved more in one single lifetime under similar circumstances.** The nearest historical parallel to Mahatma Gandhi is perhaps Mustapha Kemal who saved Turkey after her defeat in the last World War and who was then acclaimed by the Turks as the 'Gazi.'

Since 1920 the Indian people have learnt two things from Mahatma Gandhi, which are the indispensable preconditions for the attainment of independence. They have, first of all, learnt national self-respect and self-confidence—as a result of which, revolutionary fervour is now blazing in their hearts. Secondly, they have now got a countrywide organization, which reaches the remotest villages of India. Now that the message of liberty has permeated the hearts of all Indians and they have got a countrywide political organization representing the whole nation—the stage is set for the final struggle for liberty—the last war of independence.

It is not in India alone that a struggle for freedom has been heralded by a spiritual awakening. In the Risorgimento movement in Italy it was Mazzini who first gave the spiritual inspiration to the Italian people. He was then followed by the fighter and the hero—Garibaldi, who began the March to Rome at the head of one thousand armed volunteers. In modern Ireland, too, the Sinn Fein Party, when it was born in 1906, gave the Irish people a programme, which was very much similar to Mahatma Gandhi's Non-co-operation programme of 1920. Ten years after the birth of the Sinn Fein Party—that is, in 1916—the first armed revolution in Ireland took place.

Mahatma Gandhi has firmly planted our feet on the straight Road to Liberty. He and other leaders are now rotting behind the prison bars. The task that Mahatma Gandhi began has, therefore, to be accomplished by his countrymen—at home and abroad.

Indians at home have everything that they need for the final struggle—but they lack one thing—an army of liberation. That army of liberation has to be supplied from without—and it can be supplied only from without.

I would like to remind you that when Mahatma Gandhi commended his Non-co-operation programme to the Indian nation at the annual session of the Congress at Nagpur in December 1920, he said, 'If India had the sword today, she would have drawn the sword.' And proceeding further with his argument, Mahatmaji then said that since armed revolution was out of the question, the only other alternative before the country was that of Non-co-operation or Satyagraha. Since then, times have changed, and it is now possible for the Indian people to draw the sword. We are happy and proud that India's Army of Liberation has already come into existence and is steadily increasing in numbers. We have, on the one hand, to complete the training of this Army and send it to the field of battle as soon as possible. We have simultaneously to build up a new army that can go on reinforcing the Army in the field. The final struggle for liberty will be long and hard and we must go on fighting—till the last Britisher in India is either cast in prison or thrown out of the country. I would like to warn you that after our Army of Liberation—the *Azad Hind Fauj* or the Indian National Army—sets foot on Indian soil, it will take at least twelve months—and perhaps more—to liberate the whole of India from British yoke. Let us, therefore, gird up loins and prepare for a long and hard struggle.

22

A Red Letter Day

[Press statement on the achievement of Philippines regaining the complete independence of their Republic issued at Singapore, 14 October 1943][1]

Today is a red-letter day in the annals of the Philippines. Today, 18 million Filipinos will regain the complete independence of their Republic, which America robbed forty-two years ago. The re-birth of the Philippine Republic, within two and half months of the re-birth of the Independent State of Burma, is an occasion for rejoicing for all the nations of Asia and particularly for those who are still fighting for their independence. The proclamation of the Independence of the Philippines Republic to-day is of special significance and importance to India, as it is a message of hope and cheer to 388 millions of my countrymen who are fighting the British for their Independence. Having been expelled once and for all by the Japanese forces from every corner of East Asia, the Anglo-Americans have now converted India into their last stronghold in Asia. But, the day is not far off when India too will expel the Anglo-Americans and regain her Independence. Meanwhile, I extend my heartfelt felicitations to my Filipino brethren on the achievement of their cherished goal of independence after over forty years of American domination.

I also offer my most sincere congratulations to the veteran revolutionary leader General Emilio Aguinaldo on his living to see the victory of the cause for which he fought the Americans over forty years ago;

[1] *On To Delhi*, pp. 86–7.

I heartily congratulate Dr. Jose Laurel on his election as the first President of the Philippine Republic and Mr. Jorge Vargas on the achievement of the goal for which he has toiled night and day since the outbreak of the Greater East Asia War.

23

Provisional Government of Free India[1]

[i. Speech delivered at Singapore on 21 October 1943]

Indians in East Asia followed Sri Subhas Chandra Bose with unbounded enthusiasm and implicit faith and conferred on him the title of 'Netaji' (Leader). After having reorganized the Indian Independence League Netaji Subhas Chandra Bose toured Malaya and then visited Thailand and Burma. He was present at the historic ceremony of the declaration of Burma's independence at Rangoon on August 1, 1943, and had long discussions with Dr. Ba Maw, the premier, and other Ministers of Free Burma on problems of common interest.

After his return from Burma the stage was set for the formation of the Provisional Government of Free India. On October 21, 1943, a Conference of the Indian Independence League, attended by delegates from all parts of East Asia and thousands of Indians from all over Malaya, was held at Singapore. The proceedings began with a welcome address by Mr. M.K. Ramachandran, which was followed by a detailed report on the working of the League by the General Secretary Lt.-Col. A.C. Chatterji. Netaji Subhas Chandra Bose then ascended the rostrum and delivered the following stirring address:

'Friends—First of all, allow me to offer you a most cordial welcome to this Conference, which has been convened at very short notice. The purpose of this Conference is to take stock of our progress and achievement since we met here in July last and then to take the necessary steps for the early attainment of our national goal.

[1] *Chalo Delhi*, pp. 156–69.

The first task to which I addressed myself after taking over the Presidentship of the Indian Independence League in East Asia was the reorganization of the League Headquarters with a view to putting it on a war footing. This work was undertaken early in July and several new Departments were opened in the Headquarters. The reorganization of the Headquarters was effected according to the programme of 'Total Mobilization' of all the resources of Indians in East Asia—resources in men, money and materials. Following the reorganization of the Headquarters, branches of the League throughout East Asia were also reorganized on the same basis and effect was given everywhere to the new programme of 'Total Mobilization.'

The next task to which I addressed myself was the reorganization of the *Azad Hind Fauj* (the Indian National Army). To this end, I took over the direct command of our army. Since then, some changes have already been made in our army organization and, in future, some more changes will be needed. Simultaneously with changes in army organization, the morale of the Army as a whole has been considerably strengthened and improved. One indication of the present morale of our Army is the joy and enthusiasm, which light up every face, when a Unit is transferred northwards from Syonan. I am glad to tell you that today the slogan that is on the lips of every member of the *Azad Hind Fauj* is the slogan—'ONWARD TO DELHI.' In fact, it would be no exaggeration to say that the Army as a whole is earnestly longing for the day when it will be transported to the frontier of India.

While speeding up the spiritual and technical training of the existing Army with a view to making it ready for action, the work of expanding the Army has also been taken in hand. I am happy and proud to inform you that the morale of the new recruits has come up to our highest expectations. As to the number of new recruits, I may tell you that though the whole of Malaya is now dotted with our Camps, we have still a very large number of recruits in hand for whose training we have not yet been able to make the necessary arrangements. Nevertheless, we hope that in future we shall be able to make such arrangements that every recruit who volunteers may be taken care of at once. To this end, training Camps are being opened in other parts of East Asia as well—e.g. in Thailand, Burma, etc.

It is not our young men alone who have been volunteering everywhere in large numbers. Our young women also are coming forward enthusiastically to volunteer for national service of every kind. We have, therefore, found it necessary to organize a Rani of Jhansi Regiment, in which our sisters will be given military as well as Red Cross Training. The Central Training Camp for the Rani of Jhansi Regiment will be opened in Syonan on the 22nd October.

In accordance with the scheme of "Total Mobilization", strenuous efforts are being made everywhere to collect funds for the Independence Movement and also to purchase and collect supplies necessary for our Army. The response has on the whole been very encouraging. Among the middle and poorer classes the spirit of sacrifice hitherto exhibited has been remarkable and affords satisfaction and pride to every freedom-loving Indian. As for the richer classes, they are slowly coming forward and I hope that in future they, too, will not lag behind the rest of the Community in the matter of national service and sacrifice.

Since July last, besides carrying on an extensive propaganda among the Indian Community as a whole, we have been also concentrating on those sections of the Community who have been lukewarm or indifferent in the past. I am glad to be able to report that in this respect as well we have made considerable progress. There is today a general desire among all sections and strata of the Indian community in East Asia to do everything possible to further the cause of Indian Independence and they are anxiously waiting for further steps to be taken in that direction.

During the last few months, the situation inside India has been developing in a manner favourable to our cause, though it has meant more and more suffering for the people. The political attitude of the British authorities remains as reactionary as ever, though occasionally high-placed officials talk glibly of compromise. All the known and recognized leaders of Indian nationalism are behind the prison-bars, along with a very large number of our political workers and fighters. There is no possibility that this situation will change, though it is not unlikely that a futile attempt may be made once again to dupe the Indian people into a dishonourable compromise with Britain.

The political unrest in India has been greatly accentuated by the famine conditions prevailing in several parts of India—and particularly in Bengal. There can be no doubt that these famine conditions have been largely due to the policy of ruthless exploitation of India's food and other resources for Britain's war purposes over a period of nearly four years. You are aware that on behalf of our League I made a free and unconditional offer of one hundred thousand tons of rice for our starving countrymen at home as a first instalment. The British authorities in India not only did not accept this offer, but also we were abused in return. On the other hand, appeals made by public institutions in India—like the Calcutta Municipality, for instance, to President Roosevelt and Prime Minister Churchill, for food supplies for the starving millions in India evoked no response at all. The only satisfaction that we can derive out of this heart-rending situation is the thought that hunger always breeds revolution.

I am happy to be able to tell you that the general world situation remains as favourable for the success of our cause as it was before the anti-Axis powers obtained some success in North Africa and in Italy. Our countrymen at home realize this. Consequently, the only effect of the recent happenings in North Africa and in Italy has been to further strengthen the anti-British feeling in India and the determination of the people to throw off the British yoke. So far as the Indian Independence League in East Asia and the Indian National Army are concerned the determination to fight for and win liberty has been rapidly increasing with the passage of time, regardless of any developments in other parts of the world.

You are probably aware that since July last, I have toured more than once in the mainland of Malaya, in Thailand, in Burma and in Indo-China. The enthusiasm among our countrymen that I have met everywhere has not only been encouraging, but has added greatly to my feeling of confidence and optimism.

For Indians fighting for their liberty, whether at home or abroad, achievement of independence by Burma in August last and by the Philippines this month (i.e. October) has come as a very great inspiration. Indians throughout East Asia have celebrated both these occasions by holding meetings and demonstrations and have conveyed their heartfelt congratulations to the independent Governments of Burma and the Philippines. Simultaneously, they have realized more keenly than ever before the added responsibility which has now fallen on the Indian people to bring about the final emancipation of Asia by expelling the British and their allies from Indian soil.

In my visits to Thailand and to Burma, I was fortunate enough to make personal contact with His Excellency Adipadi Dr. Ba Maw and the other Ministers of the Burmese Government. From both Governments I obtained not only sympathy and goodwill for our struggle, but also assurance of help in every possible way.

I would like to inform you also that we have been planning and preparing, not only for the coming struggle, but also for post-war reconstruction. We can visualize the conditions that we shall find at home when the Anglo-Americans and their allies are expelled from our country. We have therefore set up a Reconstruction Department in our Headquarters, where the problems of post-war reconstruction are being studied. People are also being trained for work of rapid reconstruction within India simultaneously with the progress of military operations. In short, we are not leaving anything undone in our preparation for the coming fight for freedom and for the task that we shall have to undertake thereafter. From every point of view, the stage is now set for the next phase of our campaign. We have now to adopt measures both of a political as well as of a military nature.

With regard to measures of a military nature, Indians in East Asia and, in particular, members of the *Azad Hind Fauj* (Indian National Army) are eagerly looking forward to the day when we shall be able to cross the frontier of India and launch the last fight for our freedom. But before we can do that some political measures have to be adopted. We have, for instance, to form the Provisional Government of Azad Hind (Free India) and commence our struggle under the leadership of that government. The formation of such a government at this juncture will have a profound effect on Indians throughout the world, and it will afford a powerful impetus to them in the struggle that lies ahead. In fact, our countrymen in East Asia have been eagerly desiring and expecting the inauguration of the Provisional Government of Azad Hind.

The Indian Independence League, being the only representative organization of Indians in East Asia and enjoying the full confidence of the entire Indian community, is competent to form such a Government. By virtue of the powers vested in me under the Constitution of the Indian Independence League, it will be my task to form the Provisional Government of Azad Hind.

It would, naturally, have been the best thing if such a government had been constituted inside India and if that government had launched the last struggle for liberty. But things being what they are in India and all the known and recognized leaders being in prison, it is hopeless to expect the formation of a provisional government within the frontiers of India. It is equally hopeless to expect the last fight for freedom to be organized or initiated within the country. It is consequently for the Indians in East Asia to undertake this solemn task. I may, however, remark at this stage that there are several historical precedents for a provisional government being formed outside the frontiers of a country. There are also historical precedents for award of freedom being launched from outside the country.

But though the initiative in the political as well as in the military fields has to be taken outside the frontiers of India, it is no secret today that the Independence Movement abroad has been working in the closest harmony with the movement at home. Whatever we have been doing outside has the fullest support, not only of the civil population of India, but also of a large section of Britain's Indian Army. It is also no secret today that there is a regular and unbroken contact between patriots working at home and those working abroad. The British authorities have, from time to time, arrested, tortured and killed some of our liaison agents—but that has not disturbed our communications in any way. In view of all these facts, there is not the slightest doubt in our minds that when we cross the Indian frontier with our Army and hoist our National Flag on Indian soil, the real revolution will break out within the country—the revolution that will ultimately bring about the end of British rule in India.

Friends, what we are doing here at present is but a preparation for the final struggle. That struggle will begin only when we cross the Indian frontier. Then will commence the historic march to Delhi—the march that will end only when the last Englishman is either expelled from India or is thrown into prison—when India's National Flag flies over the Viceroy's House and when the *Azad Hind Fauj* holds its victory parade inside the ancient red-fortress of India's Metropolis.

Friends, I cannot end this address without expressing our heartfelt thanks to the Government and people of Nippon and to the Imperial Nipponese Army and Navy for the sympathy, help and co-operation that we have received in so generous a measure. The day will certainly come—and that too soon—when we shall give tangible proof of our gratitude for the assistance that we have received in the past and that we are going to receive in future, during one of the darkest hours in our history. In the meantime, all that we can do is to offer a humble token of our appreciation of and gratitude for the magnanimous sympathy and help that we have been receiving. As a small token of our gratitude, I have offered, on behalf of the Indian Independence League, a sum of money adequate for the purpose of manufacturing and equipping five airplanes for the Imperial Nipponese Army and five airplanes for the Imperial Nipponese Navy. Apart from this, I want to assure the Government and people of Nippon that however long and hard the struggle may be, we Indians are determined to fight shoulder to shoulder with them till our common enemy is overthrown. We are absolutely convinced of the ultimate victory of Nippon and her Allies, just as we are of our own national liberation.

And now, friends, I have to declare that I shall announce the composition of the Provisional Government of Azad Hind in the afternoon today.'

[ii. Significance of the Provisional Government of Free India]

The conference reassembled at 4 p.m. The hall was packed to overflowing, as in the morning session. Netaji Subhas Chandra Bose arrived punctually at 4 p.m., accompanied by Col. Yamamoto, Chief of the Hikari Kikan. Before proclaiming the inauguration of the Provisional Government of Free India Netaji moved a message of thanks to the Imperial Government of Japan for their kind help in the Indian Independence Movement and two messages of congratulation to Burma and Philippines on their attainment of independence. The messages were adopted by the Conference with acclamation.

Netaji then made a statement in Hindustani explaining the significance of the formation of the Provisional Government. The statement, which was translated into Tamil by Mr. M.K. Chidambaram, was as follows:

'As a student of history and, in particular, of revolutions in different parts of the world, during 22 years of public life, I always felt that what India was lacking in her fight for freedom were two things—a National Army and a National Government to lead that Army to battle. In the course of the present war, thanks to the brilliant victories achieved by the armed forces of Nippon, it became possible for Indians in East Asia to organize the Indian Independence League and the Indian National Army.

The creation of a National Army lent reality and seriousness to the whole Independence Movement in East Asia. If this Army had not been organized, the Independence League in East Asia would have been a mere propaganda organ. With the creation of the National Army, it became possible, as well as necessary, to set up a Provisional Government of Azad Hind (Free India). The Government is born out of the Independence League for the purpose of launching and directing the final struggle for India's freedom.

In setting up this Provisional Government, we are, on the one hand, meeting the exigencies of the Indian situation and are, on the other, following in the footsteps of history. In recent times, the Irish people set up their Provisional Government in 1916. The Czechs did the same during the last World War. The Turks, under the leadership of Mustapha Kemal, set up their Provisional Government in Anatolia.

In our case, the Provisional Government of Azad Hind will not be like a normal peace-time government. Its functions and its composition will be of a unique kind. It will be a fighting organization, the main object of which will be to launch and to conduct the last war against the British and their allies in India. Consequently, only such departments will be run by the Government as will be necessary for the launching and the prosecution of the struggle for liberty.

The Cabinet will consist of a certain number who will represent the civil departments of the government, while there will be others representing the Armed Forces of the Government. Since the purpose of the government is to fight for independence, the armed forces have been given a large representation on the Cabinet.

Besides the ordinary Ministers of the Cabinet, provision has been made for a number of Advisers to the Cabinet. In this manner, the Provisional Government will maintain close and organic connection with the entire Indian community in East Asia and mobilize all their resources for the coming struggle.

When the Provisional Government is transferred to Indian soil, it will assume the functions of a normal government operating in its own territory. Many new departments will then be started.

With the formation of a Provisional Government of Azad Hind, the Indian Independence Movement has obtained all the preconditions of success. It remains now to start the final struggle for freedom. This will begin when the Indian National Army crosses the frontier of India and commences its historic march to Delhi. This march will end only when the Anglo-Americans are expelled from India and the Indian National Flag is hoisted over the Viceroy's House in New Delhi.'

The conference hall resounded with loud and prolonged cheers as Netaji announced the composition of the Provisional Government as follows:

Subhas Chandra Bose (Head of the State, Prime Minister and Minister for War and Foreign Affairs)

Capt. Mrs. Lakshmi (Women's Organization)
S.A. Ayer (Publicity and Propaganda)
Lt. Col. A.C. Chatterji (Finance)

Representatives of the Armed Forces:

Lt. Col. Aziz Ahmed
Lt. Col. N.S. Bhagat,
Lt. Col. J.K. Bhonsle,
Lt. Col. Gulzara Singh,
Lt. Col. M.Z. Kiani,
Lt. Col. A.D. Loganadan,
Lt. Col. Ehsan Qadir,
Lt. Col. Shah Nawaz.
A. M. Sahay, Secretary (with ministerial rank),
Rash Behari Bose (Supreme Adviser)

Advisers

Karim Gani, Debnath Das, D. M. Khan, A. Yellappa, J. Thivy and Sardar Ishar Singh, A.N. Sarkar (Legal Adviser).

The Ministers and Advisers thereupon ascended the dais and took their seats behind Netaji.

The most touching scene was when Netaji took the Oath of Allegiance to India in the name of God. Netaji was visibly moved when he began reading the Oath in Hindustani. He seemed to feel the tremendous responsibility he was taking on his shoulders. After he had read a few words he was so overcome that he put his kerchief to his face to wipe a few drops of tears. A wave of emotion swept the whole audience, when the Head of State and Prime Minister read the following Oath:

'In the name of God, I take this sacred oath that to liberate India and the thirty eight crores of my countrymen I, Subhas Chandra Bose, will continue this sacred war of freedom till the last breath of my life.

I shall remain always a servant of India and to look after the welfare of thirty eight crores of my Indian brothers and sisters shall be for me my highest duty.

Even after winning freedom, I will always be prepared to shed even the last drop of my blood for the preservation of India's Freedom.'

Netaji was followed by the members of the Government pledging in the name of God their loyalty to Netaji Subhas Chandra Bose, the Head of the State and premier, and consecrating them entirely to the service of Mother India. Each individual Member stood at attention before Netaji and took the following Oath:

'In the name of God, I take this holy oath that to liberate India and the thirty eight crores of my countrymen, I, . . . will be absolutely faithful to my Leader Subhas Chandra Bose and shall be always prepared to sacrifice my life and all I have for fulfilling this pledge.' Netaji cordially shook hands with each of the Members to the accompaniment of hearty cheers from the audience.

[iii. Proclamation of the Provisional Government of Free India]

[The proclamation was read in Hindustani by Mr. A.N. Sahay, in Tamil by Mr. Chidambaram and in English by Netaji himself]

After their first defeat at the hands of the British in 1757 in Bengal, the Indian people fought an uninterrupted series of hard and bitter battles over a stretch of one hundred years. The history of this period teems with examples of unparalleled heroism and self-sacrifice. And, in the pages of that history, the names of Siraj-ud-doula and Mohanlal of Bengal, Haider Ali, Tippu Sultan and Velu Tampi of South India, Appa Sahib Bhonsle and Peshwa Baji Rao of Maharashtra, the Begums of Oudh, Sardar Shyam Singh Atariwala of Punjab and last but not least, Rani Laxmibai of Jhansi, Tantia Topi, Maharaj Kunwar Singh of Dumraon and Nana Sahib—among others—the names of all these warriors are forever engraved in letters of gold. Unfortunately for us, our forefathers did not at first realize that the British constituted a grave threat to the whole of India and they did not, therefore, put up a united front against the enemy. Ultimately, when the Indian people were roused to the reality of the situation, they made a concerted move—and under the flag of Bahadur Shah, in 1857, they fought their last war as free men. In spite of a series of brilliant victories in the early stages of this war, ill-luck and faulty leadership gradually brought about their final collapse and subjugation. Nevertheless, such heroes as the Rani of Jhansi, Tantia Topi, Kunwar Singh and Nana Sahib live like eternal stars in the nation's memory to inspire us to greater deeds of sacrifice and valour.

Forcibly disarmed by the British after 1857 and subjected to terror and brutality, the Indian people lay prostrate for a while—but with the birth of the Indian National Congress in 1885, there came a new awakening. From 1885 till the end of the last World War, the Indian people, in their endeavour to recover their lost liberty, tried all possible methods—namely, agitation and propaganda, boycott of British goods, terrorism and sabotage—and finally, armed revolution. But all these efforts failed for a time. Ultimately, in 1920, when the Indian people, haunted by a sense of failure, were groping for a new method, Mahatma Gandhi came forward with the new weapon of non-co-operation and civil disobedience.

For two decades thereafter, the Indian people went through a phase of intense patriotic activity. The message of freedom was carried to every Indian home. Through personal example, people were taught to suffer, to sacrifice and to die in the cause of freedom. From the centre to the remotest villages, the people were knit together into one political organization. Thus the Indian people not only recovered their consciousness, but also became a political entity once again. They could now speak with one voice and strive with one will for one common goal. From 1937 to 1939, through the work of the Congress Ministries in eight provinces, they gave proof of their readiness and their capacity to administer their own affairs.

Thus, on the eve of the present World War, the stage was set for the final struggle for India's liberation. During the course of this War, Germany, with the help of her Allies has dealt shattering blows to our enemy in Europe—while Nippon, with the help of her allies has inflicted a knockout blow to our enemy in East Asia. Favoured by a most happy combination of circumstances, the Indian people today have a wonderful opportunity for achieving their national emancipation.

For the first time in recent history, Indians abroad have also been politically roused and united in one organization. They are not only thinking and feeling in tune with their countrymen at home, but are also marching in step with them, along the path to Freedom. In East Asia, in particular, over two million Indians are now organized as one solid phalanx, inspired by the slogan of 'Total Mobilization.' And in front of them stand the serried ranks of India's Army of Liberation, with the slogan 'Onward to Delhi' on their lips.

Having goaded Indians to desperation by its hypocrisy and having driven them to starvation and death by plunder and loot, British rule in India has forfeited the goodwill of the Indian people altogether and is now living a precarious existence. It needs but a flame to destroy the last vestige of that unhappy rule. To light that flame is the task of India's Army of Liberation. Assured of the enthusiastic support of the civil population at home and also of a large section of Britain's Indian Army, and backed by gallant and invincible allies abroad, but relying in the first instance on its own strength, India's Army of Liberation is confident of fulfilling its historic role.

Now that the dawn of freedom is at hand, it is the duty of the Indian people to set up a Provisional Government of their own, and launch the last struggle under the banner of that Government. But with all the Indian leaders in prison and the people at home totally disarmed—it in not possible to set up a Provisional Government within India or to launch an armed struggle under the aegis of that Government. It is, therefore, the duty of the Indian Independence League in East Asia, supported by all patriotic Indians at home and abroad, to undertake this task—the task of setting up a Provisional Government of Azad

Hind (Free India) and of conducting the last fight for freedom, with the help of the Army of Liberation (that is, the *Azad Hind Fauj* or the Indian National Army) organized by the League.

Having been constituted as the Provisional Government of Azad Hind by the Indian Independence League in East Asia, we enter upon our duties with a full sense of the responsibility that has devolved on us. We pray that Providence may bless our work and our struggle for the emancipation of our motherland. And we hereby pledge our lives and the lives of our comrades in arms to the cause of her freedom, of her welfare, and her exaltation among the nations of the world.

It will be the task of the Provisional Government to launch and to conduct the struggle that will bring about the expulsion of the British and their Allies from the soil of India. It will then be the task of the Provisional Government to bring about the establishment of a permanent National Government of Azad Hind constituted in accordance with the will of the Indian people and enjoying their confidence. After the British and their Allies are overthrown and until a permanent National Government of Azad Hind is set up on Indian soil, the Provisional Government will administer the affairs of the country in trust for the Indian people.

The Provisional Government is entitled to, and hereby claims, the allegiance of every Indian. It guarantees religious liberty, as well as equal rights and equal opportunities to all its citizens. It declares its firm resolve to pursue the happiness and prosperity of the whole nation equally and transcending all the differences cunningly fostered by an alien government in the past.

In the name of God, in the name of bygone generations who have welded the Indian people into one nation and in the name of the dead heroes who have bequeathed to us a tradition of heroism and self-sacrifice—we call upon the Indian people to rally round our banner and to strike for India's Freedom. We call upon them to launch the final struggle against the British and all their allies in India and to prosecute that struggle with valour and perseverance and with full faith in final victory—until the enemy is expelled from Indian soil and the Indian people are once again a Free Nation.

24

Following in the Footsteps of History

[Press statement on 21 October 1943][1]

Speaking at the ceremony held today to inaugurate the Provisional Government of Free India, Netaji Bose, who was elected the Head of the State, said:

'During the last few months, the situation inside India has been developing in a manner favourable in our cause, although it has meant more and more suffering for the people. The political unrest in India has been greatly accentuated by the famine conditions prevailing in several parts of India—and particularly in Bengal. There can be no doubt that these famine conditions have been largely due to the policy of ruthless exploitation of India's food and other resources for Britain's war purposes over a period of nearly four years. You are aware that on behalf of our League, I made a free and unconditional offer of one hundred thousand tons of rice for our starving countrymen at home as a first instalment. Not only was this offer not accepted by the British authorities in India—but we were given only abuse in return.

You are probably aware that since July last, I have toured more than once in the mainland of Malaya, in Thailand in Burma and in Indo-China. The enthusiasm among our countrymen that I have met with everywhere has not only been encouraging, but has added greatly to my feelings of confidence and optimism.

I would like to inform you that we have been planning and preparing not only for the coming struggle, but also for post-war reconstruction. We can visualize the conditions that we shall find at home when the

[1] *Testament of Subhas Bose*, pp. 209–10.

Anglo-Americans and their allies are expelled from our country. We have, therefore, set up a Reconstruction Department in our headquarters, where the problems of post-war reconstruction are being studied. People are now being trained for rapid work reconstruction within India, simultaneously with the progress of military operations. In short, we are not leaving anything undone in our preparation for the coming fight for freedom and for the task that we shall have to undertake thereafter.

It would naturally have been the best thing, if a government had been constituted inside India and if that Government had launched the last struggle for liberty. But things being what they are in India and all the known and recognized leaders being in prison, it is hopeless to expect the formation of a provisional government within the frontiers of India. It is equally hopeless to expect the last fight for freedom to be organized or initiated within the country. It is consequently for the Indians in East Asia to undertake this solemn task.

There is not the slightest doubt in our minds that when we cross the Indian frontier with our Army and hoist our National Flag on Indian soil, the real revolution will break out within the country—the revolution that will ultimately bring about the end of British rule in India.

The creation of a National Army has lent reality and seriousness to the whole Independence Movement in East Asia. If this Army had not been organized, the Independence League in East Asia would have been a mere propaganda organ. With the creation of the National Army, it became possible as well as necessary to set up a Provisional Government of Azad Hind (Free India). The government is born out of the Independence League for the purpose of launching and directing the final struggle for India's freedom.

In setting up this Provisional Government we are, on the one hand, meeting the exigencies of the Indian situation, and are, on the other, following in the footsteps of history. In recent times, the Irish people set up their provisional government in 1916. The Czechs did the same during the last World War. The Turks, under the leadership of Mustapha Kemal, set up their provisional government in Anatolia.'

—SINGAPORE RADIO, 21 October 1943

25

The Rani of Jhansi Regiment

[Speech delivered on the occasion of the birthday celebration of the Rani of Jhansi and opening of the first camp for the training of volunteers for the Rani of Jhansi Regiment at Singapore on 22 October 1943][1]

The martial spirit of the Indian women in East Asia was roused when Netaji Subhas Chandra Bose called upon them to come forward in their thousands and follow the footsteps of Rani Lakshmibai of Jhansi and to take up arms against the British. The occasion was the celebration of the birthday of the Rani of Jhansi and the opening of the first camp for the training of volunteers for the Rani of Jhansi Regiment at Singapore on October 22. In an impassioned speech, Netaji Subhas Bose recalled the heroic deeds of Rani Lakshmibai and Chand Bibi, and the deeds of daring and selfless sacrifice performed by the young women of India during the last twenty years in India.

The entire audience, composed mostly of women, young and old, rose to its feet and broke out into delirious cheering when Netaji called upon the Indian women to march shoulder to shoulder with their brothers of the *Azad Hind Fauj* and be ready to lay down their lives on the battle-field for the sake of India's Freedom.

Netaji Subhas Chandra Bose was received by Mrs. M.K. Chidambaram, the President of the Women's Section, Singapore. Netaji then inspected the guard-of-honour presented by an armed unit of the Rani

[1] *Chalo Delhi*, pp. 170–4.

of Jhansi Regiment in the company of Capt. Mrs. Lakhsmi. The tricolour national flag was hoisted by Netaji with the accompaniment of a national song.

Declaring the Camp open Netaji said:

Sisters and Brothers—The opening of the Rani of Jhansi Regiment Training Camp is an important and significant function; it is a very important landmark in the progress of our movement in East Asia.

To realize its importance, you should bear in mind that ours is not a merely political movement. We are, on the other hand, engaged in the great task of regenerating our Nation. We are, in fact, ushering in a New Life for the Indian Nation, and it is necessary that our New Life should be built on sound foundations. Remember that ours is not a propaganda stunt; we are in fact witnessing the re-birth of India. And it is only in the fitness of things that there should be a stir of New Life among our womenfolk.

Our past has been a great and glorious one. India could not have produced a heroine like the Rani of Jhansi, if she did not have a glorious tradition. The history of the great women in India is as ancient as the Vedic Period. The greatness of Indian womanhood had its roots in those early days when India had its Sanskrit culture. The same India, which produced great women in the past also produced the Rani of Jhansi at a grave hour in India's history and today while we are facing the gravest hour in our history, I have confidence that Indian womanhood will not fail to rise to the occasion. If for the war of independence of Jhansi, India had to produce, and it did produce, a Lakshmi Bai, today for the war of independence of the whole of India to liberate 38 crores of Indians, India has to produce and shall produce thousands of Ranis of Jhansi.

In the same way as we have figures like Maitreyi in India's ancient days, we have the inspiring examples of Ahalyabai of Maharashtra, Rani Bhawani of Bengal, Razya Begum and Noor Jehan, who were shining administrators, in recent historic times prior to British rule in India. I have every confidence in the fertility of the Indian soil. I am confident that India, as in the past, will also produce the best flowers of Indian womanhood.

When in 1921 a new political life started in India, thousands, nay lakhs, of our sisters also joined the movement and came forward to make sacrifices. In those days it was a great thing to go to prisons. Our Indian brothers and sisters got ready to undergo the ordeal of prison life and I remember still how in December 1921 at Calcutta the jails were full. The British built two more jails and these two were also packed in a few days.

When the British found that the Indians were not restrained by fear of prison life, they changed their tactics. They resorted to the method of throwing leaders into prison and using lathis and bullets against the masses. Joining the Civil Disobedience Movement then meant willingness to face lathi charges and gun-fire and the Indians—not only men but also women—got ready to face lathi charges and gun-fire. I cannot forget an incident in Calcutta when we held a procession against the orders of the Government and when the police tried to break the procession by lathi charge, some of our sisters made a cordon around us (coming between us and the police) without flinching to face lathi charges. Thus, I have witnessed, while in India, how the spirit and determination of our sisters have been growing stage by stage.

Not only in the history of the Passive Resistance Movement but in the history of the Revolutionary Party also, we have the examples of our brave sisters who have played a noble part. I know of many sisters who became daring revolutionaries. If one type of courage was necessary for passive resistance, another and more active courage is necessary for revolutionary efforts, and in this too, I found that our sisters were not wanting. In 1931, an English Magistrate was shot dead by two girls; the age of one was 16, the age of the other was 17. In India, even ordinary men will shudder before Magistrates, but then two young sisters bravely went to the house of the Magistrate and fired at him. You can easily imagine what wonderful courage those young sisters might have had. Such courage does not descend from the skies; it comes from the soil of India; it has its roots in the age-old traditions of India's past.

Since 1928, I have been taking interest in women's organizations in India and I found that, given the opportunity, our sisters could rise to any occasion. There was one Rastra Mahila Sangh of ladies in Bengal, which did splendid work. In December 1928, a volunteer corps of 500 women was formed which was not only run on sound lines but their parades and their discipline gave us great hopes and confirmed my belief in the fact that, given the impetus and opportunity, Indian women could perform duties entrusted to them in a befitting manner. I have also seen women's organizations in India giving training in arms available in a slave country, like lathis and daggers, and the way our sisters were progressing was remarkable.

And so when I began to undertake the task of guiding the Indian Independence Movement, I felt that our sisters should also be given the opportunity to serve India at this grave emergency. I consulted many, and I was told by some that though to raise a women's regiment might be possible in India, it would be an impossible task in East Asia. What they said did not affect my conviction and my determination. And today, you have seen, before your own eyes, what our sisters have accomplished. Their work was started in July and if only now the Training Camp for them is being opened, the delay is not due to any shortcoming on their part. The delay was due to our difficulties in finding the accommodation and making the necessary arrangements. Meanwhile, I know that our sisters were getting impatient and anxious. I heard that they were intending to lead a deputation to me to ask me whether I have forgotten them. I feel happy today that the camp is ready and the camp is being opened today on the anniversary of the birthday of the Rani of Jhansi.

I may at this juncture say a few words about the Rani of Jhansi. When the Rani of Jhansi started her fight, her age was only twenty. You can easily imagine what it would have been for a girl of twenty, riding a horse, and wielding her sword in open battle. You can easily realize what courage and spirit she must have had; the English Commander who fought against her said, 'She was the best and bravest of the rebels.' He made this admission because Jhansi Rani's bravery was something which he could not hide for he himself had to fight against her. First, she fought from the Jhansi Fort, and when the Fort was besieged, she escaped with a party to Kalpi from where she put up a fight. Then she had to retreat from this battlefront, she made an alliance with Tantia Topi, attacked and captured Gwalior Fort, and using that Fort as the base continued the battle and in this last and great battle, she died fighting.

Imagine what amount of courage would have been necessary to carry on the fight in spite of more than one defeat. Yet this 20-year-old Rani had the courage and showed a valour which shall be a source of inspiration to Indians for generations to come. Unfortunately, Jhansi

Rani was defeated; it was not her defeat; it was the defeat of India. She died but her spirit can never die. India can once again produce Jhansi Ranis and march on to victory.

156 of our sisters are going to start their training in the camp, which is being opened today. But I hope that their number at Syonan will reach 1000 very soon. Training Camps for women have also been started in Thailand and Burma, but at Syonan, we have the Central Camp, and I feel that in this Central Camp we should at least have one thousand potential Ranis of Jhansi.

You have just now heard the brave words of the Commandant of the Rani of Jhansi Unit at Syonan. She expressed their determination to work ceaselessly day and night, to get prepared for the onward March to Delhi. I feel joyous at hearing that slogan 'On to Delhi' from our sisters as I have been hearing it from our brothers.

With these words, I declare the Training Camp open. And I would appeal to all the delegates present to carry my message to their localities and to make every effort to realize the programme I have now laid before you.

26

The Provisional Government of Azad Hind Declares War

[Broadcast declaring war on Britain and the USA and address to an audience of 50,000 Indians on the Padang opposite the stately municipal buildings of Singapore on 23–24 October 1943][1]

The Headquarters of the Provisional Government of Azad Hind issued the following communiqué on the night of October 23:

The second meeting of the Council of Ministers of the Provisional Government of Azad Hind met at midnight at the official residence of Netaji Subhas Chandra Bose on the 23rd and 24th of October, 1943 and resolved:.

'The Provisional Government of Azad Hind declares war on Britain and the United States of America. The Provisional Government of Azad Hind places on record its deep appreciation of the message conveying the news of the recognition of the Imperial Government of Nippon of the Provisional Government of Azad Hind. The Provisional Government of Azad Hind expresses its grateful thanks to the Imperial Government of Nippon for the generous offer of wholehearted cooperation and assistance contained in the above message.'

'The Provisional Government of Azad Hind declared war on Britain and America at 5 minutes past midnight last night' declared Netaji

[1] *Chalo Delhi*, pp. 174–87, the declaration of war being in English and the public speech translated from the original Hindustani.

Subhas Chandra Bose addressing an audience of 50,000 Indians on the Padang opposite the stately Municipal Buildings of Syonan at 4 p.m. on October 24.

The air was rent with shouts of 'Inqilab Zindabad,' 'Azad Hind Zindabad' and 'Netaji Ki Jai.'

'We have declared war because our strength has increased a hundredfold', proclaimed Netaji Subhas Chandra Bose.

He declared: "I want you to demonstrate to the world that you are resolved as one man to follow up this declaration with action that will show to the world that you mean bloody war when you declare war. The British know very well that I say what I mean and that what I mean I say. So, when I say 'War' I mean WAR—War to the finish—a war that can only end in the Freedom of India.

'But I warn every one of you to think very carefully before you raise your hand to pass this resolution of the Provisional Government of Azad Hind declaring war on Britain and America. If you too mean it, if you too are ready from this moment onward to sacrifice everything, all you have in this world and your lives to translate this declaration into action, if you mean to lay down your lives in the coming fight for India's freedom, then stand up and raise your hands', said Netaji Subhas Chandra Bose.

This was the signal for an outburst of frenzied demonstration. The audience of 50,000 rose to its feet, wild cheering broke out, fifty thousand throats shouted revolutionary slogans for full fifteen minutes without a break; where fifty thousand heads were seen a few moments earlier, was now seen only a forest of bayonets, which stood about twelve feet from the ground, the men of the *Azad Hind Fauj* and Volunteers having spontaneously raised their rifles and rested the butt-ends on their shoulders; they stood there like that and shouted revolutionary slogans; the civilians standing behind them, men, women and children raised both their hands and went on cheering their solemn assurance to Netaji; and on the 15 feet high platform Netaji stood like a lion grim and determined, witnessing this feverish enthusiasm.

Then the crowds broke the cordon; in wave after wave, they advanced towards the platform where Netaji was standing and cheered him until their throats went hoarse.

The following is Netaji's speech at the Mass Rally:

When I addressed you last on October 17th, on the occasion of our meeting to congratulate the Philippines on its achievement of independence, I told you that Burma and the Philippines had become independent and that the next would be India's turn. Today, I feel joy in informing you that the turn of India has now come, and the Provisional Government of Azad Hind has been established by us and recognized by the world.

When we look back at the succession of events which had slowly but steadily led to this important landmark in the history of our Independence Movement, we could clearly see that everything has been happening under the guidance and help of Providence. The will of God has been with us and if today, the Provisional Government of Azad Hind stands established, it is a government which has been declared to the world in the fullness of time and fitness of things.

With the beginning of the present War in Europe, our life-long enemies, the Britishers, received their first blows in the West and became weakened thereby. If they had continued to receive blows in the West only, the cause of Indian Independence could not have benefited thereby. But when the Greater East Asia War started in the East, our enemies received greater blows and became more weakened by one defeat after another. More important and significant than their losses in the East was the fact that a new door—a door undreamt of by them—was opened in the East for the emancipation of India.

The British strategists had always expected a menace to India from the North Western Frontier; little did they envisage the possibility of an Army of Liberation marching into India from the North Eastern Frontiers. They never dreamt of this possibility; nor were they prepared to defend an attack from this direction.

There is another interesting aspect of this question. Even supposing that the Britishers, suffering defeat after defeat in the West, had retreated up to the North Western Frontiers of India, even that would not have helped the cause of Indian Independence. Because there in Western Asia, we do not have any colony of Indians. On the other hand, destiny had kept three millions of Indians in East Asia. And when the enemy was driven out of East Asia and the help of Asiatics was forthcoming, the material was there in these three millions of Indians for a real bid for Independence.

With the Britishers driven to the North Eastern Frontiers of India—to the Indo-Burma borders—a golden opportunity thus arose for liberating India, and if the Indians in East Asia had not risen to the occasion, even that opportunity would have been lost. But the Indians in East Asia, I am glad to say, did not fail India at this great hour; they heard the call of the times and organized themselves into the Indian Independence League and started the formation of the Indian National Army. A retrospective survey of the events of the past few years clearly shows that Destiny had prepared the stage in an undreamt of way for the final war of Indian Independence. Things have happened steadily in the fullness of time and the fitness of things and who can deny when I say that by the grace of God, India's hour has come, that India's turn to be free has come.

When I came to East Asia and took up the leadership of this movement, my first objective was to re-organize and strengthen the Indian Independence League and to reform and stabilize the Indian National Army.

In my address to you on the 15th August, I told you that I am determined to set my foot on the holy soil of India before the end of this year. I always mean what I say. Mine was not an empty declaration or a mere boast. Since then, our preparations have been continuing slowly but steadily. You will remember the Military Review, which took place here on this Maidan on July 9, and this morning you would have noticed that the Indian National Army, which took part in the Review was far smaller than that of July last. I revealed in my address at the Military Review this morning that a considerable part of the Indian National Army had left Syonan already and that they were on the road to India. All our preparations have been proceeding in a satisfactory manner and recently it became necessary to take another and more important step, a decisive step in our march towards Independence.

The question would naturally arise as to what would be the leadership under which the Indian National Army would fight. And it was the right time for us to clear our position. The world, in general, and Indians, in particular, had to be told under whose leadership the Indian

National Army was going to fight and who would take over the territorial rights in India when the enemy is driven out. And so, at the right time, we established the Provisional Government of Azad Hind at the Conference of Indians in East Asia held on the 21st October.

If we had formed such a Government three years ago, the world would have called it a farce; and the enemy might have called it a propaganda stunt. But the Provisional Government having now risen as a natural sequence to the organization of three millions of Indians in East Asia and the establishment of the powerful Indian National Army, even our enemies would have to think twice before calling it a propaganda stunt. The present Provisional Government of Azad Hind is not a plaything; it is a solid and powerful body having as its sanction the will of the three millions of Indians united as a granite wall by the Indian Independence League and having as its support the Indian National Army.

In forming this government, we have made no innovations because it has always been part of the technique of revolution to declare a provisional government just on the eve of a final War of Independence. Many examples are available in history for the adoption of this method. We have, for instance, the case of the Czechs and the Irish as well as the case of Mustapha Kemal, who formed a provisional government at Anatolia before the Turkish War of Independence. By taking this step on the 21st October, we have not only acted at the right time but we have also adopted the right method.

It is true that it would have been better if such a provisional government could have been established within the frontiers of India. But under the present circumstances it is not practical politics to have such an organization like the Indian Independence League or such an armed force like the Indian National Army within the frontiers of India. And any provisional government declared within India without the proper organization and armed strength would be a farce; and be something, which our enemies could suppress in no time. This being the truth, and taking all the factors into consideration, patriotic Indians cannot but come to the one and only conclusion that the only practical path for the achievement of our Independence is the path which we have now chosen.

In the proclamation of the establishment of the Provisional Government of Azad Hind on the 21st of October, I have clearly defined the objectives and limits of this Government. We are not a Government like the ordinary administrations established in normal times; and hence, we have not followed the normal method nor have we opened departments, which are essential only for the administration of a country in normal times. The first and foremost function of this Government is to wage the war of Independence and hence our Cabinet is primarily a War Cabinet.

Secondly, this government would undertake to administer the liberated territories during the transition period only. We shall continue to function till the last Englishman is driven out of India, till India becomes independent, and law, order and peace are restored in Free India and till a Permanent Government of Free India is set up according to the will of the thirty-eight crores of Indians in India. I appeal to you and to every Indian in East Asia to read the Proclamation issued by us on the 21st October and to understand fully the true significance of our provisional government.

I would also take this opportunity to emphasize that if a few have been elected as members of the government, it does not mean that the vast majority are absolved of their duties or responsibilities. For the sake of administrative convenience and necessity, a few have been made members of the government, but the responsibility of the government lies equally on all the Indians in East Asia.

Those who have assumed functions in the new government machinery have not assumed any grand positions; they have assumed in fact greater burdens and responsibilities. The path of this government is not a path of roses and very soon this government will have its trial on the battlefield. You must not think even for a moment that there has been any elevation of individual position.

If there has been any elevation of position, it has been that of India and the Indians. Who can say that by the formation of this government and its recognition by the world, the status and position of the Indians have not increased in the eyes of the world? You must realize that this is your Movement and that this Government is your Government, and that your duties as members of the Indian Independence League have now increased ten-fold.

We have two great tasks before us. The first task is to make full and final efforts with a view to crossing the frontiers and setting foot on the holy soil of India before the end of this year. The second task is to continue our work and carry on our preparations for a long war. The retreat of British from India would mean the final destruction of the British Empire and so it is only natural that the British will try to cling to India with all their might.

It is not going to be an easy affair to drive the Britishers from India, but I am confident that once we are on the Indian soil we shall get the necessary help and strength from the Indians in India. The Indians in East Asia, however, should realize that their efforts must continue as ever till our final objectives are achieved.

I would once again reiterate that our programme of Total Mobilization must be carried out with greater vigour as a sequel to the formation of our Provisional Government. I would once again repeat my appeal for men, money and materials. It is the duty of the Indians in East Asia to see that there is a continuous stream of men, money and materials forthcoming till we achieve final victory.

I may say in this connection, that my call for men to rally round the Colours has been receiving satisfactory response. The way young Indians in East Asia have come forward as volunteers and the way in which our sisters have responded to my call to form the Rani of Jhansi Regiment have been inspiring indeed.

And about the offer of money and materials, I may say here that the response from the poorer and middle classes has been encouraging. I have come across instances of the spirit of sacrifice among our poor brethren, who would bring tears to eyes of even a stone-hearted man. A washerman came to me and gave his 'all' and further said that as he hailed from Jhansi he would like to march along with our sisters of the Rani of Jhansi Regiment as their washerman. A poor ill-clad Indian who was a barber came forward with 200 dollars, which represented his savings for years and gladly offered it for the cause.

Especially moving are the sacrifices of our Gowala brethren. These brothers came, gave all the cash they had, all the cattle they possessed and offered themselves as volunteers for the Indian National Army. The poorer classes have been showing by their actions and example the meaning of Total Mobilization. It is only the rich who want to know whether Total Mobilization means five or ten per cent of their savings. The poor have been spontaneously coming forward with their all and their own selves.

It is high time that the rich revolutionized their outlook. They should realize that when a volunteer joins the ranks and goes to the front he does not ask whether he should spill five per cent or ten per cent of his blood. He goes to the front to spill every drop of his blood. The life of one such volunteer is to me more precious than millions of dollars. What I would ask the rich to understand is that if they do not want to come forward to give their lives, they should at least come forward to give their possessions.

I have heard that some of the rich people have been saying that we are a nuisance and that the nuisance would be over when we leave Syonan on our march to India. I want them to know that though we may march, the Indian Independence League would still be here carrying on our 'Home Front' programme while we are engaged on the fighting front. We cannot spare the rich; we cannot spare any Indian, because ours is a life and death struggle, and we are determined to carry on our fight to victory by all means and at any cost.

I have also said that some of our rich friends are thinking of changing their nationality to dodge the Indian Independence League's demand for funds. To these misguided friends, I have to say that there are only two alternatives before them; either they must become true Indians and do their duty at this hour of need or they must say that they are friends of Britain and be treated as such. In East Asia, there is no room for Britishers or their friends, except in jails and the time is not far off when in India also their position will be the same. I hope there will soon be a re-orientation of outlook among the few rich Indians who have not satisfactorily responded to our call.

I shall now inform you of two very important decisions of the Cabinet of the Provisional Government of Azad Hind and place them before you for your ratification. There was a time when the Britishers in their propaganda tried to ignore or belittle our movement in East Asia. Now, they have taken it seriously, and for want of any other tactics, they have resorted to abusing me from their radio stations. The tactic of abuse is the last refuge of the weak, of those who are at their wits' end. But it is significant that the enemy has realized our strength, and he understands that ours is not a mere propaganda stunt. The reactions and repercussions of the establishment of our Provisional Government has been world-wide, and it will be no exaggeration if I say that it has created panic both in London and Washington.

The enemy radio stations were rather quick this time in flashing out the news of the formation of our government through their broadcasts. Meanwhile, we have received the recognition of the Imperial Government of Nippon, and this, I must say, is a historic event of tremendous importance. If this recognition was a solitary act without any precedent there could have been opportunity for people to question the *bona fides* of this gesture. But, fortunately, this has not come as an innovation. This has come as one of the corollaries of Nippon's Asiatic policy based on justice and equality. The world has heard of this policy; it has already heard of the independence of Burma and of the Philippines and so the recognition of the Provisional Government of Azad Hind has come as the natural result of this policy.

The Anglo-Americans have been proclaiming from their housetops that they were the champions of liberty and democracy, but their actions have repeatedly given the lie to their claims. Apart from their determination to maintain their hold on India, they have enslaved independent countries like Iraq and Iran. They have been and are trying to enslave free Burma.

In contrast to this, we have the action of Nippon in recognizing Independent Burma, Independent Philippines and now the Provisional Government of Independent India. Our Nippon friends have always been showing us every sympathy and now, by this recognition, they have rendered us the greatest moral assistance for which we are greatly thankful. And so, the Council of Ministers of Azad Hind has unanimously passed a resolution deeply appreciating this gesture of Nippon. I place their resolution before you for your ratification.

'The Provisional Government of Azad Hind (Free India) places on record its deep appreciation of the message conveying the news of the recognition by the Imperial Government of Nippon of the Provisional Government of Azad Hind. The Provisional Government of Azad Hind expresses its grateful thanks to the Imperial Government of Nippon for the generous offer of wholehearted co-operation and assistance contained in the above message.

'Our thanks are due to Premier General Tojo for his great interest in Indian Independence. We have to thank also Colonel Yamamoto, the Chief of the Hikari Kikan, for his co-operation, especially in the establishment of the Provisional Government of Azad Hind.'

The next Resolution, which was unanimously adopted by my Council, is a more important one. The Council after discussing the political, economic and military situations in India came to the unanimous conclusion that the hour has struck for the declaration of war against Britain and America by the Provisional Government of Free India.

Last night at 12.55 a.m., we declared war through the radio and it is interesting to note that at 2 a.m. the enemy radio stations also gave out the news of our Declaration of War. This shows how alert they are in watching what steps we are taking. The Britishers know me well enough during my fight against them in India and they know well enough also that I will not make a declaration without having the strength to enforce what I say. Our declaration is not a mere propaganda stunt. The coming events would show that we meant what we said.

Before I place our resolution declaring war on Britain and America before you for your ratification, I would ask you to realize its implications and to give your decision after full consideration. Our declaration, I repeat, is not an empty threat. We are resolved to carry it out with the last drop of our blood. And when I ask you to ratify it, I do not want to have the resolution carried in a formal ceremonial way. Your ratification would mean that you are as much resolved as we are to shed your last drop of blood in enforcing the declaration. I know that I need not put this question to the Indian National Army, because I know their mind and their anxiety to be on the Road to Delhi. I am now asking the Civilians as to whether they are one with us in making this declaration, because if they are one with us, they should come forthwith to give the fullest effect to our Programme of Total Mobilization.

Friends! I want you to realize that we are now taking part in a meeting, which is not a propaganda show; this is not a ceremonial affair. We are here at a historic meeting to decide on a life and death issue. If we succeed in the project thirty-eight crores of Indians will be free. If, on the other hand, as God forbid, we fail, for at least another century our Nation will be doomed to slavery and untold misery. I have told you at the outset how the hand of God has created this golden opportunity for us. I have shown you how we have moved from stage to stage and how we have reached the right opportunity to strike at our enemy. I have told you how we now have the organization, the Army and the Provisional Government of Azad Hind recognized by the World and how we have secured every help and support. Are we going to fail India at this great hour in her history?

Realize all these things, consider deeply all the implications of a

Declaration of War and if you decide to take the war path, if you feel in your heart of hearts ready to face anything and everything in the historic fight against the British, if you feel that you are ready to give body, soul and all to fight our enemy until victory is won, then rise and give your ratification to our War Declaration by your acclamation.'

(This was the signal for an outburst of frenzied demonstrations. The audience of 50,000 rose to its feet, wild cheering broke out, fifty thousand throats shouted revolutionary slogans for full fifteen minutes without a break. The crowds broke the cordon: in wave after wave they advanced towards the platform where Netaji was standing and cheered him until their throats went hoarse.)

Netaji continued:

'Friends! My joy and pride knows no bounds at having witnessed the outburst of enthusiasm and spirit of resolution in you, and your thirst for Independence. With this spirit permeating the hearts of the Indians in East Asia, there could only be one sequel to our Declaration of War. And that is a fight, which cannot fail to end in victory and with this demonstration of the united will and unified spirit of the Indian Nation, it may be an easy victory over our enemies. The meeting is now over, and I would appeal to you to calm yourselves and to return to your homes, resolved forthwith to make every effort to bring our war to a victorious conclusion. I would, lastly, call upon you to give three cheers for Revolution, for Free India and for the Government of Nippon.' (Cheers).

27

Where is Your Bank Book?

[Speech delivered at the All Malai Chettiars and other Indian Merchants Conference on 25 October 1943][1]

Friends! I would first give my hearty welcome to our sisters and brothers who have come to attend this conference from all parts of Malai. You have come here to take part in a conference, which, I am confident, will prove to be of great significance and importance. We have heard considerable assurances of loyalty towards our great cause, and this conference is going to put that loyalty to the test.

I do not propose to deliver a long speech because long speeches are not necessary. Firstly, I would appeal to you to realize what each one of you would do if the responsibility of liberating India was on your shoulders; to free India is a responsibility which lies on the shoulders of every Indian in East Asia, and I hope that you will realize this great responsibility which has devolved upon you.

When an army goes to the battlefield, the responsibility of fighting and winning rests equally on every individual of the army, whether he is an officer, an N.C.O. or an ordinary soldier. Only that army will win, every soldier of which is ready to do his duty. You must realize that the Indians in East Asia have today become an army which has to fight and win. As in the case of every soldier at the front, so also on every Indian in East Asia a great responsibility has fallen. I know that some of you are rich and some of you are poor. I know that some of you are

[1] *On To Delhi*, pp. 100–10.

educated while others are not. Whatever be your differences, I want you to bear in mind that all of you are equal as far as your duty in concerned. I want every Indian in East Asia to do his duty.

When in an army someone is appointed as an officer, it becomes his duty to go forward himself and to lead others to go forward. Syonan has assumed a great importance in our fight in East Asia. The Headquarters of the Indian Independence League is here; the Headquarters of the INA is here; and only recently the Provisional Government of Azad Hind has also been established here. Syonan was once a fortress of Britain, but today, it has become the Headquarters of the Indian Independence Movement in East Asia.

Syonan's relation to other places in East Asia is the same as the relation of a commander to the troops of his regiment. The success of a battle not only depends upon the way every soldier performs his duty but it also depends on the correct lead and right example given by the officer commanding the army.

You will thus realize that any voice which rises from Syonan will have its echoes all over East Asia: that any action which you take here will have its repercussions all over East Asia. The part which Indians in various parts of East Asia are going to play, will greatly depend on the example which you are going to give from Syonan. I want you to remember that your responsibilities are great because you have to give the lead, you have to provide the inspiration for Indians in other parts of East Asia.

I want you to think for yourselves and visualize what a free Indian Government would have done when faced with a grave emergency like a foreign invasion. Supposing India was a free country and supposing there was the danger of an attack by a foreign enemy, what would the Government of Free India do? Would they not have started Total Mobilization then? You could easily understand that this is the normal duty of any free government. Keeping this fact in mind I want you to realize what your duties are in our great attempt to get our independence and maintain it.

Think also of what the procedure would be in a free country when it is in a state of war. Would there be meetings and appeals as is the case with us so far? No! A free government, on the other hand, would issue only a call for all able-bodied men between specific ages to assemble at a certain place on a certain day, at a certain hour. Voluntarily, and without any grumbling, people will respond to the call. Why, because people of independent countries know that they have to make sacrifices for their liberty. And when a free government needs money to defend its independence, it does not proceed to hold meetings and start begging campaigns.

On the contrary, free governments would prepare budgets of their requirements, think of ways and means to collect that money, keeping in view the financial conditions of the people, and straightaway proceed to levy the necessary taxation. I would ask you whether any man can refuse to become a soldier or to contribute war taxes in a free country? India is not yet free but we are free in heart and spirit. And by the establishment of the Provisional Government, we have become a free people.

Now, it is our responsibility to liberate India and to establish a free Government of India. If we feel that we are fit for independence, if we really desire independence, we should straightaway live and act as we would do if we lived in free India under the aegis of our Free Government at a time of a grave national emergency. Whatever we would have done in a free India in response to the call of the Free Indian Government, it has become our solemn duty to do forthwith. Look at the people of Germany and Nippon and how in those countries, all the resources of the people have been mobilized by the governments. When it is the duty of a government to defend its own independence, they have to do it at any cost and they have to pool all the resources of their countries.

Legally speaking, there is no private property when a country is in a state of war. The government has absolute right over the lives and properties of its people during such emergencies. We too are a free people with a free government. If you think that your wealth and possessions are your own, you are living in delusion. Every life and every property belongs to the nation when it is involved in a war. Your lives and your properties do not belong to you; they belong to India and India alone.

I have every confidence that if you realize this simple truth that we have to achieve independence by any means and at any cost, and that we are now a free people in a state of war, you will realize that nothing belongs to you, that your lives, properties and everything are no more your own.

If you do not want to realize this simple truth, then you have another path clearly chalked out for you. If you do not want to shoulder your duties as a free Indian living under a free government, if you do not want independence and if you are not ready to pay the price of independence, you have only one course before you and that is the path taken by the Englishmen.

They lived as rulers once here, but now, they have only one place left here and that is the prison. If you choose, you can go to prisons and keep company with the Englishmen. But remember this, when the war is over and India becomes independent, you shall have no room in Free India. If the Indian Government condescends to have pity on you the highest act of mercy which the Free Indian Government can do is to provide you with third class tickets to leave the holy soil of India and to go to England.

I have heard that some of the rich Indians in Malai are murmuring that I am harassing them. I want to have a straight talk with them so that they can take a straight path hereafter. I have heard that some rich Indians are thinking of changing their nationality to save themselves from making contributions towards the cause of Indian Independence. I have also heard that some are thinking of handing over their properties to the custodians and of claiming them back after the war is over. Then again I have heard of people who are thinking of adopting a ruse of promising, say a lakh of Rupees, and trying to gain time by paying that amount in small instalments hoping that sooner or later we will be going away to Burma and then to India and thus they would be able to evade payments. But they are miserably in the wrong, and it is not going to be so easy for them to deceive us, and to shirk performing their duties. Whether we are here in Syonan, whether we are in Burma or in India itself, our organization shall remain here because it has to remain here to carry on its work till India becomes completely independent and the last Englishman is driven out of India.

I would appeal to every Indian whether he is a Hindu, Sikh, Muslim or a Christian not to fail in performing his duties. I know who are doing their duties and who are shirking them. I have to liberate India and I shall make India independent by all means and at any cost and I would appeal to you to realize that it is your duty too to shoulder the burden whether it pleases you or not. If you want to evade the issue, say plainly that you do not want independence, then as I have already told you, a different path lies ahead of you. So long as you say you are Indians and want to claim and make money in East Asia as Indians you cannot shirk performing the duties which devolve on you as free Indians. Do not think that it is left to your option to perform your duty or not.

I have already said in my last speech in Syonan that I am making my last appeal. Today, I am standing here not to make another appeal and I am not standing here as a beggar with outstretched hands. I stand here today representing the Provisional Government of Azad Hind which has absolute rights over your lives and properties. I assure you, friends, I am not one who is accustomed to tall talking or making empty threats. Whatever I say, I say after the fullest consideration and I mean what I say. Even my enemies know that I seldom say what I do not mean. I have said that we have to get Indian Independence by all means and at any cost and that we have to carry out Total Mobilization voluntarily if possible, by compulsion if necessary. And I would reiterate to you that I mean what I said. I am speaking at length to you today so that you shall not be under any delusion, so that you may not say afterwards that you were not given the fullest opportunity to come forward on a voluntary basis. It will be an honourable course for you and I would feel proud of you if you come forward voluntarily. But if you do not choose to come forward voluntarily, then we are not going to remain slaves on that account.

I am really surprised to hear that there are a few people who are saying that it took years for them to amass their money and that they have many children to provide for. If on this account, they had refused to make sacrifices, in a Free India under a Free Government, I would ask you to imagine, what would have happened to them. Surely, they would have been regarded and treated as enemies. You could either be a friend or foe. Do not think that only the Britishers are our enemies. Everyone who helps the Britishers, everyone who refuses to help our cause, is also our enemy because we are engaged in a life and death struggle today.

Look at those who have volunteered to join the Indian National Army and who are not getting the necessary training. They do not know how many of them would live to see India free. They are getting ready with the one thought of shedding their last drop of blood. They are getting ready to go to a free India or to die on the way. There is no programme of retreat for them. Let the programme of retreat be reserved only for Wavell and his army. The British Government has given him promotions and has now made him the Viceroy of India because he has proved himself to be a past-master in the art of saving his own life by retreat after retreat. The INA has no plan of saving its life by retreat. When the INA is getting trained either to march to victory or to spill its last drop of blood on the way, the rich people are asking me whether total mobilization means 10 per cent or 5 per cent. I would ask these people who are speaking of percentage whether we can tell our soldiers to fight and spill only 10 per cent of their blood and save the rest.

You could see with your own eyes the spirit which is permeating our young men who have become recruits and our sisters who have rallied to the Colours. Fortunately, we are not short of men. The response has been so great that we have enough recruits to get prepared even for a long war. What we are wanting is similar response in money and materials. If we are all poor, then we would be justified in seeking foreign help, but there are also rich people amongst us and our foreign friends also know it. When our own people have ample resources, it is sheer disgrace for us to stretch our hands to others for help.

When there are brothers and sisters coming forward in large numbers offering their lives, I cannot understand why those who do not want to give their lives are even grumbling to part with their possessions. What is money after all; compared with life, money is nothing. Supposing a foreign government tells you that either you have to give the crore you possess or your life, surely you would rather choose to part with your crore than your life. In the same way as young men have come forward to offer their lives, the poor classes have been coming forward voluntarily and with enthusiastic spirit to offer everything that they have. Poorer classes of Indians like, watchmen, washermen, barbers, petty shopkeepers and *gowalas* have come forward with all that they have.

And in addition to that some of them have also offered to become volunteers. Some friends ask me what I mean by the words 'Total Mobilization.' These poor men, who have volunteered not only their possessions but also their lives, have demonstrated by their own example the exact meaning of the word 'Total Mobilization.' Some of these poor people came to me, and not only did they give all the cash they had in their pockets but went further and gave me their 'savings bank books' which represent their lives' savings. Is there not one rich man among the Indians in Malai who can come forward and say in the same spirit 'here is my bank book' for the cause of Indian Independence?

The Indians as a nation believe in the ideal of self-sacrifice. Among the Hindus we have the ideal of the Sanyasins, and the Muslims have the way of the Faqirs. In our history, we have instances of numerous kings who chose to become Faqirs for the sake of faith, justice and truth. Can there be a greater cause, a nobler cause and holier cause than that of liberating 38 crores of human souls and is there not one rich man who could come and say 'here is my bank book' for such a great cause? If you are not self-sacrificing enough to offer your lives, I cannot understand why there should not be even a few among you who could say, 'spare our lives, but we give everything else.'

I shall now proceed to place before you the programme of the Provisional Government of Azad Hind. In carrying out this programme, we have to proceed slowly, steadily, and systematically as any government would do. The wealth of Indians in Malai according to pre-war estimates was 100 crores, and as you know, values have increased since then. Usually a government makes a yearly budget and, when it is necessary, supplementary budgets also during the year. I also propose to do the same thing. It is up to you either to come forward voluntarily in the spirit of Total Mobilization or you shall have to meet the demands made by us from time to time till the war is over.

My first demand from Malai is for 10 crores of Rupees, which would be approximately 10 per cent of the value of Indian possessions in Malai. And as in this conference many rich people of Malai are present, I would expect at least one crore of Rupees straightaway and I hope within a month 10 crores would be forthcoming from Malai.

28

Netaji at the Assembly of Greater East Asia Nations

[Netaji's arrival at Tokyo on 31 October 1943, exchange of views with Premier Hideki Tojo, speech at the Greater East Asia Assembly on 5 November 1943, and other statements during his tour of East and South East Asia in November 1943][1]

The Japanese Board of Information in a communiqué on the afternoon of October 31 announced that Subhas Chandra Bose, Head of the Provisional Government of Azad Hind, arrived at Tokyo.

The communiqué text was as follows:

'For the purpose of expressing gratitude to Nippon Government for the recognition and co-operation extended to his government Mr. Subhas Chandra Bose, Head of the Provisional Government of Free India, came to Tokyo today.'

It was understood that during his sojourn in Nippon Netaji Bose would exchange views with Premier General Hideki Tojo and other Nippon Government leaders on various problems, including future co-operation between Nippon Government and the Provisional Government of Free India.

[1] *Chalo Delhi*, pp. 188–94; 'Subhas Chandra Bose and Japan', 4th Section, Asian Bureau, Ministry of Foreign Affairs, Government of Japan, August 1956; and audio and video recordings of Netaji's speech at the Greater East Asia Assembly available in the archives of the Netaji Research Bureau.

Upon arrival at Haneda Airport, Netaji Subhas Chandra Bose was warmly welcomed by prominent Nippon officials, including Foreign Minister Mamoru Shigemitsu, Greater East Asiatic Affairs Minister Kazuo Aoki, and the President of the Board of Information Eiji Amau, as well as leading members of the Tokyo Chapter of the Indian Independence League.

Netaji was accompanied by a party of seven including Lieut.-Col. J.K. Bhonsle, Chief of Staff of the Supreme Command and Minister without Portfolio; A.M. Sahay, Minister without Portfolio and Chief of the Cabinet Secretariat; Lieut.-Col. D.I. Raju, attached to the Supreme Command; and A. Hassan, Private Secretary. Upon stepping from the plane Netaji exchanged greetings with the Nippon's leaders. After the exchange of greetings, Netaji and party left the airport amid rousing cheers to the residence of Viscount Keizo Shibuzawa.

Netaji Subhas Chandra Bose made an official call on Premier General Hideki Tojo at 11.20 a.m. on November 1 and took leave after remaining in conversation for 40 minutes. Foreign Minister Mamoru Shigemitsu gave a dinner in honour of Subhas Chandra Bose at his official residence on November 2. In the course of his speech welcoming the guest of honour the Foreign Minister declared: 'Now that we are comrades devoted to the same cause of emancipating and enhancing Asia, we pledge to join forces to fight this war through until ultimate victory rewards our common efforts.'

He added, 'Light comes from the East. When dawn breaks the sun may climb slowly, but as the star-spangled sky grows dim, the eastern window becomes bright with the gathered beams of the rising sun. India is now waiting the sunrise. The gray dawn that now envelops the Indian horizon will soon break into full daylight.' The Foreign Minister stressed that since the days when Mr. Bose struggled to regain India's freedom under the most difficult conditions, 'conditions have now been radically changed.' He pointed out that Anglo-Saxon imperialism had been entirely wiped out from East Asia, while the victorious forces of Nippon now stood at India's borders. He asserted that all Asia 'is now seething and stirring with the desire and determination to assert its own destiny' with the result that Indians' inspiration for independence had received added impetus.

Responding to the Foreign Minister's address, Netaji Bose declared the reawakening of Nippon to the dangers of foreign aggression, to which some Asiatic nations had fallen prey, and Nippon's brilliant victories achieved in this war of Greater East Asia, had started the whole of East Asiatic nations on the way to complete freedom. Expressing gratitude for Nippon's steps taken to liberate the whole of Asia, and the generous assistance offered, Netaji Bose stressed the 'crowning act of friendship, co-operation, and assistance has been the recognition of our Provisional Government.' 'Only when our blood flows and mingles together in pursuit of the common cause will the unity—real, lasting unity—of Asia be created,' he concluded.

At the invitation of Premier General Tojo, Netaji Subhas Chandra Bose attended the Assembly of the Greater East Asia Nations in the afternoon of November 6. In a stirring 20-minute address before the Assembly, Netaji Subhas Chandra Bose voiced deep gratitude for the unanimous pledge of sympathetic assistance by East Asiatic nations to the Indian Independence Movement, and declared this support had provided a tremendous stimulus to all Indians. He promised that a decisive battle against Britain to free India would be launched in the near future.

As he stood up to speak, he was given a great ovation by the entire assembly. He first expressed his gratitude for the honour and opportunity given him to be an observer at this historic conference and especially for the sympathy and support expressed for the coming struggle. Withholding his tears he said, 'This resolution, I assure you, Your Excellency, will travel far beyond the walls of this stately mansion and will bring hope, encouragement and inspiration to millions and millions of my countrymen groaning under the heel of British oppression, while it will also strike terror in the hearts of all those who have a guilty conscience', and asserted his firm determination to stand up against the enemy with the support of the invincible military power of Japan and the sympathy of the newly liberated countries of East Asia.

The force of his delivery compelled every member of the conference to pay attention to every phrase of his speech. For instance he said: 'Your Excellency, as I was sitting, listening to the proceedings of this august assembly yesterday and to-day, the panorama of the world's history passed before my mind's eye. My thoughts went back to the many international congresses and conferences held during the last

100 years and more. My thoughts went back to the Congress of Vienna in 1815 after the downfall of the Napoleonic Empire, to the Congress of Paris in 1856 after the Crimean War, to the Congress of Berlin in 1878 after the Russo-Turkish War in the Balkans, to the Versailles Peace Conference in 1919 at the end of the last War, to the Washington Conference held in 1921 for ensuring the Anglo-American domination of the Pacific and Far East, and to the Locarno Conference in 1925 for ingeniously binding the hands of the German people, once and for all. My thoughts also went back to the Assembly of the League of Nations, that League of Nations along whose corridors and lobbies I spent many a day, knocking at one door after another, in the vain attempt to obtain a hearing for the cause of Indian freedom.

And as I sat listening to the proceedings of this historic assembly, I began to wonder what the difference was between this assembly and similar assemblies that the world's history has witnessed in bygone days.

Your Excellency, this is not a conference for dividing the spoils among the conquerors. This is not a conference for hatching a conspiracy to victimize a weak power, nor is it a conference for trying to defraud a weak neighbour. This is an assembly of liberated nations, an assembly that is out to create a new order in this part of the world, on the basis of the sacred principles of justice, national sovereignty, reciprocity in international relations and mutual aid and assistance. I do not think that it is an accident that this Assembly has been convened in the Land of the Rising Sun. This is not the first time that the world has turned to the East for light and guidance. Attempts to create a new order in the world have been made before and have been made elsewhere, but they have failed. They have failed because of the selfishness, avarice, and suspicion in those who had to play a leading role in the creation of a new order. It is, therefore, in the fitness of things and in conformity with historic precedent that the world should once again turn to the East for light.

Your Excellency, I believe that history has ordained that in the creation of a new, free and prosperous East, the Government and people of Nippon would play a leading role. This role for the Government and people of Nippon was carved out by history as early as 1905 when, for the first time, an Asiatic nation stood up to resist western aggression.'

One of the most important and interesting aspects of his speech related to his ideas about the relation of universalism and co-prosperity and the extension of the co-sphere. He recalled how India forgot her genius of universalism since the middle ages and thus became subjugated and how even now she was suffering in misery and wretchedness and was unable to distinguish between real universalism and false universalism. He said: 'I must confess, however, to my great sorrow, in this connection, that during the Middle Ages, India developed a false type of universalism and, it is because of this false universalism, that it was so easy for European powers to settle in, and ultimately to conquer India. But we have learned through sorrow, suffering, and humiliation to distinguish now between the false internationalism and the true. We know now that that internationalism is true, which does not ignore nationalism, but is rooted in it.' He continued: 'We have also studied with great interest the attempts made in Europe and elsewhere to set up a new international order. We have learned from these experiments and from the failure which ultimately crowned these experiments. We are the wiser for this experience and today we are convinced that the establishment or the creation of an international society of nations can be possible only if we begin by setting up what I may call regional federations, like this Greater East Asia Co-Prosperity Sphere.'

'Your Excellency, may I humbly point out that the establishment of a Greater East Asia Co-Prosperity Sphere is of interest, of vital interest, not only to the people of East Asia but, if I may say so, to the people of the whole of Asia and to mankind in general.' He further said that from his personal contact with all parts of Asia, he believed that India would be more than a bridge between East Asia and West Asia and that Greater East Asia co-prosperity scheme had significance for the people of entire Asia. 'Asia for Asians', i.e. the establishment of a Greater Asia Co-prosperity Sphere and finally a World League was not to be a league of robbers, but a step undoubtedly in the direction of real international society. However, these visions of a new world, a new Asia, of a Greater Asia that would prosper in freedom—all these depended on whether we were victorious or not in this Second World War. As far as India was concerned they were indivisibly bound up with Japan and her allies in the Second World War . . . For India there was no way except to wage a relentless struggle against British Imperialism. Compromise with England meant compromising with slavery.

Turning to India's present plight, Netaji stated that India's subjugation by Europeans was originally started by errors made centuries ago. He stressed that Indians today realized this fact and they also realized that there was no room for a compromise with Britain. He declared the only way India could win its independence was to fight Britain and come out victorious.

Netaji spoke of the thousands of Indians who were dying today of starvation. With sudden emphasis he disclosed that the Indian National Army was today poised for its advance to Delhi. Netaji next expressed his deepest wishes for the successful establishment of Greater East Asia and for the completion of Nippon's great work of construction. He pointed out that the Greater East Asia joint declaration was a declaration of liberation of East Asia—the Magna Carta of 1943, which would live forever in world history. He concluded by reiterating his determination to exert his utmost efforts to drive Britain out of India and bring about early materialization of the establishment of Free India.

Bose continued: 'I, therefore, want to assure Your Excellencies, that come what may, no matter how long and hard the struggle may be, no matter what the suffering and the sacrifice involved may prove to be, we are determined to fight to the bitter end, being fully confident of our final victory. But I have no illusions about the magnitude of the task that awaits us. I do not minimize the strength of the enemy. I claim to know the British people intimately and at first hand. I have known them since I was a child of five and, knowing them so intimately, knowing the strength and the weakness of the enemy in India, and knowing also our own strength and weakness, I feel fully confident of our ultimate victory.

I do not know how many of us who are going to participate in the coming battle will survive to see India free. But whether we survive or not, whether we individually live to see India free or not, we are confident that India shall be free. We are confident that Anglo-American Imperialism will be wiped out of India, and the menace that now hangs over the whole of East Asia will be removed once and for all.'

I pray to God that this Joint Declaration which this historic assembly has unanimously adopted this afternoon may prove to be a charter for the nations of East Asia and, what is more, a charter for the suppressed nations of the whole world. May this Joint Declaration prove to be in the world's history, the charter, the new charter of liberty for the year

1943 and after. Your names will go down in history not merely as the makers of a new Nippon, not merely as the makers of a new East Asia, not merely as the makers of a new Asia, but as the makers and architects of a new world.

With this his great speech ended. It held the entire assembly in awe. His deep emotions reflected in his voice and in his tears, his foresight, the richness of the contents of his speech, his vast knowledge and finally the strength of his character which ran through his words—all combined to produce an admirable effect. His participation and his speech truly were the essence of the Greater East Asia Conference.

Immediately after Bose's speech was over, Prime Minister Tojo expressing his unswerving determination to help Indian Independence made the following important announcement: 'Japan's offer to give all help and support to India in her long cherished ambition to achieve independence is already made clear in many declarations. And now that we see that the Provisional Government of Free India has quickly established itself and that the spirit of common purpose has united them so rapidly, Japan has decided as a first step, to return in the near future the Indian territory of Andaman and Nikobar Islands, at present occupied by Japan, to the Provisional Government of Free India.'

Soon thereafter the Greater East Asia Conference came to an end. Our Subhas Chandra Bose by his participation in the conference became a shining star in Greater East Asian firmament. For him personally also, this day became the most splendid of all in the entire period of two years of his activity in East Asia. The future historians, whatever their evaluation of Greater East Asia Conference, cannot forget the imposing figure of S.C. Bose who carried the entire weight of the Indian Independence Movement on his shoulders on the occasion.

Netaji Subhas Chandra Bose was granted audience at the Phoenix Hall in the Imperial Palace at 10.30 a.m. on November 10 by Tenno Heika (Emperor of Japan). In the audience Tenno Heika was pleased to honour Netaji Bose with words of sympathetic appreciation for the latter's efforts to attain Indian Independence.

Following the Imperial audience, Netaji Subhas Chandra Bose issued the following statement:

Tenno Heika was gracious enough to receive me in audience this morning as Head of the Provisional Government of Azad Hind. That was the highest honour that India, and I personally could receive. I have renewed my determination to fight shoulder to shoulder with Tenno Heika's Government, Army and Navy, till the bitter end, until our common victory is achieved. The memory of this reception in audience by Tenno Heika will remain engraved in my memory for all time.

Netaji Subhas Bose and his party were honoured at a luncheon party on November 15, given by Mitsuru Toyama, noted Nippon patriot. Rash Behari Bose, Supreme Adviser to the Provisional Government, was also a guest at a function. The party was attended by more than 40 notables including General Shigeru Honjo, President of the Military Welfare Board of the Welfare Ministry, and Yoshihihisa Kuzuu, Director of the Imperial Rule Assistance Association.

On November 18, Netaji Subhas Chandra Bose arrived at Nanking on his return journey. As soon as he arrived in the morning, he worshipped at the Chungshan Mausoleum where the ashes of the late Dr. Sun Yat-sen, 'Father of Modern China', repose. Later, he made a courtesy call on President Wang Ching-wei. At noon, he was guest of honour at a luncheon given by President Wang and attended by other high officials of the National Government of China. In the afternoon, Netaji paid a courtesy call on General Shunroku Hata, Commander-in-Chief of the Nippon forces in China, at the latter's headquarters and also on Nippon Ambassador Masayuku Tani at the Nippon Embassy. After calling on the German as well as Manchoukuo Embassies, Netaji Bose received return calls by General Hata and Ambassador Tani at the Government's Guest Hall.

At 8:30 p.m. Netaji was guest at a banquet given by Foreign Minister Chu Min-yi. Netaji Subhas Chandra Bose, at 10:00 a.m. on November 19, received return visits from Dr. Ernest Woermann, German Ambassador to Nanking, and Lu Yung-huan, Manchoukuo Ambassador to Nanking, at the Guest Hall. At 11:00 a.m. Netaji attended the Nanking citizens' welcome meeting held in his honour at the National Public Hall.

China and India should join hands for crushing Britain and the United States in order to attain complete Greater East Asiatic freedom, declared Netaji, at the welcome rally. He called on Chiang Kai-shek and other leaders to shake off Anglo-American influence and do their utmost for the unification of China, the gaining of Indian Independence and the complete emancipation of Greater East Asia. Referring to the visit of Madame Chiang to India last year to ask Indian leaders to co-operate with the Indian Government, Netaji Bose declared that if Chiang Kai-shek actually desired the independence of China he should not have asked Indians to co-operate with their oppressors, who had enslaved 388 million Indians. Netaji stressed that China and India should both fight for the freedom and liberation of Greater East Asia.

Netaji Bose recalled that in 1938, when he was the President of the Indian National Congress, he sent a medical mission to Chungking as an expression of India's sympathy and goodwill. Netaji Bose added, 'Chungking should not take up arms against Indians, but should fight side by side with India against the common enemy, because China will never prosper under Anglo-American control.' He recalled that Dr. Sun Yat-sen was an ardent supporter of India and a torchbearer for a United East Asia.

Following the mass meeting, he was guest of honour at a luncheon party given by Masayuki Tani, Nippon Ambassador to China. At 3:00 p.m. Netaji conferred with President Wang Ching-wei at the latter's official residence and at 4:30 p.m. with Dr. Ernst Woermann. In the evening, he was guest of honour at a dinner party tendered by General Shunroku Hata, Commander-in-Chief of the Nippon forces in China.

Netaji Subhas Chandra Bose, who visited Nanking and Shanghai after attending the Assembly of Greater East Asiatic Nations in Tokyo, arrived at Manila by air at 3:15 p.m. on November 22. He was greeted at the airport by President Jose P. Laurel, Ambassador Shozo Murata, Lieut.-General Shigenori Kuroda, Commander-in-Chief of the Nippon forces in the Philippines, and other high officials of the Philippine Government. Netaji Subhas Chandra Bose called on President Jose P. Laurel at the Malacanan, expressing congratulations on the birth of the new Republic of the Philippines. In the evening Netaji received representatives of the Indian residents at the Malacanan, where he stayed during his visit. He was guest at a dinner given in his honour by President Laurel at Malacanan in the evening. The dinner was attended by Ministers of State, Nippon Ambassador Shozo Murata and other distinguished Filipino, Nippon and Indian leaders.

'British imperialism is dead; however, the United States is succeeding and replacing it in all its mercilessness and injustice,' warned Netaji Subhas Chandra Bose in an address delivered at the dinner. 'The world must choose between the perpetuation of this imperialism or establishment of a new world order based on justice and equality,' Netaji declared. 'To compromise with British imperialism is to compromise with slavery, because it always oppressed peoples economically, politically, and socially.' Regarding the rise of American imperialism, Netaji asserted, 'We must be aware of this new menace and prevent its tentacles from spreading.' Recalling that in the past Asiatic peoples, including Indians, had looked up to the United States, he said, 'But now we know the American colonial policy is actually a menace to smaller nations.' Urging total sacrifice on the part of all East Asians, he declared, 'I have always been a determined and consistent fighter against oppression. As individuals, we do not matter. We will die soon enough. We must die, but we must strive to make our nation live forever.' He recalled that the United States imperialism formerly only covered the political field; however, it had expanded to include social and economic fields as well. Hailing the convention of the Assembly of Greater East Asiatic Nations in Tokyo recently, Netaji said, 'It marked the realization of my dream to see East Asiatic nations together.' Stressing the Indian determination to fight to the last, Netaji said, 'Indians are fully prepared to die in order to salvage our country. We must die, because he who lives for India is he who dies for India. We are prepared for a long and bitter struggle.' Expressing profound thanks to his host, Netaji said, 'I am grateful to Your Excellency, the Government and people of the Philippines and wish everlasting freedom and prosperity to your Republic.'

Netaji Subhas Chandra Bose on his way back to Syonan from Nippon arrived at Saigon at 1:30 p.m. on November 24 from Manila. After a brief rest at the Nippon Hotel, Netaji paid courtesy visits to local commanders of the Nippon Army and Naval Forces. In the evening, he attended a banquet given in his honour by the Nippon Minister, Shigenori Tashiro. Later Netaji Bose addressed a mass rally of local residents at which he exhorted his compatriots to join in the crusade to liberate their motherland from British shackles. Netaji Subhas Chandra Bose returned to the Headquarters of the Provisional Government on November 25.

29

India and Ireland

[Reply to felicitations from Irish Republicans, November 1943][1]

It has given me the greatest pleasure to receive a message of felicitations from the Irish Republicans. Of all the Freedom Movements that we Indians have studied closely and from which we have derived inspiration, there is perhaps none that can equal the Irish struggle for Independence. The Irish Nation has had the same oppressors and exploiters as ourselves. It has had the same experience of ruthlessness, brutality and hypocrisy as we have. The diabolical policy of British Imperialism has brought about the partition of Ireland in the past and if British Imperialism were to survive this War, a similar fate would be in store for India. In 1916, the Irish Republicans set up their Provisional Government on the eve of the Easter Rebellion. In 1943, India's Freedom-Fighters have set up their Provisional Government before launching their last struggle for liberty. There is so much in common between us that it is but natural that there should be a deep bond of affinity and comradeship between the Irish Nation and ourselves.

With unparalleled heroism, tenacity and selflessness, the Irish fighters for Freedom have struggled against their British tyrants for many a century. They have been overpowered at times, but have never been broken. In particular, the fight that the Irish patriots have put up during the present century, the heights of sublime idealism and martyrdom that they have reached—constitute one of the noblest chapters in man's struggle for his birthright. The debt of gratitude which India's

[1] *On To Delhi*, pp. 117–18.

patriots owe to the Irish heroes for the inspiration that they have received is difficult to repay. In fact, it would not be the slightest exaggeration to say that among the fighters against alien imperialism whom I have had the honour of knowing personally, there are perhaps none whose friendship I cherish more than that of those brave men and women who have uncompromisingly stood and fought for the Irish Republic.

Sitting in a remote corner of the globe, planning and toiling for the liberation of my Motherland, the message coming from across the seas, from Irish republican friends, has sent a thrill of joy and inspiration through my soul. In the midst of my manifold preoccupations, it has brought vividly before my mind's eye the many friendships that I made in the Emerald Isle of Eire and the sacred places that I visited in that country, where many a deed of heroism and martyrdom was enacted in the cause of Freedom.

I heartily reciprocate the message of my Irish Republican Friends and send herewith a word of cheer in reply. 'Our Cause is just. Our demand is for our birthright. We are prepared to pay the price. We shall therefore triumph. Freedom will come.'

30

Plans of the INA

[Press interview, 3 November 1943][1]

Questioned about the plans of the Indian National Army and the Provisional Government, Mr. Bose replied that the army was so thoroughly equipped and so capably directed by the Provisional Government that no enemy could withstand it. He added that women soldiers had also been included, and they were as capable as the men. The following questions and answers followed:

Q. What measures have been taken by the Indian National Army and the Provisional Government to relieve India's food situation?

A. Originally Burma, and later, the Indian National Army offered 100,000 tons of rice to India's starving population, and the British Government was asked to make arrangements for taking delivery. The British Government, unfortunately, made no reply to this offer. The army is, however, determined to dispatch foodstuffs to India at all cost. A way will somehow have to be found.

Q. Why could not Burma arrange with the International Red Cross Society for the dispatch of rice?

A. When the British Government is not prepared to accept the offer, what can the Red Cross do?

Q. Have you complete confidence in the success of the Indian National Army after it had crossed the Indian border? What steps has it taken to cope with a possible rebellion in India?

A. More than 12,000 Indian troops now in the British Army have

[1] *Testament of Subhas Bose*, pp. 152–3.

assured us of their full support as soon as the Indian National Army enters India. These Indian troops have been harassed and ill treated by their British officers, and they are longing for revenge. I have also been receiving regular reports on the functioning of India's political machinery. Our agents keep us well informed of every development in India. Similarly, we have responsible people in India, who keep in touch with the latest situation abroad. Thus, the closest contact has been established between Indians at home and abroad.

Q. Can the Provisional Government efficiently control and direct the movements of the Indian National Army? Is this Army adequately equipped to carry on the war of freedom for a considerable time?

A. I consider the Provisional Government to be most competent and its army well equipped. To win any battle of freedom two institutions are essential: first, a National Army; and, secondly, a National Government. India has both. In addition, she has the recognition and full support of mighty Japan and Germany.

Q. It is believed that the Headquarters of the Provisional Government will be transferred from Shonan to Burma. What relationship exists between the Provisional Government of Free India and the Government of Burma?

A. The headquarters will be transferred when circumstances permit. As to our relationship with the Burmese Government, it is most cordial. We are like two children of the same parents. Japan has recognized the independence of Burma, the Philippines, and the Provisional Government of Free India. We three form a happy family under one guardian—Japan.

Q. What is your opinion as regards the food situation in India?

A. The situation is appalling. The fact that Churchill and Roosevelt have ignored the appeals of the Indians shows that the British Government and its American ally are quite indifferent to their misery. No satisfactory measures have, so far, been taken by the British Government. It even refuses to supply ships for the import of foodstuffs into India.

Q. It appears that you have achieved the three most important objectives, namely, the formation of an Indian National Army, the establishment of an Indian National Government, and the winning of full support from Japan. Have you any other for the immediate future?

A. Yes, one more—the last—and that is to lead the Indian National

Army to India, fight the battle of freedom, expel the Anglo-Americans from our motherland, establish an Indian National Government in India, and bring everlasting peace and prosperity to the down-trodden millions of my country.

—TOKYO RADIO (In Hindustani), 3 November 1943

31

Appeal to Chungking

[Broadcast from Shanghai on 21 November 1943][1]

I was in Tokyo at the time when Shanghai was unified under one Municipality, one Government and one Mayor. There are no longer three Shanghais, there is only one Shanghai now. It is to me an indication of coming events. I have no doubt it will not be long when the entire Chinese nation will also be unified under one Government and one leader.

From here I am on my way now to my Headquarters in the South. From there I shall soon be travelling to Burma and the Indian frontier. Duty calls me to Burma. I know that when we go to the Indian frontier to fight for Indian independence, I shall have to fight British troops, and probably also Chinese troops. I do not understand why Chinese should fight for the British in India. I fail to understand why a government which is a government for the people, calling itself a National Government, sends its troops against a friendly country in order to help a foreign power to continue its domination in that country.

The Indian people really sympathize with China and the Chinese people. You know that the Indian National Congress and Indian people actually gave help to the Chungking Government. In 1938, when I was President of the National Congress, I was responsible for sending out the first medical mission to Chungking as a token of sympathy for the Chinese people and the Chungking Government. Later on, we sent help to Chungking in various forms of medical supplies and goods in order to actually demonstrate our sympathy. I wonder if Marshal Ching

[1] *On To Delhi*, pp. 111–13.

Kai-shek and his government today want to return our goodwill by sending Chinese troops to India to fight against us on the side of the British.

I am sorry that the Chungking Government has been sending its troops to India. I always had the greatest sympathy for Chungking, yet Chinese troops are coming to India to fight against us to help British imperialism. In this connection, I tell you today, East Asia faces an entirely new situation—one no one dreamed of a few years ago. Today Nippon has adopted an entirely new policy in East Asia, demonstrated in the declaration of independence of Burma and the Philippines and establishment of the Provisional Government of Free India. The Government of Nippon by its recent new treaty with the National Government of China has declared its intention of withdrawing its troops when peace is restored.

I am an Indian nationalist and revolutionist. Every Indian should be true to the cause of India and likewise every Chinese should be true to the cause of China. From my own personal knowledge of the path Nippon actually followed since the outbreak of the War of Greater East Asia, I tell you that in view of the new situation that exists in East Asia, there is a golden opportunity for China and the Chinese people.

China's only problem is unity and this problem still remains to be solved. Otherwise what China desired has already been achieved through the new policy of Nippon. In East Asia, I have travelled extensively, and I am in a position to form this conclusion regarding the present war situation. I know the war will be a long and hard one but I am confident that in this war Britain will be defeated not only because of our just cause but also because Nippon is strategically favoured. Unless Britain is defeated in this war, you can never have peace in China or East Asia.

The day is not far off when China will be under one leader. By means of an honourable peace between China and Nippon, Nippon will withdraw her troops from China. There is no reason why you should wait till the end of this war for peace; it is possible for you in the course of this war to achieve peace and to start your national reconstruction and economic recovery of China.

32

A Blessing of Providence

[Statement on 8 December 1943][1]

This day, two years ago, began a new chapter in the history of East Asia. The changes that have taken place in the map of East Asia since then and the significance of these changes for the nations of East Asia are so well known to everybody that I need not refer to them again. Today I want to study these far-reaching changes from a different angle.

A study of history shows that the big changes in the World's History are in the nature of a wave which sweeps over the land until it reaches its farthest limit. Then, when its force is completely spent, it recedes. In other words, the big changes in the World's History are in the nature of expansion followed by contraction, or withdrawal. Thus the growth of the British Empire consisted of expansion, beginning from Britain as its base and then going up to the Far East. The last World War represented the peak of the British Empire's growth and expansion. During the next two decades the virile force of that Empire was exhausted. With the beginning of the East Asia War, the wave of expansion that had spread to far-off Hongkong began to retreat. Hence, the series of defeats beginning from Hongkong and ending in Burma. The point that now arises is, 'Is it possible to stop this retreat? Is it possible to stem the rot and to save the Empire in the midst of its decay?' To this, history replies in the negative. When decline has once set in, events will follow their predestined course, and no power on earth can ordain otherwise. The Turkish Empire that once upon a time spread from Constantinople right up to the gates of Vienna, had to return to its starting point. So

[32] *On To Delhi*, pp. 114–16.

also must the decadent British Empire return to its base. This, to my mind, is what fate and Providence have decreed.

For India, the East Asia War is nothing less than a blessing of Providence. Throughout their rule in India, the British have always thought of the North-West Frontier—the direction from which they imagined that the enemy would one day come. Never has any English general or diplomat thought of the Eastern Frontier of India. Never has any Englishman dreamt that England's enemy may suddenly appear on the Eastern frontier. Contrary to all expectation and anticipation, the Eastern frontier of India has now been thrown open. To go into India or to come out is, therefore, no problem today. What is even more significant is that beyond the Eastern frontier, there is a population of about three million Indians, who have eagerly seized the opportunity presented by the East Asia War. Even if the North-West Frontier of India had been thrown open, it would not have been possible for Indians living abroad to bring material and military assistance to their countrymen at home. Moreover, fortunately for India, the power that has succeeded in throwing open the Eastern gates of India is also the power that is determined to root out Anglo-American power and influence from our part of the world.

Whether others agree with me or not, I am firmly convinced that the British empire is fighting its last battle in India. No empire has gone down without a fight. It is therefore but natural that the British will fight hard in India and that they will muster all possible help from every quarter of the globe. But the wheels of History will grind on and they cannot be put back. The British will ultimately have to vacate India. Who will be so foolish as to think that when India is free, the suppressed nations of Western Asia will go to sleep? The Arabs, the Persians and other nations who have been groaning under British domination or pressure will naturally seize the opportunity and take up arms against their British oppressors. In fact, they are today anxiously waiting for the signal that the British retreat from India has begun. When I say this, I am not indulging in wishful thinking. During the course of this war, I have met the leaders and representatives of the suppressed nations of Western Asia. I know how closely they are following world events and how they are awaiting the further collapse of the British Empire. They are wide-awake and they will not fail to grasp the opportunity when it comes.

In 1905, Japan successfully withstood Western aggression. After consolidating her strength for 35 years she has now hurled back the tide which at one time had almost overwhelmed Asia. The tide of aggression is now flowing out. He is indeed an ignorant child who still thinks that in spite of all that has happened, the British empire can still be saved. That Empire will undoubtedly go the way of other empires of the past.

December 1941 has ushered in a new chapter in the history of Asia which is also a new chapter in the history of the world.

33

Unification of the Indian Nation

[Resolutions of the meeting of the Council of Ministers of the Provisional Government of Azad Hind adopted on 9 December 1943, and speeches during Netaji's tour of South Sumatra and the Andaman and Nicobar Islands in December 1943][1]

A meeting of the Council of Ministers of the Provisional Government of Azad Hind was held at the official residence of Netaji Subhas Chandra Bose on 9th December 1943, when the advisers were also present. The Council of Ministers discussed and adopted with certain alterations, the reports of two Cabinet Sub-Committees, namely, one of the rewards, decorations, and pensions to be granted to the *Azad Hind Fauj* warriors who would be taking part in the coming operations, and the other on the plan of National Unification.

The Council of Ministers provided liberally for the families and dependants of the *Azad Hind Fauj* warriors who might be killed, wounded, or disabled in the coming campaign. The Council of Ministers also decided that, in the case of Indian Officers and men serving in the British Indian Army, their previous service should be taken into account for purposes of pension etc., provided they came over to the *Azad Hind Fauj* during the campaign.

The recommendations of the Cabinet Sub-Committee on National Unification, as adopted by the Council of Ministers, ensured the unification of the Indian Nation, irrespective of differences of caste, creed and religion.

[1] *Chalo Delhi*, pp. 194–7.

The Council of Ministers decided that Hindustani should be the common language of India. 'Jai Hind' (Victory of India) shall be the common greeting and salutation between Indians. The present Tricolour shall be the National Flag of India, the song beginning with the words 'Subh Sukh Chai' shall be India's National song; the Tiger will be India's National Emblem; 'Chalo Delhi' will be the National War Cry till the successful conclusion of the Revolution; and 'Azad Hind Zindabad,' 'Inquilab Zindabad,' and 'Netaji Ki Jai' will be the National Slogans till the victorious conclusion of the revolution.

The plan for National Unification in the matter of food, dress, etc., was under the active consideration of the Provisional Government of Azad Hind. This plan for National Unification was to be introduced first among the Indians in East Asia.

Netaji Subhas Chandra Bose visited South Sumatra on December 10, 1943. Acknowledging the Indians' pledge to give unswerving support to the *Azad Hind Fauj* in men and material, Netaji delivered a stirring address at a mammoth rally held at Palembung by his compatriots living in all parts of South Sumatra.

In the course of his speech, Netaji Bose thanked the Indians for their absolute support and loyalty to the newly formed government and stressed the imminence of the Indian crusade to rid their motherland of British influence once and for all.

'With such unflinching determination on the part of my compatriots in every corner of Greater East Asia, and with the help of our Nippon friends, the success of our forthcoming march into Delhi and the eventual emancipation of the suffering millions cannot fail,' Netaji said.

Netaji Subhas Chandra Bose visited Andaman Islands on December 29, 1943, and immediately paid a courtesy-call on the Commander-in-Chief of the Nippon Army forces in Port Blair and expressed thanks for the support of the Nippon Army for the cause of the Indian Independence Movement as well as the creation of the Provisional Government. Later Netaji visited the Headquarters of the Nippon Military Administration and heard a detailed report on administrative activities in the islands. He also visited Ross Island. In the evening Netaji was guest at a dinner given by the Commander-in-Chief of the Nippon Army Forces and spent the night at the former official residence of the British Governor.

The next morning Netaji attended a grand rally in Port Blair. At the outset of the rally, the Indian Flag was hoisted personally by Netaji, while the Indian national anthem was being sung. In the course of his address Netaji declared that the Andaman and Nicobar were liberated from the British yoke by Nippon, which was the leader of Asia. 'These islands in the near future will become Indian territory. Entry into Delhi at the cost of our blood or to fight our way to death in the present struggle for independence are the only two ways to repay Nippon's sincerity and friendship towards India', Netaji said. Concluding he exhorted all Indians in the Andaman to 'follow either of these two courses.'

Netaji thanked Mr. Ramakrishna, Chairman of the Indian Independence League, Mr. Durga Parshad, Vice-Chairman and Nawab Ali for their loyal support. Colonel (later Major General) Loganadan, a Minister of the Provisional Government, was appointed the first Chief Commissioner of the Andaman (re-named Shaheed = Martyrs) and Nicobar (re-named Swaraj) Islands.

34

The Road to Delhi

[Statement, December, 1943][1]

From time immemorial, Delhi has been the goal of every army marching into India from outside—whether hostile or friendly. From time immemorial, Delhi has also been the objective of every Indian army that has sought to obtain control over the country. In fact, it would be no exaggeration to say that the history of India is written in stone on the plains surrounding Delhi. 'He who rules Delhi, rules India'—is a saying that is common among the people in India. Indian poets, once upon a time, went even so far as to say—'The Lord of Delhi is the lord of this world.'

Unlike Rome, towards which roads converge from all directions, Delhi has always been approached from the west—or rather from the north-west. This was the lesson of history and the British, when they finally subjugated India in 1857, tried to make the best use of this lesson. At first they tried to occupy Afghanistan, in order to safe-guard their Empire in India. But when all attempts to subjugate Afghanistan failed, the British tried to build up a wall of defence between Afghanistan and India.

The British have always believed instinctively in the value of propaganda. Just as in later times, they gave the outside world the impression that Singapore was an impregnable fortress, so also in earlier days, they gave out that the north-western frontier of India was so well-fortified that it was an impassable barrier. The fact, however, was that though the Indo-Afghan frontier was comparatively well-fortified, India could have been easily attacked from the Persian side through Baluchistan.

[1] *On To Delhi*, pp. 119–22.

But so long as Persia (or Iran) remained militarily a weak power, the British had nothing to fear. The principal fear was that Russia might one day attack India through Afghanistan. Hence all their fortifications were aimed chiefly at defending the Indo-Afghan frontier against any invading army from the north-west.

So long as Czarist Russia remained a world-power, the British in India lived in permanent dread of Russian invasion through Afghanistan. But when the Czarist regime broke down, they breathed a sigh of relief. On the other hand, the establishment of a Bolshevik regime in Moscow in 1917, professing sympathy for all enslaved nations in Asia and the accession to the Afghan throne in 1919 of King Amanullah, who professed sympathy for Indian independence, filled many Indian revolutionaries with hope that they might get help, either from Afghanistan, or from Bolshevik Russia. Consequently, in 1919 and after, many Indian revolutionaries travelled overland to Kabul and from there to Moscow, in quest of help and assistance.

King Amanullah knew that the impregnability of the northwestern defences of India was but a myth and he did not hesitate to go to war against the British in India, when disputes arose between them. When the Afghan army succeeded in breaking into India in 1919, the British got into a panic and made peace with the Afghan King on his own terms. But ten years later, British intrigue got the better of King Amanullah and he had to abdicate the throne and leave the country. In 1929, the British once again breathed a sigh of relief.

Ten years later—that is, in 1939—the situation changed once again. The Soviet-German Non-Aggression Pact in August, 1939, and the outbreak of war between Britain and Germany in September of that year, brought the Russian bogey prominently before the British mind once again. Fresh fortifications were, thereupon, started on the northwestern frontier of India with a view to repelling a possible Soviet-Russian invasion of India.

With the outbreak of war between Germany and Russia in June 1941, the feeling of panic in the British mind gave room to one of intense relief. Though, for a time, there was slight anxiety over the rapid advance of the German army towards Russian Caucasia and eventually towards Iran, the British began to feel that the Soviet-German war had saved their Empire in India.

But with the outbreak of the war in East Asia, everything was turned upside down. The north-western frontier of India suddenly lost its age-long significance—and, in its place, the north-eastern frontier came into the limelight. The jungles and mountains of the Indo-Burma frontier suddenly became passable. Through and over them, roads were opened up and along these new roads, the British Governor of Burma, his satellites and his panic-stricken forces fled to Bengal and from there to Delhi.

The British Governor of Burma is now safely installed in New Delhi where he is holding his court with the help of his fellow-refugees from Burma. But he has left behind, for our use, the roads along which he and five hundred thousand men and women travelled from Burma to India.

Since his departure from Rangoon to Delhi, these roads have been improved and other new roads have been opened up. Moreover, unlike the north-western approaches to India, the north-eastern passage to India can be negotiated—not only by land, but also by sea and by air. Consequently, from the east and north-east, there is today not one road to Delhi—but many such roads. All these roads will soon become handy and useful to us.

They say in Europe—'All roads lead to Rome.' Here in East Asia, all the above-mentioned roads lead to India's metropolis—and to the ancient Red Fortress that lies in its bosom. Delhi is our destination and to Delhi we shall travel by many roads. There are no fortifications to bar our way, as there are on the north-western frontier—though there are jungles and mountains, winds and waves. But nature has been kind to us in opening up these new roads—and nature's obstacles we shall surmount without much difficulty.

But it will be a long and weary march from here to the Viceroy's house and to the Red fortress in India's capital. So let us lose no time. Let us gird up our loins and commence the march as soon as we can. The roads to Delhi are the roads to freedom.

35

The INA is Ready

[Broadcast from Singapore on 1 January 1944][1]

Today all Indians are ready to plunge into the battle for India's freedom and the New Year is sure to bring us ultimate victory, for I become more and more confident about it when I look back on our achievements in the past. In East Asia, Japan has consolidated her power. The two newly liberated Asiatic nations, Burma and the Philippines, have shown remarkable progress within quite a short time, and the present consolidation of the Greater East Asiatic nations is an outcome of the historic conference of the six Greater East Asiatic nations held at Tokyo.

The closing year knit the 3,000,000 Indian nationals of East Asia into one compact revolutionary body, eager to sacrifice their all in the struggle for India's freedom. At their back is the invincible Indian National Army equipped with modern and up-to-date weapons of war. This Army will kindle the fire of revolution in India, which will reduce British Imperialism to ashes. The Provisional Government of Azad Hind, which is in possession of the Andaman and Nicobar Islands and which has been duly recognized by nine great powers of the world including Japan and Germany, has promised its wholehearted support to our Army. It is high time for us to launch the offensive against the British and win India's freedom. My countrymen at home, who are labouring under the atrocities of the callous British, have seen them in their true colours and have fully understood their desire to keep India in permanent bondage with the help of mercenary troops from America, China and Africa. They have also noted the evil intentions behind the speeches of Wavell. But our countrymen at home have full faith in our Army, which will soon cross the border and free India.

[1] *Testament of Subhas Bose*, pp. 68–9.

36

Indian National Army in Action

[Addresses to the INA and statements issued during the months January to March 1944][1]

After his visit to the Andaman Islands Netaji Subhas Chandra Bose arrived in Burma on January 7, 1944. The Headquarters of the Provisional Government of Free India and the Supreme Command of the Indian National Army were also shifted to Burma, which was to be the springboard for the operations of the Army of Liberation.

'Indians at home would be thrilled to hear that Netaji Subhas Chandra Bose has moved his Headquarters to within a few hours flight to Calcutta.' This was the comment made by Mr. S.A. Ayer, Minister of Publicity and Propaganda of the Provisional Government of Azad Hind on the official announcement that the Headquarters of the Free India Government had been moved to Burma. 'This is one more decisive step in Netaji's irresistible advance towards India and the British citadel in Delhi', the Minister said. 'Netaji now stands at the eastern gates of India at the Head of the Indian National Army. This Army of Liberation impatiently awaits his word of command to fire the shot that will open the campaign; the report of that shot will echo and re-echo throughout

[1] *Chalo Delhi*, pp. 197–200; Subhas Chandra Bose, *Blood Bath* (Singapore: The Publicity and Propaganda Department, Indian Independence League Headquarters, 1944; reproduced Lahore: Hero Publications, 1947; copy in the library of the Netaji Research Bureau), pp. 80–7. The message on the eve of January 26, 1944, in Netaji's own hand is preserved in the archives of the Netaji Research Bureau.

the length and breadth of India; and that will be the signal for an India-wide uprising against the British; only the unimaginative British can be blind to their present perilous position in India', Mr. Ayer asserted. Continuing, he stressed that the millions of Netaji's followers all over India were fully aware of his hurricane activities since his arrival in East Asia six months ago; they had heard every one of his momentous utterances over the Radio from Tokyo, Syonan, Bangkok and Rangoon; they knew that he had established the Provisional Government of Free India, the Headquarters of which had now moved to Burma; they knew that Netaji had moved units of the Indian National Army to within striking distance of the British bases in Eastern India; thus, Netaji's followers in India were fully aware that the stage was now set for the final showdown.

Indomitable and fighting determination to liberate India was the keynote of the fiery one-hour address by Netaji Subhas Chandra Bose given on January 11, the afternoon before troops of the Indian National Army advanced into Burma along with the Provisional Government of Free India. With the sweeping march to Delhi imminent, Netaji Bose reminded his soldiers again that 3,000,000 Indians in East Asia as well as the 380,000,000 Indians in India and powerful Axis nations stood firmly and solidly behind them. He pointed in particular to the warm and wholehearted welcome given him by various allied nations of Greater East Asia whom he visited on his way back from the historic Assembly of East Asiatic Nations.

Netaji stressed that the Indian National Army must be prepared to exert its utmost efforts to realize India's Independence in order to fulfill the hopes and aspirations of all Indians as well as repay Greater East Asiatic nations for their all-out support and sympathy.

In the morning, Netaji Subhas Chandra Bose, accompanied by Capt. Lakshmi, head of women's organization of the Provisional Government of Free India, inspected the Indian women's corps. Impressed by the intensive training carried on by the corps. Netaji Bose encouraged women members to continue to fight for the achievement of the ultimate goal of liberating India from the Anglo-Americans. Netaji Subhas Chandra Bose and members of the Provisional Government of Azad Hind were guests at a grand reception accorded to them in Rangoon by the Government of Free Burma on January 23. Speakers at the reception included, besides Netaji himself, the Foreign Minister and the Minister of Defense.

Netaji Subhas Chandra Bose declared, 'It is impossible to find words that can give adequate expression to my feelings of gratitude or express my thanks for Burma's official recognition of the Provisional Government and the hospitality so generously offered, and also the unfailing sympathy and support given by Burma to the Indian Independence Movement.' Netaji gave the solemn assurance that Free India would never forget Burma's good deeds.

Netaji made the following broadcast from Rangoon on 9 January 1944:

The last time you heard my voice over the radio, I spoke to you from Shonan. Today, I am much nearer to you, as I am now addressing you from the broadcasting station of Rangoon. The Headquarters of the 'Provisional Government of Azad Hind' has been shifted from Shonan to Rangoon. My first feelings on coming to Burma are of profound thankfulness for the hospitality that we have received at the hands of the Burmese Government, and for the help we have obtained from the Nippon authorities, without which the transfer of the Headquarters of our Provisional Government from Shonan to Burma would have been quite impossible. I am happy to be able to say that the great leader of the independent Burmese nation, and the Head of the Independent State of Burma, His Excellency Dr. Ba Maw, is one of the best friends that we now have outside India. The warm hospitality and the cordial assistance that His Excellency and His Excellency's government and nation have been giving us are of incalculable worth and value to us in our coming struggle for India's liberation. And, as for the unfailing sympathy and help that we have been receiving from Japan from the beginning of the war in East Asia, I shall only say that we shall go on fighting shoulder to shoulder with Nippon till our common enemy is completely overthrown and India is once for all emancipated from Anglo-American imperialism.

Friends! I shall now give you a very interesting piece of news, namely, that after I arrived in Burma I was able to visit the Andaman and Nicobar Islands. You will remember that on November 6, 1943, at the Assembly of Greater East Asiatic Nations held in Tokyo, His Excellency

Premier General Hideki Tojo made a historic declaration to the effect that the Government of Nippon would transfer the Andaman and Nicobar Islands to the 'Provisional Government of Azad Hind.' Following that declaration, I had conversations with the Nippon authorities on the subject both in Tokyo and in Shonan. After these conversations, the Imperial Navy authorities arranged for my visit to these islands, during which members of my Government and of my personal staff accompanied me. I have now returned here after completing that trip. The object of my journey to the Andaman and Nicobar Islands was to discuss with the local Nippon authorities preparatory measures necessary for effecting the transfer of the Andaman and Nicobar Islands to the 'Provisional Government of Azad Hind.' In pursuance of the discussions that were held there, I can now announce that I have appointed Lt.-Colonel A.G. Logonadan, a high ranking officer of the Indian National Army, as Chief Commissioner of the Andaman and Nicobar Islands. As soon as transport arrangements are made, the newly appointed Chief Commissioner will proceed to the above islands to take charge. During the visit, I, and the members of my party had the unique experience of our lives, when we stood on the soil of free India for the first time. It was an unforgettable event for us to see our tri-colour national flag fluttering in the air over the former British Chief Commissioner's residence on Ross Island. During our stay there, we occupied the former British Chief Commissioner's residence, and we wondered all the time how the wheels of victory were now moving in India's favour. The sight of our national flag flying over the Chief Commissioner's house made us all think of the day when the same flag will be hoisted over the Viceroy's House in New Delhi.

My countrymen, you remember that since August last year, I have been giving expression to my hope and belief that, before the end of 1943, we would stand on the soil of free India. That this dream has actually been fulfilled before December 31, 1943, has given us the greatest happiness. While we were in the Andaman Island we visited the notorious cellular jail in Port Blair and paid silent homage to those patriotic countrymen of ours who suffered indescribable persecution and torture in the past, and some of whom even laid down their lives as victims of British tyranny and brutality. We were informed by the former Superintendent of the jail that the last batch of political prisoners consisting of about 200 court-martialled prisoners were transported back to India along with some British officials shortly before the Japanese occupation of the island. During my visit to the island, I was able to study conditions there at first-hand, and to get acquainted with the local population. I found that they were all happy that the British have been expelled from the place, and their joy knew no bounds when they heard the declaration of the Government of Nippon regarding the islands in November last. A general national awakening was visible among the people, and they are determined to become good and patriotic citizens of India in future.

At the mass meeting, which was held there, I told the people that since they had suffered so much at the hands of British Imperialism in the past, it had pleased Providence to give them the present days of freedom and happiness. Actually, they should now forget their unhappy past, become worthy citizens of Free India, and work hard in order to create a bright and happy future for themselves. From what I have seen of the islands and of their natural resources, I am confident that as part of Free India, the Andaman and Nicobar Islands will become a place fit for free, cultured and progressive men and women to live in. I am sure that if in future the British attempt to re-conquer the islands, they will meet with fierce and stubborn opposition from the people there, who, having once tasted freedom, will never go back to their former slavery.

However, since the 'Provisional Government of Azad Hind' has an army of its own but no navy, we shall need the help and protection of the Imperial Nipponese Navy in future, even after we take over the administration of the islands, and I am profoundly happy and thankful that we shall continue to receive this assistance from the Imperial Nipponese Navy.

Friends, now that I am so near to you, you will be able to hear my voice more often, and perhaps more distinctly than in the past. But before I close for today, I should like to bring to you greetings from Burma. Here in Burma the weather is very pleasant and agreeable. A feeling of supreme optimism pervades the whole atmosphere, despite the boastful propaganda that the enemies have been indulging in for a long time and despite the occasional appearance of enemy aeroplanes in the sky. The liberated Burmese nation is determined to shed the last drop of its blood before giving up its hard-won freedom. Between the Burmese and the Indians today there is a feeling of deep comradeship—something like a blood-pact. We are determined to fight together against the common enemy, the Burmese in order to preserve liberty, and we Indians in order to expel the enemy from Indian soil. Today, India needs Burma, and so does Burma need India. United we stand, and with the help of invincible Nippon, united we shall win.

Inquilab Zindabad! Azad Burma Zindabad!
Azad Hind Zindabad!

On the eve of Indian Independence Day, 26 January 1944, Netaji wrote the following message of Indians at home and abroad:

After the outbreak of the present world-war in 1939, we are going to celebrate our Independence Day on the 26th January for the fifth time. It is necessary for us now to take stock of what we have done and what results we have actually achieved in the course of this war.

First of all, I want to say that since September, 1939, in spite of various difficulties and obstacles, the Indian Independence Movement has been progressing according to plan. The first twelve months were spent in rousing the Indian people at home to take an open stand against Britain and against Britain's war—so that India's attitude on this question could be made clear to the whole world. When this object was achieved and India's self-respect and honour were thereby vindicated—if became necessary to take such steps as would lead to the achievement of independence. If it had been possible for the disarmed Indian people at home to win liberty through a civil disobedience movement or through a secret revolutionary movement inside India, the problem would have been solved rather easily. But in the light of our life's experience and of our knowledge of the Indian situation—I and my associates were convinced that India's liberty could be achieved only if we could link up our own struggle with the world-struggle for a new order.

In order to make India's struggle a part of the larger world-struggle, it was necessary to establish contact with the outside world and to make certain investigations which were of vital interest to India. Therefore, in accordance with the will of a large section of my countrymen, I left home and homeland three years ago, with the following three objectives—firstly, to study the world—situation and forecast the ultimate result of this war; secondly, to find out the policy and attitude of the Axis Powers regarding India; and thirdly, to explore the possibilities of bringing help from outside to India's own struggle for independence.

All these three objectives were duly fulfilled. Firstly after a careful study I was convinced that however long the war might last, Anglo–American Imperialism would, in the end, be defeated. Secondly, I realized to my great satisfaction that the Axis Powers and their allies were the natural friends and supporters of India's liberty. Thirdly, I found that it was possible to bring, into India, substantial help from outside, in order to enable the disarmed Indian people to throw off the British yoke. Further, as a result of my journey abroad, I was able to help considerably in making India an international issue.

In order to mobilize help for India from outside—it was necessary, on the one hand, to organize all freedom-loving Indians living in friendly and neutral countries and, on the other, to establish close contact with friendly powers. As the whole world is by now aware, both these efforts were, in course of time, successful and, in particular, Indians living in Europe and in East Asia were organized for political and military purposes.

A technical problem that arose in this connection was as to how help from outside could be actually brought into India. This problem, too, was duly solved when, following the outbreak of the war in East Asia in December, 1941, the brilliant victories of Japan's armed forces exterminated Anglo–American power in East Asia and opened up a new road to Delhi from the East.

Three million Indians living in East Asia immediately rose to the occasion. They set up their political organization—the Azad Hind Sangh or the Indian Indian Independence League—and they also organized the Azad Hind Fauj or the the Indian National Army. When their preparations were sufficiently advanced and units of the Azad Hind Fauj began to leave for the front, the Provisional Government of Azad Hind or Free India was set up in Shonan. The Provisional Government took over the leadership of the Indian Independence Movement in general and of India's Army of Liberation in particular. The Provisional Government of Azad Hind was granted formal recognition by Japan, Germany and seven other friendly powers.

The Provisional Government took the historic step of formally linking up India's struggle for freedom with the world-struggle for a new order, by officially declaring war on Britain and the United States of America on the 23rd October, 1943.

The next important event that took place was the acquisition of the Andaman and Nicobar Islands, thanks to the generous declaration made by Japan's Prime Minister at the Assembly of Greater East Asiatic Nations in Tokyo, on the 6th November, 1943. As the whole world is by now aware, I visited the Andaman and Nicobar Islands on the 29th December last and saw our national tricolour flag flying over the resi-dence of the former British Chief Commissioner of those islands. Thus, before the end of the year, 1943, we were able to obtain the first piece of territory belonging to Free India.

The last step that we have taken is the removal from Shonan to Burma of the Headquarters of the Provisional Government of Azad Hind and of the Head Quarters of the Supreme Command of the Indian National Army.

From the above resume of the events of the last four years, it will be clear that the Indian Independence Movement, in spite of manifold obstacles, has been progressing according to plan. Our timetable might have been slightly delayed, but we have been moving forward and forward, all the time. The next step that we are looking forward to—and for which we are now busy preparing—is the march into India and, thereafter, the commencement of the long and historic march to Delhi.

We know that when we are India with the major portion of our Army, the Indian public, as well as a large section of Britain's Indian Army, will come forward to join hands with us, in order to fight the common enemy. But I would like to warn them from now that we must all be prepared for a long and hard struggle. The Indian campaign will not be a 'Blitz-krieg' like the Malayan campaign. The enemy has had time to utilize the lessons of his disastrous defeats in East Asia. He has also had time to bring reinforcements to India from remotest parts of the world. Moreover, on the soil of India, Britain will fight her last battle and before she goes down, she will certainly fight desperately. We know, as well as the British do, that the expulsion of the enemy forces from India will mean the death of the British Empire and the end of the present war. Consequently, we must launch the last struggle after we are fully prepared for a long and bitter fight. And once that struggle begins, we must carry it on with grim determination till victory is achieved and our national flag flies over the Viceroy's House and over the Red Fortress of India's metropolis.

Friends! Before I close, I should like to warn you that in spite of all the shouting and boasting that British politicians may outwardly indulge in, attempts are being made and will in future be made by the Anglo-Americans to deceive the Indian people into an unworthy compromise with British Imperialism. To this end, enemy propagandists have been straining every nerve to give the Indian people the impression that they, that is, our enemies, will ultimately win the war. Enemy propagandists are also talking incessantly of post–war reconstruction plans—as if they were confident of victory. But being fully acquainted with all that is happening in different sectors of the world-front, I can assure you that the ultimate defeat of the enemy is assured beyond any doubt. It would therefore be the height of folly—it would indeed be insanity—to think of compromising with an Empire that will soon disappear from the fact of the earth.

Therefore, countrymen at home and abroad! Go on doing your very best for our country's freedom—with unflinching and invincible faith for final victory. We, too, are doing our very best here. The zero hour will soon arrive and then together we shall march, together we shall fight and together we shall win.

Inquilab Zindabad!
Azad Hind Zindabad!

On February 4, 1944, the Indian National Army went into action and started its offensive against the British forces in the Arakan regions.

Netaji Subhas Chandra Bose issued the following Special Order of the Day on 9 February:

'The eyes of the whole world are now focused on the Arakan front, where events of far-reaching importance are taking place today. The glorious and brilliant actions of the brave units of the Azad Hind Fauj working in close concert with the forces of the Imperial Nipponese Army have helped to foil all attempts by the Anglo-American forces to start a counter offensive in this sector.

'I am sure that the brave deeds of our comrades on the Arakan front will be a source of great inspiration to all the Officers and men of the Azad Hind Fauj wherever they may be stationed at the present moment. Our long-awaited March to Delhi has begun, and with grim determination we shall continue that march until the tri-colour National Flag that is now flying over the Arakan Mountains is hoisted over the Viceregal Lodge and until we hold our victory parade at the ancient Red Fortress of Delhi.

Comrades! Officers and men of India's Army of Liberation, let there be but one solemn resolve in your hearts—either liberty or death. And let there be but one slogan on your lips—Onward to Delhi is the road to freedom. That is the road along which we must march. Victory will certainly be ours.'

Netaji Subhas Chandra Bose received the following congratulatory message from Mamoru Shigemitsu, Nippon Foreign Minister:

'Your Excellency: Allow me to tender to Your Excellency my heartfelt congratulations upon the splendid achievements of your gallant troops who have demonstrated their prowess in fighting shoulder to shoulder with the Nippon forces. I feel keenly delighted on the new successful development in the present campaign, as it will, I trust, instill fresh courage and confidence into the hearts of all Indian people who are inspired by your superb leadership and are rallying to the cause of vindication, which is no other than the harbinger of Asia's renaissance.

With very best wishes, Mamoru Shigemitsu, Foreign Minister of Nippon.'

On February 21, the Headquarters of the Supreme Command of the Azad Hind Fauj issued its first communiqué as follows:

'Latest information received from the Arakan front reporting further success achieved by our units, shows that the Indian National Army participating in the operations in the Akyab district are pushing into enemy positions in co-operation with the main forces of the Nippon Army.

Meanwhile, advance units of the Indian National Army, who in concert with the Nippon forces are now engaged in cutting off the enemy's retreat near Nyaunggyang, have destroyed bridges in that area and have advanced into the Bawli Bazaar district where they are now operating.

Another unit of the Indian National, Army, which has been pushing forward along the Mayu River since the commencement of operations, has succeeded in bringing over to our side an Indian unit of the British Indian Army. The number of officers and soldiers of this unit will not be disclosed for the time being.

The same Indian National Army unit has penetrated into the Taung Bazaar area, from where it is now pushing forward into the enemy's rear and is steadily gaining the desired war results. The main forces of the Azad Hind Fauj in the Akyab sector are preparing for further operations, according to plan.'

Netaji Subhas Chandra Bose addressed a huge mass rally [in Hindustani] to celebrate the first success of the Azad Hind Fauj against the Anglo-American enemies:

'Brothers and Sisters,

We are assembled today to give expression to our joy at the beginning of the last war of independence and at the way our first attack has been crowned with success. There cannot be an Indian whose heart would not have been thrilled at the news which has come from the Arakan front, at the news which shows that our long awaited war of liberation has begun, the news that the INA fighting shoulder to shoulder with the brave Nippon soldiers have delivered their first attack in the Indian offensive before which the enemy forces have begun to retreat. It is a matter of pride and great significance that the fight, which was launched, has started so well.

When the news went to the world first about an army in East Asia composed of patriotic Indians, there were people who were trying to ignore the existence of this army. Then came the stage when British propagandists found that they cannot suppress the news about the creation of the INA, merely by ignoring it, and so they proceeded to harp on the tune that the INA has been created under pressure by the Japanese. But when, on December 5th, the INA Radio station was established and INA officers began to speak to India in their own names, the Britishers realized that the tune would not work. Added to this, when the news was flashed out that the Headquarters of the Provisional Government of Free India as well as the Supreme Commander of the

INA had started to move and that as the first stage the Headquarters had come to Burma, the Britishers became dismayed and panicky.

This dismay and panic has now become ten-fold because the INA has actually started their offensive on the Arakan front. The beginning of our offensive is a very important event in our history because it is our first fight after the long period of our slavery. It is also the last and final fight to get back our independence. And this time, we have started the fight not with the old weapons of Satyagraha and Civil Disobedience; we have now started a fight with arms and armed forces. We have succeeded in our first stroke, and we are sure of getting more and more of success from day to day. And, having started the last war and won the initial victory, let us have a brief retrospect of what we have done so far and then look ahead as to what we have yet to do.

What has transpired on the Arakan front is not a sudden achievement or an accident, because we have been carrying out efforts for liberation according to a continuous programme. One thing after another we have been achieving, and we have been progressing towards our ideal steadily, during the past many years. Our work started with the organization of our forces in India. Especially after the last great war, a new awakening dawned on India and the Indian people started to rally their forces to get independence. They had no army and so they had to confine their activities to Satyagraha and Civil Disobedience.

The next stage was to mobilize the Indians in other free countries outside India. Indians outside also began to take more and more interest in the struggle for independence. Especially significant was the rally of the three million Indians in East Asia after the inception of the Great East Asia War. The Britishers did not anticipate even in their dreams that there would be a war of Indian Independence waged from the East of India. Their statesmen and commanders always thought that danger to their domination of India would come from the West and so all their defense preparations in the past were confined to the Punjab and the North West Frontier Provinces. The 'Komagata Maru' incident was one of them. Many of the revolutionaries were either killed or arrested. But today the situation is different. The road to India has been opened for us and we can easily reach the Indian frontiers. Even if there are no railway trains or motorcars, we can reach the frontiers on foot. The question now is how to take arms and armed forces to India. The question before us is how to carry on the fight on the soil of India till the enemies are completely driven out of India.

With the opening of the Eastern gate to India, the responsibilities of the Indians in East Asia became great. And after coming to East Asia, I placed the programme of 'Total Mobilization' before the Indian Independence League. And to the soldiers of the Indian National Army, I gave a battle cry 'On to Delhi' visualizing their goal. Both the Indian Independence League and the Indian National Army were reorganized and a new life came into them. Thanks to Providence and Destiny, with the Greater East Asia War, the Britishers were repulsed from Hongkong and Singapore, Malay and Burma, and as a result the British Empire became a thing of the past in East Asia. Three years ago, the Britishers were the Lords of Burma, but where can you see the Britishers now? They are in the jails in Burma. What happened in Burma before your own eyes is now to repeat in India. And I can say with conviction that if the Britishers are not fast enough in retreating, they would find that there is room for them in India, only in the prisons in India.

The gate to India from the East was opened when the Britishers were driven out from East Asia. The question before Indian revolutionaries a few years ago was how to send armed revolutionaries or arms to India. Many efforts were made even during the great war. When I found that our preparations had gone on according to plan, I had to make plans to start our onward march. As a first step, I formed the Provisional Government of Azad Hind so that our position could be clarified beyond the least doubt. The British propagandists were trying to make out that the Indian National Army was going to fight for Nippon. We drove the nail on the head of this allegation by establishing the Provisional Government of Azad Hind under whose leadership the Indian National Army will enter into India.

Our government was not a mere propaganda stunt because the three millions of Indians in East Asia organized into one people by the Indian Independence League was the sanction of the government, and we had a strong army as our strength. And our government had the recognition of Japan, Germany and seven other countries behind it. The

Britishers were dumbfounded and the only point that they could think of was that we had no territory, and the Delhi Radio started to make much of this. But within two days from the propaganda talk on this point came the historic announcement of Nippon handing over Andamans and Nicobar to the Provisional Government of Azad Hind. As a result, we became legally and technically as well a full-fledged government with a territory of our own. And when I travelled in East Asia such honours were given to me in Japan, China and Philippines that are not ever given to the representative of slave countries.

I regard these honours not as honour done to me individually but as honour done to India and the 38 crores of Indian people. After my tour of East Asia, I went to Andamans on the 29th December and hoisted our tricolour flag in the official residence of the British Commissioner of Andamans. To get Andamans into our hands, to free Andamans and hoist our flag there was also a very significant thing because in every revolutionary war as in France and Ireland the first attempt has always been made to liberate the prison houses. And Andamans as you know was the prison house to which the greatest Indian revolutionaries were sent by the Britishers.

After my return from Andamans, there was only one work left and that was to move forward. Previously, war detachments of the Indian National Army had gone to the front but the time had come to send all our troops to the front. And so the Headquarters of the Provisional Government of Azad Hind as well as the Supreme Commander of the Indian National Army was moved to Burma. Now there is only one question, which remains before us. That ought to be the only question, which should be in the minds of every Indian. 'How soon are we going to hoist our flag in India, and how soon can we carry on our preparations to carry out the war from stage to stage?'

For the successful consummation of every war we need a base of operations. The Britishers used India as their base to enslave Burma. History has now ordained that we should use Burma as our base to liberate India. I want every one of you in Burma to realize, firstly, that you are in the front in a war zone and secondly, that this is our base for the present war of Indian independence. To carry on our war we need three things: men, money and materials. Indians in other territories of East Asia can help and are helping, also. But you must realize that what you could mobilize from Burma is of greater value, because from Burma, we can reach the frontiers earlier.

I would appeal to the Indians in Burma to get ready for total mobilization of manpower and resources. I do not want to seek from others what Indians here are already possessing. While Indians have money and materials, it is sheer disgrace for us to go to others with outstretched hands. We are the servants of India determined to liberate the 38 crores of Indian people and so we have every right to demand from you what you have. I may say here that so far Burma Indians have been backward in carrying out our programme of total mobilization when compared to the Indians of other territories in East Asia. But that is no reason why in the future they should not go ahead of the other territories. I want every Indian in Burma, whatever religion he may profess, whatever the province he hails from, whatever the language he speaks, to come forward to do his duty towards India. From tomorrow the work of total mobilization is going to start in right earnest, and I want every Indian to come forward to give the fullest co-operation.

In the gigantic task that lies ahead of us there is room for every one of you. There is a place in our mission for each one of you whether you are rich or poor, young or old, literate or illiterate. There should be no other question or problems before you. The only question before you should be as to how you should serve India in her present hour of need. Till today some of you might have been centred in yourselves but from tomorrow I want you to forget yourselves and to think of India and India alone. I desire to see every one of you imbued with a sincere desire to serve India and a determination to give your all and do your best for liberating India. I have always been telling my army that it is not enough if 99 out of 100 soldiers are brave and sincere. Ninety-nine may be alright and one may waver but the fault of one will cloud the good work done by the ninety-nine. I have told the Indian National Army that I desire to see 100 out of every 100 proving to be brave and sincere in the test. And my message to the civilians today is this, that I desire the same thing from you. I desire to see hundred percent of all civilians as sincere patriots who consider country above everything else.

I hear that there are enemy spies in Burma. It is also said that there are Indian spies also. I do not know how far it is true. But I would say this emphatically that should there be any Indian who is an agent of the enemy or even who has the slightest inclination towards the enemy, such an Indian is not only Nippon's enemy, not only Burma's enemy, he is also the enemy of India, he is an enemy of the 38 crores of people in India. And to such traitors there could be only one penalty and that is death.

Friends! You must realise that we are in the midst of a life and death struggle. Either we are going to become free or going to be doomed to eternal slavery. We on our part are determined to become free by any means and at any cost. And anyone who tries to put obstacles in our path is an enemy, deserving the worst penalty. I would take this opportunity of warning those, if any, who try to place obstacles or carry on counter propaganda against our work. If there be cowards who do not want to fight, if there be misers who do not want to fight, if there be misers who do not want sacrifice, they may stay at their homes if they do not want to do their duty. Even as such they are condemnable, but if any such people go further and try to prevent others from coming forward, it is something which is unforgivable.

Friends! The fight is going on now and very soon we may hear that so many Indian soldiers are dead, and we will have to replace every one of them. So many demands for war supplies would be coming in. When we are fighting for our independence how can we ask others for help? We have to give our all before we would be justified to seek the help of others. It is a battle for our independence and so the men, money and materials must be ours to the last ounce of our capacity.

We need not only soldiers but also every kind of talent and ability. We need doctors and engineers, nurses, mechanics and labourers. Our slogan is 'On to Delhi,' but where is the road to Delhi? On the frontier lie mountains and jungles and we have to make our own roads, and is it not the duty of Indian labourers to make this road? I would repeat that there is a place for every Indian in Burma in our present campaign for our independence, whether he is an officer or a soldier, whether he is a technician or a labourer. All are alike, because all of us are the servants of India. There is no difference among us. All of us are alike consecrated to the cause of Indian independence.

Realize the magnitude and the sanctity of the task that lies ahead of us. Realize that if you have love for India, a greater opportunity to serve India will never come. I have confidence in my army and my people.

If you had not fully responded, partly, it was due to the shortcomings in our organization. But from tomorrow we start total mobilization with full force, and I hope to see from tomorrow a new life and a new spirit, a complete reorientation of outlook, renewed determination and unreserved response from the Indians in Burma. And as you return from this rally, I want you to keep in your mind the slogan 'Indian National Army is on the march. We are with them.' And start tomorrow to live and act accordingly.'

[On 22 March 1944, the 'Azad Hind' organ of the Indian Independence League Headquarters at Singapore flashed on its front page the most sensational and joyful news of the entry (**on 18 March 1944**) of the Indian National Army into India.] **On that occasion Netaji issued a Special Order of the Day:**

'. . . there, there in the distance—beyond that river, beyond those jungles, beyond those hills lies the promised land—the soil from which we sprang—the land to which we shall now return. Hark! India is calling—India's metropolis Delhi is calling—three hundred and eighty eight millions of our countrymen are calling. Blood is calling to blood. Get up, we have no time to lose. Take up your arms. There, in front of you is the road that our pioneers have built. We shall march along that road. We shall carve our way through the enemy's ranks—or if God wills, we shall die a martyr's death. And in our last sleep we shall kiss the road that will bring our Army to Delhi. The Road to Delhi is the road to Freedom. CHALO DELHI.'

37

Homage to the Mother of the Indian People

[Statement on the death of Shrimati Kasturba Gandhi on 22 February 1944][1]

Shrimati Kasturba Gandhi is dead. She has died in British custody in Poona at the age of 74. With 388,000,000 of my countrymen at home and with my compatriots abroad, I share the deepest bereavement over the death of Kasturba. She died under tragic circumstances, but for a member of an enslaved nation no death could have been more honourable or more glorious. India has suffered a personal loss. Kasturba Gandhi is the second fellow prisoner of Mahatma Gandhi to die under his very eyes in custody, since he was imprisoned in Poona a year and a half ago. The first was his life-long fellow worker and private secretary, Mahadev Desai. This is the second personal bereavement that Mahatma Gandhi has suffered during his present imprisonment.

I pay my humble tribute to the memory of that great lady who was a mother to the Indian people, and I wish to express my deepest sympathy for Gandhiji in his bereavement. I had the privilege of coming into frequent personal contact with Shrimati Kasturba, and I would sum up my tribute to her in a few words. She was the ideal of Indian womanhood, strong, patient, silent and self-sufficient. Kasturba was a source of inspiration to the millions of India's daughters among whom she moved and whom she met in the struggle for the freedom of her motherland. From the days of the South African Satyagraha, she

[1] *Testament of Subhas Bose*, pp. 69–70.

has shared with her great husband the trials and sufferings, which have been their lot for nearly 30 years now. Her many imprisonments seriously impaired her health, but jails held no terrors for her even in her 74th year. Any time Mahatma Gandhi launched a civil disobedience movement, Kasturba was at his side in the forefront of the struggle, an outstanding example to India's daughters and a challenge to the sons of India not to lag behind their sisters in the fight for India's independence.

Kasturba has died a martyr's death. She had been suffering from heart disease for over four months. But the callous British Government turned a deaf ear to the humanitarian pleadings of the Indian nation to release Kasturba on medical grounds. The British probably hoped that by subjecting Mahatma Gandhi to such mental anguish, they could crush him body and soul and beat him into surrender. I can only express my contempt for those brutes, who profess to fight for freedom, justice and morality and yet perpetrate such cold-blooded murder. They have not understood the Indian people. No amount of mental torture and physical suffering that the British can and may inflict on Mahatma Gandhi or the Indian nation will make him budge an inch from the stand he has taken. Mahatma Gandhi called upon the British to quit India and save India from the horrors of modern war. The insolent reply of the British was to throw him into prison like an ordinary criminal. He and his noble consort would rather die in prison than come out free in an enslaved India. The British were determined to see that Kasturba died of heart disease in custody under the very eyes of her husband. They have had their criminal desire fulfilled, and it is nothing short of murder. But to us Indians at home and abroad, Shrimati Kasturba's sad death in prison is a grim reminder that the British are bent on disposing of our leaders one after another in the most heartless manner. As long as the British remain in India these atrocities against our nation will continue unchecked. There is only one way in which the sons and daughters of India can avenge the death of Shrimati Kasturba Gandhi, and that is by the complete destruction of the British Empire in India. A special responsibility lies on the shoulders of Indians in East Asia who have launched an armed struggle against the British rulers in India. This responsibility is shared, in particular, by all our sisters here. In this hour of sorrow we will renew our solemn pledge to continue the armed fight until the last Britisher is driven out of India.

38

The INA on Indian Soil

[Broadcasts and statements from Burma, March–April 1944][1]

Netaji Subhas Chandra Bose issued the following momentous proclamation on 21 March from an undisclosed place in Burma:

'The Indian National Army under the leadership of the Provisional Government of Azad Hind and the Imperial Nippon Army, working in the closest co-operation, and fighting shoulder to shoulder, have set out on a sacred mission. At this momentous hour when the allied armies of India and Nippon are crossing the frontier and marching into India, the Provisional Government of Azad Hind makes the following proclamation:

Since the bloody war of 1857 when the armies of India were defeated in battle by the invading forces of Britain, the Indian people have never morally surrendered to the British. In spite of inhuman persecution, and in spite of forcible disarmament, they have continued their resistance to British domination. Through propaganda and agitation, through acts of terrorism and sabotage, through armed revolution, and in recent years through satyagraha or passive resistance initiated by Mahatma Gandhi—they have not only kept up the struggle for independence but have also advanced a long way towards the goal of freedom.

Since the outbreak of the present war, all attempts have been made by the Indian people and their leaders for the achievement of liberty through peaceful settlement with Britain. But all these attempts have failed. Moreover, Britain has, in the course of this war, strengthened

[1] *Chalo Delhi*, pp. 200–5.

her stranglehold over India through ruthless exploitation and brutal suppression, and has converted India into a gigantic military base for prosecuting her imperialistic war.

In pursuance of this policy, foreign troops—namely, Australian, American, Chinese and African troops—have been imported into India, and owing to the unbearable burden thrown on the shoulders of the already impoverished Indian masses, famine conditions of an unprecedented nature have broken out in large areas of the country.

In a last desperate attempt to spare India the horrors of war, Mahatma Gandhi advised the British Government to recognize India's demands for independence and quit India. The reply of the British Government was to throw him into prison along with hundreds of thousands of India's patriots. The last act of vandalism committed by the British Government was the virtual murder of Kasturba Gandhi in British custody.

Viewing the worsening situation in India, Indians in East Asia, numbering about three millions, made a solemn resolve to participate actively in the fight for the Indian people at home and their national liberation. They organized themselves politically under the Azad Hind Sangh or Indian Independence League. They organized an army, and on October 21, 1943, they set up the Provisional Government of Azad Hind. When the Azad Hind Fauj had completed all its preparations, it launched the last fight for freedom of its sacred motherland on February 4, 1944, in the Arakan region of Burma. The success achieved in this fight by the allied armies of India and Nippon has now enabled the Indian National Army to cross the frontier of India and continue its march to Delhi.

Since the outbreak of the war in East Asia, the victories achieved by the armed forces of Nippon, which are unparalleled in military history, have rendered it possible for Indians in East Asia to organize themselves for active participation in India's fight for freedom. The Government of Nippon has repeatedly declared, before the whole world, that Nippon is fighting not only for her own security but also for the destruction of Anglo-American imperialism in East Asia, and further that Nippon stands for the complete and unconditional independence of India.

In pursuance of this policy, the Government of Nippon has repeatedly expressed its readiness to give all-out aid to India in her struggle for independence, formally recognized the Provisional Government of Azad Hind, and has decided to hand over the Andaman and Nicobar Islands to the Provisional Government.

Now the Indian National Army has launched its offensive and, with the co-operation of the Imperial Nippon Army, is marching shoulder to shoulder in the common fight against the common foe—the Anglo-Americans and their allies. Until these foreign armies of aggression are thrown out of India there can be no freedom and security in East Asia, and there can be no end to the present imperialistic war of the Anglo-Americans. Nippon is therefore determined to redeem her pledge to help the Indian People to create an India for Indians.

The Provisional Government of Azad Hind hereby proclaims its solemn determination to go on fighting in closest brotherhood with Nippon until India is completely liberated. We call upon Indian people who are the bone of our bone, the flesh of our flesh, to render all help—direct or indirect—to our armies of liberation.

We call upon all patriotic Indians—men, women and children, our brothers and sisters in India, to throw themselves whole-heartedly into this last fight for India's independence. We call upon every Indian to destroy the Anglo-American war effort in India by systematic sabotage, and thereby hasten the successful conclusion of the war for our country's freedom.

We call upon, our brothers, Indian soldiers and officers in Britain's army, to refuse to fight any longer for their despotic rulers, and to come and actively joins our ranks. We call upon Indians working in various departments of the British Service to render all possible help to us in this sacred fight.

We solemnly assure the Indian People, our brothers and sisters, that they have nothing whatsoever to fear so long as they do not help the Anglo-Americans or their allies in India. We assure them, further, that in liberated territory in India, the Provisional Government of Azad Hind will be established, and that the Provisional Government will take over the administration of that territory.

We advise the Indian people, our kith and kin, to keep away from the Anglo-American armies, their aerodromes, their barracks, their munitions factories, their harbours and military installations, and their war industries, which may have to be destroyed by us before the enemy can be defeated.

Sisters and brothers in India! This is the golden opportunity for you to fulfill your long-cherished aspirations for freedom. If you rise to the occasion and do your duty, freedom will be yours before long. In this momentous crisis, India expects everyone to do his or her duty. Jai Hind!—Head of State of the Provisional Government of Azad Hind and Supreme Commander of the Indian National Army.'

On April 4, 1944, the Provisional Government of Azad Hind issued its second proclamation after entering Indian soil:

Under the leadership of the Provisional Government of Azad Hind which was formed on the 21st October, 1943, at Syonan (formerly Singapore) by the unanimous will of the three million Indians in East Asia, the Indian National Army has crossed the frontier and has penetrated deep into Indian territory.

The Provisional Government of Azad Hind, your own Government, has only one mission to fulfill. That mission is to expel the Anglo-American armies from the sacred soil of India by armed force and then to bring about the establishment of a permanent National Government of Azad Hind, in accordance with the will of the Indian people.

The Provisional Government of Azad Hind will continue the armed struggle until the Anglo-American forces are annihilated or expelled from India.

While prosecuting the armed struggle for the complete liberation of India, the Provisional Government of Free India will push on with the work of reconstruction of the liberated areas.

The Provisional Government of Azad Hind is the only lawful Government of the Indian people. The Provisional Government calls upon the Indian people in the liberated areas to render all assistance and cooperation to the Indian National Army and to the civilian officials appointed by the Provisional Government.

The Provisional Government guarantees the safety of life and property of the Indian population in the liberated areas, but will inflict severe punishment on those who carry on any activities, overt or covert, which might be of help to our Anglo-American enemies or their allies, or might disturb the work of reconstruction to be started by the Provisional Government.

The Provisional Government calls upon the Indian people to cooperate whole-heartedly with our ally, the Nippon Army, who are giving unstinted and unconditional assistance in defeating our enemies. In the last two years, the British have been strongly reinforcing themselves with troops from America, Australia, Chungking China and East and West Africa. The Provisional Government has therefore, felt compelled to avail itself of the generous offer of all-out aid made by Nippon, whose armed forces have scored unparalleled victories over the Anglo-Americans since the beginning of the war in East Asia. The Provisional Government of Azad Hind is supremely confident that the Indian National Army, with the aid of the invincible forces of our ally, the Nippon Army, will crush the Anglo-Americans and bring about the complete liberation of India.

The Provisional Government is fully convinced of Nippon's sincerity towards India. The Provisional Government is convinced that Nippon has no territorial, political, economic or military ambitions in India. The Provisional Government is convinced that Nippon is interested only in destroying the Anglo-American forces in India which are the enemies not only of India, but of Asia as well. The destruction of Anglo-American Imperialism alone will terminate this war and bring peace to the world.

In accordance with its status as an independent Government, the Provisional Government of Azad Hind is arranging to issue its own currency of Rupee-Notes of different denominations. But owing to the rapid development of the war situation culminating in our quick advance into India, it has not been possible to bring into India, in time, the currency of the Provisional Government. The circumstances have therefore, rendered it necessary for the Provisional Government to borrow from the Nipponese Government the currency (viz. military rupee notes) already in its possession and to use that currency as a temporary measure. As soon as the Provisional Government's own currency is available, the currency borrowed from the Nipponese Government will be gradually withdrawn from circulation.

Brothers and Sisters! Now that our enemies are being driven out of Indian soil, you are becoming once again what you were before—

namely, free men and women. Rally round your own Government—the Provisional Government of Azad Hind—and thereby help in preserving and safeguarding your newly-won liberty.

SUBHAS CHANDRA BOSE
Head of the State

Just before he left for the front, Netaji opened the National Bank of Azad Hind in Rangoon on April 5. The patriotic spirit of four Indians of Rangoon made it possible for the bank to be established at a very short notice with a capital of 10 million rupees. Inspired by the self-sacrificing examples of Habeeb Saheb and Srimati Betai who placed all that they possessed at the disposal of Netaji, Indians in Burma poured crores of rupees into the war chest of the Provisional Government. Habeeb Saheb's total assets were estimated at over one crore of rupees. Netaji awarded the decoration of 'Sewak-e-Hind ' to Habeeb Saheb, Srimati Betai and a few other Indians in Burma.

The Advance Headquarters of the Provisional Government of Azad Hind in Burma announced the appointment of five new Ministers of State in a special communiqué. They were Mr. N. Raghavan, Mr. A. Yellappa, Mr. Ishar Singh, Lieut.-Colonel G.R. Nagar, and Lieut.-Colonel Habibur Rahman. The communiqué said that on their appointment as Ministers, Mr. A. Yellappa and Mr. Ishar Singh would cease to hold the posts of Advisers to the Provisional Government, but, until further orders, would carry on the duties hitherto entrusted to them. The communiqué also said that Mr. S.M. Bashir of Rangoon was appointed Adviser to the Provisional Government of Azad Hind, and Lieut.-Colonel S.C. Alagappan, Minister without Portfolio, would be Minister-in-Charge of Supplies in addition to his other duties.

39

True Daughters of Mother India

[Special message for the Rani of Jhansi Regiment from headquarters, Burma on 14 May 1944][1]

Sisters,

The formation of the Rani of Jhansi Regiment is an event of unique significance in the history of our struggle for freedom. Like your brothers in the Azad Hind Fauj, you have come forward to serve your country and to fight for your country's freedom. In asking you to leave your homes and come forward to sacrifice your lives at the altar of the motherland, I have undertaken a very grave responsibility. Because of this responsibility, I have all along taken the closest interest in the work and in the progress of your Regiment. I have been praying day and night that God's blessings may always rest on you and that you may effectively participate in the struggle for liberty—to the everlasting glory of the motherland. I have been endeavouring to look after and to nurse this new regiment in such a manner that every father, every mother and every guardian may fulfill his or her responsibility satisfactorily only with your wholehearted co-operation. Therefore, you too should pray day and night that God may give you strength to fulfill your duty as true daughters of Mother India. From the progress that you have made up till now, I feel confident that the Rani of Jhansi Regiment will prove to be a success and will achieve an abiding place

[1] Archives of the Netaji Research Bureau.

in the history of our struggle for freedom. I have often lectured to you in the past that India needs today not one Rani of Jhansi but thousands of them. I want each and every one of you to do for your country what Joan of Arc of immortal fame did for France and what Rani Lakshmi Bai of Jhansi did for Bharat Mata. That honour and glory you can achieve only when you will cheerfully lay down your lives for the liberation of India. Therefore, remember that the day will come when, like your brothers, you too will need intensive training, both military and spiritual. The first contingent of the Rani of Jhansi Regiment has already moved from Rangoon towards the front. Another larger contingent is eagerly and impatiently waiting in Syonan for the transport, which will enable it to reach the front and actively participate in the coming campaign. During the past twenty years, I have seen something of what our women are capable of. I have seen that there is no work and no sacrifice of which the women of India are not capable. It is because of this confidence that I have taken the historic step in organizing the Rani of Jhansi Regiment. I am sure that each and every one of you shares the confidence that I have. I wish you all success in your present training and in your future struggle and victory.

Jai Hind.

40

Mahatma Gandhi will be Glad when the National Army Enters Calcutta

[Press statement, 18 May 1944][1]

In an interview with the Japanese newspaper Yomiuri Hochi's war correspondent, Netaji S.C. Bose said, 'It is immaterial to me how the British plan to check our advance as all their attempts will be useless. They can do nothing to shake our determination. Since January 26, 1941, when I escaped from British confinement, all their efforts to re-arrest me have failed. Now, they have posted a huge army on the Indo-Burma front to check our entry into India. But, the world has seen how the Indian National Army has successfully pierced their defences and continued its march. In a short time, this army will end British rule in India. The war of India's liberation can never be lost. Mahatma Gandhi's release was primarily due to the Indian National Army's advance. Britain wants to come to an agreement with the Congress, but that will be another defeat. Mahatmaji will be glad when the National Army enters Calcutta, and he will send me a congratulatory telegram. It is then that Indian help will be most needed. We must possess two things to win independence: (i) high and noble aspirations, and (ii) the resolution not to deviate an inch from our chosen path. The Indian National Army will continue to fight till India is free. I am glad that the efforts of this army are bearing fruit, even though slowly. The troops venerate

[1] *Testament of Subhas Bose*, pp. 157–8.

their ancestors who sacrificed their lives for their country, and their thirst for freedom knows no limits. Those who fell fighting for their country's independence rest in peace, but their spirits will be happy only when India is free. Every Indian should work on the above principles.'

—RANGOON RADIO, 18 May 1944

41

The East Asia War is Now Our Own War

[Speech at a Decoration Parade on 4 July 1944][1]

India's last war of independence began on the 4th of February 1944, in the Region of Arakan of Burma. It was on that historic day that units of the Azad Hind Fauj went into action against the forces of the enemy. The Arakan fight—though it may not be a big episode in history—has for us a special significance and for two reasons. Firstly, it was in the Arakans that our offensive against the enemy began. Secondly, it was in the Arakan fight that our troops received their first 'Baptism of Fire'. Out of this first test they emerged with colours flying, and they set a tradition for the rest of the Azad Hind Fauj to follow in future. For these reasons, the Azad Hind Fauj will forever remain grateful to those officers and men who fought bravely in the Arakan campaign and brought honour and glory to their motherland.

On the 22nd of March, I had the honour of personally decorating the Commander of our troops in the Arakans Major L.S. Misra with the medal 'Sardar-e-Jang', for bravery and efficient leadership in the battle. Thereafter, I had the honour of announcing a number of awards to other officers and men of the Azad Hind Fauj who had distinguished themselves in that campaign by their heroism and devotion to duty. One of the most outstanding amongst them—Lieut. Piara Singh—is present here today. This officer, who is an example to the members of

[1] *Blood Bath*, pp. 22–3 (translated from the original Hindustani).

the Azad Hind Fauj, has won our admiration by exhibiting a high standard of patriotism, courage and devotion to duty throughout the whole campaign. In the encounter with the enemy which took place on the 5th of February 1944 he showed bravery, initiative and resourcefulness of a very high order. For this achievement he was awarded the medal 'Vire-e-Hind,' which is an award for individual bravery of the first class. After this episode on the 5th of February, Lieut. Piara Singh distinguished himself in two other encounters—one of the 16th of February and the other on the 20th and 21st of February. It was in the latter encounter that he was injured by a trench mortar and was deprived of the use of both his legs. His condition was very serious for a time and he had to be evacuated from the field of battle. At present, he is in our hospital undergoing treatment, and I am glad to say that he is much better now. I take this opportunity of personally decorating Lieut. Piara Singh with the medal that he has earned with his blood and which he so richly deserves. By honouring such a brave officer, I am honouring myself, my army and my government.

I should like on this occasion to say a few words about the morale of our Army. After the Arakan campaign, fighting began in other sectors of the Indo-Burma frontier and, in particular, in the Haka, Tiddim and Kaladan sectors. Then came the glorious occasion when in the middle of March last, our troops—side by side with the valiant forces of the Nippon Army—crossed the frontier and marched into Manipur and Assam. Since then, our troops have been fighting the enemy on the sacred soil of our motherland. Crossing the frontier of our country has brought a unique inspiration to our army. The war in East Asia, which began in December 1941, as Nippon's war, is now our own war—India's war of liberation. Consequently, no sacrifice, no hardship, no suffering, is too great for us. It is only the price that we are paying for our Freedom. Since the beginning of the present campaign, we have received several congratulations from the Imperial Nipponese Army. Every such message has increased our determination to do even more in future and to rise to still greater heights of heroism and courage. I can assure you once again that this war is for us a life-and-death struggle—and no matter what the suffering and sacrifice involved may be, we are determined to fight to the end, being convinced of our final victory.

I am deeply grateful to the honourable representatives of the Burma Government and of the Imperial Nipponese Army for honouring us by their presence at this solemn function. With them, with their armies and their nations, we shall march shoulder to shoulder till our common victory in achieved.

42

Blood and Freedom

[Speech at a mass rally of Indians in Rangoon, Burma, at the opening of Netaji Week, 4 July 1944][1]

FRIENDS!

Twelve months ago, a new programme of 'Total Mobilisation' or 'Maximum Sacrifice' was placed before Indians in East Asia. Today I shall give an account of our achievements during the past year and shall place before you our demands for the coming year. But before I do so, I want you to realize once again what a golden opportunity we have for winning freedom. The British are now engaged in a world-wide struggle and, in the course of this struggle, they have suffered defeat after defeat in so many fronts. The enemy having been thus considerably weakened, our fight for liberty has become very much easier than it was five years ago. Such a rare and God-given opportunity comes once in a century. That is why we have sworn to fully utilize this opportunity for liberating our Motherland from the British yoke.

I am so very hopeful and optimistic about the outcome of our struggle, because I do not rely merely on the efforts of three million Indians in East Asia. There is a gigantic Movement going on inside India and millions of our countrymen are prepared for maximum suffering and sacrifice in order to achieve liberty. Unfortunately, ever since the great fight of 1857, our countrymen are disarmed, whereas the enemy is

[1] Translated from the original Hindustani and issued by the Publicity, Press and Propaganda Department, Indian Independence League Headquarters (archives of the Netaji Research Bureau).

armed to the teeth. Without arms and without a modern army, it is impossible for a disarmed people to win freedom in this modern age. Through the grace of Providence, and through the help of generous Nippon, it has become possible for Indians in East Asia to get arms and build up a modern army. Moreover, Indians in East Asia are united to a man in the endeavour to win freedom and all the religious and other differences that the British have tried to engineer inside India, do not simply exist in East Asia. Consequently, we have now an ideal combination of circumstances favouring the success of our struggle—and all that is wanted is that Indians should themselves come forward to pay the price of liberty.

According to the programme of 'Total Mobilisation', I demanded of you men, money and materials. Regarding men, I am glad to tell you that I have obtained sufficient recruits already. There has been no difficulty at all on this score and the only problem that I have had to face is as to how to train them in the speediest manner possible. I have had recruits not only from men, but from women as well and that is why the Rani of Jhansi Regiment has proved to be a success. The contingent of the Rani of Jhansi Regiment that has recently arrived from Malaya has profoundly impressed everybody by its smartness and efficiency. I am also glad to be able to say that our little boys and girls have responded enthusiastically and the 'Bal Sena' that we have organized has proved to be a success. Recruits have come to us from every corner of East Asia—from China, Japan, Indo-China, Philippines, Java, Borneo, Celebes, Sumatra, Malaya, Thailand, and Burma. The only complaint that I have is that considering the population of Indians in Burma, the number of recruits from Burma should have been larger. You will, therefore, have to exert yourselves still more in future in order to furnish more recruits from this part.

With regard to money, you remember that I demanded thirty millions from Indians in East Asia. I have actually got much more in the meantime and, from the arrangements that have been made, I am confident that a steady flow of money will be maintained in future. Our moneyed classes have realized their duty in this matter and I am thankful to them for the same. Three months ago, we established a bank of our own in Burma—the National Bank of Azad Hind Limited. This bank has already proved to be a success. Some branches of this Bank have already been opened and more will have to be opened in future.

Friends! From the very beginning I had realized the necessity of starting a Department of Supplies for obtaining necessary supplies for our Army and for our other workers. This Department has done good work during the last twelve months. Indian merchants and businessmen in all parts of East Asia have helped considerably in this work and we have also purchased a large quantity of supplies from our own funds. But we have much more to do in this sphere of activity in future. Moreover, we have to tackle the problem of transport which has hitherto hampered the collection of supplies from different parts of East Asia. Hitherto, we have depended on others for the transport arrangements—but we are now determined to do something ourselves in order to transport our supplies. In this matter, we shall need your full cooperation in the days to come.

Friends! I shall now proceed to tell you what else we have done during the past year. After three months intensive work we were able to complete the training of our Army and also to begin its expansion. When the time came to transport our troops to the front, we decided to take a most significant and important step—namely, to set up a Provisional Government of our own. The Provisional Government of Azad Hind was set up on the 21st of October, 1943, and this Government took over the leadership of the Independence Movement—that is of the Indian Independence League and of the Azad Hind Fauj. The fight that is now being fought by us is under the leadership of our own Government. The Provisional Government declared war on Britain and America on the 23rd October, last. Either simultaneously or soon after this, the Provisional Government was formally recognized by Japan, Germany and seven other friendly powers of the world. This clearly demonstrated that India's struggle for liberty was fully supported by a large section of the world-public.

When our Provisional Government was set up, we were suffering from one drawback—namely, that we had no territory of our own. Our enemies tried to make fun of us over this matter—but they were soon silenced when, on the 6th November, 1943, His Excellency Premier General Tojo declared at the Conference of Great Asiatic Nations at

Tokyo that his Government had decided to hand over the Andaman and Nicobar Islands to the Provisional Government of Azad Hind. Since then, we had sent our own Chief Commissioner to the Andaman and Nicobar Islands—Col. A.D. Loganadan—who assumed his new duties on the 21st of February 1944.

By the end of 1943, things had progressed so far that we felt that we should shift our Headquarters to Burma. Early in January, 1944, the Headquarters of the Provisional Government, of the Indian Independence League and of the Azad Hind Fauj were, therefore, moved to Burma. Then followed one month of intensive preparation.

On the 4th of February last, began our last War of Independence in the Arakan region of Burma. The fight in the Arakans will always occupy a memorable place in the history of our struggle—and that for two reasons. Firstly, it was there that we began the offensive against the enemy. And secondly, it was there that the Azad Hind Fauj was put to the first test and it came out of that ordeal with flying colours. After the Arakan campaign, no doubt remained that the Azad Hind Fauj would fight bravely and fight hard for the freedom of the Motherland.

A month after the fight in the Arakans began, we were in a position to push forward our offensive. On the 21st of March, I had the honour of announcing to the world that our troops had crossed the frontier of India and were fighting on Indian soil. Since then, the fight has become India's own fight. The war has become India's War of Liberation. This has brought a profound inspiration to our troops at the Front and also to Indians all over East Asia who are working hard on the Home Front.

After our troops crossed the frontier of India, a new problem suddenly arose—namely, the problem of administration and reconstruction in the 'Liberated Area' of India. Fortunately, we had anticipated this last year and had trained people in advance. With their help and with the help of new civilian recruits from various professions and walks of life, we set up a new organization called 'Azad Hind Dal'—in March last. Though the Azad Hind Dal is fundamentally a civilian organization, its members have been trained to work under war-time conditions in Free India and to face the same anger and hardship as members of the Azad Hind Fauj. From the enthusiasm and burning spirit of sacrifice which recruits to the Azad Hind Dal have exhibited, one can very well judge the revolutionary fervour which now inspires all Indians in East

Asia. Through the organization of the Azad Hind Dal, we are now fully prepared to undertake any work connected with administration and reconstruction in Liberated India.

Friends! From this brief resume of our activities during the past year, you will clearly realize how much ground we have covered within such a short period. From my experience of more than twenty years' work inside India, I can properly assess the worth and value of the work done here. I must, therefore, warmly thank you for the hearty co-operation that you have extended to me. At the same time, I must draw your attention to the work that still lies ahead of us. You must continue the mobilization of men, money and materials with greater energy and vigour. In particular, the problem of supplies and transport has to be solved satisfactorily. Secondly, we require more men and women of all categories for administration and reconstruction in Liberated India. We must be prepared for a situation in which the enemy will ruthlessly apply the Scorched-earth policy, before withdrawing from a particular area and will also force the civilian population to evacuate—as was attempted in Burma. Last but most important of all, is the problem of sending reinforcements in men and in supplies to the fighting front. If we do not do so, we cannot hope to maintain our success at the Front. Nor can we hope to penetrate deeper into India.

Those of you who will continue to work on the Home Front should never forget that East Asia—and particularly Burma—forms our base for the War of Liberation. If this base is not strong, our fighting forces can never be victorious. Remember that this is a 'Total War'—and not merely a war between two armies. That is why for full one year, I have been laying so much stress on 'Total Mobilization' in East Asia.

There is another reason why I want you to look after the Home Front properly. During the coming months, I and my colleagues on the War Committee of the Cabinet desire to devote their whole attention to the fighting front—and also to the task of working up the Revolution inside India. Consequently, we want to be fully assured that the work at the base will go on smoothly and uninterruptedly even in our absence.

Friends! I do not know if you are aware of the propaganda-tactics of our enemy. It is not only interesting but amusing. At first, they completely ignored the existence of our Army. Then they slowly recognized its existence, but called it a propaganda-stunt. When fighting began in the Arakan region, they could no longer ignore our Army's fighting qualities, but they maintained that our Army could never enter India. When we actually went into Manipur and Assam and the world could no longer be bluffed they could find no other argument against us and, since then, our enemies and their hired mercenaries have been indulging in undiluted abuse. Ours is a puppet army—they now say—and this puppet army will never be able to reach Delhi, for Manipur is a long, long way from India's metropolis. Well, we are not altogether ignorant of the geography of India and we know exactly how far Manipur is from Delhi. Many of our soldiers now fighting in India have come from all corners of East Asia and they have already travelled distances much longer than that between Manipur and Delhi. They are all prepared for a long march—over hills and dales and across broad rivers.

So long as our enemies continue to abuse us, we can rest assured that we are on the right path. Woe will befall us, if at any time they stop abusing and take to praising us. As for the abuse itself—well, a man does not become a puppet merely because he is called one. One man can become a traitor—but three million Indians living in different countries of East Asia cannot be metamorphosed into traitors and puppets, simply because the hirelings of the Anti-India Radio at Delhi choose to use that epithet. However, I want all of you to realize that our work has proved to be so effective that we—and we alone—have been singled out for abuse by our enemies. It is an honour that we should fully appreciate.

Friends! One year ago, when I made certain demands of you, I told you that if you give me 'Total Mobilisation', I would give you a 'Second Front'. I have redeemed that pledge. The first phase of our campaign is over. Our victorious troops, fighting side by side with Nipponese troops, have pushed back the enemy and are now fighting bravely on the sacred soil of our dear motherland. Gird up your loins for the task that now lies ahead. I had asked you for men, money and materials. I have got them in a generous measure. Now I demand more of you. Men, money and materials cannot by themselves bring victory or freedom. We must have the motive-power that will inspire us to brave deeds and heroic exploits. It will be a fatal mistake for you to wish to live and see India free—simply because victory is now within sight and within reach. No one here should have the desire to live to enjoy freedom. A long fight is still in front of us. We should have but one desire today—the desire to die, so that India may live—the desire to face a martyr's death, so that the path to freedom may be paved with the martyr's blood. Friends! My comrades in the War of Liberation! Today, I demand of you—one thing, above all. I demand of you—Blood. It is blood alone that can avenge the blood that the enemy has spilt. It is blood alone that can pay the price of freedom. Give me blood and I promise you freedom.

JAI HIND.

43

Father of Our Nation

[Message to Mahatma Gandhi, broadcast on 6 July 1944][1]

Mahatmaji,

Now that your health has somewhat improved and you are able to attend to public business to some extent, I am taking the liberty of addressing a few words to you with a view to acquainting you with the plans and the activities of patriotic Indians outside India. Before I do so, I would like to inform you of the feelings of deep anxiety which Indians throughout the world had for several days, after your sudden release from custody on grounds of ill-health. After the sad demise of Srimati Kasturbaji in British custody, it was but natural for your countrymen to be alarmed over the state of your health. It has, however, pleased providence to restore you to comparative health, so that 388 millions of your countrymen may still have the benefit of your guidance and advice. I should next like to say something about the attitude of your countrymen outside India towards yourself. What I shall say in this connection is the bare truth and nothing but the truth. There are Indians outside India, as also at home, who are convinced that Indian Independence will be won only through the historic method of struggle. These men and women honestly feel that the British Government will never surrender to persuasion or moral pressure or non-violent resistance. Nevertheless, for Indians outside India, differences in method are like domestic differences. Ever since you sponsored the Independence

[1] *Blood Bath*, pp. 24–34.

Resolution at the Lahore Congress in December 1929, all members of the Indian National Congress have had one common goal before them. For Indians outside India, you are the creator of the present awakening in our country. In all their propaganda before the world, they give you that position and the respect that is due to the position. For the world-public, we Indian nationalists are all one—having but one goal, one desire and one endeavour in life. In all the countries free from British influence that I have visited since I left India in 1941, you are held in the highest esteem, as no other Indian political leader has been, during the last century. Each nation has its own internal politics and its own attitude towards political problems. But that cannot affect a nation's appreciation of a man who served his people so well and has bravely fought a first-class modern power all his life. In fact, your worth and your achievements are appreciated a thousand times more in those countries that are opposed to the British Empire than in those countries that pretend to be the friends of freedom and democracy. The high esteem in which you are held by patriotic Indians outside India and by foreign friends of India's Freedom, was increased a hundred-fold when you bravely sponsored the 'Quit India' Resolution in August 1942.

From my experience of the British Government while I was inside India—from the secret information that I have gathered about Britain's policy while outside India—and from what I have seen regarding Britain's aims and intentions throughout the world, I am honestly convinced that the British Government will never recognize India's demand for Independence. Britain's one effort today is to exploit India to the fullest degree, in her endeavour to win this war. During the course of this war, Britain has lost one part of her territory to her enemies and another part to her friends. Even if the Allies could somehow win the war, it will be the United States of America, and not Britain, that will be the top dog in future and it will mean that Britain will become a protégé of the USA. In such a situation, the British will try to make good their present losses by exploiting India more ruthlessly than ever before. In order to do that, plans have been already hatched in London for crushing the nationalist movement in India, once for all. It is because I know of these plans from secret, but reliable sources, that I feel it my duty to bring it to your notice. It would be a fatal mistake on our part to make a distinction between the British Government and the

British people. No doubt there is a small group of idealists in Britain—as in the USA—who would like to see India free. These idealists who are treated by their own people as cranks, form a microscopic minority. So far as India is concerned, for all practical purposes, the British Government and the British people mean one and the same thing. Regarding the war aims of the USA, I may say that the ruling clique at Washington is now dreaming of world domination. This ruling clique and its intellectual exponents, talk openly of the 'American Century', that is, that in the present century, the USA will dominate the world. In this ruling clique, there are extremists who go so far as to call Britain the 49th State of the USA.

There is no Indian, whether at home or abroad, who would not be happy if India's freedom could be won through the method that you have advocated all your life and without shedding human blood. But things being what they are, I am convinced that if we do desire freedom we must be prepared to wade through blood.

If circumstances had made it possible for us to organize an armed struggle inside India, through our own efforts and resources, that would have been the best course for us. But Mahatmaji, you know Indian conditions perhaps better than anybody else. So far as I am concerned, after twenty years' experience of public service in India, I came to the conclusion that it was impossible to organize an armed resistance in the country without some help from outside—help from our countrymen abroad, as well as from some foreign power or powers. Prior to the outbreak of the present war, it was exceedingly difficult to get help from a foreign power, or even from Indians abroad. But the outbreak of the present war threw open the possibility of obtaining aid—both political and military—from the enemies of the British Empire. Before I could expect any help from them, however, I had first to find out what their attitude was towards India's demand for freedom. British propagandists for a number of years had been telling the world that the Axis Powers were the enemies of freedom and therefore of India's freedom. Was that a fact? I asked myself. Consequently, I had to leave India in order to find out the truth myself and as to whether the Axis Powers would be prepared to give us help and assistance in our fight for freedom.

Before I finally made up my mind to leave home and homeland, I had to decide whether it was right for me to take help from abroad. I had previously studied the history of revolution all over the world, in order to discover the method which had enabled other nations to obtain freedom. But I had not found a single instance in which an enslaved people had won freedom without foreign help of some sort. In 1940, I read my history once again, and once again I came to the conclusion that history did not furnish a single instance where freedom had been won without help of some sort from abroad. As for the moral question as to whether it was right to take help, I told myself that in public, as in private life, one could always take help as a loan and repay that loan later on. Moreover, if a powerful Empire, like the British Empire, could go round the world with the begging bowl, what objection could there be to an enslaved and disarmed people like ourselves taking help as a loan from abroad. I can assure you, Mahatmaji, that before I finally decided to set out on a hazardous mission, I spent days, weeks and months in carefully considering the pros and cons of the case. After having served my people so long, to the best of my ability, I could have no desire to be a traitor, or to give anyone a justification for calling me a traitor.

It was the easiest thing for me to remain at home and go on working as I had worked so long. It was also an easy thing for me to remain in an Indian prison while the war lasted. Personally, I had nothing to lose by doing so. Thanks to the generosity and to the affection of my countrymen, I had obtained the highest honour which it was possible for any public worker in India to achieve. I had also built up a party consisting of staunch and loyal colleagues who had implicit confidence in me. By going abroad on a perilous quest I was risking not only my life and my whole future career, but also what was more, the future of my party. If I had the slightest hope that without action from abroad we could win freedom, I would never have left India during a crisis. If I had any hope that within our lifetime we would get another chance—another golden opportunity for winning freedom, as during the present war, I doubt if I would have set out from home. But I was convinced of two things: firstly, that such a golden opportunity would not come within another century, and secondly, that without action from abroad, we would not be able to win freedom, merely through our own efforts at home. That is why I resolved to take the plunge.

Providence has been kind to me, in spite of manifold difficulties; all my plans have succeeded so far. After I got out of India, my first endeavour was to organize my countrymen, wherever I happened to meet them. I am glad to say that everywhere I found them to be wide-awake and anxious to do everything possible for winning freedom for India. I, then, approached the governments that were at war with our enemy in order to find out what their attitude was towards India. I found out that contrary to what British propagandists had been telling us for a number of years—the Axis powers were now, openly, the friends of India's freedom. I also discovered that they were prepared to give such help as we desired and as was within their own power.

I know the propaganda that our enemy has been carrying on against me. But I am sure that my countrymen, who know me so well, will be never be taken in. One who has stood for national self-respect and honour all his life and has suffered considerably in vindicating it, would be the last person in this world to give in to any other foreign power. Moreover, I have nothing to gain personally at the hands of a foreign power. Having received the highest honour possible for an Indian at the hands of my own countrymen, what is there for me to receive from a foreign power? Only that man can be a puppet who has either no sense of honour and self-respect or desire to build up a position for himself, through the influence of others.

Not even my worst enemy can ever dare to say that I am capable of selling national honour and self-respect. And not even my worst enemy can dare to assert that I was nobody in my own country and that I needed foreign help to secure a position for myself. In leaving India, I had to risk everything that I had, including my life. But I had to take that risk, because only by doing so could I help the achievement of India's freedom.

Their remains but one question to answer with regard to the Axis Powers. Can it be possible that I have been deceived by them? I believe it will be universally admitted that the cleverest and the most cunning politicians are to be found among Britishers. One who has worked with and fought British politicians all his life, cannot be deceived by any other politicians in the world. If British politicians have failed to coax or coerce me, no other politician can succeed in doing so. And if the British Government, at whose hands I have suffered long imprisonment, persecution and physical assault, has been unable to demoralize me, no other power can hope to do so. Moreover, as you personally are aware, I have been a close student of international affairs. I have had personal contacts with international figures before the outbreak of this war. I am, therefore, no novice, who could be duped by a shrewd and cunning politician. Last but not least, before forming an opinion about the attitude of the Axis Powers, I established close personal contact with important leaders and personalities in Axis countries who are responsible for their national affairs. Consequently, I make bold to say that my countrymen can have the fullest confidence in my judgment of international affairs. My countrymen abroad will testify to the fact that since I left India, I have never done anything which could compromise in the least, either the honour or the self-respect or the interests of my country. On the contrary, whatever I have done has been for the benefit of my nation, for enhancing India's prestige before the world and for advancing the cause of India's freedom.

Mahatmaji, since the beginning of the War in East Asia, our enemies have been carrying on a raging and tearing campaign against Japan. I shall, therefore, say something about Japan particularly because at the present moment, I am working in the closest co-operation with the government, army and people of Japan. There was a time when Japan had an alliance with our enemy. I did not come to Japan so long as there was an Anglo-Japanese Alliance. I did not come to Japan so long as normal diplomatic relations obtained between the two countries. It was after Japan took what I consider to be the most momentous step in her history—namely, declaration of war on Britain and America—that I decided to visit Japan of my own free will. Like so many of my countrymen, I had read anti-Japanese propaganda material for a number of years. Like so many of my countrymen, I did not understand why Japan went to war with China in 1937? And like so many of my countrymen, my sympathies in 1937 and 1938 were with Chungking. You may remember that as President of the Congress, I was responsible for sending out a medical mission to Chungking in December 1938. But what I realized after my visit to Japan and what many people at home do not realize, is that since the outbreak of the War in East Asia, Japan's attitude towards the world in general, and towards Asiatic nations in particular, has been completely revolutionized. It is a change that has overtaken not merely the government, but also the people of Japan. A new consciousness—what I may best describe as an Asiatic consciousness—has seized the soul of the people of Japan. That change explains Japan's present attitude towards the Philippines, Burma and India. That is what explains Japan's new policy in China. After my visit to Japan and after establishing close contact with the present day leaders of that country, I was fully satisfied that Japan's present policy towards Asia was no bluff, but was rooted in sincerity. This is not the first instance in history when an entire nation has been seized with a new consciousness. We have seen instances of it before in France during the French revolution and in Russia during the Bolshevik revolution. After my second visit to Japan in November 1943, I visited the Philippines, met Filipino leaders there and saw things for myself. I have also been in Burma for a fairly long time, and I have been able to see things with my own eyes, after the declaration of independence. And I have been to China to find out if Japan's new policy was real, or it was a fake. The latest agreement between Japan and the National Government of China has given the Chinese people practically all that she had been demanding. Japan under that agreement has agreed to withdraw her troops from China on the termination of hostilities. What then is Chungking-China fighting for? Could one believe that Britain and America are helping Chungking-China out of purely altruistic motives? Will not Britain and America demand their pound of flesh in return for the help that they are now giving to Chungking to make her continue the fight against Japan? I clearly see that Chungking is being mortgaged to Britain and America, because of past hatred and antagonism towards Japan. So long as Japan did not initiate her present policy towards China, there might have been some justification or excuse for Chinese to seek British and American aid for fighting Japan. But now that an entirely new chapter in Sino-Japanese relations has begun, there is not the slightest excuse for Chungking to continue her meaningless struggle against Japan. That is not good for Chinese people; it is certainly not good for Asia. In April 1942, you said that if you were free to do so, you would work for an understanding between China and Japan. That was an utterance of rare statesmanship. It is India's slavery that is at the bottom responsible for the chaos in China. It is because of the British hold over India that the Anglo-American could bluff Chungking into hoping that sufficient help could be brought to Chungking to enable Chungking to continue the war against Japan. You were absolutely right in thinking, Mahatmaji, that a free India would work for peace between Japan and China. I go so far as to say that the freedom of India will automatically bring about an honourable understanding between Chungking and Japan, by opening the eyes of Chungking to the folly that she is now committing. Since I came to East Asia and visited China, I have been able to study the Chinese question more deeply. I find that there is a dictatorship ruling in Chungking. I have no objection personally to dictatorship, if it is for a righteous cause. But the dictatorship that rules at Chungking is clearly under foreign American influence. Unfortunately, the Anglo-Americans have been able to deceive the ruling clique at Chungking into thinking that if Japan could be somehow defeated, then China would become the dominant power in Asia. The fact, however, is that if Japan were defeated by any chance, then China would certainly pass under American influence and control. That would be a tragedy for China and for the whole of Asia. It is through this false hope of becoming the dominant power in Asia, if Japan could be somehow defeated, that the ruling clique at Chungking has entered into an unholy alliance with the ruling clique at the White House and at Whitehall. I know something of the propagandist activities of the Chungking Government in India and of its efforts to play upon the emotions of the Indian people and win their sympathy. But I can honestly say that Chungking, which has been mortgaged to Wall Street and Lombord Street, does not deserve the sympathy of the Indian people any longer, especially after Japan has initiated her new policy towards China.

Mahatmaji, you know better than anybody else how deeply suspicious the Indian people are of mere promises. I would be the last man to be influenced by Japan, if her declarations of policy had been mere promises. But I have seen with my own eyes how, in the midst of a world war, Japan has put through revolutionary changes in countries like the Philippines, Burma and National China. In General Tojo, Japan has a leader and a Prime Minister who is true to his word and whose actions are in full conformity with his declarations, and a leader, in moral stature, towers head and shoulders above contemporary statesmen.

Coming to India, I must say that Japan has proved her sincerity by her deeds. There was a time when people used to say that Japan had selfish intentions regarding India. If she had them, why should she recognize the Provisional Government of Free India? Why should she decide to hand over the Andaman and Nicobar Islands to the Provisional Government of Free India? Why should there, now, be an Indian Chief Commissioner of the Andaman and Nicobar Islands stationed in Port Blair? Last but not least, why should Japan unconditionally help the Indian people in East Asia in their struggle for their independence? There are Indians all over East Asia and they have every opportunity of seeing Japan at close quarters. Why should three million Indians distributed all over East Asia, adopt a policy of the closest co-operation with Japan, if they had not been convinced of her bonafides and of her sincerity? You can coerce one man or coax him into doing what you want him to do. But no one can coerce three million Indians distributed all over East Asia.

If Indians in East Asia had taken help from Japan without putting forward their own efforts and without making the maximum sacrifice, they would have been guilty of wrongdoing. But as an Indian, I am happy and proud to be able to say that my countrymen in East Asia are putting forward the maximum efforts to mobilize men, money and materials for the struggle for India's freedom. I have had experience at home in collecting funds and materials and in recruiting men for national service for a period of twenty years. In the light of this experience, I can properly assess the worth and value of the sacrifice that our countrymen in East Asia are now making. Their effort is magnificent. It is because they are putting forward a magnificent effort themselves and are prepared to make the maximum sacrifice that I see no objection to taking help from Japan for such necessary articles as arms, ammunition, etc. that we ourselves cannot produce.

Mahatmaji, I should now like to say something about the Provisional Government that we have set up here. The Provisional Government of Azad Hind (or Free India) has been recognized by Japan, Germany and seven other friendly powers and this has given Indians a new status and new prestige in the eyes of the whole world. The Provisional Government has its one object, the liberation of India from the British yoke through an armed struggle. Once our enemies are expelled from India and peace and order is established, the mission of the Provisional Government will be over. It will then be for the Indian people themselves to determine the form of government that they choose and also to decide as to who should take charge of that government. I can assure you, Mahatmaji, that I and all those who are working with me regard themselves as the servants of Indian people. The only reward that we desire for our efforts, for our suffering and for our sacrifice is the freedom of our motherland. There are many among us who would like to retire from the political field, once India is free. The remainder will be content to take up any position in Free India, however humble it may be. The spirit that animates all of us today is that it is more honourable to be even a sweeper in Free India, than to have the highest position under British rule. We all know that there are hundreds of thousands of able men and women at home to whom India's destiny could be entrusted, once freedom is achieved.

How much help we shall need from Japan till the last Britisher is expelled from the soil of India, will depend on the amount of co-operation that we shall receive from inside India. Japan herself does not desire to thrust her assistance upon us. Japan would be happy if the Indian people could liberate themselves through their own exertions. It is we who have asked for assistance from Japan after declaring war on Britain and America, because our enemy has been seeking help from other powers. However, I have every hope that the help we shall receive from our countrymen at home will be so great that we shall need the minimum help from Japan. Nobody would be more happy than ourselves, if, by any chance, our countrymen at home should succeed in liberating themselves through their own efforts or if, by any chance, the British Government accepts your 'Quit India' Resolution and gives effect to it. We are, however, proceeding on the assumption that neither of the above is possible and that an armed struggle is inevitable.

Mahatmaji, there is one other matter to which I shall refer before I close and that is about the ultimate outcome of this war. I know very well the kind of propaganda that our enemies have been carrying on in order to create the impression that they are confident of victory. But I hope that my countrymen will not be duped thereby and will not think of compromising with Britain on the issue of independence under the mistaken notion that the Anglo-Americans will win this war. Having travelled round the world under war-time conditions with my eyes open, having seen the internal weakness of the enemy on the Indo-Burma frontier and inside India, and having taken stock of our own strength and resources, I am absolutely confident of our final victory. I am not so foolish as to minimize, in the least, the strength of the enemy. I know that we have a long and hard struggle in front of us. I am aware that on the soil of India, Britain will fight bravely and fight hard in a desperate attempt to save her Empire. But I know also that however long and hard the struggle may be, it can have but one outcome—namely, our victory. India's last war of independence has begun. Troops of the Azad Hind Fauj are now fighting bravely on the soil of India and in spite of all difficulty and hardship they are pushing forward slowly but steadily. This armed struggle will go on, until the last Britisher is thrown out of India and until our Tri-colour National Flag proudly floats over the Viceroy's House in New Delhi.

Father of our nation: In this holy war for India's liberation, we ask for your blessings and good wishes.

JAI HIND.

44

The Situation in Europe

[Broadcast on 8 July 1944][1]

Friends and Countrymen at home:

Today, I am going to talk to you about the situation in Europe with special reference to India and our struggle for freedom. What I shall say represents my personal views and nobody else. I hope and trust that this objective survey of mine will help you—to some extent at least—to see things as they really are. In estimating a particular situation—whether political or military—there is always a danger of unconsciously indulging in wishful thinking. Judgment that is so tainted by personal likes or prejudices or by wishful thinking is often quite untrustworthy. In the present case, in estimating the European situation, I have tried my best to guard against wishful thinking. It is not difficult for me to do so. I have no motive for being biased in my judgment, because I am convinced that the Indian situation is independent of the situation in Europe and that the Indian people can and will win their freedom, regardless of what may happen in Europe.

To get the pr̀oper background for this study, I shall deal first of all with the question as to how and why the Allies won the last World War and Germany lost it. That was due primarily to two reasons. In the last War, the French people felt that they were fighting for their hearth and homes—for all that they held dear in life—also for the recovery of Alsace-Lorraine, which they regarded as French territory. The French people were, therefore, united and they were inspired by a spiritual fervour of a high order—by what one may call the 'do or die' spirit. On

[1] *Blood Bath*, pp. 35–43.

the other hand, the German Army—though it was well disciplined and well equipped and was like an efficient machine—lacked the spiritual fervour which the French army possessed. To appreciate this fact, one has only to read the memoirs of the Allied Supreme Commander, Marshal Foch. The other reason was that Germany's internal economy was weak and could not stand the strain of a long blockade. In the present war, the situation is quite the reverse. Germany is fighting for what she considers to be her legitimate grievances and demands. The entire nation was spiritually trained prior to the outbreak of the war and the idea was ingrained in the mind of every German that defeat in this War will mean total extinction for the German people. Consequently, the moral and spiritual fervour, which belonged to the Allies—and especially to France—in the last war, now belongs to the Germans. As to her internal economy in this war, in the light of the experience gained in the last war, Germany prepared for her war requirements through her Four-Year Plan. Moreover, by occupying and controlling practically the whole of Europe, minus Russia, Germany could strengthen her economic position considerably during wartime so that she is now able to stand the strain of a long war and of a long naval blockade.

We should also remember that in the last war, the French and the Italian nations were fighting against Germany. So far as France was concerned, she was very strong, and she was fighting bravely all along. A large portion of Europe—including France and Italy—was outside German influence and control. How different is the situation today! Practically the whole of Europe minus Russia is under German influence and control—and the only serious problem that faces Germany is Russia. The Allied landings in Italy and in France have only served to strengthen the German morale, despite the extra suffering and strain that it has brought to the German people. It is a well-known fact that the Allies have been terribly disappointed at the reaction of the Italian people to the secret pact made by the Allies with the Italian King and ex-Prime Minister Badoglio. They are equally disappointed at the apathy of the French people over the Allied invasion of France. If one does not accept this statement of mine, he has only to study the American press and the reports sent from France by American war correspondents.

I know that some people are in the habit of thinking that luck always favours the British and that the British will somehow bungle through to victory at the end. But only a naïve and simple-minded person would think like this. History is a stern taskmaster and great events in history are not made by accident. Every effect has a cause. Allied victory in the last war was not the result of accident, but of certain causes and contributory factors. We have, therefore, to find out what the factors are that are working in Europe today and what result can possibly follow from these factors.

I shall now review in brief the situation from 1939 to the end of 1942 and shall, then, pass on to a review of the situation today. You may remember that in November 1940, 1941 and 1942, when the British were in a terrible plight and were suffering defeat after defeat in every theatre of war, they tried every possible means to keep up the morale of their people. At that time, they talked daily about American war production and gave astronomical figures in order to create the impression that the colossal war production and financial resources of the USA would help Britain to win the war. In their propaganda for India, the British talked unceasingly of post-war reconstruction and formed committees and set apart funds for that purpose—so that the Indian people might get the impression that Britain was absolutely confident of winning the war. But that propaganda was not of much avail—until the USA entered the war in right earnest. Since then, the tide has turned to some extent in Europe in favour of the Allies. But if one carefully analyses the recent successes of the Allies in Europe, it will be found that these successes have been due to a very large extent to the resources of the USA. If the morale in the Allied Camp is today much higher than what it was two years ago—that is also due, wholly or largely, to the USA. British morale—by itself—still remains comparatively poor. That is why Britain's Prime Minister has surrendered completely to President Roosevelt. In every theatre of war, Mr. Winston Churchill—the erstwhile haughty imperialist—has had to accept American Commanders—he has had to give up valuable British territory to his senior partner on demand—and he has had to concede what may be described as extra-territorial rights to Americans in Britain. What is more—the ruling clique behind Mr. Churchill—and its intellectual exponents and apologists—openly accept the American theory of the 'American Century'. In other words, they openly admit that Britain must make room for the USA as the bigger power and after reconciling herself to that fact Britain should try to save what she can of her Empire with the help or tacit approval of the USA. That is what explains America's reluctance to put pressure on Britain on the question of India's demand for Independence. Britain's aim clearly is to exploit India more ruthlessly when the war is over and thereby to make up—partially at least—for her present losses. To this end—plans have already been prepared in London for effectively crushing—once for all—the Indian Nationalist Movement at the end of this war. British politicians realize that they have failed, up till now, to crush the Indian Independence Movement. The policy of divide and rule, as hitherto practised, and the endeavour to exploit the Princes, the Muslims and so-called depressed classes in order to undermine the Indian National Congress—have alike failed. The remedy which British politicians have prepared for solving the Indian question in their own way in future is something quite different. But about this, I shall talk on another occasion.

Since November 1942, owing almost entirely to American help and intervention, and to American diplomacy, the Allies were able to achieve success in North Africa and later on, in Italy. Had it not been for American diplomacy, Admiral Darlan's party in France would not have come over to the side of the Allies—and it is doubtful whether the battle of North Africa would have been won by the Allies without Admiral Darlan's help. The British Government was, however, backing and are still backing General de Gaulle, as against Admiral Darlan's party. Over this question, no agreement has yet been reached between Britain and the USA—although owing to British insistence. General de Gaulle has for the present scored a victory over Admiral Darlan's success or General Giraud's. One of the results of this disagreement is that the Soviet Government has won a diplomatic victory and has established its influence in French North Africa. Another result of this disagreement between Britain and the USA is that although the war for the so-called liberation of France is going on—General de Gaulle, who is not a 'persona grata' with the Allied Supreme Commander in Europe, the American General Eisenhower, has not been given any place in it. If the Allies succeed in occupying any part of France, that territory will not probably be handed over to General de Gaulle but will be administered by Allied Military Government. On the other hand, whatever forces General de Gaulle is supposed to have, namely, the so-called Free French Forces—are made to fight for the Allies as mercenaries in Italy. The whole world knows that over European questions, there is no agreement between Britain, USA and the Soviet. The alliance that exists between these three powers is an alliance that is based solely on a common hatred and is devoid of internal unity and cohesion. Such an alliance can never achieve lasting results, nor can it win a war. This alliance is quite different from the solidarity which prevailed between the British, Americans, Belgians and French in the last World War—the solidarity which was symbolized in Marshall Foch, the Supreme Commander of the Allied Forces in France in 1918.

The Allied penetration of the European Continent appears, on the surface, to be a victory—but it is really not so. It is only a pyrrhic victory—like Napoleon's conquest of Russia and occupation of Moscow. In the case of German invasion of England, I am convinced that the British would have fought like lions. Away on the Continent, they cannot—and will not—do so. An army is not a soulless machine. It consists of human beings, who have feelings and emotions and who fight differently under different conditions. When Napoleon was young and inexperienced, the inexperienced French Army fought and won brilliant victory all over Europe. The whole of France was then fighting to save the Revolution and its fruits from the attacks of a reactionary world. But the same French Army was defeated later on by its enemies, though it was then richer in experience and was led by the Conqueror of Europe—Emperor Napoleon. In the stage of victory, the inexperienced French Army was fighting for a sacred cause under Young Napoleon. Later on, it had no holy cause to fight for—because Emperor Napoleon was then fighting for domination over Europe. The French Army was ultimately defeated under Emperor Napoleon because it had lost its morale—its will to fight. The same argument applies to the Anglo-Americans. Since they have no sacred cause to fight for—and they are only fighting for world domination—their morale cannot be bolstered up for long. I shall, therefore, hazard the prediction that as the war on the Continent drags on, the morale of the Allies will begin to sink.

I have already remarked that the morale of the British even today is comparatively poor. Nevertheless, the Allies will keep up their morale so long as exhaustion does not overtake the American Forces in Europe.

But how long will that last? According to official figures, it appears that American losses in this war have already exceeded the last war. The USA, no doubt, have a large population—but we should not forget that the Americans are not a warlike nation. They are a nation of industrialists and farmers. The war in Europe is far away from home, and it is not popular with the American nation as a whole. The people who are enthusiastic over the war in Europe are only the staunch followers of President Roosevelt—the Jews and the financial and commercial circles who are dreaming of the economic domination of the world. The influential isolationist party is apathetic towards the European War—though it is perhaps enthusiastic over the war in the Pacific. Moreover, there has been a persistent and unbroken clamour in the USA for giving up the European front and concentrating on the Pacific. Consequently, as the American losses in the war begin to mount up, grumbling will begin and exhaustion will set in. Further, from the point of view of military technique, extension of the line of communication will bring additional difficulties and problems and will add to strain, which Americans are now having to bear. As soon as the Americans begin to show signs of exhaustion, it will be the beginning of their end—and the beginning of the Anglo-American defeat in Europe.

There, now, remains the question of Soviet Russia. Will the Soviets be able to break into Germany and turn the tables on the Germans? Will they be able to reach Berlin, for instance, as Allied propagandists have been boastfully predicting. To answer this question, we should consider Russian losses in the War—as well as Russian war-production. The Soviet losses in men and materials have been colossal—nobody will deny. Consequently, there is a limit to the effort that can be put forward in future. Owing to Marshal Stalin's excellent propaganda, the morale of the Russian people was strengthened so much that the Russian people could put up with the losses and still continue the war. But they were then fighting for the fatherland—for their hearth and homes. Outside Russia, they will not have the same will to fight. Moreover, the same difficulties will overtake them, as overtook the German Army when it was marching towards Stalingrad. Consequently, I do not anticipate that the Soviet Forces will be able to move much further, after they come up to their 1939 frontiers. It has also to be borne in mind that there is no agreement whatsoever between the Anglo-Americans and the Soviets as to the fate of Europe in the event of an Allied victory. In fact, the aims of the Anglo-Americans on the one side and of the Soviets on the other are, in many areas of Europe, diametrically opposed. It is interesting to note, in this connection, that while Americans have been advertising their invasion of Europe so loudly, the organ of the Soviet Foreign Office—'War and Working Class'—has belittled the so-called 'Second Front' and has warned the Anglo-Americans that if they do not widen their front and throw in more men and materials into France—disaster may one day overtake them at the hands of the German Army.

It has also to be noted that the Anglo-Americans are anything but pleased over the Soviet Government's political offensive in Africa and in Asia—e.g. in French North Africa, in Syria, in Egypt and in Iran. Moreover, the Soviet Government's aims in Poland, in Finland, in the Baltic States and in the Balkans—also in the Dardenelles Straits—are not viewed with favour by the Anglo-Americans. It is not outside the domain of possibility that a situation may arise in the Allied Camp similar to what arose among the Balkan Powers, when they were fighting Turkey in 1912. It is also not unlikely that the advance of the Soviet Army beyond the 1939 frontiers of Russia—if that be ever possible—will raise unexpected complications and intensify the misunderstanding and friction which prevails between the Anglo-Americans and the Soviets.

This brings us to the question of Turkey. British propagandists have been trying to give the world the impression that a day will come when Turkey will throw in her lot with the Allied Powers. These propagandists think that such propaganda will influence the Indian Muslims in a pro-British sense. But nobody who knows anything about modern Turkey will put the slightest credence in such a view. Though there are circles in Turkey that are distinctly pro-Ally and though the tone of the Ankara Radio is pro-Ally—there is not the least possibility of Turkey participating in the war on either side. Come what may, Turkey is going to remain neutral.

As I have remarked at the beginning, much has been made of America's colossal war-production by enemy-propagandists, with a view to bolstering up the morale in the Allied Camp. But we should not forget that there is a limit to American war-production. American war-production has already reached its peak and, in future, it will decline instead of going up. So far as Germany is concerned, her war-production has not been appreciably impaired, despite recent air attacks. In fact, in certain items, it has even gone up. Consequently, there is every possibility that German war-production will be able to cope with the requirements of the war situation.

I shall now sum up the European situation as follows: On the eastern front, it was not possible for the Germans to defeat Russia. Likewise, it will not be possible for the Russians to defeat Germany. What appears to me to be highly probable is some sort of stalemate—with both sides digging in, as it were. In Western Europe, however, the tide will turn in favour of Germany after a time. It will, then, be possible for the Germans to push back the Anglo-Americans in France. In Italy, the Germans will put up their last defence when they leave the peninsula and come to Northern Italy. They, there, will stand fast and from there, it will not be possible for the Anglo-Americans to dislodge them.

So far as the Italian and French fronts are concerned, I am convinced that the Germans will be able to hold out, until the Allied morale begins to sink. I do not anticipate the possibility of the German morale cracking. Already, the air-attacks on Germany have begun to slow down, and Germany has taken the offensive in the air, with the help of her 'flying bombs'. This has had an appreciable effect on German morale. The next few months will be critical for Germany, but thereafter Germany will turn the corner. The only factor that could possibly upset this calculation of mine is the sudden collapse of German morale—as in the last war. But of this, I see no signs whatsoever. The Fuehrer has guarded against this in advance, by crushing all opposition inside Germany—just as Marshal Stalin did in Russia.

The war in Europe will not be merely a war of arms, but a war of nerves as well. The side that has the stronger morale will win ultimately—and that is the German side. From the purely Indian point of view, the prolonged war in Europe will be beneficial for us in the sense that it will tie up the enemy forces there. Had the Anglo-Americans left the Continent alone and had they not landed in Italy and in France, they could have diverted their land and naval forces to India and other parts of East Asia. This they cannot do any longer, because of their commitments in Europe. Consequently, the present campaign of the Anglo-Americans in Europe is a direct help in our struggle for liberty.

In conclusion, I want to repeat again that the Indian situation is independent of the European situation. No matter what happens in Europe in future, the Indian people have a God-sent opportunity for achieving their liberation. Consequently, though the European situation will continue to be interesting for us—we need not really worry about what will happen there. Freedom is now within reach. Let us grasp it while the opportunity lasts—and let us strike while the iron is hot.

JAI HIND.

45

The Situation in East Asia

[Broadcast on 9 July 1944][1]

Friends and Countrymen at home,

Yesterday I spoke to you about the situation in Europe. Today, I shall talk about the situation in East Asia with special reference to India. Like yesterday, I shall again speak to you, today, largely from personal knowledge, and not from theoretical study.

I shall introduce today's subject by a comparison of the general conditions prevailing in the last world war, with those of the present war. In the last world war, Japan was on the side of the Allies, and the enemies of the British Empire were to be found only in Europe and the Near East, that is Western Asia. For those Indian revolutionaries who were working outside India during the last war and wanted to bring help to India in the struggle for liberty, the problem of communications was well nigh insoluble. Attempts made to bring assistance to India by sea with the help of 'Komagata Maru' and other ships were easily frustrated, while the passage to India from the North West was closely guarded by the British. The present war, however, has opened up the eastern gateway of India and it is the easiest thing for us now to cross the frontier and enter our homeland.

In the last war, enemies could concentrate their entire war-effort in Europe and the Near East—because the rest of Asia was under the Allied influence or control. In the present war, since December 1941, our enemies have had to fight not only in Europe and the Near East—but in East Asia as well. This dispersion of enemy strength coupled

[1] *Blood Bath*, pp. 44–51.

with the catastrophic defeats inflicted on the Anglo-Americans by the Japanese Army and Navy, has been the greatest help to India in her struggle for freedom. The battles in Europe since September 1939 and in East Asia since December 1941 have revealed to the Indian masses that the British lion, of whom they were so much frightened at one time, has, in reality, feet of clay. This shattering of British prestige before the eyes of the Indian people has been possible because of the might of Japan in East Asia and of Germany in Europe. With its former strength seriously crippled in the course of this war and with its prestige irreparably damaged—the days of the British Empire are now numbered.

The titanic world-conflict that is now going on is not for deciding as to whether Britain will be able to continue her world hegemony in future. That problem has already been settled. For a student of history possessing insight who can look into the future, the British are as dead as a doornail. The only question that remains to be solved is whether world hegemony will pass into the hands of USA, in future, or whether it will give room to a new order in this world, which will guarantee to all nations a place in the sun. When I think of these countrymen of mine at home, who are still dreaming of a post-war world in which the British Empire will exist and in which Indians will remain as slaves—I am filled with pity for them because they have sunk so deep—morally and spiritually—as a result of slavery. The darkness of slavery has so blinded them that they cannot see the sun of liberty that is now rising.

Even Indians who are highly educated and cultured are, in some cases, so infected with the virus of slavery that they forget that empires—like individuals—age, decay and die. Once old age and senile decay have set in, rejuvenation is impossible. Neither by the grafting of glands nor by the use of crutches can an old man become young again. With the help of American crutches, old Winston Churchill and his old Empire are still managing to stand up. But the Empire that vanished from Hongkong to the Chindwin River within a few months cannot be brought back to life even by a miracle.

With regard to the situation in this part of this world, there are but two problems to solve. Firstly, will America's strength and resources be able to restore what the Anglo-Americans lost after their catastrophic defeats in East Asia. And secondly, what will the fate of India be in future? Will Britain, with America's help be able to maintain her Empire in India?

Regarding the first question, I confess that I was anxious until it was announced to the world that President Roosevelt, after meeting Premier Churchill, has decided that the Anglo-Americans would first concentrate on the European theatre of war. If they had done the reverse and if they had decided on the 'Pacific First' policy—then I would personally have been alarmed. If the Anglo-American forces had not landed in Italy and in France and they had diverted their whole strength to the Pacific, then Japan would have had a hard time. Moreover, President Roosevelt would then have been able—with his shrewd propaganda—to rouse so much enthusiasm for the war against Japan in the USA that he could have made the present war a holy war, or a crusade for the entire American nation. Besides the fact that the USA regards Japan as their greatest enemy and rival because of economic and political reasons, the Americans hate the Japanese and other Asiatics because of colour prejudice. Consequently, the war against Japan could have been popularized in the USA President Roosevelt could have roused the morale of the American nation to an unprecedented height. But he did not do so. And that he did not do so is an indication that destiny is now working for Japan, for Asia and for India.

Because fate has ordained that the Anglo-Americans will be ultimately defeated, President Roosevelt wrongly decided on the 'Europe First' policy. Now, war in Europe is not at all popular in the USA and for several reasons into which we need not enter here. Consequently, over a European war, enthusiasm in the USA cannot possibly be worked up to a level which can inspire the American people to stake everything in the war. This 'Do or Die' spirit, which is indispensable for winning a war of the present magnitude, is possessed by Japan, and this will be the fundamental cause of her final victory.

The Anglo-Americans have always been saying that they will finish the war in Europe first and then turn with all their might towards East Asia and Japan. A few months ago, Premier Churchill repeated this in his message to Marshal Chiang Kai Shek on the occasion of the seventh anniversary of Chungking's war against Japan. But it will have to be seen how the war in Europe is finished and by whom. Speaking for myself, I may prophesize that the 'Europe First' policy will sap Anglo-

American strength to such an extent that they will never be able to defeat Japan in East Asia. Once again, history will prove that to fight a big war on two fronts is a suicidal policy.

According to enemy propagandists the whole case for an Anglo-American victory rests on the so-called colossal war-production of the USA. But when we analyze American war production, we find that there is a limit to it. American production has already reached its peak, and, in future, it will decline, instead of going up. So far as Japan is concerned, from the preparations that have been made and from the measures that have been adopted, one can confidently expect that Japan's war-production will go up in future. Whoever disbelieves this statement has only to wait and see what actually happens in the days to come.

Then there remains the question of American morale. There is no doubt that American morale is today very much higher than British morale. But how long can it be kept up? If President Roosevelt adopted the 'Pacific First' policy and thereby converted the present war into a popular, national war of the American people, then American morale could have been bolstered up for a very long time—and in spite of setbacks and defeats. Apart from the fact that over a European war American enthusiasm cannot be roused to a fever pitch—the unquestionable fact remains that neither Britain nor the USA are fighting for their very existence, as Japan and Germany are. They are fighting for world hegemony—Britain in order to maintain it in future and the USA in order to win it for the future. Consequently, it will be impossible for the Americans to keep up their morale for long. Production alone cannot bolster up a nation's morale. And if richness of equipment could be a guarantee of victory, then France would never have been defeated by Germany in this war. We shall, therefore, see, in future, that as American losses in the European battlefields go on mounting up, American strength and morale will be seriously undermined. If, after that, the Anglo-Americans try to divert their whole strength and resources to East Asia, they will no longer be in a position to constitute a dangerous menace to Japan. I say this quite regardless of whether the Anglo-Americans will be able to win the war in Europe or not. As to what chances the Anglo-Americans will have of winning the battle of Europe, I have already replied in my yesterday's talk.

The war in East Asia will be long and bitter. Nobody knows that more than Japan herself. Before Japan took up the sword against the USA and Britain, every possible calculation was made and the necessary preparations were effected. Since the beginning of the war, Japan has further consolidated her position in East Asia and has speeded up her war production considerably. The morale of the Japanese nation and Japanese armed forces has also gone up a hundredfold. I do not, therefore, see any possibility of the USA being able to best Japan in future. I know quite well that, of late, the Americans have had some successes in the Pacific and that they have been able to occupy some islands that were formerly under Japanese occupation or control. But these islands belong to the outer circle of defense. The inner circle—the iron ring, if I may use that expression—remains and will remain in Japanese hands. Into that iron ring, the Americans will never be able to break. The Americans will go on nibbling at the outer circle, and Japan will go on maintaining her hold over the inner circle, until American morale ultimately begins to crack. This will be a war, not only of arms, but also of nerves, as I said yesterday. And nobody in the world will, I hope, dispute the fact that Japan's morale is much higher than that of the USA and that Japanese nerves will stand the coming strain much better than American nerves can or will.

My critics will probably raise the question of Chungking China, here and ask as to what Chungking can do to help an Allied Victory in East Asia. Nobody will minimize that military value of the prolonged resistance, which Chungking armies have put up against the armies of Nippon, and the people and soldiers of Nippon are themselves too realistic to ignore facts. But Chungking's moral foundation has been seriously undermined by Japan's New Policy in China and by the latest agreement between the National Government of China and Japan—whereunder Japan has agreed to withdraw her troops from China on the termination of hostilities. By this agreement, the Chinese people have obtained practically all their demands. What then is Chungking now fighting for? This is the question which is in the minds of everybody in East Asia today. The result of Japan's new policy in China has been that among the Chinese people themselves there is a large section now who think that since an honourable peace with Japan is possible, hostilities should be ended and the work of national restoration and national reconstruction should begin. The more the National Government of China is proceeding with national reconstruction, the more is the desire for peace spreading among the Chinese nation as a whole. Chungking is, therefore, in a morally weak position today. This weakness is further heightened by the internal difficulties which have been confronting Chungking for some time past.

With regard to the internal situation in Chungking, I shall not refer to any Axis or Nipponese observers or commentators—but shall quote an American writer. Cabling only a few days ago, Archibald Steele, the correspondent of the *Chicago Daily News*, remarked—'Weary under the accumulated burdens of seven years of war. Chungking entered the eighth year of the conflict with the realization that it will probably be the most critical of its existence. Economically and militarily, Chungking is in most difficult straits. The past year was a hard one for Chungking—by far the hardest of the war so far. Inflationary tendencies reached exaggerated forms. The Chungking Army suffered heavily from the blockade and other factors and has grown progressively weaker.' Pointing out that the remaining powers of resistance are being further sapped by the large-scale Nippon offensive in south-eastern China, the correspondent said, 'In the tempers of the people, too, can be plainly discerned the War's fatiguing effect.' He added Chungking is 'Tired, very tired.'

Knowing the critical situation in Chungking, the Americans have been trying every subterfuge in order to somehow keep up the morale of Chungking. They have, of course, tried to influence Chungking-China with the help of pro-American Chinese circles in Chungking. They have, in addition, been holding out hopes that the Burma Road will be opened before long and that large scale help and assistance will then be sent through India to Chungking. In accordance with the assurance, the Anglo-Americans began a gigantic onslaught on Burma from north to south. This offensive—which was advertised as a campaign for the re-conquest of Burma—has now fizzled out and its effect on Chungking can better be imagined than described. Another clever subterfuge attempted by the Anglo-Americans is to hold out the prospect before Chungking that in the event of Japan being defeated, China will become the dominant power in Asia. The fact, however, is that in the event of a Japanese defeat, China will definitely pass under American influence and control. Be that as it may, the American trick might have worked if things had gone on well with Chungking. But things being what they are at Chungking and Chungking's morale being so low, now as a result of the recent defeat suffered by the Chungking America at Changsha and elsewhere—American propaganda can longer be effective.

To sum up, Chungking is now in such a terrible plight and is herself so badly in need of help from the Anglo-Americans that it would be no exaggeration to say that Chungking's contribution to the Allied struggle as against Japan in East Asia, can, in future, be little indeed. From the above review of the situation in East Asia, I can safely draw the conclusion that it is impossible for the Anglo-Americans to defeat Japan. Japan is bound to come out victorious at the end. I say this regardless of what will ultimately happen in the European theatre of war.

I shall now come to India and answer the second question as to what India can achieve in the present complex of events.

Britain, during her past history, always based her strategy and her military preparations in India on the supposition that an enemy-attack could come only from the North-West. Now that the eastern gateway of India has been suddenly thrown open, I see the hand of God in it—particularly because in the region to the East of India, three million patriotic Indians are living.

These three millions of Indians have now been organized politically and militarily and they have a government of their own, which is formally recognized by nine friendly powers of the world. Indians in East Asia are united to a man. Religious and other differences, which the British have always tried to engineer in India, do not exist among them. They are pledged to fulfil the programme of Total Mobilization—Total Mobilization of men, money and materials—for effectively conducting the armed struggle for the liberation of India. They have a modern army of their own, which, since March last, has been fighting on the soil of India.

The only question is as to whether this army—the Azad Hind Fauj—with the help of the armed forces of Japan and with the assistance of freedom-loving Indians at home—can overthrow the British Power in India. I answer—'YES.'

I am talking as a realist and from experience. I know the strength of the British in India. I also know the strength the Indian people have in the country. I have seen the strength of the Anglo-American forces on the Indo-Burma frontier and in the region of Manipur and Assam inside India. I have seen and talked to the prisoners of war who have come over to our side during this campaign since February last. I have got the reports of our colleagues and of our agents who are now working inside India. From all this, I have not the slightest doubt in my mind that we shall be able to liberate India from the foreign yoke.

But it will be a long and hard struggle. On the soil of India, the British will fight desperately in the last effort to save their Empire. They will fight—as they have never fought during the course of this war. But we shall fight more bravely than the British and their mercenaries can—or will. Moreover, we have the consciousness that we are fighting for justice,—for Truth—and for our birthright of liberty. Now that we are prepared to pay the full price of liberty—and have modern arms and modern army to fight with—no power on earth can stand between us and our victory. India shall be free this time. This is our unshakeable resolve and that is also God's will.

JAI HIND

46

The Indian Situation

[Broadcast on 10 July 1944][1]

Friends and Countrymen at home,

In today's talk, I shall sum up what I have been saying about the Indian situation during the last few days and shall reiterate our plans for the future. We have progressed so far towards our goal and feel so confident of our ultimate victory that I see no objection in doing so. There are times when the soundest strategy consists—not in concealing your plans—but in laying all your cards on the table.

In India, one can find three types of men. The first type consists of those who can never think of freedom even in their wildest dream. They form, however, a despicable, microscopic minority—though some among them are even educated and cultured. We can safely ignore them. The second type consists of those who desire freedom and, at heart, hate the British—but who, owing to human frailty, do not do anything active, though from time to time, they give passive assistance to us. These people are mostly to be found in the ranks of Government officials and employees of all categories. They will come and join us openly, when our victory appears to be a certainty to the man in the street. I have myself seen in Europe how after a revolutionary change, men of this type come forward to support the new order. I have seen this in new and independent states like Croatia and Slovakia and in Austria after the Union with Germany. In Burma, too, I have seen ex-I.C.S. men, ex-High Court Judges and ex-Officials of all categories joining the new administration set up by the Independent Government

[1] *Blood Bath*, pp. 52–60.

of Burma. We, too, expect that in India, men of this type will give their support to the new Government of Azad Hind. We shall accept them, of course, provided there is no charge against them that, under British rule, they were pro-British at heart. In fact, I can make an official announcement to the effect that all those who are now in the service of the British Government and are efficient in their work, will be taken over by the new Government of Free India or Azad Hind—provided they were not pro-British at heart and, while in British service, had not gone out of their way to harm the Independence Movement. In the case of members of the British-Indian Army, who have come, or in future will come over to our side, during this War of Independence, the Provisional Government of Free India or Azad Hind has already declared that they will be treated exactly like other members of the Azad Hind Fauj and will receive pension, after retirement, for the period they previously served in the British-Indian Army, plus their period of service in the Azad Hind Fauj.

The third type of men in India consists of those who are not only freedom loving, but who do something actively for the achievement of Independence. It is to them chiefly that I am addressing this talk.

Now, for a freedom-loving Indian, what are the alternative paths to freedom? The first alternative is prayer and petition, relying on the belief that the British will grant us freedom as a gift, at the end of the war. I rule out this possibility—for no self-respecting Indian believes in this any longer.

The second alternative is the policy of 'Wait and See'—trusting in the belief that since the position of the British will become more precarious in future, they will be forced by the war situation to accept and fulfill our demand for liberty. According to these people, freedom will fall into our lap as a ripe fruit in the fullness of time and we have nothing particular to do, but to patiently bide our time. This alternative, too, I want to rule out. I have said, so often, to my countrymen that the British have decided, once for all, that, come what may, they will hang on to India till the last. The worse their position becomes elsewhere, the more greedily will they hold on to India—believing that if India can somehow be saved for the British, the British Empire will be saved.

The third alternative is the path of 'Satyagraha' or 'Civil Disobedience', which the Indian National Congress has been pursuing since

1921. Will this method bring us independence? I am definitely of the opinion that it will not. That is also what the history of the last twenty years teaches us. I know that in 1921, many people of the Congress honestly believed that 'Satyagraha' or 'Civil Disobedience' would bring us Swaraj. That idea or belief was based on two suppositions, both of which have since been falsified. The first supposition was that the British Government was capable of undergoing a 'change of heart'. The second supposition was that under the pressure of 'Satyagraha' movement, the British would see the error of their ways—would realize that the old order could no longer be kept up by force—and would, therefore, act like true statesmen—as they did in Canada and in South Africa. We have now realized that the government is devoid of heart and where there is no heart, no change of heart is possible. We have also realized that Britain's policy for a non-white race is different from her policy for a white race. Moreover, the British feel that if India goes out of the Empire, the cornerstone of the Empire will fall at once and the Empire will cease to exist. Even a grant of Dominion status will ultimately lead to India's secession from the Empire. Unlike Canada or South Africa, there is nothing to bind India to the Empire and once she reaches the status of a Dominion, she will endeavour to get out of the Empire altogether. In this connection, the recent history of Ireland has had a far-reaching effect on British attitude and mentality—which is not yet realized by many Indians at home. When British politicians of all schools of thought subscribed to the Anglo-Irish treaty in 1921—they thought the problem was solved once for all. But when President de Valera appeared on the scene in 1932, the Irish problem was re-opened, and the demand for a Republic was renewed. Since President de Valera came in power, the British have done their best to overthrow or undermine him, but they have failed. With the powers and resources of a Dominion Government, President de Valera has been fighting the British so far, and he has been fighting them more effectively than as a rebel from 1916 to 1921. The British, therefore, argue within themselves that India will follow the way of Ireland, and whatever concessions are granted to India will be used by the Indian people to fight the British more effectively in future. Therefore, it is more wise for the British to suppress the Indian Independence Movement, as long as they can do so. Now, 'Satyagraha' cannot bring about the physical overthrow of British rule or the physical expulsion of the British from India. 'Satyagraha' can only bring independence in a peaceful way, through an honourable understanding with the British. But this has been rendered impossible because of the British resolve to crush the 'Satyagraha' Movement with naked brute force. Consequently, for one who really desires freedom—there is no other alternative but to resort to the historic method of struggle. Thus, we are driven to the fourth and last alternative—namely, the use of arms for winning freedom.

A large section of the Indian people—and Indian Youths in particular—are conscious of this. That is why a secret revolutionary movement has been going on in the country, with varying tempo and vigour, during the last forty years. In the course of this movement, arms have been secured and bombs and explosives have been manufactured secretly. Now, what hopes are there of winning freedom through a revolutionary movement with or without the 'Satyagraha' Movement? Past history furnishes an answer to this question. The use of arms on a small scale and by an unorganized body of men is incapable of overthrowing a foreign government that is based on brute force and is determined to use brute force ruthlessly, whenever necessary. For winning freedom, it is not enough to use arms. Modern arms are needed, and they must be wielded by a modern army.

Had it been possible to organize a modern army inside India, and to procure arms for that army inside the country—no help from outside would have been necessary, and that would have been the best course for the Indian people. But anybody who knows the Indian situation and also knows how the Indian people were disarmed after 1857—will agree that it is quite impossible to build up a revolutionary army or to procure arms for that army within the country. But that is no reason why the struggle should be given up as hopeless. Every disease has a remedy—however difficult—and every problem has a solution—if we only discover it. The remedy, in this case, is to organize an army outside—procure the necessary arms for it there, and then march into the country. This is what Indians in East Asia are now doing.

What Indians in East Asia are doing is not without precedent in world history. For instance, during the last world war, the Irish Sinn Feiners got both money and arms from the USA and, in addition, they got arms from Germany. In the Italian struggle for freedom in 1859, the French Army of Napoleon III was invited by the Italians to help them to fight the Austrian Army of occupation in Italy. In the history of the Balkan struggle for liberation from the Turkish yoke, Bulgaria was emancipated with the help of the Russian Army. In fact, as I often said before, I have not found a single instance in the history of revolutions when freedom has been won without help from outside of some sort.

I have remarked above that the Independence of India can never be achieved through a non-violent struggle. If, however, the miracle was possible, and 'Satyagraha' by itself could bring us to our goal—nobody would be more happy than ourselves. All the gigantic effort that we are now putting forward in East Asia would, in that case, be rendered unnecessary.

In this connection, I wish to say that all those who sincerely desire freedom and have hitherto been working through non-violent means—should now support an armed struggle, when all other means have failed. I know that our youths are doing so—and will, in future, do so. But what about the older leaders? They should also do the same. I am sorry that a few of the older of the Congress leaders—out of sheer despair—are showing a tendency to fall back on the already discredited policy and method of our moderate and liberals. This is to be greatly regretted.

I shall now recapitulate in brief the strategy of our movement. We know that so long as the British Army in India is not attacked from outside, it will be able to suppress the revolutionary movement in the country. The Azad Hind Fauj has, therefore, set up the 'Second Front' in India's war of emancipation. When we advance further into India and the Indian people see with their own eyes the British force falling back—they will get the confidence that Britain's downfall is at hand. Then only will they risk their necks and come and join hands with our advancing forces to liberate the country. Together, we shall then pursue the British and expel them from the soil of India.

In working out any strategy—political or military—one should always understand the psychology of the people. This is a basic requirement for any struggle. Indians in East Asia have seen a vast Empire vanishing from Hongkong to the Chindwin River before their very eyes and within a few months. That is why they are supremely confident of defeating and overthrowing the British in India. Our countrymen at home have not had this experience. That is why they have a lurking fear in their minds that perhaps British power in India is still too powerful to be broken. We have, first, to remove the illusion from their minds before we can expect the revolution to break out. To break that illusion and to instill self-confidence into the minds of the overawed Indian people, the Azad Hind Fauj will have to fight and shed its blood. Once the British are forced to run—as they were forced to run in Malaya and in Burma—the Azad Hind Fauj will have fulfilled its first and most difficult task.

Considering the historic role of the Azad Hind Fauj, it is interesting to remember that this army was organized on one of the graveyards of the British Empire—the once impregnable fortress of Singapore. The Azad Hind Fauj, therefore, started its existence with the unshakeable conviction that destiny had already passed the death-sentence on the British Empire and that the Azad Hind Fauj was but an instrument for carrying out the execution.

The question here arises as to why we need the help of Japan in the struggle of ours. In Ireland the Irish Sinn Feiners had only five thousand irregulars, at the most, for fighting fifty thousand well-disciplined troops of the British. In Italy, Garibaldi started his military campaign with only one thousand ragged volunteers. Why then do we need the aid of Japan?

The answer to this is clear. If we had to fight the pre-war British Army in India, we would not have needed any outside assistance. But during the course of this war, the British have built up a gigantic army in our country. Moreover, they have brought additional troops, arms and equipment from all over the world—from England, from America, from Africa, from other parts of the British Empire and from Nepal. The once almighty British have been going round the world with the begging-bowl. We have, therefore, been forced to take help from generous Japan. Let the British Army in India return to its pre-war strength and I guarantee that without the aid of Japan's armed forces, we shall be able to liquidate British power in India. And if the British accept Mahatma Gandhi's 'Quit India' resolution and give effect to it—I guarantee that not a single Japanese soldier will set foot on Indian soil, in future, and that those Japanese troops that are already in India will gladly withdraw from our homeland at once.

Having outlined the whole strategy of our campaign, I shall now tell my countrymen why I feel so confident of our final victory.

First of all, I see that in accordance with the laws of history the British Empire is now in a process of decay. No artificial stimulation, like American aid, can restore that Empire to its pristine youth and glory. But an Empire in decay does not die all of a sudden. Even when the hand of Death approaches, there is a struggle, sometimes a hard struggle—before life surrenders to Death. That is why the British are still fighting, and that is why they will fight hard in future before they collapse.

Secondly, I see that the Indian people are now sufficiently advanced and sufficiently capable to be able to take charge of their own affairs. They have had sufficient schooling for this.

Thirdly, I see that there is a widespread national awakening in the country, and the people are prepared for the suffering and sacrifice that is essential for winning freedom. Moreover, they are politically well organized and well disciplined.

Fourthly, the one thing that we had been lacking so far—namely, an army of liberation—has come into existence.

Fifthly, military aid, from outside, which is indispensably necessary for India's emancipation, has now become possible, because of the opening of the eastern gateway of India and because of the strenuous efforts of Indians in East Asia.

Sixthly, thanks to a sudden development of the war situation, Britain's preparations for the defence of India in the Northwest have been set at naught. On geographical and political grounds, our advance into India from the East is to our advantage and to Britain's disadvantage.

Seventhly, we have been able to build up a strong base in East Asia for our campaign inside India. Three million Indians in East Asia have been organized into a formidable force through the 'Total Mobilization' of all their resources in men, money and materials. They will be able to effectively support our campaign inside India, as long as it will be necessary.

Eighthly, we have in Japan a first class modern power on whose help we can fall back, in crisis—particularly, if the combination of allied forces in India proves to be too strong for us.

Ninthly, there is no danger of Chungking being able to stab us in the back, when we advance into India from Burma.

Tenthly, we are led by a government of our own, which has been recognized by nine friendly powers and has their support.

Eleventh, though the general war situation is in our favour, we are, nevertheless, independent of the situation in Europe, and we shall win—regardless of what may happen in Europe in future.

Last but not least, we know the comparative strength of the enemy and of ourselves. We are strengthened by the consciousness—which the enemy does not possess—that we are fighting for justice, truth and our birthright and liberty. Our determination to fight till the end is, therefore, unshakeable. Moreover, we are now prepared to pay the full price of liberty with our blood.

Before I close today's talk, I shall say a few words about the fighting that is now going on along the Indo-Burma frontier and inside India. The most remarkable thing about this campaign is that it has finally dished the British plans for the re-conquest of Burma. To hide their discomfiture, the British are now saying that we have failed to reach Delhi, and they are inventing fictitious dates for our entry into Delhi.

Friends! Only a fool would minimize the strength of the enemy. We have seen heterogeneous armies of our enemies in the Arakans, in the Kaladan and Haka sectors, in the Tiddim area and in Manipur and Assam. As we anticipated long ago, their rations and equipment are superior to ours, because they have been looting India in order to fight us. We have, nevertheless, beaten them everywhere. Revolutionary armies everywhere in the world have to fight under conditions similar to ours—but they, nevertheless, triumph at the end. Their strength does not come from beer and rum—tinned pork and bully beef, but from faith and sacrifice—heroism and fortitude. The Azad Hind Fauj—unlike the British Army in India—has been trained to fight under conditions of extreme difficulty and hardship, and it will never let down the 388 millions of Indians for whose liberation it is now fighting.

The strategic value of Manipur and Northeast Assam is so great that it is but natural that the British should put up a stiff resistance there. Both sides know that when Manipur is liberated, the British will have to withdraw over a wide area and for a considerable depth. But we and our officers are making the fullest use of our time and experience in the campaign inside India. A long and hard struggle is beneficial to our cause, because that is the only means whereby a new revolutionary army and its officers can have their schooling. We have not only to liberate India now—but also produce the army, the officers and the Generals who will be able to preserve India's independence for all time. Therefore, whatever is happening in Manipur and Assam now is all to the good.

The war that is going on inside India is not Japan's war against Britain and America—it is India's own war of liberation. That is why we are neither impatient nor nervous. From Manipur to Delhi is a long way. We are, therefore, to fight two full years, before we can hoist our tri-colour flag over our metropolis—because we know that however long and hard the struggle may be, it can have but one outcome—namely, our victory. Meanwhile, our enemies, who had prepared to evacuate India in 1942, may enjoy themselves yet a while and continue their plunder and loot, until the day comes when from the top of the Viceroy's House in New Delhi, the death-knell of the British Empire will be rung.

Jai Hind.

47

The Great Patriot and Leader

[Speech at a ceremonial parade at the tomb of Emperor Bahadur Shah on 11 July 1944][1]

Last year in the month of September, we had a ceremonial Parade here, at the Tomb of Emperor Bahadur Shah who was our leader in the Revolution of 1857—that is, in India's First War of Independence. That ceremony last year was a historic one in India's struggle for liberty and units of the Azad Hind Fauj, who then happened to be here at that time, took part in the parade. I say that ceremony was a historic one, because after 1857, this was the first occasion when India's new revolutionary army paid homage to the spirit of the Supreme Commander of India's first revolutionary army. Last year in the parade in September, all of us who were present, took a solemn vow to continue the work of Emperor Bahadur Shah and to bring about the liberation of India from the British yoke. I am happy and proud to be able to say now that we have been able to redeem that pledge in part. Most of the troops who were then present here are now fighting at the front. The Azad Hind Fauj, after crossing the Indian frontier, is now fighting on the soil of our motherland.

It is an extraordinary—perhaps Providential—coincidence that this year, the celebration of the death anniversary of Emperor Bahadur Shah has synchronized with the celebration of Netaji Week—during which Indians all over East Asia have renewed their solemn pledge to continue the struggle till complete independence is achieved. It is also

[1] *Blood Bath*, pp. 61–5, translated from the original Hindustani.

an indication of the will of Providence that the place where the Supreme Commander in the First War of Independence laid down his mortal remains has become the base for India's Last War of Independence. It is from this place—this holy place, which is now our base—that our troops are advancing towards their motherland. That is why we have met here once again in a solemn ceremonial parade of the Azad Hind Fauj to pay homage to the soul of that great patriot and leader—to express our great joy at the partial fulfilment of last year's pledge—and to tighten our belts and reaffirm our vow to go on fighting, until the sacred soil of India is liberated from the unwanted Britisher.

It would be proper for me to say a few words about the events of 1857. English historians have falsely propagated the story that the fight of 1857 was a mutiny of the Indian soldiers in British service. In reality, it was a national revolution, in which both Indian troops and Indian civilians participated. Many of the Indian princes joined in this nation-wide struggle, though, unfortunately, some among them kept aloof. In the early stage of that war, we scored victory after victory, and it was only towards the end that we were overpowered and defeated. This is nothing unusual in the history of a revolution. In the world's history, you will rarely find a revolution where success was achieved in the first struggle. 'Freedom's battle once begun is always bequeathed from sire to son.' Even if a revolution fails for the time being and is crushed, it leaves its lessons behind. Posterity learns these lessons and then renews the struggle in a more effective manner, after making better preparations. We have learnt the lessons of our failure in 1857 and, in the light of that experience, we have prepared for this struggle—which is India's Last War of Independence.

It would be a mistake to think that in 1857 the Indian people suddenly took up arms one fine morning against the British. No revolution is fought in that hasty or haphazard manner. Our leaders in 1857 did their best to prepare for that fight, though their preparations subsequently proved to be inadequate. Nana Sahib, for instance, who was one of the prominent leaders in that holy war, had travelled all over Europe, trying to get foreign aid and assistance. Unfortunately, he had failed in that attempt and when the revolution broke out in 1857, Britain was at peace with the rest of the world and could devote all her strength and resources to the task of crushing the Indian people. Inside the country, propaganda had been carried on among the Indian Troops for some time in a most intelligent and remarkable manner, with the result that when the signal was given, fighting commenced simultaneously in different parts of the country. Victory after victory was scored. The important towns in Northern India were liberated from the hands of the British, and the revolutionary troops marched into India's metropolis with colours flying. The first phase of the campaign ended with the triumph of the revolution almost everywhere. In the second phase of the campaign, when the counteroffensive of the enemy began, our men could not hold their ground. It was then found that the revolutionaries lacked a nation-wide strategy and a dynamic leader who could co-ordinate the strategy. Moreover, in certain parts of the country, the princes remained inactive and indifferent. Referring to this, Bahadur Shah wrote to the Rajahs of Jaipur, Jodhpur, Bikaner, Alwar, etc. as follows:

'It is my ardent wish to see that the English are driven out of Hindustan by all means and at any cost. It is my ardent wish that the whole of Hindustan should be free. But the revolutionary war that has been waged for this purpose cannot be crowned with success, unless a man capable of sustaining the whole burden of the movement, who can organize and concentrate the different forces of the nation and unify the whole people in himself, comes forward to guide this rising. I have no desire left in me of ruling over India after the expulsion of the English to my own aggrandizement. If all of you Rajahs are ready to unsheathe your swords to drive away the enemy, then I am willing to resign my Imperial Powers and authority in the hands of any confederacy of Indian Rajahs who may be chosen to exercise it.'

This letter written by Bahadur Shah in his own hand broaches the spirit of patriotism and self-sacrifice, to which every freedom-loving Indian will bow his head in admiration and respect. Old and weak as he was, Bahadur Shah felt that it was beyond his capacity to conduct the war himself. He, therefore, set up a committee of six—consisting of three Generals and three civilians—who would be in charge of the whole campaign. But all his efforts failed—perhaps because the time was not ripe for the complete independence of India.

There is another fact which demonstrates the revolutionary spirit and fervour which inspired the old leader. In the proclamation, which was posted on the walls of Bareilly in the United Provinces, Bahadur Shah said:

'In this our army, the difference of small and great shall be forgotten and equality shall be the rule, for, all who draw the sword in this holy war are equally glorious. They are brethren; there is no rank among them. Therefore, I, again, say to all my Indian brethren, arise and jump into the battlefield for this divinely ordained and supreme duty.'

I have referred to all these facts in order to show you that the foundation of our present Azad Hind Fauj was laid as far back as in 1857. In this Last War of Independence, we have before us the lessons of the first war of 1857 and of its failure. This time, Providence is on our side. Our enemy is engaged in a life-and-death struggle on several fronts. Our countrymen at home are wide-awake. The Azad Hind Fauj is a formidable force, and all members of this army are united in a common endeavour to emancipate their country. We have a common strategy for conducting the campaign over a long period till complete victory is achieved. Our base has been properly organized and—last but not least—we have the memory and the example of Bahadur Shah to inspire us to heroic deeds. Can there be any doubt that ultimate victory will be ours?

As I study the events of 1857 and think of the atrocities perpetrated by the British after the revolution collapsed—my blood begins to boil. If we are men, we will certainly see to it that the heroes of 1857 and after, who suffered so much from British terror and brutality, are properly avenged. India demands revenge. The British who spilt the blood of innocent freedom-loving Indians and tortured them in an inhuman manner—not only during the war but after it was over—must pay for their crimes. We, Indians, do not hate the enemy enough. If you want your countrymen to rise to heights of superhuman courage and heroism you must teach them—not only to love their country—but also to hate their enemy.

Therefore, I call for blood. It is only the blood of the enemy that can avenge his crimes of the past. But we can take blood only if we are prepared to give blood. Consequently, our programme for the future is to give blood. The blood of our heroes in this war will wash away our sins of the past. The blood of our heroes will be the price of our liberty. The blood of our heroes—their heroism and their bravery—will secure for the Indian people the revenge that they demand of their British tyrants and oppressors.

With this prophetic insight, old Bahadur Shah said after his defeat:

Ghaziyon men bu rahegi jab talak iman ki
Takht London tak chalegi, tegh Hindostan ki

'As long as there is faith in the hearts of our freedom-fighters, the Sword of India will pierce the heart of London.' He was right. The liberation of India will pierce the heart of Britain and break up the British Empire.

JAI HIND.

48

Changing Tactics of Enemy Propaganda

[Broadcast on 12 July 1944][1]

Friends and Countrymen,

During the last few days, I have spoken to you at length about our activities in East Asia, our achievements during the last twelve months and our plans for the future. In a National Revolution of the biggest magnitude, it is not necessary to conceal one's strategy, or even the plan of operations. The success of our plans will depend on our winning over the entire Indian people to our side. Consequently, playing a game of bluff will be suicidal for us. We can impress our countrymen only by a frank and straightforward policy. We are fighting for justice, truth and our birthright of liberty. Of that, not even our enemies can have any doubt. The mass of the Indian people—we know—sympathize with us in their heart of hearts. The only question which worries them, is as to whether we shall succeed in our plans. Once they are convinced about that, they will come forward to join us openly. But having become chicken-hearted as a result of foreign servitude, they will hesitate to risk their necks, so long as the final issue of the struggle remains in doubt.

The game of our enemy is quite different from ours. They have no moral case for their domination over—and exploitation of—our country and people. The weapons that they use are, therefore, boastfulness, bluff, deceit and brute force. I know that an imperialist power will use

[1] *Blood Bath*, pp. 66–76.

every possible means for maintaining its hold over India and I am not surprised over it. What surprises and hurts me, however, is that some of our countrymen in the British service volunteer to do all the dirty work, which British imperialists should have taken upon themselves. Why should our countrymen sell themselves so abjectly for a few hundred rupees a month? The methods of British propaganda during the last war have been recorded in black and white by Englishmen themselves. One has only to read such books as 'Secrets of Crewe House' and 'Wartime Falsehoods' by Posenby to realize what British propagandists are capable of. It was an English General, Brigadier Charteris, who started the rumour in the last war that the Germans were extracting fat from the bodies of dead soldiers. He knew that it was a deliberate falsehood and after the war, he confessed that he had not hoped that this propaganda would strike roots. But the unsophisticated section of the world public thought that a British General could not lie and the trick, therefore, worked. Since then things have changed. The world public is no longer unsophisticated and thanks to the wireless and radio, propaganda from both sides can reach every corner of the world. That is one of the chief reasons why British propaganda in this war had proved to be ineffective. Nevertheless, a leopard cannot change its spots. The liar cannot stop lying, even if he knows that he is no longer trusted. He hopes against hope that there are still enough fools in this world who could be taken in. Consequently, I am not surprised that the British are continuing their game of lying and bluffing. But what is regrettable is that their hirelings in India do this dirty work for them. I know that there is a great economic distress in India and people are starving. But that is no reason why educated Indians—not only men, but sometimes also women—should come forward and sell themselves at a cheap price. On certain occasions, I have even heard men holding high degrees—lecturers of universities—doing lying propaganda from the transmitting rooms of the Anti-India Radio.

To illustrate what I say, I shall give an incidence of the enemy's lying propaganda. The Anti-India Radio has said more than once that I was so unpopular at home that I was removed from the Presidentship of the Congress and was forced to leave the country. Now, who in India does not know that in January 1939, I was re-elected President of the Congress with a decent majority, in spite of the opposition of Mahatma Gandhi and Pandit Nehru? Who in India does not know that if I had agreed to re-appoint the old Working Committee, I could have easily continued as President for another year with the approval of Mahatma Gandhi? Who in India does not know that the issue between Mahatma Gandhi and myself was that I desired and demanded a Working Committee to which I felt entitled as a result of my re-election? Who in India does not know that it was the easiest thing for me to remain at home or even in prison as a 'Security Prisoner'? Who in India does not know that it was the most difficult and most dangerous thing for me to escape from the clutches of the British? Does or does not the Anti-India Radio know that several police officers lost their jobs because they could not prevent my escape? Does or does not the Anti-India Radio know that secret agents were sent after me to try and murder me, if they failed to capture me?

There are other types of enemy propaganda, which, though not equally despicable are, at least, equally false. For instance, when, in 1943, I travelled round the world and reached Tokyo, it was a slap on the face of the British. To hide the discomfiture of our enemies, the Anti-India Radio was made to say—not once, but several times—that I had differences with the German Government and had, therefore, to leave Europe. The public reply to that lie was given when the German Government gave its wholehearted support to the Provisional Government of Azad Hind that was set up in East Asia and sent an official message, conveying the congratulations and good wishes of the German Government. Recently, to hide Lord Louis Mountbatten's discomfiture over his failure to re-conquer Burma and prevent the onward march of the Azad Hind Fauj, the Anti-India Radio has been propagating fictitious stories of differences between the Japanese Government and myself. The stories invented are to the effect that the Japanese Government is disappointed with me because no rising in the country has taken place after our troops marched into India. Everybody, who has been listening to my broadcast in India, knows, however, that I have repeatedly warned my countrymen over the radio not to commence a popular rising—or even large-scale sabotage—before we give the signal. Even a fool will realize that it will be suicidal on our part to attempt a rising or large-scale sabotage activity until our troops advance deeper into India and are in a position to bring help to those who revolt against the British. Once again I repeat that these propaganda tactics do not surprise me in the least. For those who would gladly have me murdered, such propaganda tactics are perfectly understandable. But what is surprising and humiliating is that in the year of grace, 1944, so many Indians could be found who can sell themselves for a paltry sum and do all the dirty work for our enemies. That the British should like to abuse me to their heart's content—call me Quisling, puppet and what not—is but natural. But why should they be able to find Mir Jafars and Umichands to do the lying propaganda for them? There is not a single Indian who will believe that I am capable of selling my country and myself to the Japanese or to any other foreign power.

Another dirty piece of the work that Indian mercenaries have been doing for the British is the lying propaganda about Japanese atrocities—and especially atrocities perpetrated by the Japanese on Indians. Can any Indian really believe that I and the rest of my countrymen in East Asia would co-operate wholeheartedly with the Japanese and fight shoulder to shoulder with their troops, if our countrymen had been ill-treated by them in any part of East Asia? When Japan has gone out of her way to give every support to the Indian Independence Movement and to give formal recognition to the Provisional Government of Free India, the least that our countrymen at home can do is to keep their mouths shut instead of propagating false stories about atrocities committed by the Japanese on the Indian people. Those who have not put up with ill treatment at the hands of the British, in spite of India being under British domination, would be the last persons in the world to put up with atrocities or ill treatment on the part of any other foreign power. Atrocity-propaganda is a favourite trick of the British propagandists. This time they have also become the protagonists of all the Indian religions—especially of Islam. As long as there was a pact between Germany and the Soviets and the possibility that the Soviets might give help to Indian Nationalists, the British propagandist—especially in the North West of India—carried on propaganda to the effect that the Bolsheviks were anti-religious. When the possibility of danger shifted from the Northwest to the Northeast of India, our enemies started propaganda to the effect that the Japanese were anti-religious, and, in particular, anti-Islam. Moulavis and Pandits were trained inside India and sent round to the different cantonments, posing to be new arrivals in East Asia, to do propaganda in the Indian Army to this effect. A few of the men who have been sent over to India by us were captured by the British and forced to do anti-Japanese propaganda to the effect that the Japanese were persecuting Muslims in East Asia. Our reply to that is, that Indian Muslims in East Asia are now working wholeheartedly with Hindus, Sikhs and Christians for the independence of the motherland. A still more effective reply to that propaganda is that within the ranks of the Azad Hind Fauj, there is a large percentage of Muslims and the percentage is still higher among the higher officers of that Army. These Muslim officers in the Indian National Army are not nobodies. They came of the best families in India, have been through the Military Academy at Dehra Dun and elsewhere and are widely known within the Indian Army itself.

I am saying all this not because I hope to convince or to convert those Indian mercenaries who have deliberately sold themselves for a mess of potage. I am saying this just to tell those mercenaries that we know that they are lying deliberately. In public affairs, it is a bad policy to let a lie go unchallenged. Though truth ultimately prevails in this world, we are nevertheless to fight in order that truth may triumph. In this modern age, the fight is to be carried on not only in the military sphere but also on the propaganda front. So far as the broad masses are concerned, I know that enemy propaganda does not have the slightest effect on them. That is why the Calcutta Radio has to give frequent and repeated warnings to the public not to be influenced by the propaganda of our colleagues and agents in India. The documents that we have captured during the last few months on the Indo-Burma frontier and inside India confirm the reports that we have received that the British authorities are upset over our work within the country and have had to promulgate several new ordinances of a drastic nature with a view to frustrating the activities of our colleagues and our agents in the country.

I shall come to the main issue that confronts the Indian people today—namely, India's demand for independence. I and my colleagues and fellow fighters have chalked out a plan—a concrete plan—for winning liberty for India. Whether the plan be good or bad, so long as no alternative plan is forthcoming, our plan is bound to hold the field. The only other alternative plan that has been meted is that of

Mahatma Gandhi embodied in the 'Quit India' Resolution. If that plan succeeds, our plan and our activities will be set at naught. On the contrary, if Mahatma Gandhi's plan fails—as it has failed—then all hopes of Indian independence will rest entirely on the fulfilment of our plan. Nobody would be more happy than ourselves if Mahatma Gandhi's plan were to succeed, because that would furnish a short-cut to freedom. But since that plan has failed, freedom-loving Indians, whether at home or abroad, have no other alternative but to fall back on the only other plan—that is, on our plan. If the British authorities really want to frustrate our activities, they have no other option but to make peace with Mahatma Gandhi and the Congress on the basis of the 'Quit India' Resolution.

Our enemies think that by calling me a dreamer, they will be able to discredit me. But I confess that I am a dreamer. I may tell my enemies that in dreaming dreams of India's freedom, I am in very good company. All those who have achieved big things in this world have been dreamers. A practical man and soldier like Napoleon Bonaparte was one of the biggest dreamers that the world has produced. If I did not dream dreams of India's Freedom, I would have accepted the chains of slavery as something eternal. The point is as to whether one can translate his dreams into realities. So far as I am concerned, I have redeemed all that I have promised. More than eighteen months ago, I declared that since no power on earth had been able to prevent my escape from India, no power on earth would be able to prevent my crossing the frontier again when the time was ripe. Both the Bluff and Bluster Corporation, London, as well as the Anti-India Radio, tried to ridicule me for that declaration. But they no longer speak about it because whether they officially recognize the fact or not, the whole world knows that troops of the Azad Hind Fauj are today fighting on Indian soil. The criticism that our enemies can now put forward is that we have not been able to reach Delhi yet. I know the exact distance from Manipur to India's metropolis and I have put down two years as the approximate length of the Indian campaign. With good luck, the campaign may end earlier—but we are prepared to fight for at least two years in order to hoist our National Flag over the Viceroy's House. For nearly a year, I have been saying that it is the easiest thing for us to cross the Indian frontier, but that once we are inside, the real fight will begin. The fight for India's liberation is also the fight for the destruction of the British Empire. It is, therefore, but natural that the British should, for once at least in this war, fight hard. But the death warrant of the British Empire has already been signed and all that remains is to execute the sentence.

It is a usual thing for British propagandists to resort to diversion-tactics when things go badly for them. In order to hide their own defeat, they begin to talk loudly of the success of the Americans or the Russians on some other front. If that is not possible, they try to put out some interesting story in order to divert public attention. Consequently, when things were going badly for the British on India's eastern front, they put out a story from the Anti-India Radio to the effect that 12 men who had been sent by us to India had gone over to the enemy, and they made six of them broadcast some anti-Japanese stuff from Delhi. They thought that thereby they would give the Indian people the impression that these men had gone to India to work not for us but for the Japanese. It is, of course, unfortunate for us that some of those who were sent by us to work on the home front were captured. Such incidents are bound to happen in a big struggle. I am thankful to those friends of ours who are working within the enemy camp for being able to persuade their masters to broadcast this incident. The Indian public must have realized from the Delhi broadcast that since we could send men to far-off Baluchistan, there is no part of India that we cannot reach. It is very curious indeed that the six men who spoke on the anti-India Radio, reported parrot like practically the same anti-Japanese stuff. It is also curious that after these broadcasts, enemy propagandists have again been observing a strange silence over this matter—just as in the case of Rudolph Hess, who went to England from Germany in 1941, the BBC, after noisily and enthusiastically announcing the fact, suddenly discovered that 'though speech was silver, silence was golden.' Recently, enemy propagandists have again been compelled to put out a story regarding certain desertions from the Azad Hind Fauj. Too much haste in propaganda is a bad policy. I should therefore remind the Anti-India Radio once again of the oft-quoted saying, 'he laughs best who laughs last.'

The Anti-India Radio has recently been talking of the great deeds performed by the British General, Montgomery. I am glad that it does not talk of the ever-retreating Field Marshal Lord Wavell or General Auchinleck or amphibious Admiral Lord Louis Mountbatten. But I may remind our enemies that the British by themselves have not won a single battle in this war, except where they were fighting only the Indians as in Eritrea, Abyssinia. Whatever successes General Montgomery has achieved are due almost entirely to American intervention and American support. Otherwise, the British would have won these victories before the Americans appeared on the scene.

For a fairly long time, enemy propagandists put out a story that the Azad Hind Fauj was a puppet army who has been forced to fight Japan's war. But they ultimately realized that the trick was not working. Everybody was naturally asking as to how a puppet army could fight so bravely and so stubbornly. The tactics have now been altered, and the world is being told that the Azad Hind Fauj is a ragged army with poor rations and poor equipment. I wonder if that is all that our enemies have now to say about the Azad Hind Fauj. We never claimed that we had an army as well equipped as the British Army in India. It is easy for the British to loot India in order to feed and clothe their army. But I may inform my enemies that our troops know in advance the conditions under which a revolutionary army, like ours, has to fight. Unlike the British army who can fight only with the force of beer and rum, tinned pork and bully beef, our soldiers have been trained to fight under conditions of extreme hardship. Revolutionary armies all over the world—whether in Ireland or Italy or Russia or elsewhere—have to fight under similar conditions. Everywhere they have won at the end. So, also, shall we. But we shall first have to pay for our liberty with our blood.

British propagandists are now telling the Indian people that though the Azad Hind Fauj has come into Manipur, it will never be able to reach Delhi. We never mentioned any date, by which we promised to reach Delhi. No one in his senses would do that. It is the Anti-India Radio that has been inventing fictitious dates for our entry into Delhi and has been criticizing us for not working according to timetable. A powerful empire, like the British Empire, backed by many other powers, has been fighting for nearly five years. But what has it achieved? If we, with our slender resources put down two years as the length of the Indian campaign, will that be too much? Let the Anti-India Radio wait till the 4th of February 1946, and then start criticizing us if our time-table goes wrong.

The 'leit motive' or principal motive of enemy propaganda appears to be a two-fold one—to create the impression that the British are sure to win the war and, secondly, to rouse anti-Japanese feeling in the country. To achieve the first objective, our enemies have been talking continually of post-war reconstructions as if victory was within the hollow of their hand. They have also been exaggerating every allied success in the world. But when we analyse the so-called success, what do we find? What, for instance, have the allies achieved in Italy? They had to send more men, war materials, more aeroplanes and more war-ships to Italy. At the present rate, when will the Italian campaign end? And when will the allied troops cross the Brenner to march into Germany? In France, where the German counter-attack has not yet begun in full force, what have the allies achieved in seven weeks? What have the allies won considering the heavy losses they have incurred? From the Indian point of view, the deeper the allies go into Italy and France, the better it will be for us. The so-called victories that they have achieved or may achieve in future will seriously cripple their strength. And the possibility still remains that the Allies may be ultimately thrown out of France and be held up in Italy. All this talk of finishing the war in Europe first and then coming over to East Asia to overthrow Japan is—to use a slang language—all 'Tommy Rot'. I have already said in a previous talk that the Anglo-American will never be able to win the battle of Europe. But I go so far as to say that even if they were to come out victorious, they will have no strength left to face Japan in East Asia. Let us not forget that there is a limit to war-production and a limit to human strength. Consequently, in spite of what appears on the surface today, the situation is for the Allies dark indeed.

There is one thing I forgot to mention, when I was discussing Manipur. What about the poor Maharajah of Manipur? Where is he today? Where are the pro-Congress Princes? Under what conditions are the Maharajah and his family living? When so many Maharajahs and Nawabs have been going all over the place working as recruiting sergeants, why has the Maharajah of Manipur been so silent since the beginning of the war? I know the reason. Both the Maharajah and his subjects will have nothing to do with the British. Till quite recently, people of Manipur and the Naga Hills—that is the Kohima sector—have opposed the British and even fought them. That is why they have been so friendly to our troops and have been helping them in every way.

Friends and Countrymen! During the last two and a half years, you have heard and seen an unceasing torrent of anti-Japanese propaganda. But in spite of it all, one question remains unanswered. Is there any other power besides Japan in the whole of Asia that can stand up to the Anglo-Americans—our enemies—and lend the Indian people a helping hand in their struggle? It is all right to talk of sympathy for China, for Russia and for other countries. But let us first have sympathy for ourselves. Let us first do something to liberate ourselves. Let us ask ourselves—'Who is there in this world today to give us some help in our struggle against a powerful empire, which is backed by other formidable powers?' When we come to brass tacks, we find that there is no other power except Japan to give us practical assistance in our fight for liberty. It is not the Japan of 1930 that we have to consider—but the Japan of today, the Japan that is fighting our enemies—undermining their strength and thereby making our tasks so much easier—it is the Japan that has recognized the Provisional Government of Free India and has given proof of her bonafides regarding India. Seeing the Japan of today and her new policy all over East Asia, three million Indians in this part of the world are convinced of Japan's sincerity. That is why we are determined to fight shoulder to shoulder with Japan, till the bitter end until our enemies are overthrown. The fight that is going on inside India is no longer Japan's war. It is India's own war—her way of liberation. If we, Indians in East Asia, are sincere and selfless—as we claim to be—we are bound to come out victorious. When a cause is just and the upholders of the cause are honest and sincere—as in our case—the forces of imperialism are bound to give in, in the long run. We are determined to fight and to win. Come and help us to make our task easier.

JAI HIND

49

Our Baptism of Fire

[Press statement, 21 August 1944][1]

Speaking to the chief workers of the Indian Independence League, Departmental Heads, Ministers and Advisers, Netaji Subhas Chandra Bose said:

'We started operations too late. The monsoon was disadvantageous to us. Our roads were submerged. River traffic had to be against current. Against this the enemy had first class roads. Our only chance was to take Imphal before the rain started; and we would have succeeded if we had more air support and if their forces in Imphal had not special orders to make a stand to the last man. If we had started in January we would have succeeded. In all sectors, till the rains began, we either held the enemy or advanced. In the Arakan Sector, the enemy was held. In the Kaladan Sector, we routed the enemy and advanced. In Tiddim, we advanced. In Palel and Kohima, also, we advanced. In the Haka Sector, we held them. And all this, in spite of the numerical superiority that the enemy had, plus equipment and rations.

When the rains came, we had to postpone the general assault on Imphal. The enemy was able to send mechanized divisions and thus was able to retake the Kohima-Imphal Road. The question then arose, where we should hold the line. There were two courses open: Either hold on to the Bishenpur-Palel Line and not allow the enemy to advance; or fall back and hold a more advantageous position.

What are the lessons we have learnt from this campaign? We have received our baptism of fire. A body of ex-civilians, who were ordered to withdraw when the ammunition was exhausted, preferred not to

[15] *Testament of Subhas Bose*, pp. 234–5.

withdraw, and with fixed bayonets, they charged the enemy. They came back victorious.

Our troops have gained much confidence. We have learnt that the Indian troops with the enemy are willing to come over. We must now make arrangements to take them over. We have learnt the tactics of the enemy. We have captured enemy documents. The experience gained by our Commanders has been invaluable. Before the campaign started, the Japanese had no confidence in our troops and wanted to break them up into batches attached to the Japanese Army. I wanted a front to be given to our men and this was ultimately given. Our Divisional Commander and other Officers have gained much experience from this campaign.

We have also learnt our defects. Transport and supply were defective owing to the difficult terrain. We had no front-line propaganda. Though we had prepared personnel for this, we could not use it owing to lack of transport. Henceforth, each unit of the Indian National Army will have a propaganda unit attached to it. We wanted loud speakers, but the Japanese failed to supply them to us. We are now making our own.'

—RANGOON RADIO, 21 August 1944

50

On the Gandhi–Jinnah Meeting

[Broadcast from somewhere in Burma on 12 September 1944][1]

Friends and Countrymen,

I want to talk to you today about the Indian situation. You are all aware that Gandhiji and Mr. Jinnah are discussing the Hindu-Muslim question in Bombay and that Gandhiji is prepared to come to an agreement with the League even if it means conceding the League demand of Pakistan. I know that you are all very anxious to know what we Indians abroad think about Gandhiji's attempt to pacify the League. It is clear that Gandhiji and other Congress leaders wish to compromise with Britain after settling with the League. We must act instantly, if we are to prevent this. We Indians in East Asia are today fighting for a free and united India. We are resolved to liberate our motherland, and we are confident that we shall ultimately succeed. However long and bitter the struggle, we are convinced that truth and justice will finally triumph, and that our struggle for India's liberation will be successful. Therefore, we shall never be a party to any compromise with Britain. The very idea of a compromise with the British is repugnant to us; it will, we very strongly feel, mean the perpetuation of our slavery. Friends, we have resolved to create a united and free India; therefore, we shall oppose all attempts to divide her and cut her up into bits. Ireland and Palestine have taught us a lesson. We have realized that to divide a

[1] *Testament of Subhas Bose*, pp. 76–8.

country will ruin her economically, culturally and politically. America could not have risen to her present greatness had the American Pakistanists been allowed their own way. We can easily solve the minority's problem once we are free from foreign domination. We should have the Soviet Union as our example. There are more races in the Soviet Union than in India; yet they are united today. Why? Because they are free and do not have to bow to a foreign ruler.

Personally, I have great respect for Mr. Jinnah, President of the Muslim League. I, and my party, have been in close contact with him and have co-operated with the League in the past, and I am opposed neither to the League nor to its illustrious leader. But, I vehemently oppose the Pakistan scheme for the vivisection of our motherland.

During the first three years of the present war the Anglo-Americans have suffered one reverse after another. But they never thought of capitulation or surrender. They fought on with the hope that sooner or later their luck would turn, and their hope was justified. They have achieved many victories, but that will not make them slacken their war effort, nor does it mean that our allies will slacken their efforts or surrender. I suspect that there are some in India who believe that this is possible. They have been duped by the barrage of propaganda let loose on India and the world by the Anglo-Americans. But, I still believe that my countrymen will not be fooled by Allied propaganda. All the same, I cannot but feel sorry to see that even some of the Congressmen have been taken in by it. These dupes believe that the Allies are well on the way to victory, and are, therefore, anxious to come to a compromise with British imperialism.

If we stop to think for a moment, we shall realize that final victory will go to the Axis. The war will be decided not in the West but in the East. Our attacks during the last six months have given us an idea of our enemy's strength. During these six months, in spite of his dogged attempts, he was decisively beaten in many sectors and our victorious troops drove him out of the Kaladan, Haka, Tiddim, Bishenpur, Palam and Kohima areas. True, there is a lull in the fighting just now, but that is mainly due to the monsoon, and we have been forced to take the defensive. As we have already routed the enemy more than once, we are confident that we can do so again. We are resolved to fight till the motherland is free. We are aware that the struggle ahead of us will be a long and bitter one, and that it may take as long as two years or more to liberate India. But we must remember that the Anglo-Americans were able to gain only a few successes after five years of intense warfare. We shall not be discouraged if some time passes before we meet with success. We should not compromise with the British thinking that now they are winning because then it will be impossible to liberate our motherland. The agreement between the League and the Congress will be the forerunner of a compromise with Britain. If this should happen, India will remain a slave country forever. As long as the Congress and Muslim League are separated, there will be no compromise with the British. That is why the Congressmen who want to come to a compromise with Britain have decided to swallow the bitter pill of Pakistan. I wish to remind both the Congress and Muslim League leaders that even if there is an agreement between these two parties regarding the Pakistan issue, Britain will not grant freedom to India. They have already proved this by saying that the interests of the minorities and the princes should be safeguarded. Those who believe that a compromise between the Muslim League and the Congress will persuade Britain to grant India freedom are only deceiving themselves. That being so, I fail to see the necessity for rapprochement between the League and the Congress. I am sure that even if Pakistan is conceded, it will not solve our problem. The League will never fight the British as we do. All that it wants is the division of India into Hindu and Muslim States. There will be four Muslim States, which will remain under British influence. So, instead of a single slave India, we shall have four independent slave Muslim States siding with and abetting Britain. The British will ignore the Congress–League agreement, if it is against their interest in India. They will not relinquish their hold on India. I ask the millions of Muslim young men in India, 'Will you be a party to the vivisection of your motherland? What will your status be in a divided India?' Therefore, my friends, you must remember that if you want freedom you must fight for it and kick the British out. There should be no compromise with Britain. Our divine motherland shall not be cut up.

Inquilab Zindabad! Azad Hind Zindabad!

51

The Human Spirit is More Powerful than Steel and Armour

[Broadcast on 'Army Day', 18 October 1944][1]

Sisters and Brothers in India! On the 21st October, 1943 the Provisional Government of Azad Hind (or Free India) was established at Syonan (or Singapore). Since the subjugation of India by the British in 1857, this was the first time that a Government of Free India was established and was given formal recognition, by as many as nine friendly powers—headed by Japan and Germany. The First Anniversary of the establishment of the Provisional Government is now being celebrated all over East Asia. From today, the 18th October, a full week's programme for the Anniversary celebration has been laid down and is being given effect to. According to this programme, today the 18th October, was celebrated as the Army Day. Here in Burma wherever there are units of the Azad Hind Fauj, ceremonial parades were held, at which the pledge was solemnly reiterated that the Azad Hind Fauj would continue to fight under all circumstances, and in spite of all difficulty and hardship—until India was completely liberated from the foreign yoke. Silent homage was also paid at the end of each parade to the memory of those heroes who had sacrificed their lives for the freedom of India, during the recent military operations. I had the honour of being present at one of these ceremonial parades, where a large number of our troops

[1] Transcript of recording of the broadcast by the British Government of India, INA Papers File 63/INA (National Archives of India), pp. 58–64.

were present, who had been earmarked for the next campaign against our enemies in India. I shall give you now in English a gist of my address, in Hindustani, to the Officers and men of the Azad Hind Fauj who attended that parade.

Comrades of the Azad Hind Fauj! A year has rolled by since the establishment of the Provisional Government of Azad Hind—the first Government of Free India to be formed, and recognized internationally, since our defeat at the hands of the British in 1857. The Provisional Government of Azad Hind is as you all know, a revolutionary Government, the sole object of which is to fight for, and win, freedom for India. What has given reality and significance to this Government is that, behind it, stands India's Army of Liberation. You are all soldiers of that great and historic Army. To an enslaved people like ourselves there can be no greater honour than to be soldiers in the Army of Liberation. Speaking for myself, I may tell you in all sincerity that though, through the grace of Providence, I have received the highest honour which an Indian can hope to receive at the hands of his countrymen, even that is nothing compared to the great pride and honour that I feel in being a soldier in this glorious army of ours. Like the rest of our countrymen, we too shall die one day, but we want to die fighting for our country. And we know that when we die, our names will be enshrined for ever in the history of India's struggle for liberty.

Comrades! Fifteen months ago, when I addressed you for the first time at Singapore, the graveyard of the British Empire, I gave you a new slogan. That slogan, 'Chalo Delhi' has now become your battle-cry. This battle-cry has not only inspired every member of the Azad Hind Fauj, but has also thrilled the hearts of freedom-loving Indians all over the world. With this battle-cry on their lips, the soldiers of the Azad Hind Fauj moved from Malaya to Burma and from Burma to India. And this battle-cry will remain on their lips so long as they do not reach India's metropolis.

I am sure you all remember that before the advance units of the Azad Hind Fauj left Malaya, I warned them as to what they would have to face. I warned them that they would have to face hunger, thirst, privation, forced marches and death. But I told them also that beyond all this suffering and sacrifice lay the promised land of Freedom. The recent military operations on the frontier, and inside India, have shown that my words were literally true. Our brave comrades—many of whom are no longer in the land of the living—had, in reality to face hunger, thirst, privations, forced marches and death. Nevertheless their spirit today is more indomitable and their determination more strong than ever before. I have just returned from an inspection of our front-line troops. I have seen and talked to our wounded and sick soldiers lying in their hard beds. I have spoken to them and questioned them. They have no wish, no desire, other than to resume the offensive against the enemy once again, and that, as soon as possible.

Comrades! The vanguard of the Azad Hind Fauj who took part in the recent operations, have set up a glorious and undying tradition for all those who are to follow, as well as for the future army of Free India. Through them, the Azad Hind Fauj faced its first ordeal—its baptism of fire. Out of that ordeal, the Azad Hind Fauj emerged with colours flying. Thanks to the sacrifice, heroism and achievements of our brave comrades the whole world today knows—and our enemies in particular know—that the Azad Hind Fauj is an army that will fight, and will fight till victory is achieved.

In the past, I repeatedly warned you that we would have to face an enemy superior to ourselves in numbers and in equipment. But I also told you that, nevertheless, it is we who shall triumph in the end, because of the righteousness of our cause and because of our superior morale. The present operations have proved that the human spirit is more powerful than steel and armour. In spite of manifold difficulties and hardships, in every sector from Akyab in the south to Kohima in the north, we could beat the enemy. In every sector, the enemy had either to halt his advance or to withdraw for a considerable distance. In not a single sector was the enemy able to advance one inch. It was only when, owing to tactical reasons, we decided to withdraw our forces and actually did so, was the enemy able to move up. Enemy propagandists are now loudly advertising this as a great victory—but we know what the real truth is.

Comrades! After beating the enemy in so many sectors, in spite of his superiority in numbers and in equipment, our confidence in our strength, and in our final victory, has increased a hundred-fold. We feel today that having beaten the enemy once in so many sectors, we shall beat him again when we resume the offensive. As you all know, we are now busy with our preparations for the next offensive. In carrying out these preparations we are making the fullest use of our experiences at the front, in order to remedy, as far as possible, whatever defeats or deficiencies we still have. When that offensive begins, we shall move forward and forward, until the enemy's 'MAGINOT LINE' is broken through, and his forces are put to flight.

I have been telling you again and again that the fight for India's freedom will be long and hard. The liberation of India means the emancipation of one-fifth of the human race. For such a great achievement we have to pay the price—and we have to pay that price with our own blood. Having solemnly resolved to achieve liberty through our own efforts, we cannot quail before any suffering or sacrifice, along the road to victory. The greater the price that we have to pay for our freedom, the stronger must be our determination to do or die.

You may perhaps wonder why our struggle for freedom should be long and hard. But if you think for a moment, it should not be difficult to understand that. It took the British full one hundred years—from 1757 to 1857—to conquer and subjugate India. Today, if we want to overthrow the British yoke, we cannot grudge a long and hard struggle. We know what India means for the British Empire. We know also that when India is lost to Britain, the British Empire will cease to exist. Therefore, it is but natural that the British should fight desperately in order to keep India and thereby save their Empire. That also explains why the British fought so hard for the hills and jungles of Arakan and Manipur, and at such sacrifices. The Eastern Frontier of India has become Britain's Maginot Line in India. The future fate of India will be decided not in the plains of Panipat, near Delhi, as in days old, but on the hills and in the jungles, where we have been fighting of late. The British know, as well as I do, that when this Maginot Line is broken the doom of the British Empire will be sealed. Today, our countrymen in India may feel doubtful about the final issue of this war. But when our victorious army comes into the plains of Bengal and Assam, 388 millions of our countrymen at home will be convinced that the British retreat from India has begun. Then will come the grand revolution inside the country. Then will the British Indian Army break its shackles and join India's army of liberation. Moreover, when the British are once ousted from their Maginot Line on the Eastern Frontier, they will not be able to set up a new line of defence until they cross the western frontier of Bengal and go into Bihar and Orissa. From Imphal to the River Brahmaputra, the Azad Hind Fauj will have a route march. And after breaking the enemy's improvised defence on the west bank of the Brahmaputra, the Azad Hind Fauj will have another route-march from the River Brahmaputra to the neighbourhood of Calcutta. For all these reasons, you should remember that when you fight in the Arakans, in Manipur and in Assam, you are fighting to settle the final issue of this struggle. It is in these regions, therefore, that you will have to fight the hardest battle. Knowing this, there is no reason to be discouraged if we have failed to take Imphal, in our first assault. If we have to attack not once, but ten times, before Imphal falls, we should be prepared for it. The battle of Panipat for the capture of Delhi will be fought this time on the hills and in the jungles that bar the way to Imphal and Chittagong.

Comrades! I want to repeat once again that this war—like many other wars in recent history—is a fight between the human spirit on the one side and steel and armour on the other. The Anglo-Americans hope to win this war by the sheer weight of steel and armour. But we are confident that we shall ultimately win, by virtue of our superior morale and will power. Remember always that, that side will ultimately win which has greater tenacity and power of endurance. In no revolution in the world's history have the revolutionaries ever had superiority either in numbers or in equipment. Nevertheless the revolutionaries have, in most cases, succeeded in overthrowing the foreign yoke. This will also happen in the case of India. We lost our liberty in 1857, only because we did not have sufficient tenacity and will power. In that great fight in 1857 the British were completely routed at first . . . but they did not lose heart. They reorganized their forces and launched their counter-offensive. When that counter-offensive began to succeed, it was OUR people who lost heart. By losing heart they lost their liberty. And when they lost their liberty, they easily surrendered their arms. That was India's shameful tragedy.

Those of our comrades who went forward in February and March have done their duty and have set up a glorious tradition. It will now be your turn to follow. You are among those who have been earmarked for the next offensive. Your duty will be a two-fold one—to maintain the tradition created by your predecessors and to improve upon it still more. I have no doubt that you will succeed in fulfilling this two-fold task. Before the order is given to you to move, I want to assure you once again that behind you stands not only the entire strength of the Azad Hind Fauj, but the united will and determination of Three Million Indians in East Asia who are pledged to fulfil the programme of Total Mobilization and to go on supplying you with men, money and materials. And in front of you awaits the sympathy of 388 millions of your countrymen at home.

Soldiers of India's Revolutionary Army! You have now got your Government. You have got your own army and your own commanders, who have gone through the baptism of fire and have emerged as seasoned and veteran soldiers and officers. You have got three million Indians in East Asia to provide you with men, money and materials. You have the sympathy of 388 millions of your countrymen at home. You have the whole-hearted support of the brave and unconquered people of Nippon and eight other friendly powers. All that now remains is for you to do your duty to fight for your own freedom, to pay the price of that freedom. The Provisional Government of Azad Hind has completed one year of its existence and, simultaneously, the war is entering a new phase, which is the third phase of this war. In the first phase of this war, the Axis powers had a sweeping victory on every front. In the second phase, we saw the enemy's counter-offensive. In the third and final phase of this war, we and our allies shall take the offensive once again.

This new phase is heralded by the brilliant victory scored by the Japanese Navy over the enemy's fleet in the Pacific, in the waters off Taiwan, or Formosa. I have no doubt that in spite of difficulties and set-backs that may still be ahead of us, this new offensive which is about to begin will be maintained until final victory is achieved.

In this new phase of the war, the new slogan that I have to give you is 'BLOOD BLOOD AND BLOOD'. It is only by giving our life that we can win back our liberty. It is only by giving our blood that we can pay the price of freedom. And it is only when we give our own blood that we can take the blood of our enemies. In the recent operations we had to suffer many casualties. But the casualties suffered by our enemy were at least five times that of ours. In the coming struggle, we may have to face even higher casualties than before. But that does not matter. If our casualties be higher in future, the casualties of our enemy will be even higher still.

The path to Delhi is not a path strewn with roses. The road to Delhi is not merely a road along malaria-infested jungles, and bullet-ridden hills. The road to Delhi is the road to freedom and I can see with my mind's eye that that road is red with blood—with our own blood and with the blood of our enemies. Through that blood we shall have to wade—to *Victory*, to *Freedom* and to Delhi.

52

Our First Anniversary

[Broadcast on the first anniversary of the proclamation of the Provisional Government of Azad Hind, 21 October 1944][1]

Sisters and brothers! This is the gist in English of my address in Hindustani before a mammoth meeting of Indians, somewhere in Burma, for celebrating the First Anniversary of the establishment of the Provisional Government of Azad Hind.

Exactly one year has rolled by, since the Provisional Government of Azad Hind was established at Syonan (or Singapore). Standing on the threshold of the new year, it is our duty to take stock of our past achievement and of our past failure, if any. It is also our duty to look to the future and to contemplate the task that lies ahead of us. But before I indulge in a review of the past and a contemplation of the future, I should like to say something about the struggle that is now going on all over the world. Against this world-background, the problem of India will stand out in bolder relief.

I believe that the present war is the biggest one that we have seen in history. It is not a war confined either to Europe, or to Asia or to Africa alone. It is a war that is shaking the foundations of the entire world-order of today. So long as the world remained at peace, it was easy for the big powers to maintain the status-quo and to perpetuate the subjugation of those nations that had once been conquered. Now that the

[1] Transcript of recording of the broadcast by the British Government of India, INA Papers, File 63/INA (National Archives of India), pp. 65–74.

status-quo is being turned upside down, and gigantic world forces are engaged in a deadly combat, subject nations of the world have a rare opportunity for breaking the shackles that have bound them so long. If these enslaved nations miss the golden opportunity which Providence and history have given them, not only will their task become much more difficult in future, but the day of their salvation will also be postponed to a much later date—perhaps even for a century.

So far as Europe is concerned, the present war is fundamentally a clash between the forces represented by Germany and Soviet Russia. France has, once for all, receded into the background. Britain is now playing a comparatively minor role. And taking advantage of the clash between Germany and the Soviet, the United States of America wants to extend their sway of influence over as large a part of Europe as possible. But whatever the United States of America might do to-day, the essential nature of the conflict in Europe cannot be altered.

In the Pacific and in East Asia, the conflict is one between Japan and the United States of America. In this conflict, too, Britain is playing a comparatively minor role and her one effort seems to be to recover or to save, a part of her possessions, with the help of her bigger partner.

So far as Japan and Germany are concerned, there is not the slightest doubt that their peoples feel that they have been treated unfairly and unjustly by the big powers—by the 'Haves' and they are fighting for what they consider to be their legitimate rights. Japan has made it perfectly clear that she is interested in a New Order in East Asia. Likewise, Germany is interested in a New Order in Europe. So far as Soviet Russia is concerned, there is also a limit to her dreams and desires. With regard to Britain, we can say that she is fighting only to preserve what she can of her decaying Empire. Comparing this war to a race between several competitors, we may say of Britain—'She also ran'. But, in this titanic world-struggle, there is only one power whose dreams, aspirations and ambitions have no limit. That is America. Consequently, in my opinion, world-enemy No. 1 is America. And if America were to succeed, by any chance, we would have American hegemony in this world. During the last few years, the spokesmen of America's Dollar Imperialism have been openly talking of the 'American Century' and they have made no secret of their desire to dominate the world during the next ten decades.

It is but natural that in such a world-war, there should be different phases, as well as varying ups and downs. During the first phase, the Axis powers had a sweeping victory all over the world. This was followed by the second phase when the anti-Axis powers launched their counter-offensive. At the present moment we are at the end of the second phase and at the threshold of the third and final phase of this war. During the third and final phase, the initiative will pass into the hands of the Axis Powers. And, in spite of ups and downs, they will retain the initiative until the present war comes to an end. For this third and final phase of the war, Japan has been preparing, through an intensive and complete mobilization of all her resources. The recent, brilliant victory which the Japanese Navy has scored over the American navy off the waters of Taiwan (Formosa) reminds one the oft-quoted saying in English 'Coming events cast their shadows before'. In Europe, too, the third and final phase is being heralded by what one may call the national mass uprising of the German people.

In this war, the Anti-Axis powers, being the 'haves' have the advantage of possessing bigger war-industries and they can, therefore, rely on a colossal war-production. Consequently, their aim is to beat down their enemies by the sheer weight of their steel and armour. The Anti-Axis powers know very well that there is no unity within their own camp and that their moral and spiritual strength is inferior to that of their enemies. In other words, the Anti-Axis powers can well afford to face large losses in their war materials, but they cannot hope to make up for similar losses in their human material, that is in their fighting man-power. In spite of their colossal war-production, time is not working for the anti-Axis powers. They want, therefore, to end the war, if possible, before moral and spiritual exhaustion overtakes them. Viewed in this light, it is easily understandable that the Anti-Axis powers have been continually talking of an early conclusion of the war. They know very well that the morale of their people would be badly shaken if they know that a long struggle lay ahead of them. Up till recently, the Anglo-Americans were predicting that the War in Europe would end by the end of 1944. Now that the whole world realizes that such a view is absurd to a degree, they have put off the date of the termination of the war in Europe till the spring of 1945. Simultaneously, they have been trying to bolster up the morale of their people by talking constantly of post-war reconstruction—thereby trying to give the world the impression that they are absolutely confident of their final victory. Another propaganda trick resorted to by our enemies is to assure their people that as soon as German collapse in Europe takes place, the entire war-strength of the Anglo-American powers would be transferred to the Pacific. This, however, is an eyewash. Anybody who knows anything of Europe will agree with me that if Germany's collapse were to take place—which, however is not possible—a new situation in Europe would suddenly arise which would keep the Anglo-Americans as busy and as worried over Europe, as they are to-day. Thus, these propaganda-tactics of our enemies, though they might perhaps mislead unsophisticated people in different parts of the world, cannot have the slightest impression on those who are engaged in a grim struggle with them.

Whatever the hopes and expectations of our enemies may be, this war—like many other wars of the past—will prove once again that the human spirit is more formidable than steel and armour. Once again, we shall see in this war, that that side will win which has greater tenacity and superior morale. Consequently, however long and hard the coming struggle may be, there can be but one result—namely, the defeat and overthrow of our enemies.

Viewed against this world background, the real character of India's struggle for liberty—namely that it is bound to be a long and hard struggle—should not be difficult to comprehend. The freedom of India means the emancipation from the bondage of slavery of one-fifth of the human race. For the consummation of so great an ideal, we have to pay an adequate price. The price of freedom cannot be paid in money—it can be paid only in human blood.

Moreover though the British Empire is going through a process of decay and dissolution, like other Empires of the past, it will not go down without a fight. Further, it should not be forgotten that it took the British full one hundred years from 1757 to 1857 to subjugate India. Therefore, it will naturally take us some time to turn them out. On the one hand the British are firmly entrenched in the country and they have at their beck and call, a modern army with modern arms and equipment. While the enemy is armed to teeth, we ourselves are disarmed. The fight against such vast odds will naturally take some time before it can reach a victorious conclusion. Lastly India means so much to the British Empire that the British will not leave India as easily and as quickly as they fled from Dunkirk, from Malaya and from Burma. Without Malaya and Burma the British Empire can still survive. But when India is lost to the British, their Empire will disappear from the face of the earth. Consequently on the soil of India—as on the soil of England itself—the British will fight hard. We shall consequently have to fight still harder, if we want to overthrow the British yoke and that must take time. Speaking of the time factor, I may add that if a powerful Empire like the British Empire, after fighting for five long years has achieved little, no one should grudge us at least a couple of years' time for the successful consummation of our struggle, particularly when our enemy has strengthened himself with aid and assistance from all over the world. In this connection, I should like to repeat that a long war is not disadvantageous for us or for our allies, but only for our enemies. A long war will mean for our enemies considerable loss in their fighting man-power, which will be impossible for them to recoup and replenish. On the other hand, whatever weakness we may have is not in our manpower, but in war material. There is no doubt that given time manpower will get the better of war materials. Moreover, in the course of a prolonged struggle we shall be able to acquire valuable experience, particularly in the military sphere, which will be of inestimable value to the Army of free India. Further we shall be able to further develop and strengthen unity within our own ranks which will be an example to 388 millions of our countrymen when we come into India.

Having dealt with the general character of our struggle I shall now deal with the question as to where the decisive battle will be fought. If we study every important war in history, we shall find that in every case, the decisive fight which seals the fate of the war, is fought in a particular place. If we turn to our own history, we shall find again and again that most of the decisive battles have been fought near Delhi on the plains of Panipat. This time, however, the battle of Panipat will be fought on the Eastern frontier of India. The British have fortified this eastern frontier and made it their Maginot line. They know and feel that if they do not hold this line, it will be impossible for them to hold India. If this Maginot line, stretching from Chittagong to Imphal and Kohima, is once broken, and our victorious army enters the plains of Bengal and Assam, two things will happen. The Indian people will see with their own eyes that the British are retreating. The myth of British power and invincibility will be exploded and the mass of the people will be convinced that the fall of British power in India has become a certainty. The Indian people will thereupon regain their lost confidence and rise in rebellion against their accursed oppressors. In the face of this mass uprising, the British will have but one alternative left to them—namely to flee for their lives.

The other thing that is sure to happen when Britain's Maginot line in India is broken, is that the British will not be able to put up any new line of defence until they cross over from Bengal into Bihar and Orissa. They will probably put up an improvised defence on the west bank of the Brahmaputra but it will not be difficult for us to break that line. From Imphal to Brahmaputra and from Brahmaputra to the neighbourhood of Calcutta, we shall have two long route marches.

It follows from what I have said above, that Britain's only hope of maintaining her Raj in India is to maintain her hold over the jungles and hills which bar the way to Chittagong and Imphal.

The battle for Chittagong and Imphal will be much more than a local battle. It will be, in essence, the battle of India. And the battle of Panipat will this time be fought where we have been fighting since February last. Knowing this, it is but natural that the British should throw in their whole weight in these malaria-infested jungles and mountain areas.

Since we have realized that the issue of our struggle will be decided once for all on the hills and forests of India's eastern frontier, we should not be surprised that the British have fought so hard there. Even when the Commander of the British forces in Imphal had decided to lay down arms or retreat, the British High Command, realizing the strategic importance of Imphal, insisted that the battle should be fought to the bitter end and they held out the hope to the beleaguered British forces in Imphal that General Monsoon would come to their aid before long. Since such is the great strategic value of Imphal and Chittagong, there is no need to be surprised that we could not take Imphal in our first strike. I shall go so far as to say that if we have to attack Imphal not once, but ten times, before that city falls, we should be fully prepared for it. Imphal and Chittagong will be to India's last war of Independence, what Sedan was to the Franco-Prussian war in 1856.

I shall now deal with the achievement of the Provisional Government during the last 12 months, as well as with the task that lies ahead of it. The Provisional Government of Azad Hind has, during this period, fulfilled its first task, namely, to lead the fighting forces of the Indian revolution to battle against the enemy—not only on the frontier but also inside India. The Provisional Government has thereby supplied the much-needed militant leadership to the Indian revolution. Incidentally, during the recent military operations, all doubts have been set at rest as to whether the Azad Hind Fauj will in reality fight and will be able to fight and will be able to successfully cross swords with the enemy. No longer can even our worst enemies say that Azad Hind Fauj is a propaganda stunt. After the battle that we have given them, all that our enemies can now say of the Azad Hind Fauj is that it is poorly equipped in arms and in rations. But as I have said so often, if battles could be won with beer and rum, tinned pork and bully beef, then no revolution in the world's history would have ever succeeded. The world's history does not afford a single example where the revolutionaries were better equipped or had superiority in numbers as compared with their enemies. In the case of the Irish struggle, for instance, 5000 Irish Irregulars held at bay 50,000 well-equipped British troops and brought them to their knees. It is through soul-force, through superior morale and greater tenacity that the world's revolutionaries have always triumphed. So shall we.

The recent military operations along a far-flung line, stretching from Akyab in the South to Kohima in the North, have revealed the comparative strength of ourselves and of the enemy forces. So long as we were on the offensive, the enemy forces had either to halt their advance or to retreat for a considerable distance. In not a single sector were they able to advance one inch. It was only when owing to tactical reasons—after the advent of the monsoon—we decided to withdraw our forces for some distance and actually did so, that our enemy was able to move up. This has been loudly advertised by enemy propagandists as a great victory. But we know what the real truth is.

Having beaten the enemy in so many sectors, our confidence in our strength and in our final victory has naturally increased a hundredfold. We are absolutely convinced that when we resume the offensive again we shall be able to beat the enemy once more.

Our task at present is to intensify our preparations for the next offensive—and that, in the light of the valuable experience we have gained in the recent operations. Three million Indians in East Asia have already been formed into one solid front—the National War Front.

This national war front has two wings—the home front and the fighting front. The duty of the home-front is to go on supplying men, money and materials, so long as the war continues. The greater the casualties at the front, the greater must be the contribution of the home front. Though the programme for the home front is, as I declared last year, one of Total Mobilisation I should like to make it clear now, that the maximum sacrifice demanded of the home front is not less than what is demanded of the fighting front. Between the home front and the fighting front there may be a division of work—a difference in task. But there can be no difference between the two wings of the national war-fronts, in the matter of sacrifice. Modern war has reached such a stage that one has to face death not only in the firing line, but also in one's home, on the streets, in the factories and on the parade ground. The fighting front has been told, time and again that there are but two alternatives for a soldier—either to go on fighting till victory is achieved or to lay down one's life on the road to freedom. The fighting front has also been told that the task of Azad Hind Fauj is to go on fighting till freedom is achieved, to give life so that liberty may be won in return—to pour out one's blood so that the price of liberty may be paid and last but not least to take the blood of our enemy, so that he may be overthrown and annihilated. The slogan for the fighting front for the future is therefore Blood, Blood, Blood. To the home front, too, I want now to give the same slogan. You who are now working on the home front should also be prepared to give your blood at any time. You too must be inspired by the ideal of maximum sacrifice. Only then can the entire national war front be imbued with an invincible spirit. It is not only for our soldiers to face hunger, thirst, privation, forced marches and death. You who are working on the home front should also be prepared to face the same amount of hardship, suffering, privation and even death as our comrades in the firing line. If for the emancipation of 388 million human beings, the Azad Hind Fauj has to die to the last man, that will not be a big price to pay for India's freedom. If three million

Indians in East Asia have to give their all so that India may be free, that too would be a cheap price to pay. (This was the substance of my address this evening. I shall now add the following appeal, addressed to listeners in India.)

Countrymen at home! The Provisional Government of Azad Hind is determined to fight on, shoulder to shoulder with its allies until India is completely liberated from the British yoke. The Provisional Government knows that it is engaged in a life and death struggle. It knows that the struggle will be long and hard. But it knows also that there can be but one consummation—India's victory and Freedom. The road to Delhi is a long one. That road passed over hills and jungles, over broad rivers and thick jungles. But that road is also the road to freedom. Along that road we shall travel, so long as it may be necessary, until, at long last, the tricolour National Flag proudly flies over Lord Wavell's house in New Delhi.

Countrymen at Home! We are coming. WAIT FOR US. AND COME AND JOIN US WHEN WE GIVE THE SIGNAL.

'Jai Hind'.

53

The Fundamental Problems of India

[An address to faculty and students of Tokyo University, November 1944][1]

I do not propose to speak to such a distinguished gathering on the commonplace things that you hear or read about India. I think it would be far better if I speak to you on the more fundamental problems of India. Having been a student of philosophy myself, I am naturally more interested in fundamental problems. I hope you will also agree with me that I should rather speak to you today on some of the fundamental problems that face my country, both in the present as well as in the future.

In my travels abroad, I have often found that people generally have a wrong and sometimes a rather funny idea about my country. For instance, among the people in Europe, the general idea about India is that it is a land in which three things can be found: snakes, fakirs and maharajas. Among those who have been influenced by British propaganda, the general idea about India is that it is a country where people are always fighting among themselves, and where the strong hand of Britain is required in order to maintain peace and order among the people.

If you approach the Orientalists in Europe, that is, the experts in Indology, you will find that they look upon India as a land of mystics and philosophers, a land which at one time produced a very rich

[1] From the archives of the Netaji Research Bureau.

philosophy, but which is today as dead as the ancient civilizations of Egypt and Babylon are dead today.

Now the question is, what is India in reality? No doubt we have a very ancient civilization, but unlike other ancient civilizations, such as Egypt or Babylon, Phoenicia or even Greece, the ancient culture and civilization of India is not dead. It still lives in the present. And we Indians of today think the same thoughts, fundamentally the same thoughts, and have the same feelings, the same ideals as our forefathers who lived 2,000 or 3,000 years ago. In other words, there is a continuity, historical and cultural continuity, extending from the ancient times till the present day—which is in some ways a very remarkable thing in history. Now, in order to understand India, this fundamental fact should first be understood, namely, that the India of the past is not dead. India of the past lives in the present, and will live on in the future.

Against this background, this ancient background, we see changes in our national life from age to age. During the last 3,000 years, people have come into India from outside with new ideas, sometimes with new cultures. All these new influences, ideas and cultures have been gradually absorbed into the national life of India, so that in spite of the fact that, fundamentally we have the same culture and civilization as we had several thousand years ago, we have nevertheless changed and moved with the times. Today, in spite of our ancient background, we are able to live in a modern world and adapt ourselves to that world.

Those who have been influenced, whether consciously or unconsciously by British propaganda, have the impression that India was very easily conquered by the British and also that after the British conquest of India our country was for the first time politically unified. Both these notions are entirely wrong and without foundation.

In the first place, it is not true that India was easily conquered by the British. It took the British 100 years, from 1757 to 1857, to finally subjugate India. Secondly, it is also an entirely wrong notion to think that India was politically unified by the British. The fact is that India was for the first time politically unified nearly 2,500 years ago under the Buddhist Emperor, Asoka. In reality, the India of the time of Asoka the Great was even larger than the India of today. Asoka's India included not only modern India, but also Afghanistan and a part of Persia.

After the time of Asoka, India has gone through many ups and downs in her national life. There have been periods of decay, followed by periods of progress and national upheaval. But throughout these ups and downs in our national life, we have been able, in the long run, to keep up our progress. About one thousand years after Asoka, India again reached the zenith of progress under the Gupta Emperors. This was followed by another glorious epoch in Indian history about nine hundred years later under the Mogul Emperors. Therefore, it is worth remembering that the British notion that we have been unified politically under British rule is entirely wrong. All that the British have tried to do during their regime in India is to divide the Indian people and to weaken, disarm and emasculate them.

I shall now present before you a problem which will interest scientists, and in particular, students of sociology. The question is whether the Indian people have any right to live as a free nation. In other words, have they the strength and the vitality left in them to live and to develop themselves as a free nation? I personally hold the opinion that if a nation once loses its vitality, its inner vitality, then it has no right to exist. And even if it does continue to exist after losing its vitality, that existence will have hardly any worth or value for mankind. The only reason why I stand for India's freedom and believe that as a free nation we shall have a glorious future is that I believe that we have sufficient vitality left in us to live as free men and to develop as a nation.

Now, if I have to answer this question as to whether sufficient vitality is left in us, I shall have to answer two questions: firstly, has our nation any creative faculty and secondly, is it prepared to fight and to die in order to preserve its existence? These two tests have to be applied to India.

With regard to the first question, we have seen that in spite of the British in India, in spite of the innumerable restrictions and disadvantages which follow from foreign rule, we have been able during the century to give numerous proofs that in different departments of our national life we still have creative power.

The number of philosophers and thinkers produced in India under British rule, the number of writers and poets that enslaved India has produced, the artistic revival in India in spite of British rule, the scientific progress made by the Indian people in spite of so many difficulties in the way of their education, the standard already attained by our leading scientists as compared with scientists in different parts of the world, the industrial progress made by India as the result of her own effort and initiative and, last but not least, the distinction which we have attained in the field of sport, all these go to show that in spite of being politically subjugated the vitality of the nation has remained intact.

If under foreign rule and in spite of the obstacles and restrictions that follow from foreign rule, we could give so much proof of our creative faculty, then it stands to reason that when India is free and when the masses of the Indian people are afforded educational facilities, they will be able to give much better proof of their intellectual calibre and creative faculty in different walks of life.

I have just referred to the first test of a nation's vitality, namely, creative faculty. I shall now consider the second test, namely, as to whether the Indian people are able to fight and to die for the sake of freedom. On this point I should like to say, first of all, that, since the last great fight that they had with the British in 1857, the Indian people have not given up the struggle against the enemy, even for one day.

Unfortunately, owing to what I would call the folly of our forefathers, after our final defeat in 1857, the leaders in those days had allowed themselves to be disarmed. Whatever difficulty we have subsequently experienced in winning back our freedom has been due largely to our having been disarmed. But though owing to the mistake of the leaders the people were disarmed, nevertheless they continued to fight for their freedom in other ways.

I shall not take up your time unnecessarily by giving a description of all the methods that have been used in India against the British. I will only say this, that all the methods that have been tried by revolutionaries in different parts of the world for the achievement of their own independence have been tried in India.

At the beginning of this century, particularly after the victory of Japan over Russia in 1904 and 1905, the Freedom movement in India got a new impetus and since then, during the last 40 years, our revolutionaries have been studying very closely the methods of revolutionaries in other countries and they have tried to adopt as many of their methods as possible.

They have tried also to manufacture secretly arms and explosives inside the country and to use those arms and explosives for the achievement of independence. As a development of this struggle for freedom, India tried a new experiment—Civil Disobedience or Passive Resistance—of which the best exponent was Mahatma Gandhi. Though personally I believe that this method will not succeed in bringing us complete independence, there is no doubt that it has greatly helped to rouse and unify the Indian people and also to keep up a movement of resistance against the foreign government. I should, therefore, say that the fact that in spite of all the difficulties that result from foreign rule, a nation can produce a new method and practice that method with a large measure of success is also a proof of that nation's vitality. It shows that that nation does not accept enslavement as a settled fact and is determined to struggle against it and to work out new methods for achieving independence.

I have, as a revolutionary, made a very close study of the revolutionary movements in other countries, and I can say without any exaggeration that since 1857 we have used every possible method of revolutionary struggle. In the course of this struggle, tremendous sacrifices have been made and many have given their lives. There was, however, one method that still remained for us to take up and that was the organization of a real modern national army.

That work we had not done up till recently because it was impossible to do that inside India under the eyes of the British army and the British police. But the moment this war gave the Indian people an opportunity of organizing a modern Indian national army outside India they at once seized it. As a result of that effort, and with the help of the Japanese Government and the armed forces of Japan, they have been able to build up this army.

So my point is that throughout our revolutionary struggle against the British Government and their armed forces we have shown sufficient initiative, creative power and vitality and have made tremendous sacrifices. We now hope that under the conditions, and with the advantages that this war has given us, we shall be able, after all, to fulfil our national aspirations and win freedom for India.

Having replied to the question regarding the vitality of the Indian people and their right to live as a free nation, I shall now attempt a sociological analysis of modern India. If you are to understand modern India, you have to take note of three important factors. The first factor is the ancient background, that is, the ancient culture and civilization of India, of which the Indian people of today are conscious, and of which they feel proud. The second factor is the struggle which has gone on without any break or interruption since we were finally overpowered by the British. And the third factor consists of certain influences which have come into India from outside.

Modern India is composed of this ancient background, the unbroken national struggle against Britain, and the impact of influences from abroad.

I shall now deal, in some detail, with the influences which have reacted on India from outside and which have been responsible, to some extent, in making modern India what it is today. Among these outside influences, the first factor is the influence of Western thought which was crystallized in Liberalism, Constitutionalism and Democracy.

In other words, since 1857, modern liberal and democratic thought has been influencing the intellectuals of India to a large extent.

From the beginning of the present century, a new factor came into operation. After the victory of Japan over Russia in 1904–1905, the eyes of the Indian people were opened to a new movement in Asia, the movement for the revival, not merely of Japan—but along with Japan—of other Asiatic countries. Since then, Indian thought has been greatly interested in Asiatic revival. During the last 40 years we have been thinking not merely of what was happening inside India, but also of what was happening in other parts of Asia.

Another important factor which had influence on our mind consisted of the revolutionary struggles that have gone on in different parts of the world. Indian revolutionaries studied the Risorgimento Movement in Italy under the leadership of Mazzini and Garibaldi and the struggle of the Irish people against their British oppressors. In Russia, before the last World War, there was, as you know, a movement against the Czar called the Nihilist movement. That also was studied. And nearer India the new awakening in China under the leadership of Dr. Sun Yat-sen was also studied very closely and with great interest by Indian revolutionaries.

Thus, Indian revolutionaries have been exceedingly receptive to the influences exerted by revolutionary struggles abroad. Then during the last World War, when the revolution broke out in Russia and, as a result of it, a new government—the Soviet Government—came into existence, the work of that Government was studied with great interest in our country.

People in India have not been interested so much in the Communist movement as in the work of reconstruction in Soviet Russia—in the rapid industrialization of that country and also in the way in which the Soviet Government solved the problem of minorities. It is this constructive achievement of the Soviet Government which was studied with great interest by people in our country. As a matter of fact, intellectuals like our poet Tagore, who had no interest in Communism as such, were profoundly impressed when they visited Russia by the work of educational reconstruction in that country. Then there is another influence which came to India from outside in more recent times—I mean, the new movement in Europe headed by Italy and Germany called Fascism or National Socialism. This movement was also studied by our revolutionaries.

I have just dealt with some of the influences that have reached India from different parts of the world, from England, France, Japan, China, Russia, Germany and so on. I will now take up another question viz., as to how we have reacted to these influences—how much we have accepted and how much we have rejected out of these outside influences. I must first point out that there is a big gulf between our generation and the last generation. As typical exponents of the last generation, I would like to mention Tagore and Gandhi. They represent for us the last generation, and between their thoughts and ideas and the thoughts and ideas of our generation there is a big gulf.

If you study the works of Tagore and Gandhi, you will find that all along there is a conflict in their minds as to what their reaction to Western influence should be. So far as Mahatma Gandhi is concerned, he has never given us any clear solution of this problem. He has left people in doubt as to what his attitude is towards the acceptance of Western ideas. Generally speaking his attitude is one of antagonism. But in actual practice he has not always acted in accordance with his own ideas, the reason being that the rest of his countrymen do not share that inner hostility or antagonism which Mahatma Gandhi personally has towards Western ideas and conceptions.

You all know about Mahatma Gandhi's attitude on the question of violence or physical force. He does not advocate the use of arms, or the shedding of the blood of the enemy for gaining one's freedom. This attitude towards violence or physical force is closely related to his general attitude towards foreign influence, particularly Western influence.

Our generation has followed Mahatma Gandhi as the leader of a political struggle, but has not accepted his ideas on all these questions. Therefore, it would be a mistake to take Mahatma Gandhi as the exponent of the thoughts and ideas of the present generation in India.

Gandhi is in some ways a complex personality, and I would like to analyse his personality, so that you may understand him better. In Gandhi, there are two aspects—Gandhi as a political leader and Gandhi as a philosopher. We have been following him in his capacity as a political leader, but we have not accepted his philosophy.

Now the question arises as to how we can separate the two aspects. Why, if we do not accept his philosophy, are we following him? Though Gandhi has his own philosophy of life, he is a practical politician and therefore, he does not force his own philosophy on the people. Consequently though we are following him in our political struggle, we are free to follow our own philosophy. If Gandhi had tried to thrust his philosophy on us, we would not have accepted him as a leader. But he has kept his philosophy separate from his political struggle.

I have mentioned as representatives and exponents of the last generation Tagore and Gandhi. Now let us compare their philosophies. There are some points on which they agree, but on some other points they do not. The points on which they agree are firstly, that they would like to see the national struggle being conducted without the use of arms. In other words, on the question of physical force, they have the same views. On the question of the industrialization of the country, they also have the same views. Both Tagore and Gandhi are against modern industrial civilization. But in the realm of culture, their views are not the same. So far as thought, art and culture are concerned, Tagore is prepared to accept foreign influence. He believes that in the realm of culture there should be full cooperation between India and the rest of the world and there should be reciprocity. We should not be hostile or antagonistic to the culture or art or ideas of any other nation. In the realm of culture, while Tagore advocates full cooperation between India and the rest of the world, Gandhi's general attitude is antagonistic to foreign influence. We must, however, remember that Mahatma Gandhi has nowhere given a very clear exposition of his views. I am only referring to his general attitude on this question.

I have previously remarked that there is a big gulf between the fundamental thoughts and ideas of the last generation and of our generation. I will now explain what I meant thereby. As I have just said, this problem as to what our reaction should be towards foreign influence and towards industrial civilization troubled the leaders of the old generation all their lives and we see proofs of it in their actions. But this problem does not exist for us. It does not exist for us, because our starting-point is that we want a modern India based of course on the past. We do not believe that India can achieve freedom without the use of arms. Now once you take up this attitude, that for winning freedom we have to fight and to use arms, it follows that we must have modern industries to manufacture the arms. So we take our stand on modernism. We have to fight the enemy with modern methods and with modern arms—so we must have modern industries. What constituted the biggest problem for the old leaders constitutes our starting-point. The problem for modern India is not our attitude towards modernism or foreign influence or industrialization, but how we are to solve our present-day problems.

I believe that modern Japan will understand our generation much better than modern Japan understood the last generation in India. Our stand is virtually the same. We want to build up a new and modern nation on the basis of our old culture and civilization. For that we need modern industries, a modern army and all those things necessary to preserve our existence and our freedom under modern conditions.

Having dealt with this fundamental standpoint of my generation, I will go on to discuss some of the detailed problems. For the present, of course, the biggest problem is how to fight and win this war. But that is a problem of which you are aware from what you have read in the papers or heard over the radio. I will now consider some of the problems of Free India. The moment India is free, the most important problem will be the organizing of our national defence in order to safeguard our freedom in the future. For that we shall have to build up modern war industries, so that we may produce the arms that we shall need for self-defence. This will mean a very big programme of industrialization.

After satisfying the needs of our nation in the matter of self-defence, the next problem in the degree of importance will be that of poverty and unemployment. India today is one of the poorest countries in the world, but India was not poor before we came under British rule. In fact, it was the wealth of India which attracted the European nations to India. One cannot say that in the matter of national wealth and resources India is poor. We are rich in natural resources, but, owing to British and foreign exploitation, the country has been impoverished. So our second most important problem will be how to give employment to the millions of unemployed in India and how to relieve the appalling poverty which now exists among the masses of the Indian people.

The third problem in Free India will be the problem of education. At present, under British rule, about 90 per cent of the people are illiterate. Our problem will be to give at least an elementary education to the Indian masses as soon as possible, and along with that to give more facilities to the intellectual classes in the matter of higher education.

Connected with the question of education is another problem which is important for India and that is the question of script. In India there are principally two scripts in vogue. One is the script known as the Sanskrit (or Nagri) script and the other is the Arabic (or Persian) script. Up till today, in all national affairs and conferences we have been using both these scripts. I must add that in some provinces, there are scripts in vogue which are modifications of the Sanskrit script. But fundamentally there are two scripts, and in all national affairs and conferences we have to use both these two scripts.

There is now a movement to solve this problem of scripts by using the Latin script. I personally am an advocate of the Latin script. Since we have to live in a modern world, we have to be in touch with other countries and, whether we like it or not, we have to learn the Latin script. If we could make the Latin script the medium of writing throughout the country, that would solve our problem. Anyway that is my own view and the view of my closest friends and collaborators.

I have referred to three important problems in Free India: national defence, how to remove poverty, and how to give education to the people. If we are to solve these three important problems, how are we going to do it? Shall we leave it to private agency and private initiative or will the State take up the responsibility of solving these problems?

Well, at present, public opinion in India is that we cannot leave it to private initiative to solve these national problems, especially the economic problem. If we leave it to private initiative to solve the problem of poverty and unemployment, for instance, it will probably take centuries. Therefore, public opinion in India is in favour of some sort of socialist system, in which the initiative will not be left to private individuals, but the State will take over the responsibility for solving economic questions. Whether it is a question of industrializing the country or modernizing agriculture, we want the State to step in and take over the responsibility and put through reforms within a short period, so that the Indian people could be put on their legs at a very early date.

But in solving this problem, we want to work in our own way. We will, naturally, study experiments made in other countries—but, after all, we have to solve our problems in an Indian way and under Indian conditions. Therefore, the system that we shall ultimately set up will be an Indian system to suit the needs of the Indian people.

Now if we do not tackle the economic question from the point of view of the masses, the majority of whom are poor, if we do not do that in India, we shall produce the same confusion or the same difficulties in our country, as we see in China today. You see in China today a split between the Kuomintang and the Chinese Communist Party. Personally I do not see why this should have occurred or why, if the Kuomintang Party has the interests of the Chinese masses at heart, there should be any need to have a separate party like the Communist Party under foreign influence.

Having learnt from experience, we do not want to repeat the mistake that China has made. We actually find today that because the nationalist movement in our generation has identified itself with the interests of the masses, that is, of the workers and the peasants who form more than 90 per cent of the people, because we have their interests at heart, there is no *raison d'être* for a separate party like the Communist Party. If the nationalists in India did not have the interests of the masses at heart, then you would have seen the same phenomenon as you see in China today.

Now we come to another question—namely, the political system or the Government. If we are to have an economic structure of a socialistic character, then it follows that the political system must be such as to be able to carry out that economic programme in the best possible way. You cannot have a so-called democratic system, if that system has to put through economic reforms on a socialistic basis. Therefore, we must have a political system—a State—of an authoritarian character.

We have had some experience of democratic institutions in India and we have also studied the working of democratic institutions in countries like France, England and United States of America. And we have come to the conclusion that with a democratic system we cannot solve the problems of Free India. Therefore, modern progressive thought in India is in favour of a State of an authoritarian character, which will work as an organ, or as the servant of the masses, and not of a clique or of a few rich individuals.

That is our idea with regard to the political institutions in Free India. We must have a government that will function as the servant of the people and will have full powers to put through new reforms concerning industry, education, defence, etc., in Free India.

Before I pass on to the next problem, I should like to mention another point, namely, the attitude of Free India towards religion and caste. This is a question that is frequently asked. India has several religions. Consequently, the Government of Free India must have an absolutely neutral and impartial attitude towards all religions and leave it to the choice of every individual to profess or follow a particular religious faith.

With regard to caste, that is now no problem for us, because caste, as it existed in the old times, does not exist today. Now, what is the caste system? The caste system means that a community is divided into certain groups on a professional or vocational basis and marriage takes place within each group.

In modern India there is no such caste distinction. A member of one caste is free to take up any other profession. So, caste in that sense does not exist today. Then there remains the question of marriage. In the old times, it was the custom to marry within each caste. Nowadays, intermarriage between the different castes takes place freely. Hence caste is fast disappearing. As a matter of fact, in the nationalist movement we never inquire as to what caste a man belongs to and we do not even know the caste of some of our closest collaborators, which shows that in our generation we do not think at all about caste. For Free India, therefore, caste is no problem at all.

In this connection, I should like to tell you that it was the British who created the impression throughout the world that we are a people quarrelling among ourselves, especially over religion. But that is an absolutely wrong picture of India. It may be that there are certain differences among the Indian people, but such differences you will find in every other country. If we take the so-called progressive countries of the world e.g., France before the outbreak of the present war, or Germany before Hitler and his Party came to power, you will find that there were acute differences among the people in these countries. Spain had even a first-class civil war.

But nobody ever says that, because the people in these countries had disputes and differences, they are not fit to rule themselves. It is only in the case of India that the British say that, because there are certain differences among the Indian people therefore they are not fit to be free. Again, the fact is that whatever differences there are among the Indian people are largely the creation of the British government. There are hundreds of examples to show you that throughout the history of British rule, the British have tried by every possible means to divide the Indian people. After having done so much to artificially create differences among the Indian people, the British turn around and say that we are not fit to be free.

I should also point out that if you take a modern Power like Soviet Russia and see how heterogeneous the composition of the Soviet Union is, you will realize that it, in spite of this heterogeneous character, so many different races professing so many different religions could be unified in one political system and become such a strong Power, there is absolutely no reason why India which has much more homogeneity than the Soviet Union, should not be united as one nation. As a matter of fact, you will find that outside India, where there is no British influence, there are no differences among the Indian people. In the Indian Independence Movement in East Asia and in the Indian National Army there is no question of religion or caste or class. It is just in India where the British have influence and control that you will find these differences.

On the question of national unity, I should like to give you a friendly warning that British propaganda tries to give the world the impression that the Muslims of India do not support the independence movement. This is wrong. Very often you read in the papers about certain organizations like the Muslim League or the Hindu Mahasabha. The British boost these organizations, because they are in their policy pro-British and are against the Indian National Congress, and they try to make out that the Muslim League represents the Muslims of India. But that is British propaganda. The fact is that the Muslim League and its leader, Mr. Jinnah, represent only a minority of the Indian Muslims. The majority of the Indian Muslims are nationalists and they support the independence movement, as much as anyone else. The President of the Indian National Congress is a Muslim, and so are many other members of the Congress, many of whom are in prison today.

These facts are not known to the outside world and the outside world gets the impression that Mr Jinnah represents all the Muslims of India, and that they are not supporting the nationalist movement. I would like to give out this warning about British propaganda.

I have already told you about the kind of economic and political system that we would like to have in Free India. Out of this, arises the problem as to what our political philosophy is. On this question, I gave my own views in a book I wrote about ten years ago called 'The Indian Struggle.' In that book I said that it would be our task in India to evolve a system that would be a synthesis of the systems in vogue in different parts of the world. For instance, if you take the conflict between Fascism (or what you might call National Socialism) on the one side and Communism on the other, I see no reason why we cannot work out a synthesis of the two systems that will embody the good points of both. It would be foolish for anyone to say that any one system represents the last stage in human progress. As students of philosophy, you will admit that human progress can never stop and out of the past experience of the world we have to produce a new system. Therefore, we in India will try to work out a synthesis of the rival systems and try to embody the good points of both.

Now I would like to compare some of the good points of National Socialism and Communism. You will find some things common to both. Both are called anti-democratic or totalitarian. Both are anti-capitalistic. Nevertheless, in spite of these common points, they differ on other points. When we see National Socialism in Europe today, what do we find? National Socialism has been able to create national unity and solidarity and to improve the condition of the masses. But it has not been able to radically reform the prevailing economic system which was built up on a capitalistic basis.

On the other side, let us examine the Soviet experiment based on Communism. You will find one great achievement and that is planned economy. Where Communism is deficient is that it does not appreciate the value of national sentiment. What we in India would like to have is a progressive system which will fulfil the social needs of the whole people and will be based on national sentiment. In other words, it will be a synthesis of Nationalism and socialism. This is something which has not been achieved by the National socialists in Germany today.

There are a few points in which India does not follow Soviet Russia. Firstly, class conflict is something that is quite unnecessary in India. If the Government of Free India begins to work as the organ of the masses, then there is no need for class conflict. We can solve our problems by making the State the servant of the masses.

There is another point which has been overemphasized by Soviet Russia and that is the problem of the working classes. India being predominantly a country of peasants, the problem of the peasants will be more important than the problem of the working classes.

Another point on which we do not fully agree is that, according to Marxism, too much importance is given to the economic factor in human life. We fully appreciate the importance of the economic factor which was formerly ignored, but it is not necessary to overemphasize it.

To repeat once again, our political philosophy should be a synthesis between National Socialism and Communism. The conflict between thesis and antithesis has to be resolved in a higher synthesis. This is what the Law of Dialectic demands. If this is not done, then human progress will come to an end. India will, therefore, try to move to the next stage of political and social evolution. I will now pass on to the last point in my address, and that is our conception of an international order. On this point I have already spoken several times in Tokyo. I fully support the steps that have been taken through the Joint Declaration to create a new order in East Asia on the right basis of freedom, justice and reciprocity. I have been personally greatly interested in international problems, having tried to work in several countries in order to get support for our movement and, in that connection, I also had the opportunity of studying the work of the League of Nations.

The experiment of the League of Nations has failed, and it is desirable and profitable for us to investigate as to why it failed. If I were to answer that I would say that it failed because the sponsor-nations were too selfish and short-sighted. The sponsor-nations were England, France and America. America dropped out of the League, so the Powers that controlled the League were England and France. Now these two leading Powers, instead of setting an example of unselfishness, tried to use the League of Nations for their selfish interests and for their own benefit. The only basis on which we can set up an international order is freedom, justice and reciprocity. Therefore, the work in East Asia has commenced on the right lines and on the right basis. The only task that remains for us is to see that in actual work the principles embodied in the Joint Declaration are put into effect. If they are so put into effect, then the experiment will be a success. If not, then it will again prove to be a failure.

You must have seen in my speeches and press statements that I have been very enthusiastic about this Joint Declaration. There are several reasons. Firstly, it is on the right basis and on the right lines that the work has begun. Secondly, if you want to set up an international order, it has to have a beginning in a particular region. If we make it a success in one region, it can gradually be expanded all over the world.

It is very difficult to set up a world order suddenly out of nothing and make it a success. But if you begin in one region where friendship and reciprocity between the nations can be developed, and if in that region you meet with success, then that example will be emulated by other nations in other parts of the world. So the method of setting up a regional order is the only way in which a world order can gradually be built up.

The third reason is that I have found that this idea or plan finds support among the mass of the people of this country, and especially among the youths. If I had found that this new order was being sponsored by a few politicians or leaders and that the rest of the nation was apathetic or indifferent, I should certainly not be optimistic. But it is because I have found that the people as a whole, and especially the youths are vitally interested in it and support it enthusiastically, that I believe that through the cooperation of the leaders and the people and the youths, it can be made a success.

I should like to repeat that this undertaking is for the Government and the people of this country a very great responsibility. As you know, your Government was responsible for sponsoring this idea, so you are the sponsor-nation. The success of this experiment will depend on the example set by the sponsor-nation. The League of Nations failed, because the sponsor-nations were selfish and short-sighted. This time if the nations that have joined together, and particularly the sponsor-nation, avoid a selfish and short-sighted policy and work on a moral basis, then I see no reason why the experiment should not be a success.

I should like to emphasize again the tremendous responsibility which Japan has undertaken by becoming the sponsor-nation in the task. And when I talk of the responsibility of the nation, I want also to stress the responsibility of the youths. The youths of today will be the nation and the leaders of tomorrow. An idea that is welcomed and supported by the youths will one day be supported by the whole nation. But an idea which does not find support among the youths will die a natural death. Therefore, the responsibility for making this new order a success devolves, in the last analysis, on the youths of this country. I hope and pray and trust that the youths and the students who are the future representatives of the nation will realize the tremendous moral responsibility which Japan has undertaken in initiating this new order.

There may be people who doubt whether a nation can rise to a high moral level, whether a nation can be far-sighted and unselfish and undertake the work of establishing a new order. I have every faith in mankind. If it is possible for one individual to be unselfish, to live one's life at a high moral level, I see no reason why an entire nation cannot also rise to that level. In the history of the world we have seen examples in which a revolution has changed the mentality of a whole nation and made it rise to a high level of morality. Therefore, if anybody has any doubt whether an entire nation can rise to that level, then I do not share that doubt.

I repeat, in conclusion, that the sponsor-nation should realize the tremendous responsibility that it has undertaken. This is a task not only for the leaders and the politicians, but for the whole nation and especially for those who are the hopes of the nation—the youths and the students.

54

The Fate of India

[Speech at Singapore, 17 December 1944][1]

Soon after his visit to Tokyo Netaji returned to Syonan with a view to galvanizing the flagging enthusiasm of the people in Malaya consequent upon the set-back which the INA had in July after the setting in of the monsoon. After his arrival in Syonan Netaji addressed a mammoth gathering of Indians on December 17 referring to the events of the past year and to the INA's reverses. He said:

'We have achieved a lot during the past one year. The establishment of the Provisional Government last year in the month of October was the stepping stone for our success. When our Army of Liberation started from Syonan on their march to Delhi, Indians were thinking under what government we are going to fight and to whom our victories can be attributed. History records many instances of establishment of similar Provisional Governments. But the establishment of our Provisional Government was unique in that it was recognized by nine world powers. No other revolutionary government has received so much esteem and respect as ours. India is no longer a slave country in the eyes of these nations. In the history of the world we have witnessed many revolutions. Let us take, for instance, Ireland. The Irish people established their Provisional Government. But the respect that our Provisional Government commands to-day was never commanded by Ireland. America had sympathies with the Irish cause. De Valera went to America to seek American assistance. He managed to get money, but not respect. He returned disappointed. The secret of respect commanded by us lies

[1] *Chalo Delhi*, pp. 207–13.

in the recognition of our Government by nine world powers. The Indian sisters and brothers in Malaya will have their honourable place in the history of India. It is here in Syonan that the Azad Hind Fauj was organized. It was here in Syonan that the Provisional Government of Azad Hind was established. And it was from Syonan that the Azad Hind Fauj began its march to India. We expect ceaseless help and assistance from Syonan.

While I was in Rangoon I learnt that the revolutionary spirit and enthusiasm of the people in Malai and Syonan is coming down. I have come here to see it for myself. If it is really true, I am sorry to say that it is a matter for regret. The war of independence for India is not a child's play. It is a matter of life and death for 38 crores of Indians. Either we will live like free men or we will embrace death.

I know there are British agents in Syonan, left by them when they retreated to spread false rumours and propaganda. But it does not concern us Indians. There is only one way left to us and that is the way to Delhi. There is no room for compromise. These enemy agents may be able to put obstacles in our path, but we have only one thought branded in our heart and soul and that is India and her independence.

I have brought with me Divisional Commander Colonel M.Z. Kiani to furnish you with up-to-date information about the battles in the Arakan and Imphal. I could have brought other commanders also with me. But it was not possible to bring all of them here.

Before I came here I went to Tokyo. My object in visiting Tokyo was to establish personal contact with the members of the new Cabinet and to discuss with the members of the Imperial Government and leaders of Army and Navy concerning future programme both political and military. We have settled all questions, both military and political, amicably. As regards military questions, I cannot disclose them as they are military secrets. As regards political questions, diplomatic relations will be established very soon which will strengthen our position. That will enable us to work with close co-operation and prosecute the war successfully.

At the end of December last year I toured the Andamans. On the 30th December we hoisted our National Flag on the British Chief Commissioner's residence. I had talks with Nipponese authorities and it was agreed that the Provisional Government of Azad Hind should send a Commissioner there. So Colonel A.D. Loganadan was sent to Andamans as Chief Commissioner. In January I went to Rangoon and along with me the Army and League Headquarters were shifted to Rangoon. On the 4th February, an offensive was launched in Arakan against the Anglo-Americans. The Arakan fight was a minor struggle, but great importance was attached to it. It was the first test to our Army of Liberation. Hitherto no one knew much about the Azad Hind Fauj. The world was amazed at the wonder not for us but for those who had shades of doubt in the core of their heart. Before we began the offensive Nipponese Army authorities asked a question whether the Azad Hind Fauj will be able to undergo all hardships with Nippon forces. The commanders were instructed to ensure from their officers and men before giving any definite answer. When the soldiers of the Azad Hind Fauj were questioned they all with one voice replied that they are capable of enduring as much hardships as the Nippon soldiers can endure and even more. They knew they were fighting the battle of India's independence. But in spite of this assurance, the Nipponese still had some doubts. But when it was proved that the Azad Hind Fauj is giving a bold show to the enemy, they were very much surprised.

This war is not waged by Nippon alone. It is a national war for India's liberation. We have to go to India and therefore will have to suffer more and more difficulties. Although the battle of Arakan was a minor struggle it was very important to us because it was the first test of our forces. On the 18th March the Provisional Government proclaimed that the Azad Hind Fauj crossed the Indo-Burma border and were fighting on Indian soil. In March our advance was so rapid that when our thrust into Imphal was delayed there were inquiries why Imphal was still standing against our assault. I was annoyed at persons asking such questions. These were persons who were not actually on the front line, but far behind in their homes. Those who know anything about fighting will not ask such questions. Only military observers realize the strategic importance of Imphal and Chittagong. If these cities had no military importance we would have captured them earlier. The fortifications on the Eastern Front of India are like that of the Maginot Line in France. So long as these fortifications are safe, the British are secure. When these fortifications are pierced through, our forces will easily make rapid advance towards Delhi.

In each and every battle there is a certain strategic point which will decide the course of the war. Those who are aware of the past history of India know well that Panipat always settled the fate of India. But in this war the fate of India will be settled somewhere in the jungles between Imphal and Chittagong. When once we smash enemy fortifications on the Eastern Frontier and reach the plains of Bengal and Assam then our road to Delhi will be clear. So the enemy will strive hard to hold to these fortifications. In this war when the Maginot Line was pierced, France collapsed in a few weeks. So when the fate of Chittagong and Imphal is sealed there will be no war in the Bengal Province and our advance to Calcutta will be only a route march.

I have just now told you that the battle of Imphal and Chittagong will settle the fate of India. We will get hold of these important strategic points at all cost even if we have to attempt ten times or more. When we withdrew from Imphal people were disappointed. They asked me for my opinion and I replied that there is no ground for any such doubt. We know our path and we will never waver until we reach our goal.

Friends, we should realize the importance of Imphal and Chittagong and be ready to make any sacrifice to occupy these cities. Once we take these strategic centres, our task will become easier for it will have wide repercussions throughout India. We know very well the situation in India. There is no Indian who likes the British. Every Indian hates the British and if a handful of them side with the British it is not out of love for the British but to achieve their self-interests. If the three hundred and eighty million Indians rose in revolt they could have annihilated the British with sticks and stones. Then there would have been no necessity for the Azad Hind Fauj. It is regrettable that they have not seen the destruction of the British with their own eyes as we Indians in East Asia have experienced. You are confident that the British empire will be shattered. Now it is our duty to go into India and defeat the British so that the 380 million Indians could see the destruction of the British with their own eyes. When they see it for themselves they will get courage and self-confidence and revolution will break out in every nook and corner of India and our task will become easier.

Friends, you perhaps remember that in August last year in the course of a speech at the Farrer Park I said that before the end of this year we will cross the Indo-Burma border and will stand on Indian soil. When I spoke I thought we will be able to commence fighting in the month of December. But we were delayed on account of necessary military preparations. Our forces entered India in March and we were fighting on a broad front from Akyab to Kohima. We defeated the enemy in every battle but due to transport difficulties we could not continue our advance. In the heavy rain we had only two courses open to us: either to stay in these jungles or to withdraw. The Nippon commander and our Commanders considered over the matter and it was decided to withdraw because to stay in these jungles meant disaster to the army. When the enemy saw that we have withdrawn and the road was clear they occupied the place without resistance and proclaimed to the whole world by every weapon of propaganda that they have won a great victory. But our officers and men know the real reason for our withdrawal. We are confident that we can occupy all the lost ground in no time. I would once again stress the importance of Imphal and Chittagong and we will have to occupy these places at any cost. After six months of battle we have judged correctly our strength and the strength of our enemy.

When the Azad Hind Fauj was organized the enemy began to make propaganda that the Azad Hind Fauj was not an army but only a propaganda stunt. But when our army went into action the British propagandists changed their tune and began to give out that the Azad Hind Fauj was very poorly equipped. In reply I said that our army possessed everything except meat, rum, beer and whisky which were abundantly supplied to the British forces. Our army will fight in the face of hunger and thirst. There have been many revolutions in the world history, but you can never find a single example where the revolutionary army was better equipped than their opponents. They have succeeded not because of the strength of their weapon or of numbers but by the strength of their conviction that they are fighting for a sacred cause. Take the case of Ireland. She had 5,000 revolutionaries who had dedicated their lives for their country. The British sent 50,000 troops well equipped to crush the revolution. But they miserably failed in spite of their superiority in number and weapons. I know very well the strength of our enemies and I know what we are capable of doing. We will have to make great sacrifices. Even if every soldier and officer of the Azad Hind Fauj has to lay down his life for the liberation of 380 million Indians, we are prepared for that. Even if the three million Indians in East Asia turn destitutes, that is nothing. We are proud that we are given such a golden opportunity to serve our Motherland. We are thankful to God that we have got men and material needed for the liberation of India. Three million Indians have been united. Now we have to pay the price of our independence with our blood which is not a big price. Now the responsibility that lies on our shoulders is to strengthen our army and march across into India. There is only one way for us. We have to shed our blood. So many of our comrades laid down their lives in the first campaign; nobody can say how many of us will remain alive until the war of liberation comes to a successful conclusion. Officers and men who hesitate to lay down their lives have no place in this army. Side by side with the Army the nation has to make total sacrifices. The nation must be prepared for such a sacrifice.

Last year in Bengal Province alone 20 lakhs of Indians perished due to starvation. 5 lakhs of Indians retreated along with the British from Burma and out of these more than one lakh lost their lives. If so many Indians had given up their lives for the independence of our Motherland, India to-day would have been a free country. If you are not willing to face death for the liberation of your country you have no right to call yourself an Indian. Some so-called Indians think that if India is freed they can go to India and if the British came back then also they can go back to India. I can assure these traitors that they will not go to India. We are not liberating India for them. They will have no place in a free India. We will pick up all those traitors and they will be at the mercy of the Free Government. The only favour they may expect from us will be a third class ticket to Britain.

Friends, we have to enhance our programme of total mobilization. Preparations are being made for the next offensive and we are collecting materials for this campaign. Our well-to-do brothers who are lagging behind will have to come forward and make sacrifices. Those wealthy Indians who have amassed a great fortune and are afraid to lay down their lives will have to take a Habeeb Mixture. Janab Habeeb is the first patriot who has sacrificed all his property, amounting to ten million and three thousand rupees. Those people who do not enjoy sleep thinking of their money may better take a dose of Habeeb Mixture and cure themselves by contributing all their money for our funds. I tell you as long as the entire nation is not fully prepared to sacrifice everything, our victory cannot be achieved. We must inspire and set an example to those who are obstructing our way. Fortunately their number is very small. Still they are doing harm to our movement. They think that we can only prattle and that we cannot suppress them. Now the entire nation has to come under military discipline. Those who are weak we will make them strong. And if we are forced to suppress these enemy agents disguised as Indians I know the whole nation will support us. Up to this time we entreated you with folded hands. In Nippon, Germany or in England the Governments never request but order. I can assure you that not only Syonan but the whole world, except perhaps America, is suffering from food shortage. The reason for America not suffering from such food shortage is that war has not gone to American soil. If you are prepared to sacrifice everything then the food problem will not exist at all. We also need more volunteers for the Rani of Jhansi Regiment; so I have to appeal to our sisters to come forward and join the Regiment.

I would like to ask you a question. I want you to answer honestly. When I was in Rangoon I received a report that the revolutionary spirit and enthusiasm of Indians in Syonan are fading. Now tell me how many of you are willing to work with us, prepared to make any sacrifice and to fight shoulder to shoulder with us and, if need be, to die with us?'

[Immediately the whole audience got up and expressed their willingness to lay down their lives or make any sacrifice for the liberation of India. They shouted 'Inquilab Zindabad,' 'Netaji ki Jai' and 'Chalo Delhi.']

55

We Shall Fulfill Our Promise

[Broadcast from Singapore on 1 January 1945][1]

Ladies and Gentlemen! In October last, I left Burma for a tour of East Asia. That is why I could not address you over the air. Last November, while broadcasting from Tokyo, I promised you a speech on the world situation. Before I start, I wish to offer you New Year greetings. The new year finds the war in its final and decisive stage. The people of India, particularly the Indians of East Asia, should be prepared to make the greatest sacrifices. I set out on a tour of East Asia in order to prepare the Indians there for this final battle. There is no place in East Asia where Indians are not to be found, and every Indian is enthusiastic about the battle for India's liberation. Men are joining the Indian National Army from all parts of East Asia, and money is also pouring in large amounts. This will continue until the battle for freedom is won. The Indian National Army will continue to receive monetary help. I have visited Malaya, Japan, France, Indo-China and the East Indies where I inspected the war effort of the Indian National Army. In Malaya alone, I received 7,000,000 dollars for the Indian National Army.

At this time I am reminded of my friends who are rotting in dark British dungeons in India. I am not going to relate here the brave deeds done by these patriots, whose only fault is that they worked for the freedom of their country. Justice must triumph in the end, and we shall not rest till we have won the battle of independence.

[1] *Testament of Subhas Bose*, pp. 66–8.

The war has entered its final stage. In October and November last, there were signs of it, but now it is crystal clear. Those who were saying only a few days ago that the European war would end in 1944 are now saying that it will not end in 1945 or even 1946. The German counter-attack in the West and the V-1 and V-2 has upset the Allied timetable. Allied propaganda has been exposed. Dismay prevails in England. The Germans have surpassed their enemies in the production of war material. The enemy has admitted that the German defences were strong.

On the other hand, there are deep-rooted differences between Russia, America and Britain. The bitter criticism of the British Policy in Greece, Belgium and Italy by the American Press proves the existence of differences between America and Britain over Allied policy in Europe. British troops, on the plea of liberating the people of Greece, are machine-gunning them. Recently, Mr. Churchill and Mr. Eden spoke on Greek affairs. Mr. Roosevelt let the cat out of the bag by saying that there was no such thing as the Atlantic Charter.

Whereas there is a sharp decline in manpower in America and Britain, Japanese and German war production is mounting hourly. Even if Germany is defeated, the Anglo-American armies will have to be kept in Europe in order to stem the tide of Bolshevism, and this augurs well for Japan. This policy of the Anglo-Americans will result in the ultimate destruction of their imperialism. We, who are fighting for India's liberation, should pay heed to the situation in Europe.

The Anglo-American position in the Pacific is even worse. The capture of a few islands in the Pacific by America provided the Allied propagandists with some material. But now they have realized that island hopping won't do. This has even been admitted by General Wedemeyer. The Americans said that the Japanese Navy suffered a crushing defeat in October last in the waters off Formosa and the Philippines, but the doubts expressed by American crews and British correspondents in India concerning this announcement have exposed the falsity of the whole thing. Now they realize that the American Navy suffered the same fate as Napoleon suffered while advancing towards Moscow. Coming events will bear me out. In the Philippines, the Japanese are dealing the Americans deadly blows. While the Anglo-Americans talk of linking Chungking and India by a land route, the Japanese road linking Japan with Singapore is completed. The whole Japanese nation is engaged in increasing Japan's war production. The enemy desires the end of the war, but it is improbable. Japanese and German interests lie in prolonging the war. The Japanese Kamikaze Corps are wreaking havoc on the Americans. I went to Japan several times and saw Japanese military strength. In this connection, you should read the statement of Reuter's military commentator in London, made on December 3 last, and the statement of the US Under-Secretary for War made on December 21 last. These statements will serve to show how much America and Britain are worried over Japanese military strength. The Indian National Army will shortly launch its attack and the British forces will be compelled to retreat until they are defeated.

We have gained much experience in the fighting on the Indo-Burma front, and we must make full use of it. We are certain of our victory. We know the weaknesses of our enemy, and our faith in victory has been redoubled. We know that we shall have to fight hard and bitter battles on the Indo-Burma front. The battles of Chittagong and Imphal will decide the battle of India's liberation. We shall fight the enemy with patience and steadfastness.

Brothers and sisters! We assure you that we shall fulfill our promise. The Indian National Army will soon find itself in the plains of Bengal and Assam. When we arrive there, it will be your duty to help us. Meanwhile, you should continue to make your preparations. But, do not repeat 1942 before the time is ripe for it. Convey our New Year message to those rotting in British jails, and tell them their sacrifices will not go in vain. India will be free. Jai Hind!

56

Our Immortal Heroes

[Special Order of the Day, 2 January 1945][1]

Comrades of the Azad Hind Fauj! On this auspicious New Year's Day, I want you, first of all, to look back on your achievements and on your progress since the formation of the Azad Hind Fauj. There can be no doubt whatsoever that in spite of many difficulties and drawbacks, your achievements and progress have been truly remarkable. This has been possible only because of the passionate desire for freedom which inspires the Indian people today, the many-sided assistance rendered by our countrymen in East Asia, the valuable aid offered by our allies and, above all, the hard work and sacrifice that you yourselves have put in. Before the end of 1943, units of the Azad Hind Fauj began moving in the direction of the Indo-Burma Frontier. On February 4, 1944, India's war of independence was launched in the Arakan region of Burma. On March 21, 1944, we were able to proclaim to the whole world that the Azad Hind Fauj had crossed the Eastern frontier of India and was fighting on the sacred soil of India. Since then, the fight has been going on; and in the course of that campaign, many of our comrades have laid down their lives on the field of battle. The heroism and self-sacrifice of the officers and men of the Azad Hind Fauj in India's war of independence have already become a glorious and undying tradition, which will serve as an inspiration for all times. Comrades! On this auspicious day I want you all to pay silent homage to our immortal heroes and to renew your solemn pledge to continue the fight until complete victory is achieved. India is calling you, the souls of

[1] *Testament of Subhas Bose*, pp. 174–5.

your comrades are urging you on to still braver deeds, therefore, gird up your loins for the hard battle that lies ahead. There can be no rest and no pause for us until our tri-colour National Flag is hoisted over India's Metropolis. Comrades! Our immortal heroes have paid for India's liberty with their own blood, we are proud of them, but we too must be ready for that supreme sacrifice.

Singapore, 2 January 1945

57

Bravery and Cowardice

[Statement, 13 March 1945][1]

Comrades! As you all know, the positive achievements of the officers and men of the Azad Hind Fauj last year on the field of battle and the victories that they scored over the enemy through their patriotism, bravery and self-sacrifice were marred to some extent by the cowardice and treachery of a few officers and men. We were hoping that with the advent of the New Year all traces of cowardice and treachery would be wiped out; and that in this year's operations the Azad Hind Fauj would be able to put up an unsullied record of heroism and self-sacrifice. But that was not to be. The recent treachery of five officers of the H.Q. of the 2nd Division has come as an eye-opener to us that all is not well within our ranks and that the seeds of cowardice and treachery have yet to be wiped out. If we now succeed in exterminating cowardice and treachery once for all, this shameful and despicable incident may, through God's grace, ultimately prove to be a blessing in disguise. I am, therefore, determined to take all possible measures necessary for the purification of our army. I am confident that in this I shall have your full and unstinted support. In order to destroy completely the germs of cowardice and treachery, the following measures will have to be adopted:

1. Every member of the Azad Hind Fauj, Officer, N.C.O. or Sepoy will, in future, be entitled to arrest any other member of the Azad Hind Fauj, no matter whatever his rank may be, if he behaves in a cowardly manner or to shoot him if he acts in a treacherous manner.

[1] *Testament of Subhas Bose*, pp. 175–7.

2. I am giving an opportunity to all members of the Azad Hind Fauj who may not feel inclined to work dutifully or fight courageously in future to leave the ranks of the Azad Hind Fauj. This offer will be open for one week from the time of its communication.
3. In addition to giving an opportunity to unwilling elements to leave voluntarily the ranks of the Azad Hind Fauj, I want to carry out a thorough purge of our Army. During the course of this purge, all those will be removed against whom there is suspicion that they may fail us, or betray us, at the critical moment. In order to carry out this purge successfully, I want your fullest cooperation and I want you, therefore, to give me, and my trusted officers, all available information about any cowardly or treacherous elements that may still exist in our Army.
4. It will not be enough to carry out a thorough purge now. In future also vigilance will have to continue. It will, therefore, be the duty of every member of the Azad Hind Fauj in future, to keep his eyes and ears open in order to detect in good time any tendency towards cowardice or treachery. In future, if any member of the Azad Hind Fauj detects any tendency towards cowardice or treachery, he should report at once, either orally or in writing, either to me or to the officers who may be within reach. In other words, from now onwards and for all times, every member of the Azad Hind Fauj should regard himself as the custodian of the honour and reputation of the Azad Hind Fauj and of the Indian Nation.
5. After the purge has been carried out and unwilling elements have been given an opportunity of leaving our Army, if there is any case of cowardice or treachery, the punishment will be death.
6. In order to create within our Army a moral bulwark against cowardice and treachery, we have to create an intense hatred against cowardice and treachery in any form. A strong feeling has to be created in the mind of every member of this Army that for a member of a revolutionary army, there is no crime more heinous and despicable than to be a coward or a traitor. Instructions are being issued separately as to how we can create such an intense hatred against cowardice and treachery so that there will be no more cowards or traitors within our ranks.

7. After the purge has been carried out, every member of the Azad Hind Fauj will be required to renew his oath to fight on bravery and courageously until the emancipation of our dear Motherland is achieved. Instructions regarding the form and manner of this oath will be issued separately.
8. Special rewards will be given to those who give information regarding cowardly and treacherous elements or who arrest or shoot at the front cowardly and treacherous elements.

SUBHAS CHANDRA BOSE
Supreme Commander,
Azad Hind Fauj, Burma, Dated 13 March 1945

58

End of a Dream

[Message on the eve of Netaji's departure from Rangoon for Bangkok on 24 April 1945][1]

To my Indian and Burmese friends in Burma!

Brothers and Sisters! I am leaving Burma with a very heavy heart. We have lost the first round of our fight for independence. But we have lost only the first round. There are many more rounds to fight. In spite of our losing the first round, I see no reason for losing heart.

You, my countrymen in Burma, have done your duty to your motherland in a way that has evoked the admiration of the world. You have given liberally your men, money, and materials. You set the finest example of total mobilization. But the odds against us were overwhelming, and we have temporarily lost the battle in Burma.

The spirit of selfless sacrifice which you have shown, particularly since I shifted my headquarters to Burma, is something that I shall never forget so long as I live.

I have the fullest confidence that that spirit can never be crushed. For the sake of India's freedom, I beseech you to keep up that spirit; I beseech you to hold your heads erect and wait for that blessed day, when, once again, you will have an opportunity of waging the war for India's independence.

When the history of India's Last War of Independence comes to be written, Indians in Burma will have an honoured place in that history.

[1] *India Fights On* (Bangkok: Provisional Government of Azad Hind, 1945, copy in the archives of the Netaji Research Bureau), and *Testament of Subhas Bose*, pp. 247–8.

I do not leave Burma of my own free will. I would have preferred to stay on here and shared with you the sorrow of temporary defeat. But on the pressing advice of my Ministers and high-ranking officers, I have to leave Burma in order to continue the struggle for India's liberation. Being born an optimist, my unshakeable faith in India's early emancipation remains unimpaired, and I appeal to you to cherish the same optimism.

I have always said that the darkest hour precedes the dawn. We are, now, passing through the darkest hour; therefore, the dawn is not far off.

INDIA SHALL BE FREE.

I cannot conclude this message without publicly acknowledging, once again, my heartfelt gratitude to the government and people of Burma for all the help that I have received at their hands in carrying on this struggle. The day will come when Free India will repay that debt of gratitude in a generous manner.

INQUILAB ZINDABAD! AZAD HIND ZINDABAD! JAI HIND!
SUBHAS CHANDRA BOSE
AZAD HIND FAUJ.

59

The Future Generations of Indians Will Bless Your Names

[Special Order of the Day, 24 April 1945][1]

Brave Officers and Men of the Azad Hind Fauj!

It is with a very heavy heart that I am leaving Burma—the scene of the many heroic battles that you have fought since February, 1944, and are still fighting. In Imphal and Burma we have lost the first round in our fight for Independence. But it is only the first round. We have many more rounds to fight. I am a born optimist and I shall not admit defeat under any circumstances. Your brave deeds in the battles against the enemy on the plains of Imphal, the hills and jungles of Arakan and the oil field area and other localities in Burma will live in the history of our struggle for Independence for all time.

Comrades! At this critical hour, I have only one word of command to give you, and that is that if you have to go down temporarily, then go down fighting with the national tri-colour held aloft; go down as heroes; go down upholding the highest code of honour and discipline. The future generations of Indians who will be born, not as slaves but as free men because of your colossal sacrifice, will bless your names and proudly proclaim to the world that you, their forbears, fought and suffered reverses in the battles in Manipur, Assam, and Burma, but through temporary failure you paved the way to ultimate success and glory.

My unshakeable faith in India's liberation remains unimpaired. I am leaving in your safe hands our national tri-colour, our national

[1] *India Fights On*, pp. 17–19, and *Testament of Subhas Bose*, pp. 248–9.

honour and the best traditions of Indian warriors. I have no doubt whatsoever that you, vanguard of India's Army of Liberation, will sacrifice everything, even life itself, to uphold India's national honour, so that your comrades, who will continue the fight elsewhere, may have before them your shining example to inspire them at all times.

If I had my own way, I would have preferred to stay with you in adversity and share with all the difficulties. But on the advice of my Ministers and high-ranking Officers, I have to leave Burma in order to continue the struggle for emancipation. Knowing my countrymen in East Asia and inside India, I can assure you that they will continue the fight under all circumstances and that all your sufferings and sacrifices will not be in vain. So far as I am concerned, I shall steadfastly adhere to the pledge that I took on the 21st of October, 1943, to do all in my power to serve the interests of 38 crores of my countrymen and fight for their liberation. I appeal to you, in conclusion, to cherish the same optimism as myself and to believe, like myself, that the darkest hour always precedes the dawn. INDIA SHALL BE FREE—AND BEFORE LONG.

May God Bless You!

INQUILAB ZINDABAD!
AZAD HIND ZINDABAD! JAI HIND!

Subhas Chandra Bose
Supreme Commander
Azad Hind Fauj

60

We Fight On

[Speech delivered in Bangkok on 21 May 1945][1]

Sisters and Brothers,

After I spoke to you in January last, the war situation has undergone considerable change. In Europe, German resistance has collapsed completely. Here, in Burma, we have lost the first round in our fight for freedom. Nevertheless, there is no reason why we should lose heart. If our enemies did not lose heart when they were expelled from Europe and East Asia, if our enemies, despite such staggering defeats, could continue the war and even launch a counteroffensive, we should exhibit at least as much strength and tenacity as our enemies have. You know that I have always said that we shall deserve to be free, only if we are more courageous, more tenacious, and more far-sighted than our enemies. If our enemies, after being expelled from Burma, could stage a comeback, there is no reason why we should not return to Burma again. The main point is whether our morale has broken down and whether we consider ourselves to be beaten. The Supreme Commander of the Allied forces in the last European War, Marshal Foch, once made a historic remark—'That army is beaten which considers itself to be beaten.' Among those who have come with me from Burma, there is not one man or woman who considers himself or herself to be beaten. No doubt we have lost one round in India's War of Liberation. But many more rounds are to follow and the last round will decide the final result of this war. War is in many ways like a match between two wrestlers. When the wrestlers are more or less equal in strength, victory will

[1] *India Fights On*, pp. 1–13, translated from the original Hindustani.

go to him who can hold out longer. If we have greater tenacity and staying power, if we have more spiritual strength than our enemies, then only shall we deserve to win freedom. Unfortunately, there are among us a few men who get easily upset—and even panicky—over slight setbacks. This is the psychological effect of slavery. The Indian people will have to overcome this weakness and to carry on the fight under all circumstances, if they are to win in the long run.

There is another thing I should like to tell you in this connection. In a modern war—and especially in a war of the present magnitude—many things may happen which are least expected or anticipated. A famous military strategist and one of the founders of the science of modern warfare, the German General and Writer, Clausewitz, once said—'War has many surprises.' I shall give you a few instances to illustrate the truth of this remark. In the Balkan War of 1912, the four powers—Romania, Bulgaria, Greece and Serbia—made a combined attack on Turkey. Turkey was defeated in one battle after another, until the Balkan powers almost reached the gates of Constantinople (Istanbul). Everything seemed to be lost for the Turks, and there was not even a glimmer of hope. All of a sudden, disagreement and discord broke out among the four Balkan powers, which quickly developed into a war among them. Constantinople was saved. The Turkish forces launched a counter-offensive and they managed to recover most of the lost territories. We see, therefore, that if Turkey had surrendered when all hopes seemed to have gone, she would not have been able to turn the tide of the war as she actually did.

Take another example from the recent history of Turkey. In the last world war, Turkey fought alongside of Germany and Austria-Hungary. But she was ultimately beaten. Constantinople, the proud capital of the Ottoman Empire, was occupied by the Allied forces and the Sultan, who was also the Caliph, was virtually made a prisoner. Seeing that the war was completely lost, the Sultan submitted to all the humiliating treatment imposed by the Allied forces and asked the Turks to cease all resistance. In that dark hour, there was, however, one man who would not accept defeat. Mustapha Kemal Pasha, who was then only one of the many able Turkish Officers, left Constantinople and crossed over to Anatolia. He got together a band of faithful officers and with their help organized a new army from among the Anatolian Turks. That army proved to be invincible and the Turks, by their valour, tenacity and indomitable faith, recovered the freedom and victory that they had lost when they had such powerful allies as Germany, and Austria-Hungary. It is indeed one of the miracles of history that Turkey was badly beaten when she was fighting side by side with powerful allies and that when she put up a fight all alone, after her defeat, she came out victorious in the long run. The secret of this miracle was that Kemal Pasha and his fellow fighters did not accept defeat at a time when all other Turks headed by the Sultan himself did so.

I shall now give you another instance from another part of the world, namely Ireland. During the last world war, when Ireland's enemy, Britain, was engaged in a life and death struggle, the Irish Revolutionaries made a bid for freedom. True to their motto that 'Britain's difficulty is Ireland's opportunity', they rose in revolt during the Easter Week of 1916. The Easter Revolution was, however, crushed inside of a week. At that time, there were Irish people, who called their own revolutionaries 'mad men'. But though the Easter Rebellion was crushed so easily, the forces of revolution continued to work among the rich people, and ultimately broke out in a more powerful revolution in 1919—that is, one year after the end of the war. It is a strange phenomenon in history that while the British could easily crush the Irish Rebellion of 1916 at a time when they were engaged in a life and death struggle, they had to acknowledge defeat at the hands of the same Irish Revolutionaries after they (the British) emerged victorious from the world war. If the Irish Revolutionaries had accepted defeat in 1916, the Revolution of 1919 would not have taken place, and Ireland would not have been what she is today.

A similar phenomenon took place in India also. During the world war, the Indian revolutionaries tried to organize a rebellion in order to overthrow British power in India. That attempt was easily crushed. But the spirit of the Indian people did not acknowledge defeat. After Britain's victory in the last war, and after the Jallianwalla Bagh Massacre in 1919, a political awakening of the Indian people under the leadership of Mahatma Gandhi took place on such a grand scale that the British have not been able to suppress it up to now.

The lesson to be derived from all these events is that a nation which loses its morale and its faith in ultimate victory can never hope to be victorious. On the other hand, if in spite of temporary setbacks and defeats, we continue the struggle with undiminished faith in our final success, then no power on earth can deprive us of our well deserved victory. Since we are fighting for justice and truth and for the birthright of liberty, freedom is bound to come, if only we fight on.

There is no need to hide the fact that we have lost the first round in our war of liberation. But that does not mean that the fighting in Burma has come to an end. On the contrary, the Azad Hind Fauj and the Japanese Army are still fighting on various fronts in Burma, and they will continue fighting so long as it is humanly possible to do so. Those of us who have left Burma have not withdrawn from the fight. We have come with the sole intention of continuing the struggle on other fronts. We are moving from one battlefield to another. We have but one goal before us—and only one method of achieving that goal—the method of armed struggle. Therefore, the reverses that we have suffered recently in Burma do not affect our future programme in any way. 'CHALO DELHI' continues to be the slogan and the war cry of the Azad Hind Fauj. It may be that we shall not go to Delhi via Imphal. But the roads to Delhi are many, like the roads to Rome. And along one of these many roads we shall travel and ultimately reach our destination, the metropolis of India. If our whole army of liberation becomes spirit only, we shall never stop advancing towards our homeland.

In all our recent experiences, there is one thing, which is to us tragic and humiliating. Whatever reverses we have suffered during a campaign of about fifteen months, have been due not so much to the British forces, as to the British Indian Army. In the spring of 1944, it was the British Indian Army that barred our way to Imphal, Calcutta and Delhi. This year, it has been the British Indian Army more than anybody else that has been responsible for the re-entry into Burma of the British. In the last century, it was with the help of India that the British conquered Burma. Now it is again with the help of India that the British have re-entered Burma. There is, however, one silver lining in the cloud that has overtaken us, and that is, the British Indian Army of today is not the British Indian Army of the last war. Soldiers of the Azad Hind Fauj have had numerous opportunities of coming into close contact with members of the British Indian Army. Very often our soldiers were told by the latter that if they (i.e. Azad Hind Fauj) succeed in advancing further, members of the British Indian Army would then come and join them. There is no doubt that at heart large sections of the British Indian Army sympathize with the Azad Hind Fauj and its fight for freedom. But the British Indian Army is not yet prepared to take the risk and line up with the revolutionaries. As a result of foreign rule, members of the British Indian Army have lost their self-confidence and they are afraid that the British might ultimately win, in which case they would be in a difficult situation. Moreover, they have been influenced, to some extent, by the propaganda of our enemies that the Azad Hind Fauj (Indian National Army) is a puppet army of the Japanese. After coming into Burma, the eyes of the British Indian Army will be opened. They will see for themselves what the Provisional Government of Azad Hind and the Azad Hind Fauj have done and how they have fought for India's freedom. They will hear 'Jai Hind', which is the greeting of all free Indians. They will also hear India's inspiring national anthem sung by freedom-loving Indians in Burma. The effect of this experience on the British Indian Army, and all other Indians, who have come into Burma alongside of the British, is bound to be great in the days to come.

Friends! I shall refer once again to the war in Europe. There was a time when the German armies had advanced inside Russia right up to Stalingrad. I wonder how many people there were who, in those days, could imagine that the tide would turn and that one day, the Soviet Army would be in Berlin. Germany's defeat is one of the surprises of this war. Clausewitz was perfectly right when he said that, 'War has many surprises.' But there are more surprises to come, and some of these surprises will not be welcome to our enemies. You know very well that I have been always of the opinion that if Germany collapsed, it would be a signal for the outbreak of an acute conflict between the Soviets and the Anglo-Americans. That conflict has already broken out, and it will be intensified in the days to come. The time is not far off when our enemies will realize that though they have succeeded in overthrowing Germany, they have indirectly helped to bring into the arena of European politics another power—Soviet Russia—that may prove to be a greater menace to British and American imperialism than Germany was. The Provisional Government of Azad Hind will continue to follow international developments with the closest interest and endeavour to take the fullest advantage of them. The fundamental principle of our foreign policy has been and will be—Britain's enemy is India's friend.

It is clear by now that the war aims of the Soviet Union are quite different from those of the Anglo-Americans, although they had a common enemy in Germany. This has been further confirmed at the San Francisco Conference where the Soviet Foreign Commissioner, Mon. Molotov, refused to submit to the Anglo-American demands. In fact, Mon. Molotov went so far as to challenge the credentials of the puppets of Britain and America who came to represent India and the Philippines, respectively. The differences that became visible at the San Francisco Conference are only a precursor of a much wider and deeper conflict between the Soviets and the Anglo-Americans, which the future has in store for the world.

While the conflict between the Soviets and the Anglo-Americans is going on, we should not fail to understand the real position and strength of our principal enemy, Britain. So long as Britain was fighting without the aid of America, whether in Europe or in East Asia, she was beaten in every battle. Britain's recent successes have been due first and foremost to American leadership and American assistance. I have said so again in the past, that the days of the British Empire are drawing to a close. The British Empire is a decadent and decaying empire, and it is endeavouring now to prolong its life with the help of the United States of America. But though the life of an old man may be prolonged with the help of skilfull doctors and efficacious medicines and injection, it can never be restored to youthful vitality. The British Empire is endeavouring to march on with the help of American crutches, but these American crutches cannot help Britain very long. All that we have to do is to deliver a knockout blow to British Imperialism in India, which is the basis of Britain's world imperialism.

Our programme in East Asia remains unaltered. I demand from my countrymen in East Asia 'Total Mobilization'. We want more men, more money and more materials to replenish the losses we have recently suffered. Above all, we want an indomitable will and unshakeable determination. Let me remind you that it took the British full 100 years—from 1757 to 1857—to finally subjugate India. Therefore, if we are to fight on for a few years more in order to recover our liberty, nobody should grudge it. It is no doubt encouraging to us in East Asia to find that Indians all over the world—even in enemy countries—are wide-awake. You have seen this recently in the case of the San Francisco conference where Indians in America, headed by Srimati Vijaylakshmi Pandit, demanded complete Independence for India. Even a flunkey of British Imperialism, Sir Feroz Khan Noon, had to say in public that no power on earth could deprive India of her freedom. According to him, the forces of nationalism inside India and world forces outside India, make India's demand for independence irresistible. In conclusion, I call upon you—my countrymen in Thailand—to come forward and do your duty to India in the difficult days that are still ahead of us. Above all, I want you to cherish the same optimism and confidence in final victory as we have. It is this spiritual strength that is our sheet-anchor. India shall be free and before long. With this unshakeable belief, let us continue the struggle for India's emancipation.

Jai Hind.

[At the end of this speech, Netaji asked the audience how many of them were prepared to continue the struggle till a victorious conclusion was reached. The entire audience composed of men and women stood up in response and gave vent to their feelings in prolonged and enthusiastic cheering. With singing of the National Anthem, the proceedings came to a close.]

61

The German Defeat

[Statement on the situation in Europe from an undisclosed base outside Burma on 22 May 1945, and broadcast by the Provisional Government of Azad Hind Radio, Singapore, on 25 May 1945][1]

The war situation in Europe developed with dramatic suddenness during the last week of April and first week of May. Though it was apparent to every observer since the beginning of this year that the German armed forces would not be able to hold out for an indefinite period, nobody could predict how and when the end would come.

The courage, tenacity and fortitude with which the armed forces of Germany fought till the moment of Herr Hitler's death must compel the admiration of the whole world. In my own view, the defeat of Germany was not a military but a political one. It was the foreign policy of Germany vis-à-vis Soviet Russia and other countries that was fundamentally responsible for the military disaster, which has now overtaken the German nation. One of the blunders committed by the German Government in the realm of foreign policy was the total disregard of Bismarck's advice to the German nation, 'never to fight on two fronts.' The turning point in European affairs came in 1940 when, M. Molotov, the Soviet Foreign Minister, visited Berlin. That was the hour when German statesmanship should have risen to its fullest height and reached an understanding with Soviet Russia by any means. If Bismarck had been alive, he would have done that. But, unfortunately for the German

[1] *India Fights On*, pp. 26–31, and *Testament of Subhash Bose*, pp. 79–81.

nation, just as faulty statesmanship was responsible for their defeat in the First World War, so also has it been responsible for their defeat in the present war.

The problem that should now engage the attention of every student of international affairs is as to what will happen to Europe in future. On this point, my views are perfectly clear, and I firmly adhere to what I have consistently said in the past—namely, that the collapse of Germany will be the signal for the outbreak of an acute conflict between the Soviets and the Anglo-Americans. The whole world knows that the war aims of Soviet Russia are quite different from those of Anglo-Americans. The Soviet Government knows that the defeat of Germany has been due first and foremost to the heroism, tenacity and sacrifice of the people and armed forces of the Soviet Union. Consequently, the Soviet Government, being conscious of its own strength, will never give in to the Anglo-American powers in the post-war reconstruction of Europe. The truth of this remark has been already exemplified at San Francisco, where the conference virtually resulted in a fiasco when M. Molotov left that city.

The San Francisco Conference is only a precursor of the events that are to follow in the domain of European affairs. Europe now stands at the crossroads of history. Prior to the outbreak of the present war, the affairs of Europe were in a chaotic condition, with the big powers pulling in different directions. Germany, however, had a plan for the reorganization of Europe, and during the last five years she endeavoured to work out that plan. Now, with the collapse of Germany, that plan has come to naught. In post-war Europe, there is only one other power that has a plan, which is worth giving a trial, and that power is Soviet Russia. The only plan—if we call it a plan—which Britain can have is to maintain the balance of power in Europe in her own selfish interest, with the help of France and, possibly, of the United States. That plan will never be accepted by the European nations. So far as the United States are concerned, however keen and ambitious they may be to establish the 'American Century' in world history, they will never succeed in controlling the affairs of Europe from across the Atlantic. Moreover, neither Britain nor the United States of America, who are capitalist-imperialist countries, can produce a plan of social reconstruction which will be acceptable to the nations of Europe. Consequently, we come to the conclusion that there is no other alternative for the nations of Europe than to give a trial to the experiment that has proved to be eminently successful within the Soviet Union. No doubt, Britain and America, and Britain even more than America, will do everything in their power to stop and frustrate Soviet plans for the reconstruction of Europe. But these attempts are bound to fail, primarily because, during the last five years, public opinion all over Europe has swung so violently to the left that after the collapse of National-Socialist Germany, no government and no social order can endure which is not predominantly 'Leftist' in character. So far as Germany's future is concerned, we have to remember that the Nationalist-Socialist Government, during a period of twelve years, virtually destroyed the old capitalist regime. The only alternative before the German people, therefore, seems to be a socialist order of a radical type, which will be on friendly terms with the Soviet Union. Whether this development will actually take place depends on how Germany will be treated by the Allied Powers.

If Germany is not humiliated and is not made to nurse a desire for national revenge, it is inevitable that there will be a peaceful transition from National-Socialist trend, and the German people will be drowned for the time being, and we shall see once again the seeds of an ultranationalist revival, which may prove to be the starting point of another European War—and, perhaps, of World War number three. If there is one man in Europe today who holds in his hands the destinies of the European nations for the next few decades, that man is Marshal Stalin. The whole world, and above all, Europe will, therefore, follow with breathless anxiety the moves of the Soviet Union in the days to come. In this hour of Germany's sorrow, I cannot help reiterating, on behalf of the Indian people and myself, my heartfelt gratitude to the German people and nation for the sympathy and support that they gave us in our struggle for freedom.

62

Ill-Treatment of Prisoners of War

[Statement on the treatment of members of the Azad Hind Fauj captured by the Anglo-Americans in Burma, Bangkok, 30 May 1945][1]

Information that has reached us from reliable sources in Burma goes to show that vindictive and brutal treatment is being meted out to officers and men of the Azad Hind Fauj (Indian National Army) who have been captured by the Anglo-Americans in Burma. As the whole world knows, the Anglo-Americans and, in particular, the British have always been in the habit of condemning Germany and Japan for their supposed ill-treatment of Anglo-American prisoners-of-war. But I would now like to ask what the Anglo-Americans are themselves doing with the members of the Azad Hind Fauj, who happened to fall into their hands in Burma. Though the Allied forces in Burma belong to several nationalities, the responsibility as regards the ill treatment of officers and men of the Azad Hind Fauj devolves solely on the British authorities. The British authorities cannot even invent the excuse that we ill-treated their troops who fall into our hands. The only allied troops who fell into our hands were those who voluntarily came and joined the Azad Hind Fauj. And even the Delhi Radio admitted some days ago that all those who joined the Azad Hind Fauj received good treatment.

[1] *India Fights On*, pp. 32–4.

It may be that the British authorities think that we are not in a position to retaliate and they can, therefore, do with our officers and men what they like. But I would like to warn the British authorities that that is not the case. If we are forced to do so, we can find ways and means for adopting retaliatory measures, in case they continue to ill-treat and persecute the officers and men of the Azad Hind Fauj. But before we are forced to think of retaliatory measures, there is one remedy open to us, which is not only efficacious but also easy. If our countrymen at home take up this matter and carry on a raging and tearing campaign inside India, I am absolutely sure that the British authorities will be brought to their senses and will see the error of their ways. Public opinion in India may not be strong enough to force the British to concede independence to India, but it is certainly strong enough to stop the ill treatment and persecution of members of the Azad Hind Fauj who have become prisoners-of-war at the hands of the British. Members of the Azad Hind Fauj are honest patriots and revolutionaries fighting for the freedom of their motherland. They, no doubt, fought bravely and stubbornly against the British, but they fought with clean hands and with a clear conscience. They are, therefore, entitled to decent treatment during captivity in accordance with international usage and convention. Consequently, I appeal to my countrymen at home to take up the cause of their own prisoners-of-war, who fought for India's liberation and who are now receiving brutal and vindictive treatment at the hands of the British. I appeal to them, also, to compel the British authorities to divulge correct information about the fate of these prisoners-of-war, so that the world may judge how far the British themselves observe the rules and canons of international warfare to which they pay so much lip homage.

63

Comment on First Wavell Offer

[Statement broadcast by the 'Provisional Government of Azad Hind Broadcasting Station', Saigon, on 18 June 1945][1]

Sisters and brothers! I listened with great attention to the speech which the Viceroy of India, Lord Wavell, broadcast on June 14, from New Delhi conveying the offer of the British Government to India. That was the offer to bring which Lord Wavell made a long pilgrimage to London. Though the manner and tone of the Viceroy's speech gave one the impression that he himself had very little hope that nationalist India would accept this offer, I have no doubt that the Indian public is now busy discussing the offer.

At such a juncture, it would neither be untimely nor out of place to inform my countrymen at home as to how Indians in East Asia reacted to the British Government's offer. First of all, we found out, as the Viceroy has himself confessed, that the only motive of the British Government is to mobilize India's support in the war against Japan. The British people are war-weary and after the termination of the war in Europe they badly need rest, and as such, they want others to fight their battles while they themselves reap the fruits of victory. But the British Indian troops, too, are war-weary, and after the recent successes of the Anglo-Americans in Burma they also desire rest and relaxation. It is, therefore, vital for the British to make the Indian people pour out their

[1] *Testament of Subhas Bose*, pp. 83–7.

money and shed their blood for the preservation of the British Empire. While the fighting was going on inside India and along the Indo-Burma border the British could bluff the British Indian Army with the preaching that it was their duty to fight for the defence of India. The British could also bluff them later on by preaching that the Burma campaign was merely a continuation of the campaign for the defence of India.

But now that the British want India's blood and money for the campaigns beyond Burma and for the campaigns in the Pacific, a new scheme must be found in order to obtain India's support for such campaigns. That is why the British Government has now put forward this new offer, which is in reality Sir Stafford Cripps' old offer in a slightly altered garb.

In deciding what reply we, Indians, should give, we will have to consider what we stand to gain by fighting Britain's war against Japan. It is one thing for Britain to forcibly exploit India for her war of aggression, but it is quite a different thing for Indian nationalists to voluntarily fight Britain's war. To co-operate in Britain's war effort at this stage will mean that we have completely nullified our moral struggle against the British. It will mean political suicide on the part of the Indian National Congress and for us Indians as well.

At an earlier stage of the war British propagandists and their trumpeters could possibly bluff and bamboozle the Indian people that India's defence was at stake as the Japanese were then knocking at India's gates. But now with the change in the war situation in East Asia, no Indian can have the slightest interest in fighting Britain's war against Japan. It is, therefore, crystal clear that any acceptance of Lord Wavell's offer will be tantamount to a voluntary shedding of precious Indian blood and draining our resources in fighting Britain's imperialistic war. But what would India gain in return? Nothing, except a few jobs on the Viceroy's Executive Council.

We cannot even argue that by accepting the offer we shall be reaching the 'goal of self-government', which Lord Wavell and the British Government want us to believe. India does not care any longer for self-government within the British Empire, and India will never be content with anything less than complete independence. But even if any Indian is prepared to accept self-government, he would have a much better chance of achieving that objective by continuing the resistance now than by accepting the present offer. The moment we accept the offer it will be inferred by the British Government that we are prepared to compromise by taking something very much less than even self-government. I have no doubt in my mind that the acceptance of this offer will seriously jeopardize all chances of securing even self-government in future, not to speak of complete independence. In short, by accepting the offer we shall gain nothing but we shall lose a lot, and it is Britain that will profit by our lack of strength.

Under normal circumstances there would not be even a ten to one chance for any Indian nationalist to be enamoured of the present offer, but the British are cunning politicians and they have chosen the proper psychological moment for aiming this offer at India. British politicians are hoping that the Indian people are, now, overawed by recent Anglo-American victories. The Indian people may, therefore, feel that we stand no chance of achieving independence during the course of the present war, and might as well make the best of a bad bargain and take whatever is being offered by the British. This is going to be the attitude of pessimists and moderate politicians like Sri Rajagopalachariar, but this attitude is entirely mistaken and unjustified and will inevitably result in putting back the clock of freedom by many years.

The first surprise of this war has been the defeat of Germany. But there are many other surprises in store for us, and some of them will not be welcome to our enemies. Although the war in Europe has ended, the war in East Asia will go on for a long time and India will have plenty of opportunities in future for working for and achieving her liberation. There is, accordingly, no reason whatever to enter into a humiliating compromise which British imperialism has offered us in the hope that, in view of her strong position, we will be overawed into accepting it. Firstly, Britain has not yet won the war; and, secondly, even if we fail to win independence during the course of the present war, we shall still get a last opportunity when the present war terminates and the changeover from war to peace takes place. History affords similar instances of successful revolutions, which have broken out immediately after a big war, and on several occasions the revolutionaries have emerged victorious out of the place following the war. For instance, in Ireland, the Easter Rebellion of 1916 was crushed, but the Irish

Revolution of 1919 after Britain's victory in the First World War was successful. Similarly, Turkey was badly defeated during the First World War, but after her defeat in 1918, she launched a war of liberation and came out triumphant in 1921. After the Allied victory in Europe in the present war Syria and Lebanon are already waging their war of liberation, and I have no doubt that they will ultimately come out victorious. Consequently, there is no reason whatsoever why we should humiliate ourselves by accepting the offer, which we proudly rejected in 1942 when Sir Stafford Cripps brought it to India.

I shall now refer to the merits of the British proposal. On close and careful analysis, it will be found that the present proposal is in essence and in substance identical with that of Sir Stafford Cripps' offered to us in 1942. Three more seats on the Viceroy's Executive Council have been offered to us this time, for example, those of Home, Finance and External Affairs; for these and other portfolios the others will be appointed by the Viceroy and will be responsible to him and not to the representatives of the people. On the other hand, the most important portfolio, that of the War Member, has been reserved for a Britisher, namely the C.-in-C. While the present offer is the old offer of Sir Stafford Cripps appearing in a slightly altered form, there are other obnoxious features, which render the offer totally unacceptable. In his speech the Viceroy has clearly indicated that he regards the Congress as one among many parties as has been the traditional policy of the British Government. This attitude was indignantly repudiated by Mahatma Gandhi at the Round Table Conference in London in 1931, when, as representative of the Congress, he represented the Indian People. If the Congress accepts the offer now, it will repudiate once for all what it has consistently maintained, namely, that it represents the people of India; and it will accept what the British Government has repeatedly held, namely that the Congress is one among many parties in India. I cannot, for the slightest moment, imagine how any Indian nationalist can think of accepting this offer.

There is another mischievous feature in Lord Wavell's offer. He has ordered the release of the members of the Working Committee of the Congress, but has maintained that unless his offer is accepted, all those who participated in the rising of 1942 will have to remain in custody. There is, nowhere, mentioned in his speech that even if his order is accepted, those who were imprisoned in the year 1939 and 1942 will be set free. It is a well-established convention in all democratic countries that a constitutional change is heralded by an amnesty for all political prisoners. In the case of India, however, this convention has been given the go-by.

The British Government has been telling us that no constitutional changes can be introduced during the course of the war, though we have seen that throughout the world far-reaching political changes are being carried out. Here in East Asia, we have seen quite a different state of affairs. Right in the midst of the war, several independent governments have been set up and power has been handed over to people. So, you see that this British plea is completely hollow, and it is intended to delay and deny the Indian demand. If Britain really wants to set up a responsible government, she should lose no time in declaring India a self-governing nation and hand over power to the people's representatives.

Sisters and brothers in India! You have suffered long and suffered much from the political persecution and economic exploitation of British capitalism. Let us suffer a little longer. We have to resist British imperialism by all the moral and material means at our disposal, and above all, let us keep the flag of independence flying. By continuing our fight against imperialism, and by refusing to compromise over independence, we shall be able to keep burning the question of India's freedom before the bar of world opinion. That is the way to freedom. On the other hand, by accepting the offer, we will be humiliating ourselves and losing the moral sympathy of the world.

It may be that some of you are asking what is the best way for achieving the liberation of India. To that my answer is perfectly clear. Firstly, from outside India, we shall carry on the armed struggle for our freedom to the last man and to the last round. Secondly, there are numerous friends of India abroad who advocate our cause before the bar of world opinion and all international conferences. And, lastly, my countrymen, you too must be prepared to launch a revolution at the opportune moment, which will spread like the wild fire of the prairies and may even be supported by the British Indian forces.

Sisters and brothers! In conclusion, I appeal to you not to give up hope. I repeat that the forces that are now working inside India and outside are irresistible. There is no earthly power that can stop the Indian people from achieving their goal of freedom. With patience and determination we shall achieve our goal. The Viceroy has asked for your goodwill and co-operation. Tell him that your goodwill and co-operation have been reserved for India's struggle for liberty and for none else.

64

No Compromise on Independence

[Broadcast from Singapore on 19 June 1945][1]

Sisters and brothers in India!

Yesterday, I spoke in a general way about Lord Wavell's offer and what our reaction to it should be. Today, I want to speak to you again on the same subject. But before I do so, I should like to draw your attention to the communiqué issued by the 'Provisional Government of Azad Hind' on the same topic. That communiqué has been broadcast to you from this station yesterday and again today. The importance of this communiqué lies in the fact1 that it represents the considered opinion of politically minded Indians in East Asia. The communiqué has also added significance in so far as Indians in East Asia will stand by the policy enunciated therein. In other words, if the Congress decides to accept Lord Wavell's offer and if, as an inevitable consequence of it, the Congress leaders come at the head of the Indian troops to fight Britain's imperialist war in the Far East, then there will be no option for us but to fight with the 'Azad Hind Fauj' against our own countrymen, who would then be allies of British imperialism.

British and American news agencies have been giving detailed reports of the daily developments inside India. With the help of these reports it is possible to form a correct picture of what is going on inside our country. From the reports coming from India, it is clear to me that most people are absorbed in the consideration of the secondary features and the insignificant details of the British offer; while, on the other

[1] *Testament of Subhas Bose*, pp. 87–95.

hand, they do not give sufficient attention to the fundamental issues involved in that offer, as well as the inevitable consequences of it. I would, therefore, beg you to consider, first of all, what the inevitable results of accepting Wavell's offer will be, because the Congress leaders will have to take the responsibility of sending at least half-a-million Indian troops to fight Britain's imperialist war, not on the Indo-Burma border or inside Burma, but in the regions beyond Burma and in the Pacific. With all due respect, I would like to ask Mahatma Gandhi, Maulana Abul Kalam Azad, Pandit Jawaharlal Nehru, Sardar Vallabhbhai Patel and other leaders whether they will take the responsibility of fighting Britain's imperialist war in the Far East and sacrificing half-a-million Indian lives for the same.

Our countrymen at home do not perhaps realize what is the real origin of the present offer of the British Government. As I have said in a separate statement, I have definite information obtained from reliable sources that the British Government was asked by the United States of America to provide sufficient men, money and material for the future campaigns in the Far East. The British Government was prepared to produce the required money and material, but was unable to provide the manpower from Britain, for reasons to which I shall subsequently refer. The British Government thereupon called upon Lord Wavell to obtain half-a-million Indian troops from India in order to meet the demand of the United States of America. Lord Wavell, knowing the Indian situation, was unable to comply with this request, because the big portion of the British-Indian Army has been engaged in the war in Africa, Asia and Europe over a long time and has now become war-weary. Lord Wavell informed the British Cabinet that unless sufficient public enthusiasm was aroused in India, it would not be possible to find half-a-million Indian troops who would be willing to fight Britain's war in the Far East. Thereafter, communications took place between Lord Wavell and the British Cabinet as to how India's support could be mobilized for the future military operations in East Asia, that is, in Malaya, Thailand, Indo-China, China and Japan proper. The real motive underlying the British offer is to somehow get, with the approval of the Indian nationalists, and the full connivance of the Congress, half-a-million troops with necessary material to fight Britain's imperialist war in East Asia. Hence it is Chungking that will profit greatly if Indian troops are made available for the war in Far East. It is, therefore, not surprising that the Chungking Government and its propaganda organs are now jubilant over Lord Wavell's offer and want the Congress to accept it. It may be that there are a few Indians at home, who know that Indians troops sent out to the Far East in the future will be opposed by the Azad Hind Fauj or the Indian National Army. But, there is no Indian who can be indifferent to this nor can anyone approve of this plan of sacrificing half-a-million Indian lives for Britain's imperialist war in East Asia.

I have already said that there are definite reasons as to why the British Government is unable to obtain from Britain itself the necessary fighting men needed for the future campaigns in the Far East. First of all, the British have suffered tremendous losses during the war on many fronts over a period of five years and nine months. As a result, the British people are war-weary, and British troops are not willing to face another long campaign, which will have to be fought under conditions much harder than in Europe. Secondly, unlike the First World War, this war has well nigh brought about the financial bankruptcy of Britain. Owing to the pressure of war and the colossal demand for war material, British industries had to switch over almost entirely to war production. This was not the case with American industries. The result was that, during the war, Britain has been fast losing her pre-war markets and these markets were steadily going into the hands of American industry. If this process goes on for a long time during this war, then Britain, in spite of an Allied victory, will lose the greater portion of her pre-war foreign trade and will be economically ruined. Owing to this reason, British leaders find it imperative to release their factory workers from the fighting forces and war services as soon as possible and thereby restart peacetime industries. It is absolutely impossible for Britain to do both things at the same time, namely, to fight another long campaign in the Far East and to restart her peacetime industries.

Therefore, the other big source of manpower within the British Empire, namely, India, is to be exploited in order to produce cannon fodder for the future campaigns in East Asia. If it had been possible to get the required half-a-million troops from India without popular sympathy and support, Wavell's offer would never have seen the light of day; but since the British Indian Army has already been fighting over a long period and is war-weary, it is absolutely essential for Lord Wavell and the British Cabinet to win over the Congress in order to get the required cannon-fodder for their future campaigns.

I have no doubt in my mind that under normal circumstances, nobody belonging to the Congress would have even looked at Lord Wavell's offer. In order to give their consideration to that offer, Congressmen will have to give a go-by to the fundamental principles and beliefs of the Indian National Congress. The Congress stands for complete independence. Lord Wavell's offer, as has been rightly pointed out by Mahatma Gandhi, does not even mention the word 'independence'. Secondly, the Congress stands for non-participation in and resistance to Britain's imperialist war. Thirdly, the Congress is still pledged to the 'Quit India' resolution adopted three years ago, and the national slogan for the Indian people since then has been 'Do or Die' in the fight for India's freedom. No Congressman can, consistent with his principles, therefore look at Lord Wavell's offer not to speak of giving consideration to it. Nevertheless, the fact that so many Congressmen and leaders are actually considering the British offer is because a wave of defeatism has swept over India since the Anglo-American successes in Europe and in Burma. In a fit of pessimism and defeatism, some Congressmen are forgetting their life-long principles and are now reconsidering the offer, which they rejected in 1942.

What I want to tell my countrymen at home, clearly and frankly, is that the pessimism and defeatism which seems to have overtaken them is altogether unjustified. Whether one considers the international war situation or the international political situation, there is no cause for pessimism or despondency. The war in East Asia, whatever its ultimate result may be, is going to be a long and bitter one. The whole world knows that there is no real unity in the camp of the so-called United Nations. The war aims of Soviet Russia are quite different from those of the Anglo-American Powers, and the conflict between the Soviet and the Anglo-American is growing from day to day. Both sides have of late been trying to patch up their differences in Europe, but that is because they are preparing for a showdown in the Far East. Since the collapse of Germany in Europe Soviet Russia has been taking an increasing interest in the affairs of Asia. Had it not been for this, M. Molotov, the Soviet Foreign Minister, would not have declared at

San Francisco that the day was not far off when the voice of Free India will be heard in the world.

While the war in the East will be going on, surprising developments are bound to take place in the domain of international affairs. Some of these developments will not be favourable to our enemies, and they will afford India further opportunities for achieving her independence. Syria and the Lebanon, in spite of the Allied victory in Europe, are fully utilizing the international situation for achieving their independence. By using England and the United States of America against French imperialism, Syria and the Lebanon are setting an example to India as to how India can utilize the present international situation for winning her freedom. There is no doubt that if today Syria and the Lebanon are using Britain and America against France, the day is not far off when other Arab States will use their friendly powers against Britain. British politicians realize this, and they realize also that India will utilize the support of friendly powers for winning her independence, and some of these friendly powers may come from inside the camp of the United Nations. During the course of this war, India has become a live issue in world politics, and there is no doubt that in all international conferences in future the Indian issue will be raised. British politicians, therefore, want to prevent India remaining an international issue any longer and want to convert India into a domestic issue of the British Empire. Let us not forget that the moment there is a compromise between nationalist India and Britain, India will become a domestic issue of the British Empire, and it will then be impossible for foreign powers such as Soviet Russia to intervene on behalf of Indian independence.

In spite of the recent military successes of our enemies, India has been making rapid progress towards her goal of independence. In addition to what the Indian people have been doing at home, two distinct forces have been working for India's independence. Firstly, those who have been fighting with arms against India's enemies, and secondly, those who have been advocating India's independence before the bar of world opinion. Those, who have, hitherto, been fighting with arms against India's enemies, shall go on fighting in future. So far as the Indian National Army is concerned, it will go on fighting to the last man and to the last round. Similarly, those who have made India an international issue and who have been advocating on India's behalf before the world, will also go on doing so. The forces working outside India, coupled with the resistance inside India, are irresistible. If, you, my countrymen at home, cannot fight British imperialism with arms, then at least keep up moral resistance to our enemy by refusing to compromise with him or to fight his imperialist war.

In this connection, I want to make an honest appeal to Mahatma Gandhi, to the President and members of the Congress Working Committee and to the millions of Congressmen and Congresswomen, who stand behind them, that they should not judge the international situation wrongly at this critical moment. A mistake in appraising the international situation is likely to lead to a wrong step in Indian politics. India is not beaten. We have not fallen yet. The present international situation is not unfavourable to us. On the contrary, it is much to our advantage and will become more so in the days to come. Why then should we think of a compromise now, why then should we accept the offer, which we deliberately rejected three years ago?

I speak now as an ordinary member of the Congress, who throughout his whole public life has faithfully served the Congress and the cause of India's independence. Even if you, my sisters and brothers at home, feel that our allies will be ultimately defeated and that the Anglo-Americans will ultimately emerge triumphant, there is still no reason to despair so far as India is concerned. No matter what happens in world politics in future, India is bound to win. India's star is definitely in the ascendant. Do not try to drag it down by a wrong step at this juncture. We have suffered long and have suffered much. Let us suffer a little more and a little longer. But, by all means let us stick to our guns till the end of this war. Sisters and brothers at home, don't you understand why Lord Wavell is in such a beastly hurry? Don't you understand why he has rejected the suggestion of Mr. Jinnah to postpone the Simla Conference? To us outside India, the matter is very simple and very clear. The general election in Britain takes place on July 5. The Conservative Party wants to prevent India becoming an election issue. That is why Wavell's offer was flung upon us one month before the general elections in England. Nobody knows what the result of the general election may be. But everybody knows that whether the Labour Party gets a clear majority or not, it will, in any case, emerge much stronger in Parliament after July 5. The Conservative Party is afraid that if the

Labour Party comes to power and if in the meantime the Indian problem is not settled, the Labour Party is bound to make another attempt to solve the Indian question. Personally, I do not believe in bargaining, because, for me, there can be no compromise over India's independence. But if you are keen on bargaining, and if you are determined to compromise over India's independence, then, I beg you not to commit yourselves before July 5. I do not know what was in the mind of Mr. Jinnah when he asked for the postponement of the Simla Conference, but if he intended to avoid playing his trump card before July 5, then I must express my admiration for his political sagacity and farsightedness. I can make a clear prediction that Lord Wavell will move heaven and earth to arrive at a decision before July 5. If he succeeds, it will be a feather in the cap of the Conservative Party and will help considerably to swell the votes of the Conservative Party's candidate at the elections. Moreover, if Lord Wavell succeeds in arriving at an agreement with the Congress before July 5, and if thereafter the Labour Party comes to power, then the Conservative Party will be able to prevent the Labour Cabinet reopening the Indian issue.

It is not my intention to say that I believe in bargaining with the Labour Party. Far from it, my own plan is clear, and that is to go on fighting with the Azad Hind Fauj to the last man and to the last drop of our blood. But if you are not prepared to go that way because you regard it as a perilous adventure, and if you are determined on bargaining with the British Government, then I should say that the time for bargaining is after July 5. If you do not come to an agreement with Lord Wavell before July 5, then you will help to swell the votes of the Labour Party's candidates at the general elections. We won't forget that both the Cripps offer, and the Wavell offer have been made under the auspices of a predominantly Tory Cabinet. The Labour Party has, on both occasions, been a minority party, and the initiative and responsibility did not rest with the Labour leaders. If Lord Wavell fails in his endeavour, it is inevitable that the British public would like to give the Labour Cabinet another chance to tackle the Indian issue. Therefore, to sum up, if you believe in bargaining, then break with Lord Wavell and reject his offer. It will undoubtedly aid the Labour Party at the polls and will enable them to come into office. After that, the Labour Party will certainly take the initiative in reopening the Indian issue, hoping that it will succeed where the Conservative Party had failed. Remember, my conviction is that if there is any other Cabinet after July 5, that Cabinet will consider it as a matter of duty and necessity to solve a problem which has remained unsolved for a long time. Therefore, with the Labour Cabinet, you can strike a bargain, which will be much more advantageous to India than a bargain with Lord Wavell dictated by the Conservatives.

Sisters and brothers at home! I shall address you again tomorrow at about this time. Today before I close, I should like to say one thing more. You are, now, violently condemning the Viceroy, and you are criticizing him for giving an equal number of seats in the Executive Council to caste Hindus and Muslims. But why don't you go deeper into the question and find out the idea behind it? So far not one single Indian leader has done so, judging from the reports that are before me. I regret that the members of the Hindu Mahasabha have taken what appears to be their own peculiar line. Our objection should not be to Muslims getting a majority of seats on the Executive Council. The moot question is what type of Muslims will come to the Executive Council? If we have Muslims of the type of Maulana Abul Kalam Azad, Asaf Ali and Rafi Ahmed Kidwai, the destiny of India will be safe. And, I, personally, believe that it is only right to give all the freedom to such patriots. There is no difference between a patriotic Muslim and a patriotic Hindu. The British intention in the present case is to give all the Muslim seats to the nominees of the Muslim League. Seats reserved for the caste Hindus should all be given to the Congress. For the remaining seats, the Viceroy will appoint his own nominees, who will act according to the Viceroy's directions.

Consequently, with the Muslim League acting in full co-operation with the British Government, the Congress Party in the Executive Council will become a permanent minority. Thus, by a clever stratagem the Viceroy will not only continue to rule India arbitrarily as he has done up till now, but he will continue to do so in the future with the help of the Congress.

Now, the question arises as to whether the Muslim League members in the Executive Council will co-operate with the Viceroy. Personally, I am absolutely certain that they will do so because the Viceroy has agreed to give them a weightage in his Executive Council. If the Muslim

League co-operates with the British Government in its war effort, then the British purpose of exploiting Indian manpower and resources for fighting Britain's imperialist war will be easily fulfilled.

I have no doubt in my mind that in the offer of Lord Wavell there is a secret understanding, either explicit or implicit, between the Muslim League and the British Government. But it is Mr. Jinnah and his colleagues who will outwit Wavell. In the Executive Council, the Muslim League Party will carry out Britain's war policy in order to realize their plan of Pakistan as a reward for the Muslim League's cooperation in Britain's war effort. The Congress Party, if it accepts this offer, will become a permanent minority in the Executive Council. Nevertheless, she will have to carry out Britain's war policy as part of the compromise. After co-operation of the Congress has been secured by the British Government through this clever stratagem the British will try to get the Congress to agree to bring about the vivisection of India, namely, Pakistan. In the meantime, the Congress will have committed political suicide by accepting a position in which it will have admitted that it is not the representative of the Indian people, but only one party among several parties in India.

I, therefore, ask you, nay, I implore you, to ponder deeply over the matter and reject this shameless and sinister plan of Lord Wavell. I can understand those leaders who have so far declined to say anything about the merit of Lord Wavell's offer. But I am painfully surprised to find that some of those leaders who have spoken, like Pandit Jawaharlal Nehru, have not insisted on the release of all the political prisoners prior to the Simla Conference. They have not even criticized the Viceroy for ignoring altogether those who were imprisoned prior to the disturbances of 1942, as well as those who were imprisoned after these disturbances. All that the Viceroy has said is that the Congressmen should behave like good boys and accept his offer, and that the release of those who were imprisoned in connection with the 1942 disturbances should be considered by the new Executive Council. There is not even a guarantee that they will all be released by the new Executive Council.

In conclusion, I want to say that though I do not agree with the line of approach of the members of the Hindu Mahasabha and of the anti-Pakistan front, I feel very strongly that they have done a great service to India by giving an outspoken expression of their opposition to Lord

Wavell's plan. In fact, I should go one step further and say that at this critical juncture it is the duty of all right-thinking and patriotic Indians, particularly of all progressive Congressmen, to start a raging and tearing campaign all over the country against Lord Wavell's offer. Mahatma Gandhi has always been responsive to public opinion as a leader should be. By declining to represent the Congress officially at the Simla Conference, he has done the right thing and has kept himself free to adopt the line which he thinks is right and in accordance with the wishes of the people and in the true interests of India. I have no doubt in my mind that public opinion, and in particular, the opinion among the rank and file of the Congress, should oppose this plan without delay. Mahatma Gandhi will not fail to take notice of it, and he will then advise the Congress to reject the unwanted offer. Sisters and brothers, the destiny of India now lies in your hands; be up and doing and see to it that Lord Wavell's offer goes the same way as the Cripps offer of 1942.

Jai Hind.

65

Wavell's Offer Exposed

[Broadcast from Singapore on 20 June 1945][1]

Sisters and brothers in India!

I am going to speak you today, as I would have done if I had been with you at this critical juncture. I shall speak to you as one who has been with the Congress and has served the Congress with loyalty and devotion since 1921, through fair weather and foul. You remember very well, I hope, what political developments took place in India after September 1939 when the war broke out in Europe. At that time the British Government wanted to use the Congress Ministries in the Provinces for the prosecution of the war, but the Congress refused to co-operate in the war effort, and for two reasons: firstly, because India's national demand for independence had not been conceded by the British Government, and, secondly, because Britain's war was an imperialist war, in which India had no interest. At that time, there was no question of Congress cooperating with the British Government at the centre, but only in the eight provinces out of eleven where there were Congress Ministries. Since the Congress decided not to cooperate in Britain's war in 1939, the Congress Ministries resigned, although it was very clear to every Congressman that if these Ministries had remained in office, they could have done a lot of good to the Indian people in other matters. After the resignation of the Congress Ministries, the Congress, gradually, once again, resumed the fight for freedom. The climax came in 1942 when the 'Quit India' Resolution was passed and when the people were given a new slogan in their renewed struggle for liberty: the slogan of 'Do or Die'.

Now, in the year of grace, 1945, we are confronted with Lord

[1] *Testament of Subhas Bose*, pp. 96–101.

Wavell's offer. We are told that if the Congress agrees on whole-hearted participation in the coming campaign in the Far East, then the Congress can get two things now plus a promise of self-government for the future. These two things are: firstly, some jobs on the Viceroy's Executive Council, and, secondly, the restoration of the Congress Ministries in the Provinces.

From the reports coming from India, it appears that some Congressmen are very favourably disposed towards Lord Wavell's offer, which means that they are satisfied with the promise of self-government, not independence mind you, provided the Congress Ministries in the Provinces are restored and a few jobs in the Viceroy's Executive Council are made available to Congressmen. But all these alluring offers have been before the Congress for a long time. First of all, the British have all along promised us self-government. Secondly, in the Provinces, there were eight ministries under our control in 1939, and it is we who decided that they should resign. Thirdly, jobs in the Viceroy's Executive Council have always been open to Congressmen who were prepared to sell themselves.

There are two new conditions in Lord Wavell's offer. Firstly, the number of jobs on the Viceroy's Executive Council has been increased. Secondly, there is the explicit condition that acceptance of the offer will mean their pledge of wholehearted participation in the coming campaign in the Far East. This was not the case when the Congress Ministries tendered their resignation in 1939. The Congress Ministries, if they had so desired, could have accepted the offer after 1939, without giving a clear pledge of wholehearted participation in Britain's war.

To those who are now eager to accept Lord Wavell's offer, I should like to put a few questions in order, to clarify the issue before us. (i) What has happened to our goal of independence, to which there is not even a partial reference in Lord Wavell's offer? (ii) Does Purna Swaraj mean only Indianization of the Viceroy's Council, or does it mean complete independence and total severance of the British connection? (iii) Why did the Congress Ministries resign in 1939? (iv) What has happened to our slogan, 'Do or Die'? (v) Why did we condemn Congressmen like Shri Aney and Dr. Khare for accepting jobs on the Viceroy's Executive Council?

Friends! It cannot be argued by those who want a compromise today, that the new Executive Council, as envisaged in Lord Wavell's offer, is fundamentally different from the Executive Councils of the past. The Viceroy himself has left no doubts on the matter. He has made it crystal clear that his proposal comes within the four corners of the existing constitution and that his plan does not imply a constitutional change. Further, it is the Viceroy who will appoint his Executive Council, and the members of the Council will be responsible to him and not to the Legislature.

The most appalling position is that in the Executive Council, the will of the majority will not prevail, and the Viceroy will have full powers to veto the decisions of that Council. This is the type of freedom and democracy; this is the type of 'new deal' that India is to receive at the hands of Britain. I have to add that though new jobs have been thrown open to us, for example, the Home, External Affairs, and Finance portfolios, nevertheless, the key-position, namely, the War portfolio remains in the hands of the British C.-in-C. The War member will control not only his own department, but on the plea of war requirements, he will exercise effective control over all other departments. Whatever the War member will bring before the Council will, of course, be endorsed by the Viceroy, and all other Executive Councillors will have to agree to it. The Executive Councillors will be legally bound by their responsibilities to the Viceroy and Governor-General, and they will be morally bound by their pledge of wholehearted participation in Britain's war.

Consequently, Lord Wavell's proposal may best be described in the words of the late Vithalbhai Patel, as 'Swaraj for the Viceroy', but not even swaraj for the Executive Council. As to the Department of External Affairs being handed over to an Indian member, I feel that it will prove to be an eye-wash, because the affairs of Indian States, as well as those relating to tribal and frontier affairs, will be outside the jurisdiction of this member. Though there is no question of collective responsibility or majority rule in the new Executive Council and though the Viceroy and Governor-General will remain the same autocrat as before, he has, nevertheless, to hide his autocracy in the new Executive Council through an ingenious political device or strategy. This stratagem consists in providing for a permanent majority in the Executive Council, which will stand by the Viceroy in all circumstances.

It is, I believe, the intention of Lord Wavell to give to the Muslim League all the seats in the Executive Council reserved for Muslims, if the Muslim League makes that demand. Similarly, he will give to the Congress all the seats reserved for caste Hindus, if the Congress insists, while the members from the other communities will be appointed by Lord Wavell according to his own sweet will, and it goes without saying that these members will be completely subservient to him. It follows, therefore, that if the Viceroy can win over either the Congress bloc or the Muslim League bloc in the Executive Council, then he will have a permanent majority to stand by him at all times. Now the question is, which of the two blocs is likely to sell itself to the Viceroy? It will be difficult for the Congress bloc to do so, because it will then be repudiated by the general public and by the rank and file of the Congress. But it will be possible for the Viceroy to win over the Muslim League bloc to his side by throwing a bait that if they behave like good boys and co-operate wholeheartedly in the war, then the British Government will, as a reward, help them to realize their dream of Pakistan. On the other hand, if the Muslim League bloc gives him any trouble, the Viceroy will put out a threat that the British Government will lend its support to the plan of a unified India as against the Pakistan plan.

In this connection, I shall venture the remark that it should be no surprise to anybody if there is already a secret understanding, whether explicit or tacit, between the British Government and the Muslim League that both of them will make common cause against the Congress in the Executive Council. If the above analysis is correct, as I am sure it is, then it follows that if the Congress accepts the offer, the Congress bloc in the Executive Council will become a permanent minority. Nevertheless, the Congress bloc will be constrained to carry out Britain's war policy in view of the pledge of wholehearted co-operation in the war effort, which is an integral part of the compromise.

It is, therefore, incumbent on us to consider coolly and dispassionately at this stage what the Congress and the country will gain by accepting the offer, and what the inevitable consequences of such acceptance will be. So far as I can judge, the only thing that the Congress will gain by accepting the offer will be a few jobs in the Executive Council, but both the British Government and the Muslim League will stand to gain much. So far as the British Government is concerned, it will be able to prosecute the war with the help of the Congress in the name of Indian people, and it will thereby be able to exploit the country's resources in men and material much more than ever before. So far as the Muslim League is concerned, it will succeed in outwitting the Congress by reducing it to a permanent minority in the Executive Council. The Muslim League will also succeed in realizing its dream of Pakistan with the help of the British Government.

When the British Government once succeeds in achieving her immediate objective, namely, the prosecution of the war through the help of the Congress, it will then have no further need for the co-operation of the Congress. The British Government will then keep off the Congress and openly embrace the Muslim League and bring about the vivisection of India. In the meantime, the Congress will have humiliated and debased itself and made itself ridiculous in the eyes of the whole world. It would have to trade its fundamental principles and give a go-by to the goal of independence. Further, by fighting Britain's imperialist war, the Congress will have forgotten its revolutionary purposes and lost its spirit of militant nationalism. The Congress will also have committed political suicide by voluntarily accepting the position that it is not the representative of the Indian masses, but it is only one party among many parties in India. Last, but not least, by compromising with British imperialism the Congress will have lost the sympathy of freedom-loving men and women all over the world and will also have lost the support of several friendly Powers including Soviet Russia.

Sisters and brothers! This is what you will lose by accepting Lord Wavell's offer. All that you will gain will be a few jobs in the Viceroy's Executive Council for some ambitious Congressmen. I shall not try your patience any further today, but before I close I shall repeat a few salient points from my talk yesterday. Firstly, do not forget what the original motive of Lord Wavell's offer is. That motive is to bamboozle you and get half-a-million Indian troops to fight Britain's war in the Far East; that is, in regions beyond Burma and in the Pacific. Secondly, if you believe in India's independence, then there is no reason to feel disheartened or discouraged because of the recent military successes of our enemies. India's position in the international field has never been so strong as it is today. By a combination of uncompromising resistance at home, armed struggle in East Asia and diplomacy in the international field, we shall win our independence by the end of this war. That will bring real independence, not self-government within the British Empire, nor Indianization of the Viceroy's Executive Council. Probably the greatest hindrance to independence has appeared in our life, namely, pessimism and defeatism. The people who fight and shed their blood do not succumb to defeatism. It is the armchair politicians and those who are cowards, who easily fall a victim to pessimism and despondency.

Our Azad Hind Fauj has suffered many losses in the recent campaign in Burma, but this has made our determination to fight to the last man and to the last round more intense. The major portion of our army is still intact and will continue fighting. Fortunately, in spite of all the propaganda of the Anglo-Americans, their military position in East Asia is not what they have been trying to make out. In Burma, hard and bitter fighting is still going on, and in the rest of East Asia, the Anglo-Americans will have to face a long and bitter struggle before any decision can be reached.

Countrymen! Do not forget our comrades in prison and those who have suffered so much in the cause of independence. Remember also that the Viceroy has ignored all those who have been in prison before 1942, as well as those who were imprisoned from 1942 onwards but not in connection with 'Quit India' disturbances. Last, but most important of all, if you are determined to go on bargaining with the British Government for a compromise, then wait till the British general elections are over. Whether a Labour Cabinet comes into office or a Conservative Cabinet, you will get far better terms, if you negotiate after July 5. Lord Wavell will move heaven and earth to come to a settlement of the issue before July 5, because that decision will help the Conservative Party. But you should not fall into the trap he has laid for you.

Sisters and brothers at home! At this critical hour the destiny of India lies in your hands. Now is your time for starting the 'Quit India' campaign all over the country and thereby making it possible for anyone to arrive at a compromise. 'Jai Hind!'

66

Consign Wavell's Offer to the Scrap Heap

[Broadcast from Singapore on 21 June 1945][1]

Sisters and brothers in India! During the last three days I have been speaking to you from a broader point of view, both national and international, and I have also been considering the Indian problem in its proper setting, that is, against the international background. Judging from the reports reaching us through various news agencies, it appears that those who are giving vocal expression to their views today are approaching the Indian problem from a very narrow and shortsighted point of view. Most of those who view the Indian problem from the correct point of view cannot easily make their voice heard outside India, particularly because some of them are now in custody. If Mahatma Gandhi and the members of the Congress Working Committee had insisted on the release of all political prisoners prior to any negotiations with the British Government, then we would have had no cause for anxiety. If the release of all political prisoners had taken place and a full meeting of the All-India Congress Committee been held, then the opinion of the entire Congress organization would have made itself heard. But the British Government, cunning it is, has deliberately kept the rest of the political prisoners in custody and released only the members of the Congress Working Committee, so that the opinion of the entire Left wing of the Congress Organization may be effectively muffled.

[1] *Testament of Subhas Bose*, pp. 101–9.

I have no doubt in my mind that public opinion in India, and in particular the Congress Organization, has moved much further in a revolutionary direction since the beginning of the present war in 1939. Consequently, if a plenary session of the Congress were held today or even a full meeting of the All-India Congress Committee, Lord Wavell's offer would be rejected by an overwhelming majority. The British Government and Lord Wavell know the Indian situation and they realize that if the British offer had been left to the verdict of Congressmen in general or even to the All-India Congress Committee, then there would not be the slightest chance of its acceptance. They have, therefore, created a situation in which only the members of the Congress Working Committee will decide about Lord Wavell's offer on behalf of the Congress. According to the Congress constitution, the Working Committee cannot make a final decision on behalf of the Congress on such an all-important issue.

I am, however, prepared to admit that if the Congress Working Committee had represented all sections of the Congress or if there had been a real emergency, there might have been some moral, though not legal, justification for the Congress Working Committee to handle this all-important issue on its sole responsibility. But, it is well known that the Left Wing of the Congress, which is quite influential, is not represented on the Working Committee at all. And, nobody can maintain that there is such an emergency in the country that the Working Committee is obliged to make a momentous decision behind the back of the All-India Congress Committee and of the rank and file of the Congress. I can understand that the British Government, to achieve its own ends, has manoeuvred in such a way that Lord Wavell's offer has been placed not before the All-India Congress Committee or a plenary session of the Congress, but only before the Congress Working Committee, but I cannot understand why members of the Working Committee are walking into the trap cleverly laid by Lord Wavell. Apart from the provision of the Congress constitution according to which the Working Committee is a mere executive body and not its deliberative or law-making body, from the purely moral point of view, it is wrong and unfair for the Working Committee to dispose of a matter which will affect the entire future of the Congress and India for several decades. Even at this late hour, I honestly and humbly appeal to Mahatma

Gandhi not to make a decision behind the back of the Congress. I make this appeal particularly because by accepting the Wavell offer, we shall be receding from the progress already made and nullifying the fundamental principles and resolutions of the Congress, and we shall be undoing the work and sacrifices of the Congress over a long period.

I shall now say a few words as to what will be the effect of accepting Lord Wavell's offer. First and foremost, the goal of the Indian National Congress is complete independence, whereas Lord Wavell's offer scrupulously avoids even mentioning the word independence. Secondly, in 1938–9, the Congress had refused to participate in Britain's imperialist war, and the Congress has suffered much because of its anti-war policy. But, the fundamental basis of Lord Wavell's offer is that all those who accept the offer will have to pledge themselves to wholehearted participation in Britain's war in the Far East, and this war cannot be described by any stretch of imagination as a war for the defence of India. Thirdly, acceptance of the offer will mean the rescinding of the 'Quit India' resolution of 1942. After the acceptance of the offer the Congress will have to give up the slogans 'Liberty or Death' and 'Do or Die' and devise other slogans, which will express the ideas embodied in Lord Wavell's offer.

I should like to know how the Congress can be distinguished from the Indian Liberal Federation, if it agrees to give up its fundamental principles and resolutions and accepts the present offer? As I have stated in my previous talks, under normal circumstances, no Congressman would have even looked at Lord Wavell's offer, not to speak of giving consideration to it. The only psychological explanation of the present compromising attitude of several Congress leaders is that they probably feel that the Anglo-Americans are going to win the war and that there is no hope of our achieving our independence. This appreciation of the situation is entirely wrong. In spite of the recent successes of the Anglo-Americans in Europe and in Burma, the Indian issue has become a live issue in international affairs. Whatever the ultimate issue of the war in East Asia may be, even the Anglo-Americans have had to admit that the coming campaign in East Asia is going to be a very long and bitter one and that the armed forces of Japan will fight every inch of the ground. Even in Burma, in spite of our recent reverses, bitter fighting is going on in many sectors and in several parts of the country. While

Japan is capable, Indians in East Asia will continue their fight against the British and their allies. In spite of the recent losses in Burma, the main force of the Azad Hind Fauj remains intact, and the Azad Hind Fauj will go on fighting to the last man and to the last round.

If Indians at home do not give up resistance to British imperialism, nothing can prevent the attainment of India's independence by the end of this war. By a combination of resistance inside India, armed struggle in East Asia and the adoption of a realistic policy in the international field, India will certainly emerge as an independent nation by the time this war ends. But, for the achievement of our liberation, internal struggle against the British has to be guaranteed. Armed struggle in East Asia I am in a position to guarantee. I can also give this assurance that if resistance to British imperialism is kept up inside India, then India will remain an international issue, and diplomacy in the international field will be able to help our cause considerably. For the present, the British do not have much to worry about trouble inside India, but they are, nevertheless, afraid of two things. They are afraid that if moral resistance inside India continues, India will remain an international issue. They are also afraid that if the Indian people remain hostile to the British, it will be impossible for them to obtain adequate help from India in men and resources for the coming campaign in the Far East. The British know that without India's help in a large measure and in particular without the help of India's manpower they cannot win the war in the Far East. Lord Wavell's offer is calculated to kill two birds with one stone; firstly, the offer is a bait to guarantee India's wholehearted participation in Britain's imperialist war; secondly, it will convert the Indian issue into a domestic issue of the British Empire and thereby bring about a withdrawal of all help to India by the United Nations including Soviet Russia.

In this connection, I should like to repeat what I said in a statement issued by me on the 19th instant. In that statement, I disclosed information received from very reliable sources to the effect that the origin and the basis of Lord Wavell's sinister offer is the demand of the British Government that India should supply half-a-million troops for the coming campaigns in East Asia in regions beyond Burma and in the Pacific. If the British Government could have obtained from India that much-needed help without the co-operation of the Indian people,

Wavell's offer would in all probability not have seen the light of day. But, the British Indian Army, like the British Army, is war-weary and the British Government and Lord Wavell think that it is now necessary to win public sympathy and enthusiasm in India in order to obtain military aid in so large a measure.

Before the members of the Working Committee decide to accept Lord Wavell's offer, they should be prepared to sacrifice half-a-million Indian lives for Britain's imperialist war in the Far East. I have envisaged what the Congress stands to lose, if it were to accept Lord Wavell's offer. Consequently, before deciding to accept the offer, members of the Working Committee will have to calculate carefully what they will gain thereby and whether that gain will compensate in adequate measure what we shall lose. It stands to reason that if what we gain is much less than what we lose, we should reject that offer as we rejected Sir Stafford Cripps' offer in 1942. There may be Congressmen who think that what we are thinking of doing now, we shall have to do that in the long run. This view is completely erroneous; I have already remarked in a previous talk, that even if the worst happens and India fails to obtain her freedom during the course of the present war, then we shall have another opportunity as soon as the present war comes to an end.

The changeover from war to peace is a period of unrest. During this period of unrest, even a victorious power is at a disadvantage because it needs rest and relaxation. That is why the revolutions of Ireland and Turkey after the First World War, revolutions, which failed during the war period, attained complete success after the termination of the war.

On reading a report, which is before me today, I find that the Congress President, Maulana Abul Kalam Azad, said: 'If the present negotiations fail, the Congress will wait till the end of the war before launching a further attempt.' I cannot agree with the Congress President that we should not renew the struggle at home while the war is on, but I agree with him that at the end of the war, if India still happens to be enslaved, Indians will again have another opportunity of launching a large-scale offensive against British imperialism, and I have no doubt in my mind that in that post-war campaign the demobilized members of present British-Indian Army will play a very important role.

Since it is apparent that most of the Indian leaders who are now free are considering Lord Wavell's offer not from the broader but from a very narrow and short-sighted point of view, I shall now consider what our comparative losses and gains would be if we were to accept that offer. What Lord Wavell has offered us if we agree to wholehearted participation in the coming war in the Far East is as follows: (i) The promise of self-government; (ii) some jobs on the Viceroy's Executive Council and (iii) the restoration of Congress Ministries in the Provinces. All these three things have always been before us. The British Government has always promised us self-government. We had eight Ministries under our control in the Provinces in 1939, and these we resigned voluntarily. Jobs in the Viceroy's Executive Council have always been open to such Congressmen as were prepared to sell them. It may be remarked that the Wavell offer gives us more seats in the Executive Council, but, as against that, there is an express stipulation that acceptance of the offer will mean wholehearted participation in Britain's war. Was this not the reason why the Congress Ministries resigned in 1939? They could have remained in office after 1939 without giving a pledge of wholehearted participation in the war. But, they preferred to resign rather than sacrifice the country's resources in fighting a war to keep British imperialism alive.

In Britain, many people are waxing eloquent over the merits of the offer on the ground that a considerable advance has been made in the Indianization of the Executive Council. I hope that no Congressman will adopt a similar attitude, because the Congress demand is not Indianization of the services or of the Executive Council, but the withdrawal from India of the British Power, wherein are included the Viceroy, as well as the British Commander-in-Chief. Lord Wavell has in fact made it quite clear that his offer does not imply any constitutional change. Moreover, the newly constituted Viceroy's Council will only be an advisory body, and it is the Viceroy who will finally select these members who will be responsible not to the Central Legislature but to the Viceroy personally. Moreover, inside the Executive Council, the will of the majority will not prevail, and the Viceroy will have full powers to veto recommendations or proposals of the Executive Council. There is no question of collective responsibility or majority rule in the Executive Council. The Executive Council cannot, therefore, be called a Cabinet by any stretch of imagination. In the Executive Council, the chief position will be held by the British War Member, namely, the

Commander-in-Chief. What the War Member will demand the Viceroy will certainly endorse. Consequently, next to the Viceroy the War Member will be all-powerful. So long as the Viceroy and the C.-in-C. act in concert they will be able to control all the departments. The other Executive Councillors will not be able to object, because they will be illegally bound by their responsibility to the Viceroy; and they will be morally bound by their pledge of wholehearted participation in the war. The Department of External Affairs, which is to be run by an Indian, will prove to be an eyewash, because foreign affairs will be excluded from its jurisdiction. The Member in charge of this department will become like the Indian Defence Member of the Viceroy's Council who is in charge of army canteens.

I should like to ask those Congressmen, who are today so keen about accepting Lord Wavell's offer, with what face we shall go back to the Ministries, which we voluntarily gave up in 1939? I should also like to ask why the Congress condemned Mr. Aney and Dr. Khare who accepted jobs on the Viceroy's Executive Council, when the Congress is now going to do the same. The more I think of this, the more I am convinced that incalculable harm will be done to the status and prestige of the Congress and to India by accepting this offer. We shall be putting back the clock by at least 25 years. All that we shall gain in return for this wholesale sacrifice of principles will be a few jobs on the Executive Council for some ambitious and power-mad Congressmen.

I shall now try to show that if the Congress accepts the offer, the British Government and the Muslim League will profit at the expense of the Congress. It is, I believe, the intention of Lord Wavell to give to the nominees of the Muslim League all the seats in the Executive Council reserved for the Muslims, if the Muslim League makes that demand. Similarly, he will give to the Congress all the seats reserved for caste Hindus if the Congress insists. The remaining members will be appointed by Lord Wavell according to his sweet will, and it goes without saying that these members will be completely subservient to him. It follows, therefore, that if the Viceroy can win over to his side either the Congress bloc or the Muslim League bloc in the Executive Council, then he will have a permanent majority to stand by him at all times. I take it that the Congress bloc in the Executive Council cannot and will not consent to a pact with the Viceroy, because if it does, the rank and file of the Congress will ridicule it. But if the Viceroy throws a bait to the Muslims that the British Government will help them to realize their dream of Pakistan, then there is every likelihood of the Muslim League bloc making a pact with the Viceroy. The moment it is done, the Viceroy will have a permanent minority in the Executive Council to stand by him at all times, and the Congress bloc will thereby be reduced to a permanent majority. Nevertheless, the Congress block will be constrained to maintain its pledge of wholehearted participation in Britain's war by carrying out the Viceroy's policy. Thus, if the offer is accepted, the British Government will profit by prosecuting the war with the help of the Congress and in the name of the Indian people. The Muslim League will also have succeeded in reducing the Congress to a permanent minority in the Executive Council and by realizing its dream of Pakistan with the help of the British Government.

I have pointed out what we shall lose by accepting the offer. I shall now say something as to what more we shall lose if the Congress co-operates with the British Government for a period of time. Firstly, the independence movement as well as the freedom mentality of the Indian people will suffer a serious setback. By fighting Britain's imperialist war, the Congress will forget its revolutionary purpose and lose its spirit of militant nationalism. And, lastly, by compromising with British imperialism, the Congress will forfeit the sympathy of freedom-loving men and women all over the world and will lose the support of those friendly powers like Soviet Russia who have full sympathy for our cause and are willing to lend us active help.

Friends, up to today I have been considering Lord Wavell's offer from the purely political point of view, but I have not considered its communal implications. But I shall do so now. By accepting the offer, the Congress will incidentally, though it may be indirectly, accept the principle of communalism in politics. It will acknowledge the Muslim League as the sole representative of the Indian Muslim, and it will thereby betray all those Muslim organizations like the Azad Muslim League, Jamiat-ul-Ulema, Shia Conference, Majlis-e-Ahrar, Proja Party, Muslim Majlis, All-India Momin Party, etc., that have been following a nationalist line at very great sacrifice. Moreover, the Congress will be forced to admit that the word 'Congress' is synonymous with the word 'caste Hindus' and not even only with the word 'Hindu'.

I am making this statement on the supposition that the seats reserved by the Viceroy for the caste Hindus will be given to the nominees of the Congress; and those reserved for the Muslims will be given to the nominees of the Muslim League, and that the member or members from Scheduled Castes will be appointed by the Viceroy himself. Now I would like to put a question to Lord Wavell. Amongst the Muslim members of the Executive Council, will he include outstanding Muslims of the type of Maulana Abul Kalam Azad, who are not members of the Muslim League, and since the vast majority of the Scheduled Caste votes were given to the Congress in the last elections, will the Viceroy leave it to the Congress to put up an Executive Councillor from amongst the Scheduled Castes and not make the selection himself? If he does not do these, then it will be crystal clear that the Viceroy's sinister intention is to reduce the Congress into an organization of the caste Hindus. Let somebody apply this acid test to Lord Wavell. The result of this test will then speak for itself.

Whatever the other objections to the Viceroy's offer may be, this single objection, namely, the communal implications of it, is enough to condemn that offer and render it totally unacceptable to any nationalist party. The Congress is a national institution representing Indians of all religious faiths, and it has fought hard and suffered much to maintain its national character. It will commit veritable suicide if at this stage of its career the Congress were to renounce its national character and accept a communal label. Likewise, it will stultify itself once and for all, if it gives up its role as a representative of Indian Nationalism and if it accepts the position of one party among many parties in India. I should like to repeat what I said the day before yesterday that the Conservatives are keen on bringing about a compromise with the Congress, and Lord Wavell is anxious to get a decision before July 5. The acceptance will help the Conservative Party considerably at the polls and possibly ensure its return to power. If Lord Wavell succeeds, and the Conservatives fail to return to office, he will then be able to prevent the Labour Cabinet from revising Britain's India policy because the British Government will have already been committed to the Wavell offer. It is likely that if we do not accept his offer now and the Labour Party comes to power then that Party is bound to take up the Indian issue, when he shall be able to get better terms. And, if the

Conservative Party returns to office it will also be constrained to make another offer, otherwise India will remain an international issue to the great disadvantage of Britain. But, we will get another chance, and a better chance, of bargaining after the war. I say this for the consideration of only those who are really in favour of a policy of compromise with Britain and who are not prepared to fight for complete independence.

In conclusion, let me remind you once again, as I said yesterday, that in this fateful hour the destiny of India lies in your hands, and the responsibility is exclusively that of the Indian people and not the Congress Working Committee. Therefore, carry on a raging and tearing campaign against this sinister offer and see that this offer is consigned to the scrap heap before July 5, 1945.

67

Reflections on the Wavell Offer

[Broadcast from Singapore on 22 June 1945][1]

Sisters and brothers in India! Latest news reaching us from India is to the effect that the Congress Working Committee decided last night to accept Lord Wavell's invitation to participate in the Simla Conference. To those who are acquainted with the present attitude of the Indian National Congress, this news has not come as a surprise. Referring to the opinion inside the Congress Working Committee, the political correspondent of the Associated Press of India has reported as follows: 'The opinion among the Congress leaders about the Viceroy's proposal divides itself into three groups. The first party is led by Mr. Gandhi and Sardar Vallabhbhai, who take strong exception to the use of the term "caste Hindus" in the Viceroy's broadcast. The middle group is led by Mr. Nehru and Maulana Abul Kalam Azad who, not being satisfied with the quantum of power contemplated to be transferred, take the view that the scheme can be given a fair trial as an interim measure, provided there is sufficient possibility of advancing India's demand for national independence and to improve the lot of the poor. The third group, led by Mr. Rajagopalachari and Mr. Bhulabhai Desai, feel that the terms of reference of the Simla Conference are so wide and elastic that all fears of the Congress are groundless. They advocate that the Congress should accept the proposal without picking holes in it and give it a fair trial and thus demonstrate the determination of the Congress to get on with the business.'

[1] *Testament of Subhas Bose*, pp. 109–14.

I cannot judge from this distance if the analysis of the political correspondent of the Associated Press of India is correct or not, but I would not be surprised if it is. In fact this analysis conforms with what I said yesterday about the political character of the present Congress Working Committee. It appears that the Radical Democratic Party has condemned the Simla Conference on the ground that Labour representatives have not been invited to the conference. Judging from the analysis of the political correspondent of the Associated Press of India, the opinion of the Radical Democratic Party on this question is not supported by any member of the Congress Working Committee. The argument seems to be that even while agreeing to accept the invitation to the Simla Conference, the Working Committee has not committed itself in any way. But, this argument cannot seriously be accepted because the offer as it stands and the implications of its acceptance are clear. Everybody who attends this conference will have to accept the policy of wholehearted participation in the coming campaign in East Asia, and the Congress will have to repudiate the policy it laid down regarding participation in the war, when the Congress Ministries resigned office in 1939. Moreover, everybody attending this conference will have to accept the present constitutional position of the Viceroy and the Governor-General in the Executive Council and will have to accept the humiliating position of functioning as mere advisers and not responsible ministers. Lord Wavell has made no secret of this, and in fact, he has made it quite clear that it is he who will appoint the members of the Executive Council. So, the members of the Executive Council will be responsible not to the Legislature but to him, and there is no question of majority rule or of collective responsibility in the Executive Council. Consequently, everybody who attends the Simla Conference will have to give up the demand for independence. They will have to give up also the usual demand for a National Government at the Centre, responsible to the Legislature, and will have to be content with Indianization of the Executive Council functioning within the framework of the 1935 Act. Presently, there can be no doubt whatsoever that acceptance of the invitation to the Simla Conference after all this will amount to giving up the fundamental principles and policies of the Indian National Congress, including the 'Quit India' resolution for which so many of our brethren and comrades are still rotting in prisons. Moreover, it is very unfortunate and painful that not a single member of the Congress Working Committee has put forward the demand for the release of all political prisoners, prior to negotiating with the British Government, although many of them have issued statements dealing with certain points in Lord Wavell's offer.

I said in my talk yesterday that the Working Committee is an executive body and is not constitutionally empowered to decide the destiny of so many million peoples and to commit the country to a course of action which is contrary to the fundamental ideals and policy of the Congress. Since the Working Committee does not represent all sections within the Congress and since there is no agreement on this question inside the country, there is no moral—not to speak of legal—justification for the Working Committee to deliberate on such vital issues behind the back of the All-India Congress Committee and the Congress as a whole. There is also no justification for the Working Committee to accept on its own responsibility the invitation to the Simla Conference, especially when the whole offer is contrary to the fundamental principles and policy of the Congress.

I beg and implore Mahatma Gandhi and the Working Committee, even at this late hour, to pause and ponder over this great responsibility, which they are taking upon themselves by ignoring the All-India Congress Committee and the Congress on such a momentous occasion. I fail to understand why the Working Committee should act in such an unfair manner. That Lord Wavell and the British Government are in a hurry I can understand. They are acting under their motives; firstly, Lord Wavell and the British Government know that the Indian people are overawed by the recent military successes of the Anglo-Americans and that the Indian people are at last beginning to realize that the Anglo-Americans are bound to win this war. Lord Wavell and the British Government want to exploit this psychological moment and strike while the iron is hot. They are afraid that after a few months the whole world will realize that despite the collapse of Germany, the overthrow of Japan in the Far East is not an easy proposition. Secondly, Lord Wavell and the British Government must somehow bamboozle these leaders and secure at least 500,000 Indian troops and vast quantities of military supplies for Britain's imperialist war in the Far East. Thirdly, Lord Wavell and the British Government must come to some agreement with the Indian leaders before July 5, when the general elections in England will commence. All these three motives afford sufficient explanation as to why Lord Wavell and the British Government are in a beastly hurry. But that is no reason why the Congress Working Committee should fall into their trap. In this connection, I would like to repeat what I said previously as to why Lord Wavell is moving heaven and earth in order to come to an agreement with the Indian leaders before July 5.

Though the Labour Party has agreed to the terms of Lord Wavell's offer, the main responsibility of putting through that offer rests with the Conservative Party, who are in a majority in the present government. If, therefore, Lord Wavell succeeds in arriving at an agreement with the Indian leaders, it will be an achievement for the Conservative Party, and will help to swell the votes of the Conservative Party's candidates at the polls and thereby help the return of that party to power. If, in spite of Lord Wavell's success, the Conservative Party fails to secure a majority and if the Labour Party is returned to office, the Conservative Party will at least be able to prevent the reopening of the Indian issue by the Labour Cabinet. If, on the other hand, Lord Wavell fails, his failure, which will be the Conservative Party's failure, will help the Labour Party at the polls. The Labour Cabinet will then have to take up the Indian issue again, because in the domain of foreign affairs the Labour Cabinet must justify itself to achieving something which the Conservative Party failed to do. And, if in spite of the failure of the Simla Conference the Conservative Party returns to power, it will be forced to reopen the India Issue. If the Conservative Party is back in office, and if the deadlock in India continues, the Indian question will remain an international issue, and the Indian issue will have to be brought up before the international conferences of the future, including the Big Three conferences then to be held.

Now, I want my countrymen to understand that the Conservative Party will do everything possible to prevent the Indian issue being brought up before an international conference. Ultimately, there is no doubt whatsoever that if Lord Wavell's offer is turned down by us, as I hope it will be, there will be another opportunity for bargaining with the British Government after the general elections, no matter which party secures the majority on the 5th of July. The fact that a long and bitter campaign in the Far East lies ahead of the British Government is an additional guarantee that Britain will have to placate India.

I want to make it clear before I proceed further that there is no question of bargaining except that the British quit India. But—since there are so many Indians at home who are thinking in terms of a compromise with British imperialism, it is their duty to consider when and how to make this bargain. On this point, I am quite sure that the best time for bargaining is after July 5, and though there is very little hope of the Labour Party recognizing India's independence, it would be possible to strike a better bargain with that party. A compromise with the British Government on the issue of Lord Wavell's offer can be justified only on two conditions. First, if there had been no chance of winning independence, and secondly, if, this had been the last chance for arriving at a compromise with the British Government. As to the first condition, I may say that in spite of the recent successes of the Anglo-Americans, India has, now, a better chance of achieving her independence than ever before. As to the second condition, I will repeat that no matter which party in Britain is called upon to form a Cabinet, India will get another chance of bargaining with the British Government after July 5.

In my view, there are three factors, the immediate effects of which will help India to win her independence by the end of this war. They are (i) resistance to British imperialism inside India; (ii) armed struggle against the British outside India; and (iii) diplomacy in the international field. Even moral resistance inside India will be enough. India must remain an international issue, and our diplomacy in the international field should be directed towards mobilizing support for Indian independence. India must take the assistance—moral and material—of those nations which are fighting Britain and are, therefore, her enemies. So far as armed struggle is concerned, in spite of our recent reverses in Burma, the main forces of the Azad Hind Fauj will not give up the struggle. We shall continue fighting, and we shall fight to the last man and to the last round. We in East Asia can take a much more objective view of the war situation than our countrymen at home, who are easily misled by British propaganda and have begun to believe in an exaggerated view of the strength of the Anglo-American powers. If our countrymen at home believe in our word, they should accept our reading of the war situation and change the policy of the Congress in accordance with this.

Those countrymen who are thinking of accepting Lord Wavell's offer should look ahead and prepare themselves for the day when they will have to provide half-a-million Indian troops as cannon-fodder for Britain's imperialist war in East Asia, and they should also be prepared for fighting their own countrymen in the Azad Hind Fauj, who are prepared to fight the British wherever they happen to meet them. Even if these Congressmen are not ashamed to take up arms against their brothers and sisters in the Azad Hind Fauj, they should at least refuse to provide half-a-million Indian lives as cannon fodder for the perpetuation of the British Empire. To those who doubt that India can achieve her independence by the end of this war, I should like to say that India would never get another opportunity like this for fighting for her freedom. As soon as the war ends in the complete victory of the Axis Powers, as it inevitably will, India will become free and be able to take her proper place in the New World Order, which will replace the Anglo-American domination of Asia. And, even if Japan were to lose, India will have another opportunity of bargaining with Britain. But, to agree to the mass-slaughter of our youth and the waste of our material resources in fighting Britain's imperialist war will be a criminal folly. My appeal to you, therefore, is to reject the Wavell offer and continue your struggle till the end of the war, and then, choose your course of action in the light of circumstances. I earnestly appeal to Congress leaders not to be stampeded into a compromise.

68

Reject the Wavell Offer

[Broadcast over the Provisional Government of Azad Hind Radio, Singapore, on 23 June 1945][1]

Sisters and brothers in India! Yesterday, I told you that in any case, it is wrong, according to the Congress constitution, and also morally unfair for the Congress Working Committee, which is an executive body, to exceed its powers and make decisions on behalf of the All-India Congress Committee or the Congress. I should have added it is also unwise and impolitic for the Working Committee to do so. To an outside observer it appears as if the Working Committee was acting with indecent haste. I feel constrained to say that as compared with Mahatma Gandhi and the Working Committee, Mr. Jinnah acted wisely and cautiously. He declared, according to the report before me that he could not advise the representatives of the Muslim League to attend the Simla Conference until after his interview with Lord Wavell on the 24th. Whatever Mr. Jinnah's inner motives might have been, he did not show any anxiety to jump at the offer made by Lord Wavell. Mr. Jinnah took another prudent and cautious step in asking Lord Wavell to postpone the conference.

I think that if the Congress Working Committee had also asked for and insisted on a postponement of the Simla Conference, Lord Wavell's hand would have been forced. However, it is good that the Congress Working Committee has decided to meet before and during the Simla

[1] *Testament of Subhas Bose*, pp. 114–17.

Conference to make a final decision. It would have been another unwise step, if some of the members of the Working Committee had proceeded to Simla in order to be available for giving necessary advice to Mahatma Gandhi and other Congress representatives at Simla. If this had been done, it would have shown indecent eagerness on the part of the Working Committee to grab at the British offer. Now, some time has been gained, and I hope that before the final decision is taken on behalf of the Congress, a meeting of the All-India Congress Working Committee will be summoned. There should be no acceptance of the Wavell Offer purely on the decision of the Working Committee on the ground that several members of the All-India Congress Committee are in prison. If Mahatma Gandhi and the Working Committee insist on it, then the Viceroy will have to order their release and to come to terms with the Congress on this point. If the Viceroy refuses to release the members of the All-India Congress Committee, his bona fides will then be open to question.

By urging that the All-India Congress Committee should be summoned in order to consider Lord Wavell's offer, I do not suggest that the body, as it is at present constituted, is the sole custodian of our national conscience. Owing to the decisions taken of late by the supreme executive of the Congress against those members of the All-India Congress Committee in agreeing to a compromise with Britain, even the All-India Congress Committee has to some extent lost its representative character. Was it not infamous and ridiculous for the Congress High Command to take disciplinary action against those veterans who were insisting on a struggle with British imperialism, and on the other hand, let off scot-free those Congressmen like C. Rajagopalchari, who were consistently advocating in public a policy virtually amounting to unconditional co-operation with the British Government? Was it not unfair and ridiculous to make Shri Bhulabhai Desai the leader of the Congress Party in the Central Assembly, when he did not play his part during the last Civil Disobedience Movement? Be that as it may, why I insist that the All-India Congress Committee and not the Congress Working Committee should decide this all-important question is not because the former is not full of differences, but because it will be, at least, constitutionally correct and proper. The issue is one which affects the fundamental principles and resolutions of the Congress, and in particular, the Congress goal of complete independence, and therefore, it is only just and proper that the decision should be taken by direct representatives of the people.

I have already said that unless Mahatma Gandhi is exceedingly careful he might be outmanoeuvred by the Viceroy and Mr. Jinnah into a position in which the Congress will nominate the members of the Executive Council for only those seats which have been reserved by the Viceroy for the caste Hindus. In other words, there is every danger that Mahatma Gandhi might be manoeuvred into a position in which he will make a hasty admission that the word 'Congress' is synonymous with the words 'caste Hindus'. That would be the political death of the India National Congress from which it will be impossible for the Congress to retrieve itself.

This danger could be avoided if the Congress representatives to the Simla Conference submit a panel of names concerning all the seats, barring that of the Commander-in-Chief. Will the Congress representatives do so? I am glad to find that the Working Committee has been thinking along these lines. But it is not enough to think. Congress representatives will have to insist that the Viceroy give up, altogether, the religious and communal basis for the composition of the Executive Council, and adopt a political and national basis instead. We must not forget what the difficulties before us are. I have always been of the view that as in a peace conference, so also in a political round table conference, it is only belligerent parties who are entitled to participate. That the British have, now, a stepping stone to other far-reaching changes is not because of Mr. Jinnah and the Muslim League, but because of the Congress, which has consistently fought the British Government with all the means at its disposal.

At the time of the Round Table Conference in 1931, I pointed out that it was only the Congress and those who fought with the Congress who were entitled to represent India at the Round Table Conference held in London. I reminded my countrymen on that occasion that Ireland, where the British Prime Minister, Mr. Lloyd George wanted to outmanoeuvre the Sinn-Fein Party by summoning a national convention representing all Irish parties, the Sinn-Fein Party refused to attend the convention because in their view such a convention did not represent Ireland. The Sinn-Fein Party continued its fight and the day, ultimately, arrived when the British were forced to hold a Round Table Conference with only the representatives of the Sinn-Fein Party. In our case, we should never forget that it is only those who have fought the British Government who are entitled to speak for India and represent India at a Round Table Conference with the representatives of Britain. After all, the importance of the Muslim League is due largely to the fact that it has the backing of the British Government. By giving undue importance to the Muslim League, the Congress is betraying its old friends in such nationalist organizations as the Jamiat-ul-Ulema, Majlise Ahiar, Khudai-Khidmatgars, Azad Muslim League, Shia Conference, Proja Party, All India Momin Party, etc., in addition to a large and influential section of Muslims in the Indian National Congress who have stood for national independence at very great sacrifice.

From reports coming from India, it appears that opposition to Lord Wavell's offer has been voiced from several platforms. Unfortunately, this opposition is not being pooled together. In 1940 when there was a danger that the Congress was drifting towards a compromise with British imperialism, we held an All-India anti-compromise conference at Ramgarh in order to rally all the radical elements in India's public life. A similar conference should be held now and without delay. It would be highly beneficial if an All-India anti-Wavell conference could be held now to fight, organize and combine opposition to Lord Wavell's offer. On behalf of this conference, whose meetings would be held all over India on a particular day, resolutions should be passed giving expression to India's real opinion about Lord Wavell's offer, and it would be a good idea to celebrate an 'All-India Anti-Wavell Day' on July 5, when the general elections in England will be held.

Here in East Asia, we are going to have a celebration on July 4. The 4th of July is known all over the world as the day of American independence. In East Asia, it is the day on which the Indian Independence League in East Asia was imbued with new light and commenced a new phase in its career. Celebration on July 4, which will be held all over East Asia wherever there are Indians, will be in the nature of a referendum. We shall call upon Indians in East Asia on that day to give their verdict on Lord Wavell's offer, and if that verdict is to be one of condemnation to renew then and there our determination to continue the armed struggle for India's freedom under all circumstances, even if the Congress Working Committee were to accept Lord Wavell's offer.

Sisters and brothers at home! I shall now close for the day. On Monday, the 25th, I shall address a special talk for the revolutionaries in India, giving my directions as to what they should do in the event of the Congress Working Committee accepting Lord Wavell's offer. Viceroys may come and Viceroys may go, but India will continue to live, and India's fight for freedom will ultimately succeed.

Jai Hind.

69

No Compromise with Britain

[Summary of speech at a mass rally of Indians in Singapore, broadcast from Singapore, on 24 June 1945][1]

Friends! After nearly six months I stand before you again to speak to you on the present situation and our future task. I am sorry that I cannot bring you good news from Burma. After our failure to take Imphal last year, the enemy was able to advance into Burma. While the main force of the enemy was held up by the forces of the Imperial Japanese Army and the Indian National Army, advanced mechanized units of the enemy consisting of tanks, armoured-cars, etc., were able to break through our defences and threaten our headquarters. We had to decide whether we should keep our headquarters there, inviting attacks from the enemy's advanced mechanized units, or withdraw to a safer place. It was not easy for us to withdraw from danger zone in Rangoon leaving behind our comrades of the Azad Hind Fauj fighting at the front. But, after very careful consideration, the Ministers of the Provisional Government of Azad Hind unanimously decided that, owing to certain reasons, we should withdraw to a safer place.

After we left Rangoon, it was still possible for us to keep our headquarters in Burma, as the Burma Government, the Government of Adipadi Dr. Ba Maw, did. But that was also considered advisable in the interests of India. The present position in Burma is that fighting is going on in all parts of the country in the Shan States, in the Toungoo

[1] *Testament of Subhas Bose*, pp. 117–23, translated from the original Hindustani.

area, near Prome, and in the Arakan. The main force of the enemy is still being held up, and nobody can say how long the fight will go on, or when the enemy will succeed in capturing Burma. Though the strength of the Azad Hind Fauj is small compared to the Japanese Army, our comrades of Azad Hind Fauj are fighting valiantly under very difficult conditions. Our main force is with our comrades who are now fighting in Burma, but we have to withdraw our headquarters from Burma, leaving our army in charge of the newly organized Burma Command of which Major-General Loganadan is the Commander with Lieut.-Col. Arshad as his Chief of Staff.

The Provisional Government had to withdraw its headquarters from Burma in order to organize its forces outside Burma and continue the fight on other fronts. If we had no other forces outside Burma then in all probability, we would have remained with our comrades in Burma and fought to the last, facing any situation that would have arisen thereafter. There was another reason, which persuaded us to withdraw our headquarters from Burma. It was clear to us that after his recent military successes, the enemy would launch a new military and political offensive on other fronts, and it was necessary for us to prepare in time for that offensive and meet it when it was launched. Our misfortune was that the crisis in Burma came almost simultaneously with the crisis in Europe. The enemy took full advantage of it and immediately launched a political offensive directed towards India. That political offensive was Lord Wavell's offer.

The motives behind Lord Wavell's offer are principally two in number: firstly, to extract help from India for the future war in East Asia, and, secondly, to reach a compromise with the Indian people and thereby make India a domestic issue of the British Empire. The British had to produce men, money and material in large quantities to help America in the future war against Japan. But the British Army and also the British Indian Army is war-weary and does not want to face a long campaign in the Far East, under conditions much more difficult than in Europe. Therefore, the required cannon fodder could be obtained only from India. But, unless the full strength and resources of the Indian people are mobilized and their enthusiasm roused, the British can never obtain from India the manpower they need for the future war in East Asia. The other motive behind Lord Wavell's offer is to make India a domestic issue of the British Empire and thereby prevent friendly foreign powers from intervening on behalf of India's independence. The Allied Powers have talked so much about freedom and democracy for all nations that the enslaved nations of the world have begun to take full advantage of this in working for their own independence. Syria and the Lebanon are examples of this. The remark made by the Soviet Foreign Minister, M. Molotov, at the San Francisco Conference, while acknowledging the credentials of the India representatives, and his statement that the day is not far off when the voice of Free India will be heard in the world was given as a warning to Britain. The British Government realized that if there is no compromise with the India people, India would remain an international issue, and it would be open to friendly foreign powers to intercede on behalf of India's independence, even if the Indian people did not take up arms against the British Government.

If you want to understand Britain's future aims in India, you have only to remember that Britain is determined to prevent friendly foreign powers from espousing the cause of India's independence. Our policy should, therefore, be to prevent the British from making India a domestic issue of the British Empire by preventing any understanding between India and Britain, which is not on the basis of India's complete independence.

Several years before the outbreak of this World War, when the League of Nations was in existence, the late Vithalbhai Patel and myself went to Geneva with the object of bringing India's demand for independence before the League of Nations. At that time, we failed because no member of the League of Nations wanted to offend Britain by advocating India's independence before that body. But conditions have changed considerably since then, and now, there is a better chance of bringing India's case for independence before the bar of world opinion. The fact that Japan and eight other friendly powers have recognized India's independence by formally recognizing the Provisional Government of Azad Hind has strengthened India's position considerably before the whole world.

Before I deal with Lord Wavell's offer, I want to say something about the world situation. As I predicted six months ago, the collapse of Germany has brought about an acute conflict between the Soviet and the

Anglo-Americans. At the present moment, they have patched up their differences in Europe, but that is only superficial and is a preparation for a real showdown in Asia. Moreover, in spite of differences temporarily patched up, the fundamental differences between the two sides still remain, and they are irreconcilable. The result of the German collapse has been that Soviet power and influence in Europe has increased very much more than that of the Anglo-American Powers.

America is now concentrating on the war against Japan and is demanding adequate help from Britain. In my personal opinion, in a future war in East Asia, two main battles will be fought. One is on the mainland of Japan, and the other in China. I cannot say at the present moment which battle will come first, but there is no doubt that Japan is fully prepared for both these main battles. I know also that in every part of East Asia, the armed forces of Japan are organized on a self-sufficient basis. Consequently, if there is a setback in one theatre of war, that will not affect the fighting strength of Japan's armed forces in another theatre. The Anglo-Americans know fully well that a long and bitter struggle is ahead of them. In this connection, it is interesting to note what a distinguished British Commander, General Slim of the British 14th Army, who fought in Burma recently, said the other day in an interview in England. He remarked that though many nations talk of fighting to the last, there is only one nation that actually does so and that is Japan. While Japan will go on fighting under all circumstances, we will also do the same for the sake of India's independence, and the Azad Hind Fauj will fight to the last man and to the last round.

In my personal opinion, I doubt very much if the coming conference between Marshal Stalin, President Truman and Prime Minister Churchill to deal with the problems of East Asia can come to anything. I do not think that the problem of China can be successfully tackled in view of the strained relations between Chungking and Yenan and in view of America's ambitions in China. I am of the opinion that it is easier for the Yenan Government to come to an agreement with Nanking than with Chungking. So long as Chungking is dominated by America I do not see how the unification of China will be possible. So far as Japan is concerned, her new policy in China and her promise to withdraw troops from China on the termination of hostilities have made it clear that Japan will welcome the unification of China, and her only interest is and always has been that Anglo-American power and influence is kept out of China. Every Indian has only goodwill towards China and wants to see a strong and unified China progressing along the lines laid down by China's great leader, Dr. San Yat Sen. A free Asia is not possible without a free China and a free India.

In spite of our recent reverses in Burma, our optimism and our confidence in our final victory remains unimpaired. India's independence can be won by the end of this war, because of three principal factors; firstly, our armed struggle in East Asia, secondly, diplomacy in the international field; and, thirdly, resistance inside India. It goes without saying that the greater the resistance inside India, the less time will it take for us to win our independence. But even if resistance inside India is only moral in character, India will remain an international issue, and there will be ample scope for discussion in the international field. The most important problem for us is to continue the bitter struggle against the British in East Asia. This will have a two-fold effect in that it will influence the cause of India and it will also help to purge our countrymen at home of the defeatist mentality, which is the result of successful enemy propaganda. Secondly, it would tend to reveal our rightful claim before the world, and enable us to secure the support of friendly powers. To continue the armed struggle, we must keep our confidence in our final victory. In this connection, I want to refer to what the Allied Supreme Commander in the last World War, Marshal Foch, wrote in his memoirs. Talking of victory and defeat, Marshal Foch said: 'That enemy is beaten which considers itself to be beaten. So long as an army does not consider itself to be beaten, defeat in any particular area does not mean real defeat.' The British, for example, were expelled from Burma in 1942, but they have managed to re-enter Burma. Who can say that we shall not recapture in Burma what we have lost? When we were withdrawing from Burma, I reminded my comrades of the above remarks of Marshal Foch, and I pointed out that we were not beaten by any means, because not one of us felt that he was beaten, or that the battle was lost.

A true revolutionary is one who never acknowledges defeat, who never feels depressed or disheartened. A true revolutionary believes in the justice of his cause and is confident that his cause is bound to prevail in the long run. Though we have lost the first round in the battle of Burma, I find that we have been able to influence even the enemy.

After entering Burma, the enemy was able to see and hear something of the work of the Provisional Government of Azad Hind and of the Azad Hind Fauj. Previously, the enemy used always to refer to us as the 'Japanese Puppet Army'. After entering Burma he began to call us the 'Japanese-inspired India National Army.' But now they refer to us as Indian National Army. When the British took Mandalay they issued an order that no Indian was to use the greeting 'Jai Hind' which, as you know, means 'Victory to India'. The result of this order was that boys and girls of our Balak-Sena in Mandalay came out in the streets and greeted British Officers with 'Jai Hind'. Our point is that if we go on fighting bravely and shedding our blood, we shall not only be able to influence our countrymen, who are indifferent and lukewarm, but we shall also be able to impress the enemy.

I shall now come back to Lord Wavell's offer. That offer contains three principal points: firstly, a promise of self-government within the British Empire; secondly, more seats on the Viceroy's Executive Council, and, thirdly, restoration of the Ministries in the Provinces. There is nothing in this offer which can commend itself to any nationalist Indian, and under normal circumstances, not a single Congressman would have even looked at that offer. Firstly, the British have been, always, promising self-government. Secondly, since the members of the Viceroy's Executive Council are responsible to the Viceroy and nobody else, more seats on that Council do not mean any advance towards our appointed goal of independence. Furthermore, the Viceroy will have the power of veto and so he will be able to turn down any decision of the Executive Council, even if it is unanimous. In short, the Viceroy's Executive Council will not function as Cabinet but as an advisory body, the power remaining in the hands of the Viceroy. Thirdly, the restoration of the Ministries in the provinces has no importance, because the Congress Ministries in eight provinces voluntarily resigned in 1939, since they were opposed to participation in Britain's war.

Unfortunately for us, the Indian leaders, who are, now, outside prison, have been so overawed by the recent military successes of the Anglo-Americans that they have developed a defeatist mentality. That is why Mahatma Gandhi and the Congress Working Committee have decided to attend the Viceroy's Conference at Simla on the 25th when Lord Wavell's offer will be discussed. We are, now, doing what is possible to persuade our countrymen at home not to accept Lord Wavell's offer, and thereby make the Simla Conference a failure. If we fail in this and if the Congress accepts the offer of entering the Viceroy's Executive Council, we shall, then, find created a situation inside India whereby the Congress will be forced to resign from the Executive Council. We are determined to prevent a compromise between India and Britain, so that India may remain an international issue, so as to enable us to work for the complete independence of India.

Our task in East Asia is a two-fold one. Firstly, to continue the armed struggle which we launched on the 4th February, 1944; secondly, to agitate for Indian independence in the international field and to utilize every conflict within the camp of the so-called United Nations, and in particular, the conflict between the Soviet Union and the Anglo-Americans. For our fight in East Asia, Malaya is our base. So long as the British are kept out of Malaya, our work for India's independence will continue uninterrupted. Therefore, if, at any time, the British try to land in Malaya, we will fight with all the strength that we have.

When the history of Indian independence is finally written, Indians in Malaya will have a glorious place in that history. The contribution of Indians in Malaya for India's struggle for freedom in men, money and material has been great. India will always remain grateful for the same. In particular, Malaya has been the birthplace of the Azad Hind Fauj and of the Provisional Government of Azad Hind. Malaya has contributed a large number of young men, who have fought bravely and died for India's freedom, and Malaya has made the largest contribution to the ranks of the 'Rani of Jhansi Regiment'. Indians in Malaya must maintain the brilliant record that they have already set up. It is from Malaya that the call for total mobilization first went out.

Today, I want to appeal to you for more men, more money and more material. After our most recent reverses in Burma, your responsibility has become greater. Knowing what you have done in the past, I have no doubt that you will do even more in future. I only want you to keep up your faith in the justice of our cause. So long as you keep up this faith you will also keep up your optimism and your confidence in final victory.

'Jai Hind'.

70

Britain's Burma Policy

[Broadcast from Singapore on 25 June 1945][1]

The first stage in the gradual disillusionment of the people of Burma has been reached. As a compensation for the loss of their newly won independence, the Burmese people have been presented with a new bill, which is now before the British Parliament. This bill is accompanied by the usual vague promise of self-government for the future. For the present, the only possible thing that Burma will get will be an Executive Council which will be responsible, not to the Burmese people or their Legislature, but to the Governor himself. A few officials and non-officials and some Britishers will be given seats in the Executive Council. There will be a debating society in the shape of a legislature, which will have no control over the Governor or his Executive Council and which will serve as an entertainment to those who love to talk.

If the British think that the people of Burma, who have had a taste of independence, however short-lived, will be deceived by such tricks, then I must say that they have learnt nothing since they were driven out of East Asia. It goes without saying that the disillusionment which has begun to overtake the Burmese people will be complete, when they finally realize that the British promise of self-government, not of independence, is nothing more than similar promises made in the past. I have no doubt in my mind that when complete disillusionment ultimately overtakes them, the Burmese people will turn against their British rulers with the weapons that they recently secured when they were enjoying their independence.

It is very interesting to note, in this connection, that there is no talk whatsoever of a national army for Burma. Independent Burma had an

[1] *Testament of Subhas Bose*, pp. 124–5.

army of its own, however small it might have been. But under the benign scheme of their British liberators, the Burmese people will not have an army of their own. If the British think that this will not be noted by the Burmese people, then they are living in a fool's paradise. What is adding to the general disillusionment that is stepping in, is the provisional order issued by the British military authorities in Burma, which virtually abolishes, without any compensation, the prevailing currency. It is well known that whenever there is a change of government in any country in the world the new government accepts for a certain period of time the prevailing currency at par until a changeover to the new currency takes place. In a way, I am glad that the British authorities in Burma have issued this order abolishing the prevailing currency, because it will bring acute economic distress to the Burmese people and thereby help more than anything else to rouse their resentment and indignation.

The proposals made by Mr. Amery, Secretary of State for Burma, and Prime Minister Churchill have truly proved to be of the worst order. I hope and trust that they will go on making similar blunders so that the revolution that is inevitable in Burma will come sooner than one might expect today. While the bill that is now before Parliament takes Burma politically back to the year 1909, on the economic side the British Government has assured Burma of a return to the status quo ante, that is, to the exploitation of Burma by the Burma Oil Company, Burma Corporation, and so many other British firms. Only one who has taken leave of his senses can believe that the Burmese people would welcome a return to their pre-war economic status.

According to London reports, the Labour Party has given its support the other day to this measure sponsored by the Coalition Cabinet. This is a further proof, if such proof is needed, that with regard to dependent countries like India and Burma, there is no difference between the policy of the Conservative Party and that of the Labour Party. Those Indians who still think that the advent of the Labour Party to power will bring an advantage to India, should take a leaf out of Burma's experience. Speaking for myself, I may say that I hope and trust that the Conservative Party will be returned to power, so that under the lashes of British imperialism the people of India may come out in open revolt in order to break once for all the shackles of slavery.

71

Co-operation with Japan

[Broadcast from Singapore on 26 June 1945][1]

India is now facing a political crisis, and if a wrong step is taken, we might suffer a setback in our march towards independence. I cannot tell you how worried I feel today, because on the one hand, independence is within sight, while on the other, if a wrong step is taken that independence may recede into the distance. At the outset, let me tell you that enemy propaganda in India has been so successful that influential leaders, who were once convinced that independence was within our grasp, and who were determined to do or die in order to win that independence, are now thinking in terms of becoming members of the Viceroy's Executive Council.

We, who are outside India at this critical juncture, can take a much more objective view of the entire world situation than most of our countrymen at home. It is, therefore, our duty to tell you frankly what we think, and to advise you accordingly. After we withdrew our headquarters from Rangoon, it was open to us to move to another place inside Burma, just as the Government of Independent Burma did at a time when our troops were still fighting inside Burma. But we hoped that the enemy would immediately exploit his recent military successes in Europe and in Burma, and launch a new political and military offensive. Consequently, we should be ready to meet that offensive, and we should be at a place from where we could speak to India if necessary. That is the principal reason why I am in Shonan or Singapore today.

The crisis that faces India today has arisen because some influential sections among our countrymen, who only three years ago were shouting

[1] *Testament of Subhas Bose*, pp. 125–9.

'Liberty or Death', are now prepared to enter into a compromise with the British Government on Lord Wavell's own terms. This attitude is altogether mistaken and unjustified for two reasons. Firstly, there can be no compromise over the question of independence. Secondly, the situation is not what these countrymen of ours think, and if we continue our resistance to British imperialism, we shall win our independence by the end of this war.

If among those who are listening to me now there is anyone who has any doubts as to whether I am in close touch with what is happening all over the world, he can himself judge from one simple fact. He must have noticed from my talks during the last week that I am in intimate touch with daily developments inside India, and if I am in touch with daily developments at home, I can easily be in touch with what is happening all over the world. On the other hand, for those who are inside India and who cannot see what is happening in that part of the world that is not dominated by the Anglo-Americans and who are victims of enemy propaganda, it is difficult to form an objective opinion of the entire world situation.

Today, the whole world is in the melting pot, and India's destiny is bound up to some extent with what is happening all over the world. Now, why am I so optimistic at a time when some of our prominent leaders have developed a defeatist mentality? It is because of two principal reasons. Firstly, we are carrying on an armed struggle against the British and their allies, and we are not pessimistic about the present situation in East Asia, in spite of our recent reverses in Burma. Secondly, India has become an international issue, and if that issue is not converted into a domestic issue of the British Empire, India's case will come up before the bar of world opinion. Can't you see with your own eyes or hear with your own ears how Syria and Lebanon are exploiting the war situation to their advantage by creating a split within the camp of the so-called United Nations? We are no less intelligent or less far-sighted than the leaders of Syria and Lebanon. But, if we want to bring the Indian issue before the bar of world opinion, we have to do two things: firstly, we have to prevent any compromise with British imperialism; and, secondly, we have to assert India's right to freedom with arms.

If our countrymen at home cannot take up arms and if they cannot even continue civil disobedience against Britain's war effort, let them, at least, keep up their moral resistance to British imperialism and refuse to come to any compromise. We shall continue to assert India's right to freedom with arms, and so long as we do so, no power on earth can prevent India remaining an international issue, provided you do not let us down by compromising with the British Government.

I understand that some of the leaders at home are furious with me for opposing their plans for a compromise with the British Government. They are also furious with me for pointing out the blunders of the Congress Working Committee and the Congress; and they are furious with me for pointing out that the Congress Working Committee does not represent national opinion in the Congress or in the country. These imperialist leaders are abusing me for taking the help of the Japanese. I am not ashamed of taking the help of Japan. My cooperation with Japan is on the basis that Japan recognizes India's complete independence, and it has already granted formal recognition to the 'Provisional Government of Azad Hind' or Free India. But those who now want to co-operate with the British Government and fight Britain's imperialist war are prepared to accept the position of subordinates responsible to Britain's Viceroy in India. If their leaders co-operate with the British Government on the basis that Britain grants formal recognition to the Government of Free India, that would be a difficult matter. Moreover, Japan has given us the arms with which to organize an army of our own with which we can fight British imperialism, which is our sole enemy. This army, the Azad Hind Fauj, has been trained by Indian instructors, using the Indian language. This army carries India's national flag, and its slogans are India's national slogans. This army has its own Indian officers and its own officers' training schools run entirely by Indians. And, in the field of battle this army fights under its own Indian commanders, some of whom have now reached the rank of Generals. If this army is called a 'puppet army', then it is the British Indian Army that should be called a 'puppet army', because it is fighting Britain's Imperialist War under British officers. Am I to believe that in an army of 2,500,000 only a microscopic number of Indians are found fit to obtain the highest honour in the British army, namely, the Victoria Cross? Not one single Indian has yet been found fit to hold the rank of General.

Comrades! I have said that I am not ashamed to seek the help of Japan. I can go forward and say that if the almighty British Empire can go down on its knees in order to obtain the help of the United States of America, there is no reason why we, an enslaved and disarmed nation, should not take help from our friends. Today we are taking the help of Japan; tomorrow, we shall not hesitate to get help from any other power, if that be possible and if that be desirable in the interest of India. Nobody will me more happy than myself, if we could achieve India's independence without foreign help of any sort. But I have yet to find one single instance in modern history where an enslaved nation has achieved its liberation without foreign help of any sort. And, for an enslaved India, it is much more honourable to join hands with the enemies of the British Empire than to curry favour with British leaders or British political parties. Our whole difficulty is that we do not hate our enemies enough, and our leaders are always eager to help India's enemy.

Is it not ridiculous that some of our leaders spout anti-imperialist venom abroad while shaking hands with imperialism at home? Comrades! I would never have opened my mouth and said one word to you, if I had been sitting as an armchair politician here. I and my comrades here are engaged in a grim struggle. Our comrades at the front have to play with death. Even those who are not at the front have to face danger every minute of their existence. When we were in Burma, bombing and machine-gunning were our daily entertainment. I have seen many of my comrades killed, maimed and injured from the enemy's ruthless bombing and machine-gunning. I have seen the entire hospital of the Azad Hind Fauj in Rangoon razed to the ground with our helpless patients suffering heavy casualties. That I and many others with me are still alive today is only through God's grace. It is because we are living, working and fighting in the face of death that I have a right to speak to you and to advise you. Most of you do not know what bombing is. Most of you do not know what it is to be machine-gunned by low-flying bombers and fighters. Most of you have had no experience of bullets whistling past you, to your right and to your left. Those who have gone through this experience and have kept up morale dare not even look at Lord Wavell's offer.

Comrades! We have to consider what to do about Lord Wavell's offer. First of all, though the time at your disposal is short, you will have to do everything possible to prevent the acceptance of this offer by the Congress Working Committee. Secondly, if you fail in that, you will then have to create a situation which will force the Congress Representatives to resign from the Viceroy's Executive Council. This will not be difficult. You will have to bring about a crisis between the Viceroy and the Congress Members of the Executive Council. There is no doubt that when the new Executive Council is formed, the Viceroy will begin to exploit India's resources in men, money and material for fighting Britain's future war in the Far East. This will naturally raise numerous issues in which India's interests will clash with those of Britain. In that situation, you will have to let loose a barrage of agitation and propaganda. Then the Congress Members of the Executive Council will be sure to stand up for India's interests against those of Britain, and this will lead to a clash with the Viceroy and inevitably end in their resignation. Then, you will have to agitate in order to prevent Indian troops being used as cannon fodder. You will have to undertake to sabotage Britain's war effort in India and prevent Indian troops being sent to the battlefront. As you are aware, during the last five years the British were giving valuable instructions for organizing and carrying on underground movements in countries which went out of their control and influence. If you follow all those instructions and apply them against the British in India, you will achieve valuable results.

Comrades! I shall now close for the day, but before I conclude I would like to remind you again that a revolutionary is one who believes in the justice of a cause, and he believes that the cause is bound to prevail in the long run. He who gets depressed over failure is not a revolutionary. The motto for a revolutionary is 'Hope for the best, but be prepared for the worst.' I am confident that if we fight on and if we play our cards well in the international field, we shall win our freedom by the end of this war.

'Jai Hind!'

72

I Am a Revolutionary

[Broadcast from Singapore on 27 June 1945][1]

Comrades! During the last few days, I have been speaking to you as a revolutionary addressing fellow revolutionaries in India as I would have done if I had been at home today. By revolutionary I mean a person who stands for the complete independence of his country and who is not prepared to compromise over the question of independence. Furthermore, a revolutionary believes that the cause for which he is fighting is a just one, and that cause, therefore, is bound to triumph in the long run. A revolutionary can never get disheartened or depressed over any failure or setback, for his motto is, 'Hope for the best, but be prepared for the worst.' As revolutionaries fighting for the freedom of India, our faith in our final victory is unshakeable, just as our determination to fight on under all circumstances is unflinching. It is with this invincible spirit that we face the British and look forward to the future. For us as revolutionaries, the independence of India is a settled fact. There is no power on earth that can stand against our goal of freedom. The only uncertain factor is the time factor.

On that question, I should like to say that the exact time as to when India will attain her freedom depends on two factors: Firstly, how much effort we can put forward and how much sacrifice we are prepared to make. Secondly, how we are prepared to utilize the present war situation to our advantage. And from this standpoint, we have to do at least three things. Firstly, whether inside India or outside, we have to assert India's right to freedom with arms. Secondly, inside India, we have to

[1] *Testament of Subhas Bose*, pp. 130–5.

keep up resistance, at least moral resistance, and prevent a compromise with Britain by all means. Thirdly, we have to make India an international issue and put India's case before the bar of world opinion.

I have already said in my previous talk that we, in East Asia, will continue to assert India's right to freedom with arms. So long as we do so, India will remain an international issue, provided people at home do not let us down by compromising with British Imperialism and thereby make India a domestic issue of the British Empire. By a combination of military successes and lying propaganda, the British have managed to create an atmosphere in India which is favourable for a compromise. Among a certain section of our countrymen, the British have been able to create the impression that the Anglo-American Powers are going to win this war, and that India has no hope of achieving her independence during the course of the present war, and further, therefore, the Indian people should accept what they are now being offered.

As soon as the British realized that their propaganda in India was becoming effective, they struck while the iron was hot, and they put forward an offer, an offer, which is, in essence and in substance, the old offer of Sir Stafford Cripps with very slight modifications. Under normal circumstances, not one single genuine Congressman would have looked at Lord Wavell's offer, or would have touched it with a pair of tongs. But because of their defeatist mentality, some of our countrymen, thinking that everything is lost, are trying to grab at this offer just as a drowning man catches at a straw.

Since our enemies have suddenly thrown an obstacle in the path of our independence, our task as revolutionaries is to remove the obstacle by all means at our disposal, so that the forces now working inside India and outside may carry us forward towards our destined goal. Though the time at our disposal is short I am nevertheless hopeful that we can succeed in the effort, provided we can open the eyes of our countrymen in time to the danger that will overtake us if we accept Lord Wavell's offer, and agree to give material support to Britain in her war against Japan. Because, on the one hand, Lord Wavell's offer, if accepted, will divert us from the path of independence. On the other hand, the acceptance of that offer will create a situation in which the Congress will cease to be the representative of the Indian masses, reducing itself to the position of one party among many parties in the country, and at the same time, it will make the Congress refute its national character as an organization representing Indians of all religious creeds.

I am surprised and pained to find that there are some Indians to-day who do not realize that the Viceroy and his masters have laid a trap for the Indian people. These gentlemen go so far as to believe in the bona fides of Lord Wavell and praise his sincerity, but I find that the Viceroy has himself exposed his own character, his motives and intentions. While opening the Simla Conference on June 25, Lord Wavell delivered a sermon to the Indian leaders and said, 'You must accept my leadership for the present until there is some agreed change in the constitution. I am responsible to His Majesty's Government for the good government and tranquillity of India.' But that is not all. Earlier in his speech Lord Wavell said, 'I have called you together from all parts of India at this critical moment in our history to advise and help you in advancing India towards prosperity, political freedom and greatness.'

It is impossible for a self-respecting Indian to put up with this type of patronizing. As far as I am aware, nobody has appointed Lord Wavell as the guardian of India nor has anybody placed India's destiny in his hands. I should like very much to know if the Congress Working Committee accepts this role of Lord Wavell as the arbiter of India's destiny. While the whole world is talking today of aggression and the Anglo-American Powers, in particular, claim to be fighting aggression in this world, let us not forget that British rule in India is based on aggression, brute force, plunder and loot. Let us not forget also that the British have no right to be in India and that it is high time that they had shown some repentance for all their misdeeds in India, instead of posing as our well-wishers or as the saviours of India. Only vanity of the meanest order will explain Lord Wavell's sanctimonious attitude at the Simla Conference.

Another interesting fact, which reveals Lord Wavell's real intentions, is that in the arrangement of seats at the conference table, the seat to his right, which should have been given to the representatives of the most important party attending the conference, was not given to the Congress President, Maulana Abul Kalam Azad. This was announced over Radio New Delhi yesterday; but it was not stated if a protest has been lodged on behalf of the Congress. If no such protest has yet been lodged then it must be assumed that the Congress representatives are so keen about attending the Simla Conference that they are prepared to forget any insult or humiliation in doing so.

I wonder if your attention has been drawn to another relevant and interesting fact. While Lord Wavell was making an announcement about the new offer of the British Government, the India Ofiice in London was making an announcement to the effect that recruitment in England for the Indian Civil Service was being resumed. This is the clearest proof, if any, further proof were needed, that Britain has no intention of relaxing her hold on India. Commenting on this, Prof. Harold Laski, Chairman of the Labour Party of Great Britain, said in a statement issued from London on June 25, 'It suggests to the Indian nationalist mind and the nation that the British seem to envisage a considerable lapse of time before they quit India or alternatively, saddling India for many years with the payment of considerable sums of money of Britishers as compensation for possible loss of office.'

I do not know if any of my listeners have felt intrigued as to why Lord Wavell has converted the Simla Conference into a seret conference behind closed doors. I am told that something like an oath of secrecy has been administered to all the gentlemen attending the conference. Why is it so? I have never heard of a conference in which the fate of a country is going to be decided being held in camera. The only explanation I can find is that Lord Wavell is afraid of public opinion in India. Behind closed doors, he is trying to bamboozle the Indian leaders, and he is apprehensive that if the proceedings are made public, public opinion in India might assert itself in time and spoil all attempts to lead India's leaders into his trap.

While talking of the Simla Conference, I must offer my respectful congratulations to Mahatma Gandhi on the wise step he has taken in not attending the Simla Conference. To me, it is a clear indication that Mahatma Gandhi remembers how the British Government threatened him at the Round Table Conference held in London in 1931. Then, it was so manoeuvred that Mahatma Gandhi's position as the sole representative of the Congress was brought down to the level of the representatives of the other parties attending the conference. In the present case by refraining from attending the Simla Conference, Mahatma Gandhi has been able to keep himself above party level. His non-attendance not only enhances his personal prestige but may even be ultimately helpful to the cause of India.

Comrades! We have, now, to consider what to do about Lord Wavell's offer. First of all, though the time at our disposal is short, we will have to do everything possible to prevent the acceptance of this offer by the Congress Working Committee. We should carry on a raging and tearing campaign against Lord Wavell's offer throughout the length and breadth of the country. You will also have to see to it that an organized opposition is put up. From this distance, I gather the impression that there is plenty of opposition in the country to Lord Wavell's offer. But the oppositionists do not seem to be joining hands in a common campaign for preventing the acceptance of that offer. In your campaign for the rejection of the offer, it will help you considerably if you challenge the Congress Working Committee to produce a programme, which the new Executive Council will carry out. The country will, then, be able to judge from the programme whether the task of the new Executive Council will be to fight Britain's imperialist war in the Far East and provide 500,000 Indian lives as a cannon fodder or to help India along the path of prosperity, political freedom and greatness as Lord Wavell promises.

It is essential that before the Congress Working Committee accepts Lord Wavell's offer, it should place before the Viceroy the programme, which the new Executive Councillors will work out. This programme, if approved by the Viceroy, will be the acid test as to whether the new Executive Council will be able to serve the interests of India or not. If you fail to prevent the acceptance of the offer, you will then have to create a situation, which will force the Congress representatives to resign from the Viceroy's Council. This will not be difficult. You will have to insist on the release of all political prisoners, which will, in itself, bring about a crisis between the Viceroy and the Congress members of the Executive Council, as in 1938 when the Congress Ministries in Bihar and the United Provinces demanded the release of all political prisoners, and there was a conflict with the Governor. Further, there is no doubt that when the Executive Council is formed, the Viceroy will begin to exploit India's resources in men, money and material for fighting Britain's imperialist war in the Far East. This will naturally raise numerous issues in which India's interests will clash with those of Britain. If you keep up your agitation and propaganda against the Congress members of the Executive Council, the Congress members will be forced to stand up for India's interests against those of Britain. A conflict with the Viceroy will be inevitable. Then, you will have to agitate in order to prevent Indian troops being sent as cannon fodder to the Far East. If you fail in that, you will have to undertake sabotage in order to prevent war production, interrupt transport and disrupt lines of communication.

As you are aware, during the last five years, the British have been giving valuable instructions for organizing and carrying on an underground movement in countries which went out of their control, for instance, France, Belgium, Holland, Denmark, Yugoslavia and Greece. There are people in India, as in Britain, who have been trained in underground activities in other countries. If you can utilize these men or if you can at least make use of the instructions for underground activity in other countries issued by the British authorities and apply them against the British in India, you will achieve valuable results.

Last but not the least, you will have to do propaganda work in order to incite a revolt within the Indian armed forces, and thereby prepare for a revolt from within. The Indian Army of today is not the Indian Army of 1939. The Indian Army according to British reports is 2,500,000-strong. In this army, there are many who are politically minded and nationalist in thought. The time for an armed revolt will have come when this army is demobilized and if India is not free by then. Thanks to this war, 2,500,000 Indians have been trained in the use of arms. When the time comes for their disbandment, you can raid the armoury and get the arms with which to fight our British rulers. The Chittagong armoury raid in 1930 was an excellent example of how arms belonging to our enemy can be procured and then used against them.

I am confident that if we fight on, refusing to compromise with British imperialism, and if we play our cards well in the international field, we shall win our freedom by the end of this war. But, that does not mean that if by any chance we fail to succeed, we should be disheartened or depressed. Outwardly, if the worst happens and India does not emerge as an independent state by the end of this war, our next plan should be for a post-war revolution; and if we fail in that too, then there will be World War No.3 to give us another opportunity to fight for our freedom. I have no doubt that World War No.3 will break out within ten years of the end of this war and perhaps much earlier, in case all the suppressed nations of the world are not liberated during the course of the present war.

As I have already said, India's independence is certain, the only uncertain factor is the time factor. At the worst—at the very worst—it may take a few more years for India to be free. Why then should we be so eager to rush to the Viceroy's House for a compromise? Your task as revolutionaries will be to keep the flag of independence flying and to keep it flying until such time as the masses of India rise in open rebellion and hoist the tri-colour National Flag over the Viceroy's House in New Delhi.

'Jai Hind!'

73

Carry on the Struggle

[Broadcast over the Provisional Government of Azad Hind Radio, Singapore, on 28 June 1945][1]

Comrades-in-revolution! Last night I wanted to prove that by accepting the Wavell's offer, we stand to gain nothing. On the other hand, we stand to spoil our nation's future. If we accept the offer we will undoubtedly secure some high posts for the nominees of the Congress, but that is all. We, as a nation, will be doomed, and the Congress will have to discard all that it has stood for all these years.

When revolutionary movements gain strength in any independent country, the foreign dominating government always tries to come to some understanding with the revolutionaries so that it might retain its hold intact by agreeing to a few superficial concessions. When the Sinn-Fein Party launched a revolution in Ireland, the British Government proposed a national convention of all the parties to draft a future Irish Constitution. But the Sinn-Fein Party boycotted the so-called national convention saying that only those who fight for freedom have the exclusive right to frame a constitution for their country. They continued their national revolution, and some time later, the British Government was forced to come to terms with the Sinn-Fein Party to the exclusion of all other parties.

You may recall that when the question of participating in the Round Table Conference in 1931 arose, I said that the Congress alone had the right to join the conference and none else. Those who do not fight for freedom cannot claim the right of participating in such conferences.

[1] *Testament of Subhas Bose*, pp. 135–8, translated from the original Bengali.

Congress leaders did not pay any heed to my words then. Mahatma Gandhi attended the Second Round Table Conference along with other reactionary delegates, but soon after, he realized that the British Government wanted to pitch Indians against one another in that conference. Mahatmaji never forgot the lesson he learnt there. That explains why he did not join the Simla Conference. He has enhanced his prestige by refusing to attend the Simla Conference, and I have no doubt that his non-participation will ultimately lead to good results. Though he supported the Desai-Liaqat Ali Pact, which prompted Lord Wavell to go to England and return with a new offer, Mahatmaji has done the right thing by not participating in the conference. He alone can save the Congress and the country from impending humiliation. I am of the opinion that the Congress has committed the same blunder by joining the Simla Conference as Mahatmaji did in 1931 by joining the Round Table Conference. The Congress, today, is the same Congress, which has been fighting for freedom for the last half a century. It is, therefore, the exclusive right of the Congress to make and arrive at a settlement with any power. The Congress will, therefore, lower its prestige by attending conferences along with diverse political elements. The Congress is the only national and representative organization of India, and it alone has the right to speak for and represent the people of India as a whole. The plan, however, betrays the Viceroy's designs. He has allowed parity between the Hindus and Muslims in his council. He has invited both the Congress and the Muslim League, thereby reducing the status of the Congress to that of a sectarian organization. But Mahatmaji has played his hand well. He has forced the Viceroy to invite Maulana Azad to the conference, and he himself remained away from the conference. Thus, he has defeated both Wavell and Jinnah in their subtle and evil designs. Jinnah, however, will not feel comfortable with Maulana Azad, a Muslim, representing the Congress. So he carries on parleys with Pandit Pant and not with Maulana Azad.

The proposed Executive Council will have Muslim League and Congress representatives; besides this, the minority communities like the Sikhs, Anglo-Indians and others will also be represented. The Congress representatives will, of course, remain loyal to the cause of the country, but the Leaguers might be won over by the Viceroy. In that case, he can have his own way. Even if the Congress and the League nominees agree on anything, the Viceroy's veto will always be there to nullify it. So almost in all cases, he will have his own way. And when we remember that he wants 500,000 troops to fight Japan, we can realize that it is a blunder to take part in the Simla parleys.

The British authorities hold out assurances that the Viceroy's veto will be seldom exercised, but the very treatment meted out to the Congress belies such hopes. In the first instance, the first seat was given to the President, not of the Congress, but of some other organization. Everywhere the first seat is given to the representative of the greatest organization. According to the Delhi Radio, the Congress President was given a seat not to the right of the Viceroy but to his left. This is not a question of personal prestige. It is an insult to the institution we all love. I want to know if any protest has been lodged against this arrangement. If not, the Congress proved to the country that it is only too eager to accept even if it has to put up with this insult.

Some of our countrymen praise Lord Wavell for his sincerity and goodwill. In the inaugural speech before the conference, he is reported to have said, 'I have invited you to help me bring India nearer to her goal of self-government. We must not disperse without coming to a settlement. I am responsible to His Majesty's Government for the peace and welfare of India. I appeal to you to help me in my task.' It is really strange that Wavell still considers himself an arbiter of India's destiny. It should be made clear to him that Indians are the arbiters of their own destiny. The day is long past when Indians felt proud of such compliments, now they feel humiliated at being patted on the back by the British.

Friends, we make the following suggestions to our countrymen to rectify the wrong done by the Congress by participating in the Simla Conference. Bring home to our countrymen that the Working Committee has no right to decide such a grave issue. This right belongs to a plenary session of the Congress. The present Working Committee contains no Leftist elements, which should be duly consulted.

Friends, I have finished. Remember we are revolutionaries. We are optimistic. We must carry on our struggle despite all allurements, and we must succeed.

'Jai Hind!'

74

A Silver Lining

[Broadcast from Singapore on 29 June 1945][1]

Sisters and brothers in India! The latest news from Simla affords a silver lining in the cloud that is ahead of us today. Today, the representatives of the Muslim League have insisted that all the seats in the Viceroy's Executive Council earmarked for Muslims should go to the Muslim League and to the Muslim League alone. It is but natural that the Congress should refuse to accept this position and to insist that at least some of the seats earmarked for Muslims should go to Nationalist Muslims, who are outside the Muslim League. I only hope and pray that the Congress will not budge an inch from this position out of extreme eagerness to accept the British offer. To submit to the unreasonable demand of the Muslim League on this question would amount to political suicide for the Congress.

I have no doubt in my mind that should the unexpected happen and the Congress surrender to the Muslim League on this fundamental and all-important question, there will be a revolt within the Congress. Not only will the entire left-wing revolt against such a decision, but large numbers of Congressmen, who are not left-wingers, will also join in the revolt. I am extremely happy to learn that representatives of five Nationalist Muslim organizations have recently held a conference in New Delhi and have reiterated their declaration that the Muslim League is not the only representative organization of the Muslims of India. The summoning of this conference is an indication that party differences in India are beginning to assert this. I only hope that those organizations and individuals who are hostile to it or are suspicious of Lord Wavell's

[1] *Testament of Subhas Bose*, pp. 138–40.

offer put up a combined opposition. In the first place, it appears to me eminently desirable that all Nationalist Muslim organizations in India should make their voice heard. Perhaps the Azad Muslim League or the Jamiat-ul-Ulema will take the initiative in convening a representative conference of Nationalist Muslim organizations from all over India. From the report, which is before me, I find that in the recent conference held in New Delhi, representatives of the Khudai-Khidmatgars of the Frontier Province and of the Proja Party of Bengal did not participate. It is also not clear if the Majlis-I-Ahrar took part in that conference. In the conference that I have suggested, it may even be possible to invite representatives of the Unionist Party of the Punjab, because it is possible that the Muslim members of the Unionist Party will not accept the position that the Muslim League is the sole representative of the Muslims of India.

All those who feel as strongly as I do that in the interests of India and for the early achievement of India's independence, Lord Wavell's offer should be rejected lock, stock and barrel, must continue their agitation until we are completely out of danger. Moreover, if we lose the first round and if the Congress ultimately accepts Lord Wavell's offer, we must, nevertheless, continue our activity so that a situation may be created in which the Congress will be compelled to resign from the Viceroy's Executive Council. In a revolutionary struggle, we can never afford to be disheartened, discouraged or depressed, especially at a time when so much depends on the success of the campaign.

Mahatma Gandhi's wise decision in not participating in the Simla Conference gives us some hope that the tragedy may yet be averted. I can understand why the Muslim League representatives have resented the invitation to Maulana Azad to attend the conference. What Mahatma Gandhi has done is not only magnificently proper, but has been a particularly wise step. It would have been a very great injustice to Maulana Abul Kalam Azad, personally, and to the large number of the Congress Muslims who have made tremendous sacrifices in the cause of India's freedom, if the Congress President had not been allowed to lead the Congress delegation to the Simla Conference simply because he happens to be a Muslim.

I am surprised to find that in his negotiations with the Congress, Mr. Jinnah did not deal directly with the Congress President, but paid commodious lip service to Pandit Govind Ballabh Pant as an intermediary between himself and the Congress President. Maulana Abul Kalam Azad, by leading the Congress delegation, has been able to render a great service to India by making the voice of India felt in the conference. There is no doubt that by his non-participation in the Simla Conference, Mahatma Gandhi has enhanced his personal position and prestige. It is also not new to him to keep out of the whole situation, thus making it possible for him to put himself at the forefront at the right moment and advise the rejection of the proposed offer. Meanwhile, the danger continues and we can't afford to waste our time. I, therefore, hope and trust that all lovers and supporters of Indian independence will continue their efforts to secure a rejection of the British offer, which is a great menace to the cause of India's freedom. Once this obstacle is removed from the path of India's freedom, the Indian people will be able to regain their mental balance and to prepare a first-class plan to continue the national struggle till complete independence is achieved.

'Jai Hind!'

75

Liberty or Death

[Summary of speeches, July 1945][1]

In spite of recent setbacks, the three million Indians in East Asia celebrated on July 4, 1945, the second anniversary of the historic day on which Netaji Subhas Chandra Bose assumed the leadership of the Indian Independence Movement in East Asia. The day was celebrated with mass meetings and demonstrations, and Indians in East Asia renewed their pledge of loyalty to the Provisional Government of Azad Hind and to their leader, Netaji Subhas Chandra Bose. They also reaffirmed their grim resolve to wage the war of India's liberation until victory was achieved. These observances in connection with Netaji Week lasted for the entire week and concluded on July 10.

In Syonan on July 4, prayers were held in all mosques, churches and temples for the long life of Netaji Subhas Chandra Bose and the complete success of his mission in life, i.e., the complete liberation of India from the British yoke. The day's activities commenced with the singing of the National Anthem. The climax was reached in the evening when tens of thousands of Indians rallied at a huge mass meeting, which was addressed by their beloved leader Netaji Subhas Chandra Bose.

Before the proceedings commenced, Netaji stressed the importance of the new National Anthem for India that had been in vogue in East Asia since 21st October 1943—the day on which the Provisional Government of Azad Hind was formed. Netaji stated that the new National Anthem had been composed by Janab Syed Mumtaz Hussain of the Publicity Department of the Indian Independence League

[1] *Chalo Delhi*, pp. 218–22.

Headquarters in East Asia. Netaji appreciated the composition and adopted it as the future National Anthem of Free India acceptable to all Indians without any distinction of caste or creed. In appreciation of Janab Hussain's services for the cause of Mother India, Netaji presented him with a beautiful silver casket containing a cheque for ten thousand dollars.

Then Netaji addressed the meeting in Hindustani for well over two hours. Netaji asked the gathering whether they were prepared to continue the armed struggle against the Anglo-Americans until India was completely free. For a couple of seconds the whole atmosphere was tense and then the whole gathering stood up as one man and signified their willingness to follow their leader to freedom or death.

An event of great importance in the history of the Indian Independence Movement in East Asia took place on July 8, when the foundation stone for a memorial to the Indian martyrs, who laid down their lives in the cause of India's battle for freedom, was laid by His Excellency Netaji Subhas Chandra Bose, Head of the Provisional Government of Azad Hind and Supreme Commander of the Azad Hind Fauj on the waterfront on Connaught Drive, Syonan. The function was attended by the Azad Hind Fauj and the volunteers of the Rani of Jhansi Regiment, who were drawn up to form three sides of the square, while a number of others were lined up on the road. The Balak Sena unit and girls of the Indian National School also took part in the ceremony. High ranked Nippon officials, high officials of the Provisional Government of Azad Hind of the INA and of the Indian Independence League and prominent members of various communities were present.

The ceremony began punctually at 11 o'clock with the arrival of Netaji Bose followed by the hoisting of the national flag, the band playing the National Anthem. Netaji then gave an address in Hindustani extolling the supreme sacrifice made by the martyrs.

Addressing the gathering Netaji said: 'Today is for us Indians a memorable day—a day that will live in our history for all time. We have assembled here today in a solemn ceremony to pay our respectful homage to all those who have given their lives for the freedom of our motherland, under the leadership of the Provisional Government. As you know, the Provisional Government of Azad Hind declared war on Britain and America on the 23rd October 1943, and the armed struggle for India's liberty was actually launched on the 4th of February 1944.

Since then, we have, on several occasions, paid our homage to those heroes who died for the freedom of India. But this is the first occasion when we are erecting a memorial to our Glorious Dead. It is, I believe, in the fitness of things that our first War Memorial should be put up in this city. Syonan is also the birthplace of the Azad Hind Fauj; Syonan is also the birthplace of the Provisional Government of Azad Hind.

It is from Syonan that the troops of the Azad Hind Fauj and members of their auxiliary organizations like the Azad Hind Dal marched to Burma, on their way to India. Furthermore, Syonan and Malai have contributed a large number of recruits for our army and a large number of workers for our independence movement. That is why the Provisional Government of Azad Hind decided to erect the first memorial to the heroes of Azad Hind in this city, which was once the bulwark of the British Empire in the East and which became, later, the starting-point of India's last War of Independence.

There are occasions when thoughts lie too deep for words, and this is one of those solemn and sacred occasions. Let us, therefore, pay our respectful homage to the immortal dead in solemn silence. And, while paying our homage, let us pray to the Almighty Father to give us strength to continue and complete the work that our heroes left unfinished. Their immortal souls are with us today to inspire us to greater deeds of heroism and valour. With God's blessings and with the inspiration given us by our heroes, let us continue the struggle without faltering and without compromising, until the complete independence of India is achieved. And let us have unshakeable confidence in our final victory, as well as unflinching determination to achieve that victory in spite of all difficulties and tribulations.'

Netaji then laid the foundation stone by placing a marble plaque bearing an inscription in Hindustani with the flag standing at half-mast. The whole parade was brought to attention, and two minutes silence was observed with the guard of honour standing with arms reversed. Netaji and the Nippon Administration and leaders of various communities placed wreaths to the high-ranking officers of the Provisional Government of Azad Hind.

With three salvoes of feu de joie by the guard of honour, followed by the singing of the National Anthem, and with the flag flying full mast, the ceremony came to an end.

76

Face Any Situation Like Brave Soldiers

[Special Order of the Day, Singapore, 14 August 1945][1]

COMRADES,

All sorts of wild rumours are now afloat in Syonan and other places, one of them being that hostilities have ceased. Most of these rumours are either false or highly exaggerated. Till this moment, fighting is going on, on all fronts, and I say this, not only on the basis of reports from friendly sources, but also of reports given out by the enemy radio. If there is any change in the war situation, I shall be the first to inform you. Therefore, I want all of you to remain perfectly calm and unperturbed and carry on your duties in a normal way. Above all, do not allow yourselves to be influenced in any manner by wild bazaar rumours. We have to face any situation that may arise, like brave soldiers fighting for the freedom of their motherland.

JAI HIND.

Subhas Chandra Bose
SUPREME COMMANDER,
AZAD HIND FAUJ.

Syonan, 14th August 1945.
1500 hours

[1] Archives of the Netaji Research Bureau.

77

The Roads to Delhi are Many

[Special Order of the Day, 15 August 1945][1]

To Officers and Men of the Azad Hind Fauj,

Comrades, in our struggle for the independence of our motherland, we have now been overwhelmed by an undreamt of crisis. You may perhaps feel that you have failed in your mission to liberate India. But let me tell you that this failure is only of a temporary nature. No setback and no defeat can undo your positive achievements of the past. Many of you have participated in the fight along the Indo-Burma frontier and also inside India and have gone through hardship and suffering of every sort. Many of your comrades have laid down their lives on the battlefield and have become the immortal heroes of Azad Hind. This glorious sacrifice can never go in vain.

Comrades, in this dark hour I call upon you to conduct yourselves with the discipline, dignity and strength befitting a truly Revolutionary Army. You have already given proofs of your valour and self-sacrifice on the field of battle. It is now your duty to demonstrate your undying optimism and unshakeable willpower in the hour of temporary defeat. Knowing you as I do, I have not the slightest doubt that even in this dire adversity, you will hold your heads erect and face the future with unending hope and confidence.

Comrades, I feel that in this critical hour, thirty-eight crores of our countrymen at home are looking at us, the members of India's Army of Liberation. Therefore, remain true to India and do not for a moment

[1] Archives of the Netaji Research Bureau.

waver in your faith in India's destiny. The roads to Delhi are many and Delhi still remains our goal. The sacrifices of your immortal comrades and yourselves will certainly achieve their fulfilment. There is no power on earth that can keep India enslaved. India shall be free and before long.

JAI HIND.

15th August, 1945 SUBHAS CHANDRA BOSE

78

India Shall be Free

[Special message to Indians in Malaya, Thailand, Indo-China, Java, Sumatra, Borneo, Philippines, Japan and other parts of East Asia, 15 August 1945][1]

Sisters and Brothers,

A glorious chapter in the history of India's Struggle for Freedom has just come to a close and, in that chapter, the sons and daughters of India in East Asia will have an undying place.

You set a shining example of patriotism and self-sacrifice by pouring out men, money and materials into the struggle for India's independence. I shall never forget the spontaneity and enthusiasm with which you responded to my call for 'Total Mobilization'. You sent an unending stream of your sons and daughters to the camps to be trained as soldiers of the Azad Hind Fauj and of the Rani of Jhansi Regiment. Money and materials you poured lavishly into the war chest of the Provisional Government of Azad Hind. In short, you did your duty as true sons and daughters of India. I regret more than you do that your sufferings and sacrifices have not borne immediate fruit. But they have not gone in vain, because they have ensured the emancipation of our motherland and will serve as an undying inspiration to Indians all over the world. Posterity will bless your name, and will talk with pride about your offerings at the altar of India's Freedom and about your positive achievement as well.

[1] Archives of the Netaji Research Bureau.

In this unprecedented crisis in our history, I have only one word to say. Do not be depressed at our temporary failure. Be of good cheer and keep up your spirits. Above all, never for a moment falter in your faith in India's destiny. There is no power on earth that can keep India enslaved. India shall be free and before long.

Jai Hind.

15th August, 1945 — Subhas Chandra Bose

Letters

1

To The Hikari Kikan
CONFIDENTIAL

Unity-Faith-Sacrifice
Indian Independence League Headquarters
P.O. BOX NO. 82 No. 7 Chancery Lane,
TELEGRAMS-JAYABHARAT
Syonan.

PHONE 31505
26th August, 1943

Ref. HQ/HK/137
The Headquarters,
The Hikari Kikan,
Syonan.

Dear Sirs,

We are grateful for the material assistance in cash and in kind that we have received from time to time and that we are going to receive in future through the Hikari Kikan from the Imperial Japanese Army Authorities. We desire very much to treat the above material assistance as a loan from a friendly power, which the Government of Free India will duly honour and repay. I shall, therefore, feel obliged if the above material assistance given to us is put under one account—to be called the 'India Account'—and the interest thereon is duly calculated.

When the Provisional Government of Free India is formed and is recognized by the Imperial Japanese Government, the above material assistance given to the Indian Independence League, East Asia, should be debited to the Provisional Government as a loan duly incurred—which the Government of Free India will honour and repay.

I shall be thankful if this arrangement is approved.

Yours truly,
Subhas Chandra Bose
President,
INDIAN INDEPENDENCE LEAGUE
East Asia.

2

To Sisir Kumar Bose[1]

Unity-Faith-Sacrifice
The Indian Independence League

Chancery Lane
Syonan
Sri Sri Kali Puja
29th October, 1943

The bearer of this letter is going to our country for special, urgent work. I shall be grateful if my friends, colleagues and supporters were to help him.

Yours
Subhas Chandra Bose

[1] Translated from the original Bengali, this letter was handed over to Sisir Kumar Bose by the leader, 'T.K. Rao', of a secret group sent by submarine from Penang by Netaji. A similar letter in Netaji's own hand from the 'Indo-Burma frontier' was received by Sisir Kumar Bose after the end of the war in 1945 from another secret agent who had been unable to deliver it in 1944. The first letter had to be destroyed in 1944, but the second letter is preserved in the archives of the Netaji Research Bureau.

3

To the parents of Pratima Pal[2]

Rangoon
22.1.44

Dear Friend,

It has been two weeks since I arrived here with my Headquarters. I will be here from now on. I had sent you a telegram, but I do not know whether you received it. I had informed you that arrangements were being made for your family's accommodation as you had requested. I have made the arrangements here, so you need not have any worry. Your brother is working here in our reconstruction department.

Please reply to my letter. Both of you are always in my thoughts. May God bless you and may your noble enterprise be crowned with success—that is my constant prayer.

Your well-wisher,
Subhas Chandra Bose

[2] Translated from the original Bengali.

4

To Brahmachari Kailasam

Syonan

ARZI HUKUMATE AZAD HIND
(THE PROVISIONAL GOVERNMENT
OF FREE INDIA)

Rangoon,
13.3.44

Respected Brahmachariji,

I am grateful to you for all your letters (three, I think). It is very kind of you to take so much interest in my future.

Please convey my respectful pranams to Swamiji and accept the same yourself.

The work here is increasing by leaps and bounds, and I cannot cope with it—even after working day and night.

I was hoping to come to Syonan on a flying visit—but I could not manage at the last moment.

The situation is developing very favourably for us, and this is keeping me here.

Please send me any book that you consider useful for me.
Hope this will find Swamiji and all of you well.

Jai Hind
Subhas Chandra Bose

5

To Brahmachari Kailasam

Syonan

ARZI HUKUMATE AZAD HIND
(THE PROVISIONAL GOVERNMENT
OF FREE INDIA)

Burma,
18.3.44

Respected Brahmachariji,

Many thanks for your kind letter of the 7th March and the book, which Lt. Col. Chatterjee brought here.

If you have any mail for me, please give it to Lt. Col. Alagappan or whoever is in charge of the League Rear Headquarters.

We are all frightfully busy here—particularly because events are moving fast.

Please convey my best regards to Swamiji and accept the same yourself.

Jai Hind
Subhas Chandra Bose

6

To Brahmachari Kailasam

Syonan

Personal & Confidential

SADAR DAFTAR ARZI HUKUMATE
AZAD HIND (THE PROVISIONAL GOVERNMENT
OF FREE INDIA)

16.4.44

Jai Hind,

I have an opportunity of sending mail to Rangoon, and I am taking this opportunity of scribbling a few lines before crossing the frontier. Once I do so, I do not know when I shall be able to communicate with you again.

Things are going on very well at the front—on the whole—and the spirits of all are high.

Please convey my respectful *namaskar* to Swamiji and accept the same yourself.

Besides our troops, many—many men of the Reconstruction Department from Syonan and Rangoon have gone forward. We shall be meeting them in Free India. Azad Hind Zindabad!

Jai Hind
Subhas Chandra Bose

7

To Lieutenant M Satiavati Thevar

PJR/4/M

INA SADAR DAFTAR, ALA KAMAN
AZAD HIND FAUJ
(HEADQUARTERS, SUPREME COMMAND, INDIAN NATIONAL ARMY)

Headquarters
Burma.
14th May, 1944

Lieut. Thevar

Rani of Jhansi Regiment
Syonan

'Jai Hind'

I have been watching your work with the greatest interest since Captain Lakshmi left Syonan for the first time. It was in appreciation of your good work that I was glad to promote you to the rank of Lieutenant. I am sending herewith some new orders with regard to the administration and training of the Rani of Jhansi Regiment in future. You will see therefrom that I desire that the discipline of the Camp should be further tightened up. I want you to be particularly careful in the matter of allowing visitors inside the Camp and also in allowing volunteers to go out. I noticed in Rangoon that from the very beginning the volunteers were allowed to go home on Sundays with the result that the discipline was slacker than in Syonan. Fortunately in Syonan most of the volunteers came from outside. With regard to the volunteers coming from Syonan city itself, I leave it to you to further control their going out, should you deem it necessary in the interests of discipline.

I read with great interest the report you sent me, dated the 26th February, 1944.

There are a few points to which I should like to draw attention:

(i) It would be desirable to get the volunteers trained in sentry duty. To begin with, they should do sentry duty at night inside the Camp. Gradually, when the time is ripe, they could also undertake sentry duty outside the Gate during day time.

(ii) I do not approve of the system of naming platoons after personalities. I should like you to discontinue this practice and use numbers instead.

(iii) If you find it possible, please introduce a fortnightly weighment. This will enable you to observe more closely the health of the volunteers.

(iv) I do not like the volunteers to waste their time unnecessarily in cooking and other domestic duties. These duties they have done enough at home. In the Camp they should concentrate on the task that lies ahead of them. Consequently, if at any time you can employ Cooks of reliable character, I should like you to utilize their services.

(v) I should like to know in detail as to what steps have been taken to train N.C.O.'s.

On receipt of this, please let me have an up to date report. I should like particularly to know the present strength of the Regiment. If you have any recommendations to make with regard to promotion, please let me have them along with the report. I should also like to know whether the food supplied to the volunteers is satisfactory.

I hope you are receiving necessary help and assistance from the Rear Headquarters of the Indian Independence League and from the Rear Headquarters of the Azad Hind Fauj in Syonan. I am asking Sri J.A. Thivy and Col. Bhonsle to give you all assistance that you may need. I am asking Colonel Bhonsle, in particular, to supervise the training of N.C.O's and to arrange for the further training of the Officers of the Regiment.

I should like in future to have a monthly report from you as to the progress of the work.

I am extremely disappointed over the delay in transporting the first contingent to Burma. I have done my best from this end to arrange for the transport, but luck has been against us so far. However, I still hope that in the near future, arrangements will be made for bringing them to Burma.

I am enclosing herewith a short message for the members of the Regiment which I would like you to read out to them in the different languages.

With best wishes for the success of your work,

JAI HIND
Subhas Chandra Bose

8

To Brahmachari Kailasam

Syonan

ARZI HUKUMATE AZAD HIND
(THE PROVISIONAL GOVERNMENT
OF FREE INDIA)

Burma
18.6.44

Jai Hind!

I have just arrived here from Bangkok after a comfortable journey. There is nothing much to write except that things are going on all right. We have, however, a hard fight before us—which, of course, I welcome.

I have an opportunity of writing to you today.

I hope that the affairs of the Welfare Association will be settled satisfactorily. I hope also that the Orphanage will get all the help, which Swamiji and you may require.

With respectful namaskar to Swamiji and yourself.

Jai Hind
Subhas Chandra Bose

9

To Lieutenant M. Satiavati Thevar

INA

SADAR DAFTAR, ALA KAMAN
AZAD HIND FAUJ
(HEADQUARTERS, SUPREME COMMAND,
INDIAN NATIONAL ARMY)

Dated 18th June 1944

Lt. M.S. Thevar,
Commandant, Rani of Jhansi Training Camp
Syonan

Jai Hind,

I received your letter dated 15th June which you handed over to my Adjutant, containing your recommendations regarding some promotions. I am expecting the Jhansi contingent to arrive here within a day or two. After their arrival I shall go into the matter in a comprehensive way and issue orders pertaining to promotions in the different Units of the Rani of Jhansi Regiment.

Before I left Syonan, I had a talk with Col. Bhonsle and Sri Thivy. I have asked Col. Bhonsle to supervise the training of the Rani of Jhansi Regiment, Syonan. I want him to arrange for special training for Officers and N.C.O.'s. I have also asked him to arrange for additional training for the Special Service Group of that Regiment. Regarding the training of the Special Service Group, it will have to be considered if that training could be carried out in the same Camp or in a special Camp. It may not be easy to find or build a special Camp for the Special Service Group. Consequently, the possibility of sending the Special Service Group to Burma for training may also have to be considered.

I have already told Col. Bhonsle that the Chief Instructor has not been doing his work properly and that he should be changed.

Apart from training, other matters pertaining to the Rani of Jhansi Regiment will be dealt with by Sri Thivy as before.

I hope you will introduce more strictness in the matter of allowing the volunteers to go out of Camp, and also in the matter of interviews inside the Camp. Please tell all the girls of your Regiment that while greeting anyone they should simply say 'Jai Hind' and not 'Jai Hind Sahib'.

As I told you verbally, I want you to delegate your work as much as possible to your assistants and to concentrate on the training of the Regiment. You will also have to devote more attention to your own training. And remember always that a real leader is one who not only works hard himself (or herself) but also gets the maximum work out of others.

Please take up with Mr. Thivy the question of sending a group from your Regiment to do propaganda work in the principal towns in Malaya that can be reached by train. All those who go with this group should carry their rifles. This propaganda tour should be in addition to the tour of Mrs. Lukshmeya and other ladies.

With all good wishes, Jai Hind.

Subhas Chandra Bose
SUPREME COMMANDER
AZAD HIND FAUJ

10

To R.K. Sekharan

ARZI HUKUMATE AZAD HIND
(THE PROVISIONAL GOVERNMENT
OF FREE INDIA)

Sri R.K. Sekharan

Tokyo.

18 June, 1944

'Jai Hind '

I am extremely happy to receive your letter and to hear that you are getting on very well with your studies. It gives me very great pleasure indeed to know that you are determined to derive the maximum benefit from your stay in Nippon, and to return to Free India as worthy sons of our motherland. You have gone to Nippon to undergo training, which will enable you to become full-fledged soldiers who will defend India's Independence with the last drop of their blood. Meanwhile, the heroism and self-sacrifice with which Officers and men of the Azad Hind Fauj are fighting on the battlefields of Arakan, Kaladan, Imphal and Kohima should serve as a shining example to you to follow all your life.

Though you are yet in your teens, you have left your homes and parents and brothers and sisters, and you have travelled thousands of miles to far-off Nippon and will stay there for some years. Though physically you are thousands of miles away from me, you are always in my thoughts.

There was much that I wanted to tell you when I addressed you in Syonan. But the thought of parting from you so overpowered me that I could hardly speak. I wanted to go back to Syonan again in March to see you off—but I could not, owing to the military operations then going on at the Indo-Burma frontier. In future, I shall be moving further and further from you and may not, therefore, be able to write to you. But do write to me, my dear boy, whenever you have a chance of writing. Wherever I may be, I shall think of you and pray for your success.

I hope you will continue singing the National Anthem everyday during your stay in Nippon. And pray every morning and night that you may become a worthy Son of Mother India.

Jai Hind
Subhas Chandra Bose
SUPREME COMMANDER,
AZAD HIND FAUJ.

11

To The Secretary, Ceylon Department

ARZI HUKUMATE AZAD HIND
(THE PROVISIONAL GOVERNMENT
OF FREE INDIA)

RANGOON,
21st June 1944.

Secretary, Ceylon Department,
Rear Headquarters, Indian Independence League,
Syonan

Jai Hind,

I wrote to you on the 18th inst. acknowledging receipt of your letter of the 14th inst. from Bangkok. But I am afraid that I did not acknowledge your previous letters.

I duly received your previous letters of the 27th April, 28th April and 12th May.

Re: the Ceylon Burghers, the main point is as to whether they regard themselves as children of the soil and whether they are trustworthy. If they are, then there is no objection to their joining the IIL. You have only to be careful that they do not come in with an ulterior motive—viz. come in to pump out information re: our organization.

So far as secret work is concerned, you will have to be extra-cautious. Even if Ceylon Burghers are allowed to participate in the public activity of the Indian Independence League, they should not easily be admitted into our secret revolutionary activities. In this matter, you should not be carried away by our emotions, but should rather be extra-cautious.

There is one question which I have often been asked and which I should like to answer here. A Ceylonese is not compelled to work in the Ceylon Department of the IIL, if he does not like to do so. He may work in any other Department of the IIL, if he prefers to do so. Similarly, an Indian, if he so chooses, can work for the Ceylon Department and can join the Lanka Unit, if he feels the urge to concentrate on work for Lanka. It follows, therefore, that a Ceylonese, who wants to join the

Army is not compelled to join the Lanka Unit—if he does not choose to do so.

In my last letter, I asked you to have a talk to Major Swami about the special training of the Lanka youths—subsequent to their training at the Azad School. I hope that you will be able to talk the matter over with Major Swami before he leaves Syonan. There is one thing that I would like to stress in this connection. For the special training, we must have the very best men. What is wanted for this talk is quality, not quantity. Therefore, do not be eager to put all the Azad schoolboys into the special training unless they pass the moral test. Revolutionary activity is much more difficult than fighting with an army, and it requires a much higher degree of courage and heroism. I was told by Major Swami that all the boys in Penang were not up to the mark.

Wishing you all success in your work and with cordial greetings to all of you,

Jai Hind
Subhas Chandra Bose

12

To Lieutenant M. Satyavati Thevar

SADAR DAFTAR, ALA KAMAN
AZAD HIND FAUJ
(HEADQUARTERS, SUPREME COMMAND,
INDIAN NATIONAL ARMY)

Confidential

RANGOON,
21st June, 1944

Lt. M.S. Thevar,
Commandant, Rani of Jhansi Regiment Training Camp
Syonan

Jai Hind,

I am sending herewith a copy of a circular which was issued by me some time ago and which did not probably reach you.

I hope you have duly received the letter which I wrote to you from here dated the 18th inst.

You will be glad to know that the Jhansi contingent arrived here safely today after an uneventful journey. Capt. Lee of the INA accompanied the party from Thailand, under my instructions, and the Administrator of the Jhansi Training Camp, Rangoon, met the party at Moulmein. They are all in high spirits.

When I was in Syonan it was reported to me that you wanted a Car for the use of the Regiment. I went into the matter and found that it was difficult to spare a Car exclusively for the Regiment. Whenever you want a Car, you can ring up the IIL Rear Headquarters and they will comply with your wishes as far as possible.

As the number grows, your work will become more and more difficult. Above all, you will have to be strictly impartial towards girls coming from different parts of India and speaking different languages. In addition to this, you will have to be firm, but friendly, to all those who are in your care. It is a difficult task and will need your utmost effort and attention.

I should like to remind you once again not to bother yourself with work which others can manage. You must concentrate your whole attention on Training—the training of those who are in the Camp and of yourself. A Commandant is the Officer in-charge of a Training Camp and not the manager of a lodging-house. Moreover, your own promotion will depend on the progress you make in your military duties.

It is worthwhile considering if there should be an elderly lady in the Camp for looking after the household, thereby relieving others of this work. If you consider this desirable, the League Headquarters can then look out for such a lady.

With all good wishes,

Jai Hind
Subhas Chandra Bose

13

To Lieutenant M. Satiavati Thevar

ARZI HUKUMATE AZAD HIND
(THE PROVISIONAL GOVERNMENT
OF FREE INDIA)

Confidential

Burma
4th August, 1944

Lieutenant Thevar
Commandant,
Rani of Jhansi Regt.Training Camp
Syonan

'Jai Hind'

I am writing this in haste because there is a chance of sending mail to Syonan by air tomorrow morning. I duly received your letter a few days ago. I shall reply to it later on. I hope the work is going on satisfactorily and that more recruits will come in, in future. Please keep me informed of all the developments. The Syonan contingent is keeping good health here. They will be given further training. Only the Nurses have been sent further up to work in one of our hospitals.

With all good wishes,

Jai Hind
Subhas Chandra Bose

P.S.: I hope you are taking advanced military training yourself. This is necessary if you desire further promotion.

S.C.B

14

To Lieutenant M. Satyavati Thevar

Personal and Confidential

INA

SADAR DAFTAR, ALA KAMAN

AZAD HIND FAUJ

(HEADQUARTERS, SUPREME COMMAND, INDIAN NATIONAL ARMY)

Burma,
19th August, 1944

Captain M.S. Thevar,
Commandant,
Rani of Jhansi Regiment Camp,
Syonan

Jai Hind!

Enclosed you will find the latest orders regarding promotions in the Rani of Jhansi Regiment. I have much pleasure in promoting you Captain. This is in recognition of the good work you have done as Commandant of the Camp. There is, however, something I want to tell you quite frankly. I want to see the Rani of Jhansi Regiment Officers as efficient as the men Officers of the INA, so that nobody can have any justification for thinking that promotions in the Rani of Jhansi Regiment are easy. From the strictly military point of view, you are not yet fit to be a Captain, but I hope that you will exert yourself to the utmost to become fit. When I was in Syonan I told you that your job is not to be merely a good household manager. You have to be also an efficient Army Officer. In order to be able to give more time to your own training, you must divide the work among your assistants. I noticed a tendency in you to keep too much power and responsibility in your hands. Please remember that an efficient organiser is one who not only works hard himself or herself, but also makes other people work hard. An organizer is judged not merely by the output of his or her own work, but by the total output of the work of the whole organisation.

In Syonan I also heard some complaint about your being partial. I do not know how far this complaint is justified. The complaint was to the effect that you were more partial to the Tamil-speaking members of the Regiment. I hope you will see to it that nothing is done which may give any cause for complaint about your being partial. We all have to face complaints even when we are absolutely just and fair. Consequently, such complaints are bound to increase considerably, if there is the slightest justification for them.

In your original recommendation, you suggested promoting Rasamma from Sepoy to Havildar. This sort of thing cannot be done and I hope you will not make such recommendations in future. We had to make a few rapid promotions at the beginning—but now that the Regiment is fairly well-organized, all promotions must be according to the usual procedure. The moment you promote a Sepoy as Havildar straightaway, you will expose yourself to a charge of favouritism. This is bound to happen, especially when no case has been made out for such rapid promotion. I have, therefore, promoted Rasamma from Lance Naik to Naik, in the accompanying orders. She must wait for her turn before she can be promoted Havildar.

With the exception of Rasamma, I have given effect to all your recommendations. I have done so more or less blindly, trusting your judgment. You ought to know by now that promotions in the Army, if not strictly just and fair, cause a great deal of heart-burning. I hope you will try to make your recommendations so impartially that I may not have any ground whatsoever for distrusting your judgment.

I am glad that you have been maintaining good discipline in the Camp. I feel, however, that there is room for improvement in discipline—especially in girls going out of the Camp.

I hope this will find you all in good health and spirits.

Jai Hind
Subhas Chandra Bose

15

To Brahmachari Kailasam

Syonan

ARZI HUKUMATE AZAD HIND

(THE PROVISIONAL GOVERNMENT OF FREE INDIA)

Confidential

MEMO

Rangoon
20.8.44

Jai Hind!

I hear that you have gone with the party to inspect conditions of our labourers in Thailand. I am glad. Perhaps you are back in Syonan by now. I am eagerly awaiting the report of the inspection party. I hope that you are quite well, despite a trying tour. Please give my respectful 'pranams' to Swamiji.

I am keeping good health. Perhaps you are aware by now that we have had to go over to the defensive against our enemies. It was not possible to take Imphal owing to the heavy rains, which put us at a disadvantage. We have now fallen back to a more advantageous line of defence. We are preparing for the next offensive.

Our troops have fought magnificently. As long as we were on this offensive, we could beat the enemy everywhere. Having beaten the enemy, our troops have the confidence born of victory. We have seen that we are more than a match for the enemy. We are now busy preparing for the next offensive—in the light of the experience gained in six months' fighting.

The morale here is excellent—both among civilians and among the army. I am sorry to hear that the morale in Malaya has gone down. Why is it so?

With respectful greetings, and Jai Hind.

Subhas Chandra Bose

16

To Brahmachari Kailasam

Syonan

ARZI HUKUMATE AZAD HIND

(THE PROVISIONAL GOVERNMENT OF FREE INDIA)

MEMO

Burma
22.8.44

Jai Hind!

I wrote to you the other day. Today, I am writing this just to inform you that I have received your long letters from Thailand.

I am grateful to you for taking the trouble of joining the Inspection Party. I hope your health is none the worse for the long journey.

With respectful 'namaskar'
Jai Hind
Subhas Chandra Bose

17

To the mother of Pratima Pal[3]

ARZI HUKUMATE AZAD HIND
(THE PROVISIONAL GOVERNMENT
OF FREE INDIA)

Burma
22.8.44

Dear Friend,

Jai Hind!

I suddenly heard from Pratima one day that she had lost her father. I am deeply worried about you and everyone else in your family. Please accept my heartfelt sympathy. May God give you solace and the strength to bear this great calamity—that is my ardent prayer.

I have tried to console Pratima. I have told her that since her father of his own free will had gifted her for the service of the country she must bear all her anguish like a true heroine. Pratima is a good girl, a brave girl, she has understood. She has composed herself. You are her only concern. If she gets news of your well-being, she will be able to focus on her own work. I shall be grateful if you would please send news that you are alright as soon as possible.

You will, of course, be glad to know that your daughter has performed well in her work and has been promoted to the rank of 'sub-officer'.

I hope and believe that you will remain brave of heart in this crisis. If you stay calm, your children too will be able to follow your example. Merciful God will give you peace, consolation and strength.

Jai Hind!

Yours sincerely,
Subhas Chandra Bose

[3] Translated from the original Bengali.

18

To Brahmachari Kailasam

ARZI HUKUMATE AZAD HIND
(THE PROVISIONAL GOVERNMENT
OF FREE INDIA)

Burma
19.10.44

Jai Hind!

This is just a line to inform you that I am doing well. I have just returned from an inspection of our front-line troops. In spite of the suffering and hardship that our troops have suffered, their morale is excellent. The civilian morale is also quite good. I am sorry to hear that the morale in Malaya has fallen. I may be visiting Syonan after some time.

With pranams to Swamiji and yourself.

Jai Hind
Subhas Chandra Bose

19

To the INA Cadets

Tokyo

ARZI HUKUMATE AZAD HIND
(THE PROVISIONAL GOVERNMENT
OF FREE INDIA)

Fukuoka
29.11.44

My dear boys,

On the eve of my taking off from the soil of Nippon, I want to send you my love and good wishes for the success of your work. I have no son of my own—but you are to me more than my son—because you have dedicated your life to the cause, which is the one and only goal of my life—the freedom of 'Bharat mata'.

I am confident that you will always remain true to the CAUSE, and to 'Bharat Mata'.

I am sorry that I could not see you again before leaving—but you know that I am always with you in spirit.

God bless you,
Jai Hind
Subhas Chandra Bose

20

To Sri Rama Murti

Tokyo

ARZI HUKUMATE AZAD HIND
(THE PROVISIONAL GOVERNMENT
OF FREE INDIA)

Fukuoka
29.11.44

Jai Hind,

I am enclosing herewith a letter for our cadets which I would like you to deliver to them. We have been detained here owing to bad weather, but are hoping that we shall be able to take off tomorrow. Otherwise there is nothing else to write to you. Hope that the work will go on better now. Don't forget to have the 'printed Prayer' sent to the boys from the General Staff. In case the copies get lost, you may try to get more copies printed there. Otherwise, please inform me and we shall have fresh copies printed in Syonan and forwarded from there. Here are a few points which you will have to follow up:

(a) A small library for the use of the cadets.
(b) National Anthem in its revised form to be distributed to all the League Branches.
(c) Investigate the diet of Indians in Japan and whether there is a case for asking for more rations.
(d) Examine the industrial scheme of Mr. Mehra and draw up a practical scheme for submitting to the General Staff.
(e) Investigate further the bad elements among the Indians with a view to putting the matter up before the authorities.

Planes are always flying from Tokyo to Syonan. If you keep in touch with the proper quarters, you may be able to send mail frequently to Syonan.

Jai Hind
Subhas Chandra Bose

P.S.: Please give the copies of all my recent broadcast speeches to the General Staff and the Board of Information. Please tell the Board of Information that I have no objection to their printing them in the Tokyo press if they so desire.

S.C.B.

21

To Sri Rama Murti
Tokyo

ARZI HUKUMATE AZAD HIND
(THE PROVISIONAL GOVERNMENT OF FREE INDIA)

Taiwan
(Formosa)
9.12.44

Jai Hind!

We have had rather bad luck this time with the weather. A cold wave seems to be accompanying us everywhere—and moreover, at every aerodrome we have been delayed. That is why we are still on our way. At Shanghai we met Sri A.M. Sahay—he will be going to Tokyo after some time—after his work in China is finished. Please inform Mrs. Sahay about Sahayji's safe arrival at Shanghai.

I wrote to you from Fukuoka, through a member of the Foreign Office who was returning to Tokyo. Along with that letter, I enclosed a letter from myself to the boys (cadets)—asking you to deliver the letter to them.

A member of the Burmese Embassy is going to Tokyo and I am taking this opportunity of scribbling a few lines to you. Please inform Sri Sivaram about my movements.

I would like to have the *Nippon Times* and all journals published in English from Japan and China. Please preserve these papers and journals serially and whenever there is an opportunity of sending them by any messenger, going to Syonan or Rangoon, please seize the opportunity. If you are sufficiently alert, I am sure that you will find many people going from Tokyo to Syonan or Rangoon. You will have to make the right contacts. Moreover, the general staff often have people going in that direction by aeroplane. The Thai and Burmese Embassies also have people going. The members of the Thai Embassy going to Bangkok can deliver the mail to the Indian Independence League at Bangkok.

The IIL can then forward the mail from Bangkok to Rangoon by air—which is easy. I know the Thai Ambassador very well and I am sure that the Thai Embassy will gladly help in this matter.

Hope you are all well. We are all well.

With all good wishes,

Jai Hind
Subhas Chandra Bose

Sri Rama Murti
Chairman, Territorial Committee, IIL
Tokyo

22

To the INA Cadets

Tokyo

ARZI HUKUMATE AZAD HIND
(THE PROVISIONAL GOVERNMENT
OF FREE INDIA)

Saigon
14.12.44

My dear boys,

I am leaving for Syonan today. Today a gentleman is going from here to Tokyo. I am taking the opportunity of sending a bundle of 'papar' for you. I could have sent a few other things, but he could not carry any more weight.

I hope you are all well. We had a safe journey; but we were delayed at every stage of the journey owing to bad weather.

With all good wishes and affection,

Jai Hind
Subhas Chandra Bose

23

To Sri Rama Murti

Tokyo

ARZI HUKUMATE AZAD HIND
(THE PROVISIONAL GOVERNMENT
OF AZAD HIND)

Saigon
14.12.44

Jai Hind!

I do not know when this letter will reach you. Today Major Abe of the Hikari Kikan is going to Tokyo on a transfer and he is taking with him a bundle of 'papar' for our boys. I could not send anything more, because more weight cannot be carried by him.

I am enclosing a cutting from an American Journal—'Nation'—on the Imphal operations. I would like you to send this to H.E. General Tojo on my behalf.

I could not hand over this letter to Major Abe in time, but he is taking the 'papar' all right. Lt. Col. Habibur Rahman has written a forwarding letter to you, along with the 'papar', on my behalf.

From Fukuoka, I wrote you a letter and also enclosed a letter for our boys. I hope you got my letter in time and forwarded the letter to the boys.

I am arranging to send some butter from here for our boys from time to time. The difficulty is about finding someone who can carry a parcel. If that could somehow be arranged, then a periodic parcel could easily be sent from Saigon to Tokyo.

I am enclosing a letter for the boys.

Please send me a copy of the radio-talk that I delivered at Tokyo, addressed to America. I think you will find a copy with Mr. Sivaram or with the Broadcasting people.

If I can manage, I shall send you copies of the extempore speeches that I delivered at Tokyo. I shall have to sit down and reproduce them from memory. You can then bring out these speeches in booklet-form, if necessary.

On my arrival at Syonan, I shall expect a message from Tokyo about opening a Broadcasting station for USA.

Mr. Ayer is on his way to Syonan to meet me there. I am leaving for Syonan today.

Hope all well there. With all good wishes,

Jai Hind
Subhas Chandra Bose

24

From Benito Mussolini

[Telegram]

January 2, 1945

H. EXC. SUBHAS CHANDRA BOSE

HEAD OF THE PROVISIONAL GOVERNMENT OF FREE INDIA

WHILE CONVEYING MY THANKS TO YOUR EXCELLENCY FOR THE GREETINGS THAT YOU HAVE SENT TO ME AND THE ITALIAN PEOPLE ON THE RUCURRENCE OF THE NEW YEAR I BEG YOU TO ACCEPT MY MOST CORDIAL AUSPICES FOR YOUR PERSONAL WELFARE AND A HAPPY FUTURE FOR INDIA, FREE AT LAST FROM THE OPPRESSION OF OUR COMMON ENEMY.

MUSSOLINI

25

To Dr Majumder

Rangoon
15. Feb. 1945

Dr. Majumder,
Chairman, Indian Independence League,
Seremban.

Jai Hind,

Sri H.P. Bhowmick is going back to Malaya. He has suffered some severe injuries at the front line. He himself wishes to be with his relatives and believes he would be better off there. Hence, I have no objection to his going back to Malaya.

I request you to do the following things for him:

1. He shall be given a suitable monthly allowance by the Indian Independence League Branch, Seremban.
2. Ration shall be supplied to him regularly (on the INA or AHD Scale).
3. You shall give whatever and whenever medical help is required by him.
4. If possible, a servant be appointed who shall attend to him always. His pay and rations shall be borne by the League, Seremban.

I desire that all help be given to him to make him feel happy and comfortable.

Hoping the work in your State is progressing satisfactorily.

Jai Hind
Subhas Chandra Bose

26

To M. Satyavati Thevar

ARZI HUKUMATE AZAD HIND

(Provisional Government of Free India)

Bangkok
21st May 1945

Capt.M.S. Thevar
Commandant
Rani of Jhansi Regiment Training Camp

Jai Hind,

I duly received your recommendations regarding promotions. But I did not have time to go through them. Lt. Col. Habib-ur-Rehman will be coming up here shortly and I am asking him to go through your recommendations and give his opinion thereon. Please place all your recommendations before him and all the facts connected therewith, so that he may be able to give his opinion thereon.

Please let me know if the proposed extension of your camp has already been completed and if so, for how many persons extra accommodation is available in the camp.

I hope that the work is going on satisfactorily and that all of you are doing well.

Jai Hind
Subhas Chandra Bose

27

From M. Satyavati Thevar

RANI OF JHANSI REGIMENT
TRAINING CAMP

22nd May, 1945

To

HIS EXCELLENCY
NETAJI SUBHAS CHANDRA BOSE
SUPREME COMMANDER, A.H.F.

Dear Netaji,

I have received your letter of the 21st May, 45 and as per your instructions, I have put all the recommendations for promotions before Lt. Col. Habib Ur Rahman and I am sending a list of same to you.

Regarding the extension of camp, the officers' Qrs. is almost complete and a new barrack and a new office is to be started in a few days time. The delay in construction was due to lack of materials. The construction of the above two will be completed soon as the materials have arrived already.

There will be enough of accommodation for 100 in three weeks' time. It may be necessary to occupy the rest of one-third of the land left for public use, as there is not sufficient space for parade. I shall try to approach the municipality sometime through the Hikari Kikan.

For about a period of four months the camp suffered a good deal from scabies, malaria and Influenza etc. At present the Camp is free from all these and the health of all the Sepoys have improved and are more cheerful at present.

It has been suggested by Col. Alagappan that all the educated or at least 150 sepoys to be trained in nursing for which arrangements are being made.

The Deputy Chief of Staff has been a great help in connection with regular and good supplies of vegetables, fish and other supplies as well. All are quite happy and healthy in this camp at present.

The work of the camp has been carried on as usual. A 4th N.C.O.'s course has been started and a few more sepoys joined the nursing section. Captain Das Gupta has been sent as a M.O. in charge in place of Major (Mrs.) K.S. Narula. More information if required regarding these changes, may please be got from Lt. Col. Habib-ur-Rahman. As I feel that this petty matters should not worry you omit them in this letter.

The spirit of the sepoys ... [illegible] is given to us most of us would prefer to fight and die, yet, we leave everything to your will our supreme Commander. Whichever way you want us to be useful we are ready and our greatest desire is to stand by you till the last.

We hope that you are keeping good health as well as the rest who are with you.

'Jai Hind'

M. Satiavati Thevar
Captain
Commanding Rani of Jhansi Regiment
Trg. Camp.

28

Bangkok
10. 6. 45

Brahmachari Kailasam

Syonan

Jai Hind,

This is just to say that I am doing well. The fight goes on, despite what has recently happened in Burma. We shall win and India will be free.

Please convey my respectful pranams to Swamiji. With respectful greetings,

Jai Hind
Subhas Chandra Bose